D1616636

COLONIALITY IN THE MAYA LOWLANDS

COLONIALITY IN THE MAYA LOWLANDS

ARCHAEOLOGICAL PERSPECTIVES

EDITED BY

Kasey Diserens Morgan and Tiffany C. Fryer

UNIVERSITY PRESS OF COLORADO
Louisville

© 2022 by University Press of Colorado

Published by University Press of Colorado
1624 Market Street, Suite 226
PMB 39883
Denver, Colorado 80202-1559

The University Press of Colorado is a proud member of
the Association of University Presses.

The University Press of Colorado is a cooperative publishing enterprise supported, in part, by Adams State University, Colorado State University, Fort Lewis College, Metropolitan State University of Denver, Regis University, University of Alaska Fairbanks, University of Colorado, University of Northern Colorado, University of Wyoming, Utah State University, and Western Colorado University.

∞ This paper meets the requirements of the ANSI/NISO Z39.48-1992 (Permanence of Paper).

ISBN: 978-1-64642-283-8 (hardcover)
ISBN: 978-1-64642-284-5 (ebook)
https://doi.org/10.5876/9781646422845

Library of Congress Cataloging-in-Publication Data

Names: Diserens Morgan, Kasey, editor. | Fryer, Tiffany C., editor. | Douglass, John G., 1968– writer of foreword.
Title: Coloniality in the Maya lowlands : archaeological perspectives / edited by Kasey Diserens Morgan and Tiffany C. Fryer.
Other titles: Global colonialism.
Description: Louisville : University Press of Colorado, [2022] | Series: Global colonialism | Includes bibliographical references and index.
Identifiers: LCCN 2022017920 (print) | LCCN 2022017921 (ebook) | ISBN 9781646422838 (hardcover) | ISBN 9781646422845 (ebook)
Subjects: LCSH: Mayas—Mexico—Quintana Roo (State)—Antiquities. | Excavations (Archaeology)—Mexico—Quintana Roo (State) | Quintana Roo (Mexico : State)—Antiquities. | Mexico—Colonial influence. | Guatemala—Colonial influence.
Classification: LCC F1435.1.Q78 C65 2022 (print) | LCC F1435.1.Q78 (ebook) | DDC 972/.6701—dc23/eng/20220420
LC record available at https://lccn.loc.gov/2022017920
LC ebook record available at https://lccn.loc.gov/2022017921

The University Press of Colorado gratefully acknowledges the support of Princeton University.

Cover illustration: A section of the public mural "La Creación de Noh Cah Santa Cruz Balam Nah Kampokolche," by Israel Dzib Carvajal. Felipe Carrillo Puerto, Quintana Roo, Mexico. Photograph by Kasey Diserens Morgan.

Contents

Foreword

John Douglass

It is my pleasure to write this foreword to *Coloniality in the Maya Lowlands: Archaeological Perspectives*, edited by Kasey Diserens Morgan and Tiffany C. Fryer. This first book in the Global Colonialism series is more than a valuable collection of some of the latest research in historical archaeology of the eastern Maya lowland region, though it is also that. The editors seek to go beyond the better-known transition from pre- to post-Columbian by focusing on the eighteenth through twentieth centuries—a period during which, as Rosemary A. Joyce points out in chapter 12, Indigenous people continued to experience and participate in profound changes to their territoriality and material worlds. The introductory chapter and a number of other chapters in the book think through important concepts such as the historical period, settler colonialism, postcolonialism, and many other topics related to Indigenous peoples living and experiencing life in a world changed dramatically around them by colonialism.

The essays collectively assert the importance of both archaeology and living descendant memory for recovering and analyzing the history of events, technologies, labor strategies, and settlement patterns. All the chapters show how

https://doi.org/10.5876/9781646422845.c000

archaeologists of the more recent past deal with sometimes frustrating gaps in the material and documentary record, as well as their own positionality vis-à-vis descendant communities. Where there are site overlaps, the chapters complement, rather than repeat, one another. That said, the wide range of issues addressed in the chapters of this book—including piracy, smuggling, refugees, violence, race, land, labor, futures—illustrates the diversity of ways scholars can focus and dive deeply into topics of colonialism. These vastly different themes, though all somewhat related in systemic ways, illustrate the importance of understanding the ebb and flow of daily life, as well as larger socioeconomic and political systems at play in regions during times of colonialism.

We are so pleased to have this volume begin the series' conversation about colonialism across time and space. Whether one is interested in the eighteenth and nineteenth centuries in the eastern Maya lowlands, in colonialism writ large, or even pirates, *Coloniality in the Maya Lowlands* offers scholars and students an opportunity to think more comparatively about colonialism.

COLONIALITY IN THE MAYA LOWLANDS

Characterizing an Archaeology of Coloniality in the Maya Lowlands

Kasey Diserens Morgan and Tiffany C. Fryer

Archaeologists working in historically Maya-speaking territories (today's southeastern Mexico, Belize, northern Honduras, and Guatemala) have long influenced developments across the discipline. These researchers have produced a rich body of scholarship exploring Maya society before Spanish invasion and settlement. They have contributed regionally and internationally, creating and testing new standards for archaeological practice, perfecting innovative scientific techniques, exploring the inclusion of ethnographic and epigraphic methods, and helping illuminate the processes involved in the rise, mainte-nance, and collapse of intricate state-level societies (Marcus 2003; Nichols and Pool 2012; Chase and Chase 2016). Unlike archaeology in other settler colonial societies such as the United States and Australia, however, Mayanist archaeol-ogy has been slower to embrace the study of post-fifteenth-century life in the region (but see Rice and Rice 2004; Kepecs and Alexander 2005; Alexander and Kepecs 2018; Alexander 2019).

Maya experiences with European colonialism have instead typically been the domain of intrepid revisionist ethnohistorians (Farriss 1984; Clendinnen [1987]

https://doi.org/10.5876/9781646422845.c001

2003; Jones 1989; Restall 1997; on Latin America as settler colonial society, see Gott 2007; Castellanos 2017). Scholars of the New Philology—the study of the Colonial period using documents authored in native languages by Indigenous subjects—have greatly shifted the conversation about so-called Conquest and the Colonial periods toward interpretations that center native peoples' understanding of the life of colonialism (Restall 2012). Legal and religious documents authored in Latin script by Maya—much like the tablets and stelae that preceded them—provide a window into how Maya incorporated and pressed back against the technologies of colonialism at play in their lives (Restall 1997; Hanks 2010; McCrea 2010; Sigal 2013; Quezada 2014; Christensen 2016; Dutt 2017). The vantage point offered by the material record may help to amplify these efforts, allowing archaeologists to contribute to offsetting the frequency with which taken-for-granted assumptions based on colonial documentation authored by the "conquerors" are replicated across the fields of (post)colonial Maya history and anthropology.

The few archaeological works in this area tend typically—and importantly—to focus on the transitional phase between the Late Postclassic and Early Colonial periods (roughly AD 1350–1650; e.g., Lee 1979; Graham, Pendergast, and Jones 1989; Emery 1990, 1999; Hanson 1995; Kepecs 1997, 1999, 2005; García Targa 2000; Nance, Whittington, and Jones-Borg 2003; Andrews, Benavides Castillo, and Jones 2006; deFrance and Hanson 2008; Oland and Palka 2016), leaving the Middle Colonial period through Early National period (roughly AD 1650–1910) largely unexplored. Archaeological studies of the twentieth and twenty-first centuries in the Maya lowlands are almost nonexistent. Post-transitional historical archaeologies have not been entirely ignored in the subfield of Maya studies, but they tend to be represented by one-off articles or as a single chapter in a larger volume dedicated to work on the deeper past (Miller and Farriss 1979; Arías López and Burgos Villanueva 2001; Yaeger et al. 2004; Mathews and Lizama-Rogers 2005; Palka 2005; Andrews, Burgos Villanueva, and Millet Cámara 2006; Martos López 2010; Andrews 2012a; Ramsey 2016; Kaeding 2017; Mathews and Gust 2017). Work on transitions from the Late Postclassic to Early Postconquest periods may be thriving, but archaeological research on eras following that transition is scarce.

There may be a less rigid line drawn between the "prehistoric" and "historic" periods in Mesoamerican archaeologies broadly (Fowler 2009, 429) because of works on these transitional periods, but the simultaneous devaluation of historical archaeologies in Mesoamerica, and specifically the Maya region, endures. Indeed, the question of the archaeological significance of the material remains of (post)colonial history still biases researchers against this work (Mrozowski, Delle, and Paynter 2000, xxii). That is: what is archaeology able to add to our knowledge about this period that productively adds to the already robust ethnohistorical scholarship? Moreover, characterizations of the future of the field over the past four decades consistently chart exciting and ever-innovative paths for Mayanist archaeologists yet make no mention of the efficacy of engaging in archaeological studies of Mayan history post-fifteenth century (Marcus 1983, 1995; Demarest 2009). Pioneering in her field, Hattula Moholy-Nagy at Tikal conducted work in Guatemala in the 1950s (Moholy-Nagy 2012), which blazed the way for the serious study of the Colonial period by archaeologists as part of the long-term history of Mayas in the region. Despite its marginalization, a handful of scholars working across post-fifteenth-century sites since the 1980s charted the way for the growth of historical archaeologies in the region (see, esp., Andrews 1981, 2012b; García Targa 1995; Alexander 1997, 2003, 2004; for recent useful reviews, see Fowler 2009; Palka 2009; Alexander 2012; Joyce, Gómez, and Sheptak 2015). Recent monographs such as Rani Alexander's (2004) *Yaxcabá and the Caste War of Yucatán*, Jorge Victoria Ojeda and Jorge Canto Alcocer's (2006) *San Fernando Aké*, Jennifer P. Mathews and Gillian Schultz's (2009) *Chicle*, Allan Meyers's (2012) *Outside the Hacienda Walls*, and Sam Sweitz's (2012) *On the Periphery of the Periphery* have all made way for deeper archaeological engagements with more recent periods of Mayan history.

This volume builds on the decades of work by these few determined scholars of the Maya region who do focus on the historic period, defined as the Colonial era and its aftermath (roughly 1500 to present). We are exceedingly grateful for those who laid the groundwork and attested to the value and relevance of historical archaeology in the region early on. We are especially motivated by the proliferation of doctoral and master's dissertations focused on the post-fifteenth-century Maya world since the early 2000s, including Jennifer Dornan's (2004) "'Even By Night We Only Become Aware They Are Killing Us,'" Kira Blaisdell-Sloan's (2006) "An Archaeology of Place and Self," Olivia Ng's (2007) "View from the Periphery," Maxine Oland's (2009) "Long-Term Indigenous History on a Colonial Frontier," Steven Morandi's (2010) "Xibun Maya," Adam Kaeding's (2013) "Negotiated Survival," Erin Schmidt's "An Examination of Capitalism in Nineteenth-Century Haciendas in Yucatan, Mexico," Russell Sheptak's (2013) "Colonial Masca in Motion," Collin Gillenwater's (2014) "Agency at Hacienda Pancota," Alison Hodges's (2015) "Resistance, the Church, and a Comparison of Ceramics from Sixteenth-Century Caluco, El Salvador," Guido Pezzarossi's (2014) "New Materialist Archaeology of Antimarkets, Power and Capitalist Effects in Colonial Guatemala," Tracie Mayfield's (2015) "The Nineteenth Century British Plantation Settlement at Lamanai, Belize," Alyssa Bonorden's (2016) "Comparing Colonial Experiences in Northwestern Belize," John Gust's (2016) "Bittersweet," Christopher Thrasher's (2017) "Surviving Spanish Conquest," Alejandra Badillo Sánchez's (2018) "Rumbo al Corazón de la Tierra Macehual," and Tiffany Cain's (2019) "Materializing Political Violence." The chapters here will demonstrate how we have moved beyond the study of the (Post)Colonial periods as an after-thought that was tacked on obligatorily as archaeologists attempted to account for historic materials recovered on their ancient Maya-centric field projects.

Transitional archaeologies focused on changes in Maya lifeways since the onset of Spanish colonialism are incredibly important, and we hope that such studies will continue to grow. But the contributors to this volume highlight an even more marginalized period: the Late Colonial period to the Early National period (roughly, the eighteenth to twentieth centuries), at which point Spanish colonial—and later Yucatecan and Mexican settler colonial—systems had become well ingrained, giving way to new social categories and cultural practices. Together, our contributors push for making historical archaeology a part of a critical tool kit for scholars of the Maya region. They are principally concerned with interrogating broader processes of (post)colonial change over time, and how the impacts of those changes continue to resonate in and influence life in the region today. We also think critically about the impact of our studies on local communities and the communities within which we work. By doing so, we join efforts to create a more inclusive and dynamic practice of archaeology broadly.

Historical Archaeologies of Coloniality

Although the contributors to this volume have each come to engage historical archaeology through different avenues, the pieces are united by an understanding of historical archaeologies as those archaeologies that concern themselves with "the last 500 years . . . a period of the differential penetration of European-inspired practices of domination around the globe" (Paynter 2000, 170). Historical archaeologies, thus, are archaeologies of colonialism, capitalism, and the notion of modernity itself. By examining colonialism and postcolonialism as a set of dynamic long-term processes of social, economic, and political control manifest through quotidian relationships, historical archaeologists can address processes such as imperialism, capitalism, racialization, globalization, modern warfare, ethnogenesis, and cultural tourism. They can effectively shed light on how the social constructs of Indigeneity, race, place, power, resistance, agency, history, and heritage materialize (McGuire and Paynter 1991; Lyons and Papadopoulos 2002; Kazanjian 2003; Gosden 2004; Jordan 2009; Liebmann and Murphy 2010; Liebmann 2012; Oland, Hart, and Frink 2012; Voss and Casella 2012; Ferriss, Harrison, Wilcox 2014; Orser 2019).

But, because historical archaeologies address so many histories we might characterize as transitional—from native autonomy to colonial rule to Republican nationhood to transnational entanglements—periodization can become messy. Throughout the volume, readers will encounter references to the Colonial or Republican period but also to colonial and (post)colonial spaces. Such differences lie in the juridical distinction between formal colonial subjugation under competing European imperial powers and the social engineering of colonialism whose systems maintain power long after juridical decolonization. As historical anthropologist Ann Stoler (2016, ix–x) insists, the notion (post)colonial references a skepticism of and lack of clarity about the assumed line between the postcolonial present and the colonial—and, we would add, precolonial—pasts.

Latin Americanist postcolonial theorists at the end of the twentieth century began to think of this permeable boundary in terms of what they called *coloniality*—or the ongoing systems of social order and knowledge production engendered by European colonialism and left unimpeded after Independence (Lander 2000; Quijano 2000, 2007; Wynter 2003, Lugones 2010). Coloniality refers to how colonialist logics become intertwined with material practices to provide the necessary conditions for the maintenance of oppressive, hierarchically gendered, and racialized power structures. Coloniality is a critique of the *performance* of colonial dominance that relies on the myth of cultural and genealogical absorption of Indigenous peoples rather than their outright nonexistence or apparent elimination (as the myth in many British colonial contexts goes; Castellanos 2017, 778). Coloniality positions the "real *indio*" at the point of contact—the point from which Indigeneity begins to be disavowed through a process of racial dilution. The same process is deployed against African descendant peoples in many Latin American countries when the capitalist usefulness of the category "Black" becomes antithetical to the post-Independence national project (Restall 2009). Coloniality provides a framework for comprehending how so-called Conquest was not a homogenous event but a long-term (and yet unfinished) process (Oland and Palka 2016). The coloniality literature can be critiqued because it obscures the strategies of elimination and dispossession that occurred—and continue to occur—under colonialism (Speed 2017). In Spanish-speaking contexts, *colonialismo* implies settlement (Castellanos 2017, 778). Thus, studies of Spanish colonialism are always studies of postinvasion settlement. Postinvasion settlement implies the ushering in of new sets of social relationships, some of which were foreseen and orchestrated by the Crown, others of which could never have been predicted (Bianchi Villelli 2011).

However, coloniality is a premise of modernity in the American context (and arguably elsewhere; see Ndlovu-Gatsheni 2013). Over the past two decades, a proliferation of research on modernity as a subset of historical archaeology has emerged (Thomas 2004; González-Ruibal 2008, 2013; Dawdy 2010). This work opens the door to understanding not only how the mentality of power delimited by the notion of coloniality undergirds the modern project but also how that mentality is reinforced through material practices. Attention to the materiality of coloniality allows us to break down the conceptual divide between coloniality and settler colonialism, as well as to confront the difficulties of periodization that can occur when investigating the unfolding of modernity in a "postcon-tact," postinvasion settled world. These cooccurring histories shape space and place across temporal boundaries. Understanding contemporary inequities set in motion by colonial processes requires us to understand space as a physical expression of both past and present power structures (Manuel-Navarrete 2012). By studying Maya history since the Postclassic period, and drawing connections between those histories and present-day social concerns, Mayanist archaeolo-gists may position their work to expose the breakdown of colonial systems, or the continuity of those systems as resonant structures of power that seek to subjugate particular kinds of people (Liebmann and Rizvi 2008).

It is critical to acknowledge how colonialism differentially impacted regions and people. By tacking back and forth between time periods and traversing geopolitical boundaries in this volume, we show how new cultures formed as a result of colonialism—how "what was previously understood as acculturation has come to be viewed instead as transculturation, creolization, and ethnogen-esis, [global] processes that were shaped by local factors and resulted in varied outcomes" (Van Buren 2010, 157–158). Mary Van Buren (2010) describes recent trends in the archaeological study of colonialism, with an increased focus on bottom-up approaches to understanding the agency of local actors and the pro-duction of new identities. She addresses the varied responses of members of colonial and postcolonial society to "identity and culture change, demographic effects of European Expansion, missionization, the changing nature of eco-nomic activities, and urbanization" (159). Other anthropologists have drawn attention to the variety of colonial practices and pressures that lead to uneven assimilation, ethnogenesis, and, in some spaces, extreme attempts to secure autonomy where racialized oppressions preclude the possibilities of recognition (Montejo 1999; Gabbert 2004; Vanthuyne 2009; Joyce, Gómez, and Sheptak 2015; Balaton-Chrimes and Stead 2017). Understanding these processes as growing out of a settler colonial milieu and as enabling the performance of coloniali-ty strengthens the theoretical frameworks from which archaeologists may explore the complicated history of postinvasion, settlement-based modernity in Mesoamerica and beyond.

Thus, historical archaeologies of the Maya region center not only on the mechanics and materials of the colonial past but also on the presence of colonial structures today (Gosden 1999; Stoler 2016). They are necessarily archaeolo-gies of coloniality. Joel Palka's (2005) study of the "unconquered" Lacandon Maya offers an interesting example of how contact and colonialism reshaped the lives of those groups seen as on the edge of the influence of colonialism. His study shows that colonialism is a multidirectional process, the outcomes of which are only so predictable. Through recent investigations like this, schol-ars rework the histories of Maya America, moving beyond tropes of collapse and conquest (Restall 2003), to include broader histories of a multicultural societies that were homogenous neither before (Yaeger and Robin 2004) nor after (Tiesler, Zabala, and Cucina 2010; Wesp, chapter 3 in this volume) the onset of European colonialism.

These variabilities result from the negotiation of power, social life, and the formulation of identity under inequitable conditions (Van Buren 2010; Kaeding 2013, 2017; Bührer et al. 2017). By recognizing the Maya lowland region as a settler colonial context, within which coloniality is performed and reproduced daily, we can identify how studies of the sixteenth century might have important ramifications for the goings-on of the twenty-first. Addressing the present-day issues that are a result of the continuation of colonial power structures under new regimes, as well as more specific concerns—such as migration (Meierhoff, chapter 8 in this volume), food insecurity (Dedrick, McAnany, and Batún Alpuche, chapter 2 in this volume), violence (García Lara and Olán, chapter 4 in this volume; Fryer, chapter 5 in this volume; Badillo Sánchez, chapter 6 in this volume), and control over historic resources (Diserens Morgan, chapter 11 in this volume)—becomes possible. For instance, some scholars show that racial and social domination can be manifested in the design of colonial structures and towns (Gutiérrez 1983; Solari 2013; Nemser 2017). Studies of space, power, and urbanism in pre-Spanish invasion Mayanist archaeologies have been influential, providing comparative baselines for archaeologies being conducted in the region and across the globe. Such emphases could easily be reworked to address the study of colonialism in the Maya region. In fact, studies such as Allan Meyers's (2012) investigation of Hacienda Tabi in northwestern Yucatán have already shown how investigating discrete spaces of (post)colonial life—for instance, plantations—can change the conversation about how people negotiate power and individuality in policed spaces of domination.

Acknowledging Colonialist Thought in Mayanist Archaeologies and Anthropologies

The ways in which historians, anthropologists, and archaeologists throughout the nineteenth and twentieth centuries studied "the Maya" were themselves often artifacts of colonialism. Ethnohistorian Nancy Farriss (1983, 2) suggested that many of the modern studies of Maya by scholars are comparable to their exploitation during colonial times. Indeed, the very shaping of a people called "the Maya" indexes the durability of colonialist ideals such that even the subject of study, notwithstanding considerable increases in self-reflexivity on the part of Mayanist researchers, becomes a unified and unquestioned subject—one for which widespread and generalizable conclusions may be drawn (Castañeda 1996, 2004; Gabbert 2004; Joyce 2005; Armstrong-Fumero 2009). Widely regarded anthropological studies such as Robert Redfield and Alfonso Villa Rojas's ([1934]

1967) *Chan Kom: A Maya Village* and the subsequent *A Village That Chose Progress: Chan Kom Revisited* (Redfield 1957) illuminated little-understood aspects of Maya social life while concretizing ahistorical representations of Maya communities and suggesting their eventual extinction due to encroaching forces of globalization (see Armstrong-Fumero, chapter 13 in this volume).

Ethnicization and objectification of "the Maya" by archaeologists, anthropologists, government, and tourism industries give rise to other forms of power imbalances, whereby millions of today's Maya peoples (those Indigenous peoples who are Maya language family speakers and descendants) are characterized as unworthy of their histories, lesser than their genealogical predecessors, and culturally consumable but politically expendable (Watanabe 1995; Pyburn 1998; Cojti Ren 2006; Breglia 2006). Such studies perpetuate long standing colonially derived biases toward Indigenous peoples—they are the artifacts of the coloniality of power in Maya America. Some current scholarship examines discursive practices of othering and/or homogenizing in Mayanist anthropology and archaeology, producing work that instead complicates the complex relationships between colonizer and colonized, people of differentially racialized identities, researcher and researched across the historically Maya regions of Central America (e.g., Pyburn 2004; Ardren 2004; Cojti Ren 2006; Armstrong-Fumero and Hoil Gutierrez 2017; Kaeding 2017). The continued othering of "the" Maya by governmental agents and researchers, as well as the expansive cultural and archaeological tourism industry across historically Maya territories, further distances Maya-identified peoples from each other and from their respective histories (McAnany and Parks 2012).

Coloniality in the Maya Lowlands: This Volume's Approach

This volume began as an organized session entitled "Recent Shifts in Maya Archaeology: Investigations of the Colonial and National Periods of the Yucatan," at the Society for American Archaeology in 2017. We aimed to bring together scholars who were braving unconventional dialogues about postinvasion experiences across the historically Maya region to share and exchange findings, challenges, and achievements with one another. We are together nineteen archaeologists and anthropologists working in what are today southeastern Mexico, Belize, Guatemala, and Honduras—though in order to provide some cohesion, we have tried to limit our case studies to lowland contexts. Some contributors started as ancient Mayanists and others as historical archaeologists; some are just beginning their academic journeys as graduate students, and some are seasoned senior scholars. When we decided to pursue this volume, we wanted to demonstrate that the study of the Colonial and Postcolonial periods offers great value for the expansion of Mayanist archaeologies. The contributors to this volume are committed not only to the expansion of knowledge about these marginalized time periods in Maya archaeology but also to addressing some of the field's most pressing theoretical and methodological questions—how to conceive of and grapple with the material realities of coloniality, for example—at a regional level.

As Richard Wilk noted in his 1985 article "The Ancient Maya and the Political Present," our archaeological research interests are never far from the current political moment. But, as editors, we believe that by reflexively embracing those agendas, we can mobilize archaeology to address critical social, economic, and political issues facing the communities within which and with whom we work. We address violence, resource insecurity, land rights, refugees, the control of borders, the movement of contraband, surveillance, individual and collective agency, consumption, uses of historic resources, and the futures of Maya archaeology—all colonial endurances. Although not every project focused on the recent past will be overtly political, the reality of coloniality means that such projects will be difficult to disentangle from the sociopolitical concerns of the present moment, and we remain unconvinced that they should be. Aligning with recent trends in archaeology and anthropology (e.g., Colwell-Chanthaphonh and Ferguson 2007; Hale 2007; Atalay 2012; Atalay et al. 2014; McAnany 2016; Fryer and Diserens Morgan 2021), many of our authors thus combine their archaeological research with ethnographic, engaged, and activism-oriented methodologies, examining the impact of their work on modern-day descendant communities and the ways engagement with modern-day communities in turn impacts their research.

The wide variety of case studies presented here seek a better understanding of what living through shifting power dynamics and social, cultural, and religious transformations requires; what living through tumultuous political regimes, revolt, and the precarity of newly formed nation states requires; what frequent migration due to political and economic upheaval requires; and what newly globalizing economies require. These chapters respect Maya people, both past and present, as actors in the shaping of a globalized, modern world. They attend to how change is managed, adapted to, and eventually leaves its mark in the archaeological record.

Organization of the Volume

The volume is divided into three parts, grouping the essays along semichronological and thematic lines. Each part opens with a preface where readers will find short background essays briefly outlining histories (and highlighting additional sources not cited in this introduction) to contextualize the chapters that follow. Following this Introduction, "Part I: Colonial Lives" focuses on the construction and maintenance of new lifeways throughout the Middle and Late Colonial periods. Dedrick, McAnany, and Batún Alpuche (chapter 2) discuss how economic strategies and agriculture changed over the course of the Colonial period. They argue that communities forcibly gathered under the Spanish colonial system of *congregación* organized to use *rejolladas*, or soil-filled sink holes, to achieve food security under otherwise precarious conditions. In chapter 3, Wesp explores some of the ways in which peoples of African descent adapted to life in colonial Mexico and how that story has been obscured over time, especially in the Maya region. She argues that ongoing discrimination against Black Mexicans is exacerbated by the dichotomous characterization of colonial life as an exclusive opposition between Spanish and Indigenous peoples. Attention to colonial society as multiracial is a first step toward more fully illuminating the experiences of life under colonialism throughout the historically Maya region. Finally, in chapter 4, García Lara and Olán explore the clash of empires as reflected in changes to the landscape through fortification practices on the eastern frontier of the Yucatán. They address the violence of piracy and the movement of contraband across international borders—a problem that continues to resonate today.

Opening "Part II: (Post)Colonial Lives," Fryer (chapter 5) picks up on the theme of violence by examining the same region as García Lara and Olán but moving us into the latter half of the nineteenth century following the region's Independence from Spain. Drawing on work with a collaborative heritage initiative, she shows how the prolonged violence of the so-called Caste War of Yucatán (*guerra de castas*, 1847–1901) altered human geographies across the area, arguing that attention to core objects of social life such as rock walls and corn-grinding stones can illuminate how collective violence transforms the sphere of daily life. The Caste War figures prominently in the three chapters that follow Fryer's. In chapter 6, Badillo Sánchez interrogates the military operations of the final years of the conflict as the Mexican Army swept through the jungle, plowing toward the sanctuary and former stronghold of the insurrectionists still controlling what is today southeastern Quintana Roo. She shows how the grafting of new biopolitics onto the occupied territories during and following the final affront engineered new social relations and geographies.

In chapter 7, "Living on the Edge," Houk, Bonorden, and Kilgore investigate the formation of new communities after war-induced migration. Comparing three refugee communities in British Honduras, they show how people tried to achieve a sense of normalcy in their daily lives as they simultaneously constructed new lives and did what they could to maintain their individual social and cultural identities—a process that has been documented among today's global refugee communities. Meierhoff (chapter 8) shifts the conversation about refugee livelihoods from the logging regions of northern British Honduras to the ruins of Tikal, Guatemala. His study speaks to the temporal circulation of places, how a place once abandoned can become home again to people who find themselves removed from the places they once knew as home. Together, these two chapters make a compelling case for the contribution archaeology can make to refugee studies while reinforcing Wesp's call in chapter 3 for archaeologists to take the reality of multiethnic societies at both the heart and edge of empire seriously. Still, in times of war, some people cannot or choose not to leave war-torn areas. Often, the social structures that lead to war become amplified in those spaces (Lubkemann 2010), creating paradoxical social geographies. Part II closes with Gust's piece (chapter 9) on the intensification of debt peonage and the expansion of the plantation system in northern Yucatán from the late nineteenth century, as the Caste War raged on, until the Mexican Revolution. Through careful archival research, he shows how labor and land are intimately connected and how nuanced differences in access to and control over land can variously intensify or diminish the insecurities felt by people trapped within systems of unfree labor.

"Part III: Futures for Recent Maya History" opens with Mathews, Gust, and Fedick's retrospective (chapter 10) on taking up historical archaeology in the Yucatán. Situated between the themes of global commodity exchange, capitalist expansion, and postwar life, their study mobilizes ethnographic, ethnoarchaeological, and archival methods to illuminate the importance of small-scale commodities industries throughout the history of the region. In chapter 11, Diserens Morgan turns to a contemporary example of the reinhabitation of ruins and what happens when those resettled places come under the influence of modern-day heritage. She introduces the concept of the "living dead" as a precaution and call to action for archaeologists, alongside heritage specialists and historic preservationists, to reconsider how ideals around loss—and which places and objects are significant enough to pursue programs that stall loss—can distract from the heritage *and* livelihood value of these places to the local communities that continue to inhabit them. Both of these chapters present a foray into archaeological ethnography as an essential component of historical archaeologies of the Maya world for the future.

The volume concludes with two commentaries on the major themes presented in the book and the future of historical archaeology across the historically Maya regions of what are today southern Mexico and Central America. In chapter 12, Joyce underscores that the historical archaeology of this region is poised to help us understand how new ways of being in the Maya world were formed and have changed over time, and that these types of analyses can be done on a regional level. Finally, Armstrong-Fumero (chapter 13) highlights the shared investments of historical archaeologists and sociocultural anthropologists working in the Maya region, tracing four major themes of the book that would provide fruitful points of engagement for ethnographers working in this space: ethnicity, agricultural change, political geography, and historical migrations.

This introduction is by no means exhaustive, but we hope that it is illustrative of both the trajectory of historical archaeology in the Maya region as well as the spaces of opportunity for studying life following Spanish invasion in Mayanist archaeologies. We advocate approaching the Maya region as a settler colonial context and attending to the material practices of coloniality that continue to unfold there. As such, we reimagine where "Maya archaeology is headed" (re: Marcus 1995) with the hope that readers, whether new to the field or well seasoned, will think twice before disregarding the (post)colonial lenses in their excavation units, take seriously the knowledge held and shared by Maya communities with whom they work, and embrace the opportunity to contribute to wide-reaching conversations about the history (and presence) of colonialism in the Americas.

Acknowledgments. As scholars beginning our journey in the field of Maya historical archaeology, we are grateful to those who came before us, whose work is highlighted in this introduction. We are also exceedingly grateful to all of our authors and the participants of the original SAA 2017 session and the Maya communities who have welcomed us all year after year to conduct the research reflected in this collection. Finally a special thank you to our discussants, Rosemary A. Joyce and Fernando Armstrong-Fumero, and the anonymous reviewers whose generous commentary strengthened the volume immensely.

References

Alexander, Rani T. 1997. "Haciendas and Economic Change in Yucatán: Entrepreneurial Strategies in the Parroquia de Yaxcabá, 1775–1850." *Journal of Archaeological Method and Theory* 4 (3–4): 331–351.

Alexander, Rani T. 2003. "Introduction: Haciendas and Agrarian Change in Rural Mesoamerica." *Ethnohistory* 50 (1): 3–14.

Alexander, Rani T. 2004. *Yaxcabá and the Caste War of Yucatán: An Archaeological Perspective.* Albuquerque: University of New Mexico Press.

Alexander, Rani T. 2012. "'Prohibido Tocar Este Cenote': The Archaeological Basis for the Titles of Ebtun." *International Journal of Historical Archaeology* 16 (1): 1–24.

Alexander, Rani T. 2019. *Technology and Tradition in Mesoamerica after the Spanish Invasion: Archaeological Perspectives.* Albuquerque: University of New Mexico Press.

Alexander, Rani T., and Susan Kepecs. 2018. *Colonial and Postcolonial Change in Mesoamerica: Archaeology as Historical Anthropology.* Albuquerque: University of New Mexico Press.

Andrews, Anthony P. 1981. "Historical Archaeology in Yucatan: A Preliminary Framework." *Historical Archaeology* 15 (1): 1–18.

Andrews, Anthony P. 2012a. "The Henequen Ports of Yucatan's Gilded Age." *International Journal of Historical Archaeology* 16 (1): 25–46.

Andrews, Anthony P. 2012b. "Historical Archaeology in the Maya Area: A Working Bibliography." Accessed September 4, 2017. http://sites.ncf.edu/andrews/.

Andrews, Anthony P., Antonio Benavides Castillo, and Grant D. Jones. 2006. "Ecab: A Remote Encomienda of Early Colonial Yucatan." In *Studies in Mesoamerican and Central American Prehistory*, edited by David M. Pendergast and Anthony P. Andrews, 5–32. Oxford: British Archaeological Reports International Series S1529.

Andrews, Anthony P., Rafael Burgos Villanueva, and Luis Millet Cámara. 2006. "The Historic Port of El Real de Salinas in Campeche, and the Role of Coastal Resources in the Emergence of Capitalism in Yucatán, México." *International Journal of Historical Archaeology* 10 (2): 179–205.

Ardren, Traci. 2004. "Where Are the Maya in Ancient Maya Archaeological Tourism? Advertising and the Appropriation of Culture." *Marketing Heritage: Archaeology and the Consumption of the Past*, 103–113. Walnut Creek, CA: AltaMira Press.

Arías López, José Manuel, and Rafael Burgos Villanueva. 2001. "Rancho Uaymitún: Un sitio histórico en la Costa Norte de Yucatán." *Arqueología* 2 (25): 89–107.

Armstrong-Fumero, Fernando. 2009. "A Heritage of Ambiguity: The Historical Substrate of Vernacular Multiculturalism in Yucatan, Mexico." *American Ethnologist* 36 (2): 300–316.

Armstrong-Fumero, Fernando, and Julio Hoil Gutierrez. 2017. "Settlement Patterns, Intangible Memory, and the Institutional Entanglements of Heritage in Modern Yucatán." In *Legacies of Space and Intangible Heritage: Archaeology, Ethnohistory, and the Politics of Cultural Continuity in the Americas*, edited by Fernando Armstrong Fumero and Julio Gutierrez, 15–32. Boulder: University Press of Colorado.

Atalay, Sonya. 2012. *Community-Based Archaeology: Research with, by, and for Indigenous and Local Communities*. Berkeley: University of California Press.

Atalay, Sonya, Lee R. Clauss, Randall H. McGuire, and John R. Welch, eds. 2014. *Transforming Archaeology: Activist Practices and Prospects*. Walnut Creek, CA: Left Coast Press.

Badillo Sánchez, Alejandra. 2018b. "Rumbo al Corazón de la Tierra Macehual: La Campaña Militar de Yucatán contra los Mayas 1899–1904." PhD diss., CIESAS Peninsular, Mérida.

Balaton-Chrimes, Samantha, and Victoria Stead. 2017. "Recognition, Power and Coloniality." *Postcolonial Studies* 20 (1): 1–17.

Bianchi Villelli, Marcia. 2011. "Coloniality in Patagonia: Historical Archaeology and Postcolonial Critique in Latin America." *World Archaeology* 43 (1): 86–101.

Blaisdell-Sloan, Kira. 2006. "An Archaeology of Place and Self: The Pueblo de Indios of Ticamaya, Honduras (1300–1800 AD)." PhD diss. Berkeley: University of California.

Bonorden, Alyssa Brooke. 2016. "Comparing Colonial Experiences in Northwestern Belize: Archaeological Evidence from Qualm Hill Camp and Kaxil Uinic Village." MA Thesis. Texas Tech University, Lubbock.

Breglia, Lisa. 2006. *Monumental Ambivalence: The Politics of Heritage*. Austin: University of Texas Press.

Bührer, Tanja, Flavio Eichmann, Stig Förster, and Benedikt Stuchtey. *Cooperation and Empire: Local Realities of Global Processes*. New York: Bergahn Books.

Cain, Tiffany. 2019. "Materializing Political Violence: Segregation, War, and Memory in Quintana Roo, Mexico." PhD diss., University of Pennsylvania, Philadelphia.

Castañeda, Quetzil E. 1996. *In the Museum of Maya Culture: Touring Chichén Itzá*. Minneapolis: University of Minnesota Press.

Castañeda, Quetzil. 2004. "'We Are Not Indigenous': An Introduction to the Maya Identity of Yucatán." *Journal of Latin American Anthropology* 9 (1): 36–63.

Castellanos, María Bianet. 2017. "Introduction: Settler Colonialism in Latin America." *American Quarterly* 69 (4): 777–781.

Chase, Arlen F., and Diane Z. Chase. 2016. "Urbanism and Anthropogenic Landscapes." *Annual Reviews of Anthropology* 45: 361–376.

Christensen, Mark Z. 2016. *The Teabo Manuscript: Maya Christian Copybooks, Chilam Balams, and Native Text Production in Yucatán*. Austin: University of Texas Press.

Clendinnen, Inga. (1987) 2003. *Ambivalent Conquests: Maya and Spaniard in Yucatan, 1517–1570*. Cambridge: Cambridge University Press.

Cojti Ren, Avexnim. 2006. "Maya Archaeology and the Political and Cultural Identity of Contemporary Maya in Guatemala." *Archaeologies* 2 (1): 8–19.

Colwell-Chanthaphonh, Chip, and T. J. Ferguson, eds. 2007. *Collaboration in Archaeological Practice: Engaging Descendant Communities*. New York: Rowman Altamira.

Dawdy, Shannon Lee. 2010. "Clockpunk Anthropology and the Ruins of Modernity." *Current Anthropology* 51 (6): 761–793.

deFrance, Susan D., and Craig A. Hanson. 2008. "Labor, Population Movement, and Food in Sixteenth-Century Ek Balam, Yucatán." *Latin American Antiquity* 19 (3): 299–316.

Demarest, Arthur A. 2009. "Maya Archaeology for the Twenty-First Century: The Progress, the Perils, and the Promise." *Ancient Mesoamerica* 20 (2): 253–263.

Dornan, Jennifer Lynn. 2004. "'Even by Night We Only Become Aware They Are Killing Us': Agency, Identity, and Intentionality at San Pedro Belize (1857–1930)." PhD diss., University of California, Los Angeles.

Dutt, Rajeshwari. 2017. *Maya Caciques in Early National Yucatán*. Norman: University of Oklahoma Press.

Emery, Kitty F. 1990. "Postclassic and Colonial Period Subsistence Strategies in the Southern Maya Lowlands: Faunal Analysis from Lamanai and Tipu, Belize." MA thesis, University of Toronto.

Emery, Kitty F. 1999. "Continuity and Variability in Postclassic and Colonial Animal Use at Lamanai and Tipu, Belize." In *Reconstructing Ancient Maya Diet*, edited by C. D. White, 61–81. Salt Lake City: University of Utah Press.

Farriss, Nancy M. 1983. "Indians in Colonial Yucatan: Three Perspectives." In *Spaniards and Indians in Southeastern Mesoamerica: Essays on the History of Ethnic Relations*, edited by Murdo J. MacLeod and Robert Wasserstrom, 1–39. Lincoln: University of Nebraska Press.

Farriss, Nancy M. 1984. *Maya Society under Colonial Rule: The Collective Enterprise of Survival*. Princeton, NJ: Princeton University Press.

Ferris, Neal, Rodney Harrison, and Michael V. Wilcox, eds. 2014. *Rethinking Colonial Pasts through Archaeology*. Oxford: Oxford University Press.

Fowler, William R. 2009. "Historical Archaeology in Yucatan and Central America." In *International Handbook of Historical Archaeology*, edited by Teresa Majewski and David Gaimster, 429–447. New York: Springer.

Fryer, Tiffany, and Kasey Diserens Morgan. 2021. "Subversive Heritage, Indigenized Tourism, and Heritage Activism in Maya Quintana Roo." In *Trowels in the Trenches: Archaeology as Social Activism*, edited by Christopher Barton, 81–107. Gainesville: University Press of Florida.

Gabbert, Wolfgang. 2004. *Becoming Maya: Ethnicity and Social Inequality in Yucatán since 1500*. Tucson: University of Arizona Press.

García Targa, Juan. 1995. "Arqueología colonial en el área maya: Aspectos generales y modelos de estudio." *Antropología Americana* 25: 41–69.

García Targa, Juan. 2000. "Análisis histórico y arqueológico del asentamiento colonial de Tecoh (Estado de Yucatán, México), Siglo XVI." *Ancient Mesoamerica* 11 (2): 231–243.

Gillenwater, Collin R. 2014. "Agency at Hacienda Pancota: Early Colonial Daily Consumption of a Contested Age and Material Culture." MA thesis, Illinois State University, Normal.

González-Ruibal, Alfredo. 2008. "Time to Destroy." *Current Anthropology* 49 (2): 247–279.

González-Ruibal, Alfredo. 2013. "Reclaiming Archaeology." In *Reclaiming Archaeology: Beyond the Tropes of Modernity*, edited by Alfredo González-Ruibal, 1–29. New York: Routledge.

Gosden, Chris. 1999. *Anthropology and Archaeology: A Changing Relationship*. New York: Routledge.

Gosden, Chris. 2004. *Archaeology and Colonialism: Cultural Contact from 5000 BC to the Present*. Cambridge: Cambridge University Press.

Gott, Richard. 2007. "Latin America as White Settler Society: The 2006 SLAS Lecture." *Bulletin of Latin American Research* 26 (2): 269–289.

Graham, Elizabeth, David M. Pendergast, and Grant D. Jones. 1989. "On the Fringes of Conquest: Maya-Spanish Contact in Colonial Belize." *Science* 246 (4935): 1254–1259.

Gust, John R. 2016. Bittersweet: Porfirian Sugar and Rum Production in Northeastern Yucatán. PhD diss., University of California, Riverside.

Gutiérrez, Ramón. 1983. *Arquitectura y urbanismo en Iberoamérica*. Madrid: Ediciones Cátedra.

Hale, Charles R. 2007. *Engaging Contradictions: Theory, Politics, and Methods of Activist Scholarship*. Berkeley: University of California Press.

Hanks, William F. 2010. *Converting Words: Maya in the Age of the Cross*. Berkeley: University of California Press.

Hanson, Craig A. 1995. "The Hispanic Horizon in Yucatan: A Model of Franciscan Missionization." *Ancient Mesoamerica* 6 (1): 15–28.

Hodges, Alison D. 2015. "Resistance, the Church, and a Comparison of Ceramics from Sixteenth-Century Caluco, El Salvador." PhD diss., Illinois State University, Normal.

Jones, Grant D. 1989. *Maya Resistance to Spanish Rule: Time and History on a Colonial Frontier*. Albuquerque: University of New Mexico Press.

Jordan, Kurt A. 2009. "Colonies, Colonialism, and Cultural Entanglement: The Archaeology of Postcolumbian Intercultural Relations." In *International Handbook of Historical Archaeology*, edited by Teresita Majewski and David Gaimster, 31–50. New York: Springer.

Joyce, Rosemary A. 2005. "What Kind of Subject of Study Is 'The Ancient Maya'?" *Reviews in Anthropology* 34 (4): 295–311.

Joyce, Rosemary A., Esteban Gómez, and Russell Sheptak. 2015. "Doing Historical Archaeology in Central America." In *The Oxford Handbook of Historical Archaeology*, edited by James Symonds and Vesa-Pekka Herva. Oxford: Oxford University Press. https://www.oxfordhandbooks.com/view/10.1093/oxfordhb/9780199562350.001.0001/oxfordhb-9780199562350. Accessed March 19, 2022.

Kaeding, Adam R. 2013. "Negotiated Survival: An Archaeological and Documentary Investigation of Colonialism in Beneficios Altos, Yucatan, Mexico." PhD diss., Boston University.

Kaeding, Adam R. 2017. "Negotiating Colonialism on the Southern Frontier of Spanish Yucatan." In *Frontiers of Colonialism*, edited by Christine D. Beaule, 59–88. Gainesville: University Press of Florida.

Kazanjian, David. 2003. *The Colonizing Trick: National Culture and Imperial Citizenship in Early America*. Minneapolis: University of Minnesota Press.

Kepecs, Susan. 1997. "Native Yucatán and Spanish Influence: The Archaeology and History of Chikinchel." *Journal of Archaeological Method and Theory* 4 (3/4): 307–329.

Kepecs, Susan. 1999. "The Political Economy of Chikinchel, Yucatán: A Diachronic Analysis from the Prehispanic Era through the Age of Spanish Administration." PhD diss., University of Wisconsin, Madison.

Kepecs, Susan. 2005. "Mayas, Spaniards, and Salt: World Systems Shifts in Sixteenth Century Yucatan." In *The Postclassic to Spanish-Era Transition in Mesoamerica: Archaeological Perspectives*, edited by Susan Kepecs and Rani T. Alexander, 117–138. Albuquerque: University of New Mexico Press.

Kepecs, Susan, and Rani T. Alexander, eds. 2005. *The Postclassic to Spanish-Era Transition in Mesoamerica: Archaeological Perspectives*. Albuquerque: University of New Mexico Press.

Lander, Edgardo, ed. 2000. *La colonialidad del saber: Eurocentrismo y ciencas sociales, perspectivas latinoamericanas*. Consejo Latinoamericano de Ciencias Sociales, Buenos Aires.

Lee, Thomas A., Jr. 1979. "Coapa Chiapas: A Sixteenth Century Coxoh Maya Village on the Camino Real." In *Maya Archaeology and Ethnohistory*, edited by Norman Hammond and Gordon R. Willey, 208–222. Austin: University of Texas Press.

Liebmann, Matthew. 2012. *Revolt: An Archaeological History of Pueblo Resistance and Revitalization in Seventeenth-Century New Mexico*. Tucson: University of Arizona Press.

Liebmann, Matthew, and Melissa S. Murphy, eds. 2010. *Enduring Conquests: Rethinking the Archaeology of Resistance to Spanish Colonialism in the Americas*. Santa Fe, NM: School of American Research Press.

Liebmann, Matthew, and Uzima Rizvi. 2008. *Archaeology and the Postcolonial Critique*. Lanham, MD: Altamira Press.

Lubkemann, Stephen C. 2008 *Culture in Chaos: An Anthropology of the Social Condition in War*. Chicago: University of Chicago Press.

Lugones, Maria. 2010. "Toward a Decolonial Feminism." *Hypatia* 25 (4): 742–759.

Lyons, Claire, and Jon K. Papadopoulos, eds. 2002. *The Archaeology of Colonialism*. Los Angeles: Getty Research Institute.

Manuel-Navarrete, David. 2012. "Entanglements of Power and Spatial Inequalities in Tourism in the Mexican Caribbean." Working Paper Series No. 17, https://www.desigualdades.net/Resources/Working_Paper/17_WP_Manuel-Navarrete_online.pdf.

Marcus, Joyce. 1983. "Lowland Maya Archaeology at the Crossroads." *American Antiquity* 48 (3): 454–488.

Marcus, Joyce. 1995. "Where Is Lowland Maya Archaeology Headed?" *Journal of Archaeological Research* 3 (1): 3–53.

Marcus, Joyce. 2003. "Recent Advances in Maya Archaeology." *Journal of Archaeological Research* 11 (2): 71–148.

Martos López, Luis Alberto. 2010. "Arqueología de la Guerra de Castas en Quintana Roo: El Baluarte de Yo'okop y el Camino a Chan Santa Cruz." *Boletín de Monumentos Históricos* 3 (18): 113–131.

Mathews, Jennifer P., and John Gust. 2017. "Cosmopolitan Living? Examining the Sugar and Rum Industry of the Costa Escondida, Quintana Roo, Mexico." In *The Value of Things: Prehistoric to Contemporary Commodities in the Maya Region*, edited by Jennifer P. Mathews and Thomas Guderjan, 144–162. Tucson: University of Arizona Press.

Mathews, Jennifer P., and Lilia Lizama-Rogers. 2005. "Jungle Rails: A Historic Narrow Gauge Railway in Quintana Roo." In *Quintana Roo Archaeology*, edited by Justine Shaw and Jennifer P. Mathews, 112–126. Tucson: University of Arizona Press.

Mathews, Jennifer P., and Gillian P. Schultz. 2009. *Chicle: The Chewing Gum of the Americas: From the Ancient Maya to William Wrigley*. Tucson: University of Arizona Press.

Mayfield, Tracie D. 2015. "The Nineteenth-Century British Plantation Settlement at Lamanai, Belize (1837–1868)." PhD diss., University of Arizona, Tucson.

McAnany, Patricia A. 2016. *Maya Cultural Heritage: How Archaeologists and Indigenous Communities Engage the Past*. Lanham, MD: Rowman and Littlefield.

McAnany, Patricia A., and Shoshaunna Parks. 2012. "Casualties of Heritage Distancing." *Current Anthropology* 53 (1): 80–107.

McCrea, Heather. 2010. *Diseased Relations: Epidemics, Public Health, and State-Building in Yucatán, Mexico, 1847–1924*. Albuquerque: University of New Mexico Press.

McGuire, Randall H., and Robert Paynter, eds. 1991. *The Archaeology of Inequality*. Cambridge, MA: Basil Blackwell.

Meyers, Allan D. 2012. *Outside the Hacienda Walls: The Archaeology of Plantation Peonage in Nineteenth-Century Yucatán*. Tucson: University of Arizona Press.

Miller, Arthur G., and Nancy Farriss. 1979. "Religious Syncretism in Colonial Yucatan: The Archaeological and Ethnohistorical Evidence from Tancah, Quintana Roo." In *Maya Archaeology and Ethnohistory*, edited by Norman Hammond and Gordon R. Willey, 223–240. Austin: University of Texas Press.

Moholy-Nagy, Hattula. 2012. *Historical Archaeology at Tikal, Guatemala: Tikal Report 37*. University Museum Monographs. Philadelphia: University of Pennsylvania Museum of Archaeology and Anthropology.

Montejo, Victor D. 1999. "The Public Eye: Becoming Maya? Appropriation of the White Shaman." *Native Americas* 16 (1): 58–61.

Morandi, Steven J. 2010. "Xibun Maya: The Archaeology of an Early Spanish Colonial Frontier in Southeastern Yucatán." PhD diss., Boston University.

Mrozowski, Stephen A., James A. Delle, and Robert Paynter. 2000. "Introduction." In *Lines That Divide: Historical Archaeologies of Race, Class, and Gender*, edited by James A. Delle, Stephen A. Mrozowski, and Robert Paynter, xi–xxxi. Knoxville: University of Tennessee Press.

Nance, Charles R., Stephen L. Whittington, and Barbara E. Jones-Borg. 2003. *Archaeology and Ethnohistory of Iximché*. Gainesville: University Press of Florida.

Ndlovu-Gatsheni, Sabelo J. 2013. *Empire, Global Coloniality and African Subjectivity*. New York: Berghahn Books.

Nemser, Daniel. 2017. *Infrastructures of Race: Concentration and Biopolitics in Colonial Mexico*. Austin: University of Texas Press.

Ng, Olivia. 2007. "View from the Periphery: A Hermeneutic Approach to the Archaeology of Holotunich (1865–1930), British Honduras." PhD diss., University of Pennsylvania, Philadelphia.

Nichols, Deborah L., and Christopher Pool. 2012. "Mesoamerican Archaeology: Recent Trends." In *The Oxford Handbook of Mesoamerican Archaeology*. Oxford: Oxford University Press. https://www.oxfordhandbooks.com/view/10.1093/oxfordhb/9780195390 933.001.0001/oxfordhb-9780195390933.

Oland, Maxine H. 2009. "Long-Term Indigenous History on a Colonial Frontier: Archaeology at a Fifteenth–Seventeenth Century Maya Village, Progress Lagoon, Belize." PhD diss., Northwestern University, Evanston, IL.

Oland, Maxine, Siobhan M. Hart, and Liam Frink. 2012. *Decolonizing Indigenous Histories: Exploring Prehistoric/Colonial Transitions in Archaeology*. Tucson: University of Arizona Press.

Oland, Maxine H., and Joel W Palka. 2016. "The Perduring Maya: New Archaeology on Early Colonial Transitions." *Antiquity* 90 (350): 472–486.

Orser, Charles E., Jr., ed. 2019. *Archaeologies of the British in Latin America*. Cham, Switzerland: Springer.

Palka, Joel W. 2005. *Unconquered Lacandon Maya: Ethnohistory and Archaeology of Indigenous Culture Change*. Gainesville: University Press of Florida.

Palka, Joel W. 2009. "Historical Archaeology of Indigenous Culture Change in Mesoamerica." *Journal of Archaeological Research* 17 (4): 297–346.

Paynter, Robert. 2000. "Historical Archaeology and the Post-Columbian World of North America." *Journal of Archaeological Research* 8 (3): 169–217.

Pezzarossi, Guido. 2014. "A New Materialist Archaeology of Antimarkets, Power and Capitalist Effects in Colonial Guatemala." PhD diss., Stanford University, Stanford, CA.

Pyburn, K. Anne. 1998. "Consuming the Maya." *Dialectical Anthropology* 23 (2): 111–129.

Pyburn, K. Anne. 2004. "We Have Never Been Post-modern: Maya Archaeology in the Ethnographic Present." In *Continuities and Changes in Maya archaeology: Perspectives at the Millennium*, edited by Charles W. Golden and Greg Borgstede, 257–272. New York: Routledge.

Quezada, Sergio. 2014. *Maya Lords and Lordship: The Formation of Colonial Society in Yucatán, 1350–1600*. Norman: University of Oklahoma Press.

Quijano, Aníbal. 2000. "Coloniality of Power and Eurocentrism in Latin America." *International Sociology* 15 (2): 215–232.

Quijano, Aníbal. 2007. "Coloniality and Modernity/rationality." *Cultural Studies* 21 (2–3): 168–178.

Ramsey, Jason. 2016. "Sedimentation and Sentiment." In *Elements of Architecture: Assembling Archaeology, Atmosphere, and the Performance of Building Spaces*, edited by Mikkel Bille and Tim Flohr Sørensen, 287–301. New York: Routledge.

Redfield, Robert. 1957. *A Village That Chose Progress: Chan Kom Revisited*. Chicago: University of Chicago Press.

Redfield, Robert, and Villa Rojas, Alfonso. (1934) 1967. *Chan Kom: A Maya Village*. Chicago: University of Chicago Press.

Restall, Matthew. 1997. *The Maya World: Yucatec Culture and Society, 1550–1850*. Stanford, CA: Stanford University Press.

Restall, Matthew. 2003. *Seven Myths of the Spanish Conquest*. Oxford: Oxford University Press.

Restall, Matthew. 2009. *The Black Middle: Africans, Mayas, and Spaniards in Colonial Yucatan*. Stanford, CA: Stanford University Press.

Restall, Matthew. 2012. "The New Conquest History." *History Compass* 10 (2): 151–160.

Rice, Don S., and Prudence M. Rice. 2004. "History in the Future: Historical Data and Investigations in Lowland Maya Studies." In *Continuities and Changes in Maya Archaeology: Perspectives at the Millennium*, edited by Charles Golden and Greg Borgstede, 71–87. New York: Routledge.

Schmidt, Erin. 2013. "An Examination of Capitalism in Nineteenth-Century Haciendas in Yucatan, Mexico." MA thesis, New Mexico State University, Albuquerque.

Sheptak, Russell. 2013. "Colonial Masca in Motion: Tactics of Persistence of a Honduran Indigenous Community." PhD diss., Leiden University, Netherlands.

Sigal, Peter. 2013. *From Moon Goddesses to Virgins: The Colonization of Yucatecan Maya Sexual Desire*. Austin: University of Texas Press.

Solari, Amara. 2013. *Maya Ideologies of the Sacred: The Transfiguration of Space in Colonial Yucatan*. Austin: University of Texas Press.

Speed, Shannon. 2017. "Structures of Settler Capitalism in Abya Yala." *American Quarterly* 69 (4): 783–790.

Stoler, Ann Laura. 2016. *Duress: Imperial Durabilities in Our Times*. Durham, NC: Duke University Press.

Sweitz, Sam R. 2012. *On the Periphery of the Periphery: Household Archaeology at Hacienda San Juan Bautista Tabi, Yucatán, Mexico*. New York: Springer.

Thomas, Julian. 2004. *Archaeology and Modernity*. New York: Routledge.

Thrasher, Christopher Adam. 2017. "Surviving Spanish Conquest: Yucatec Maya Social and Cultural Persistence." PhD diss., University of West Florida, Pensacola.

Tiesler, Vera, Pilar Zabala, and Andrea Cucina, eds. 2010. *Natives, Europeans, and Africans in Colonial Campeche: History and Archaeology*. Gainesville: University Press of Florida.

Van Buren, Mary. 2010. "The Archaeological Study of Spanish Colonialism in the Americas." *Journal of Archaeological Research* 18 (2): 151–201.

Vanthuyne, Karine. 2009. "Becoming Maya? The Politics and Pragmatics of 'Being Indigenous' in Postgenocide Guatemala." *PoLAR: Political and Legal Anthropology Review* 32 (2): 195–217.

Victoria Ojeda, Jorge, and Jorge Canto Alcocer. 2006. *San Fernando Aké: Microhistoria de una comunidad afroamericana en Yucatán*. Tratados 24. Mérida: Ediciones de la Universidad Autónoma de Yucatán.

Voss, Barbara L., and Eleanor Conlin Casella. 2012. *The Archaeology of Colonialism: Intimate Encounters and Sexual Effects.* New York: Cambridge University Press.

Watanabe, John M. 1995. "Unimagining the Maya: Anthropologists, Others, and the Inescapable Hubris of Authorship." *Bulletin of Latin American Research* 14 (1): 25–45.

Wilk, Richard R. 1985. "The Ancient Maya and the Political Present." *Journal of Anthropological Research* 41 (3): 307–326.

Wynter, Sylvia. 2003. "Unsettling the Coloniality of Being/Power/Truth/Freedom: Towards the Human, after Man, Its Overrepresentation-An Argument." *CR: The New Centennial Review* 3 (3): 257–337.

Yaeger, Jason, Minette C. Church, Richard M. Leventhal, and Jennifer Dornan. 2004. "Maya Caste War Immigrants in colonial British Honduras: The San Pedro Maya Project, 2000–2003." In *Archaeological Investigations in the Eastern Maya Lowlands: Papers of the 2003 Belize Archaeology Symposium*, edited by Jamie J. Awe, John Michael Morris, and Sherilyne Jones, 103–114. Belmopan: Print Belize.

Yaeger, Jason, and Cynthia Robin. 2004. "Heterogenous Hinterlands: The Social and Political Organization of Commoner Settlements near Xunantunich, Belize." In *Ancient Maya Commoners*, edited by Jon C. Lohse and Fred Valdez Jr., 147–174. Austin: University of Texas Press.

COLONIAL LIVES

Tiffany C. Fryer and Kasey Diserens Morgan

One of the greatest strengths of Mayanist archaeology is, perhaps, its long-standing relationship to ethnohistory (Jones 1977; Hammond and Willey 1979; Bryant 1988; Rice and Rice 2004). Interpretations founded on *both* artifactual and textual remnants—whether hieroglyphic stelae or Spanish- and Maya-language colonial documents (including such texts as parish records and prophetic codices; Restall 1997; Chuchiak 2010)—provide a wealth of possible analytical avenues to Mayanist archaeologists studying the post-fifteenth century (see Golden and Borgstede 2004; Alexander and Kepecs 2018). Yet, archaeological contributions to Maya studies remain overwhelmingly geared toward understanding precolonial Maya societies, despite the demonstrated successes of historical archaeologies of colonialism in other regions of the Americas. A notable early exception was Suzanne Miles's (1957) article that—apart from her having produced it at a time when both the subject matter of the Colonial period and the participation of women in archaeology remained marginalized—innovatively drew on both archival and archaeological evidence to reconstruct Pokom-Maya society as it would have been at earliest contact with the Spanish (another project

https://doi.org/10.5876/9781646422845.p001

worth noting for its early establishment is the Coxoh Colonial Project [Lee and Markman 1977]).

Those few archaeologists working on the transition between late postclassic sociopolitical systems and early colonial ones have laid the foundations for more sustained engagement with historical archaeologies of Spanish and British colonialisms in the Maya world (Gasco 1992, 2005; Kepecs 1999; Kepecs and Alexander 2005; Rice and Rice 2005, 2018; Sampeck 2007, 2010; Oland and Palka 2016; Orser 2019). Such archaeologies trace the morphologies of these cultural transformations from the earliest periods of contact around 1518 to the mid-1800s as the yoke of colonial subjugation was replaced by the complexities of nationhood and citizenship following Independence (with the exception, of course, of British Honduras, which did not gain Independence as Belize until 1981).

Of special importance to this topic is the history of missionization (a history that historical archaeologists working across the formerly Spanish territories of the Americas have consistently attended to; see Panich and Schneider 2014, 2015). The relationship between military and religious conquest was a complicated one that left unmistakable material signatures (Miller and Farriss 1979; Graham 1998; Carruthers 2003; Pugh, Rómulo Sánchez, and Shiratori 2012; Pugh et al. 2016). Maya themselves played a central role in the effectiveness of religious subjugation (Sigal 2000; Hanks 2010; Christensen 2013, 2016), though the more spectacular acts of religious violence, such as Fray Diego de Landa's burning of the Maya codices, continue to capture the imagination. Archaeologists are showing more interest in the period of early contact, invasion, and colonial subjugation, though it too remains understudied.

We know that Maya were not passive recipients of colonialism. Many fought for centuries to maintain control over their lands and lifeways (Chamberlain 1948; Clendinnen [1987] 2003; Jones 1989, 1998; Bracamonte y Sosa 2001). The efficacy of their resistance often facilitated the maintenance of at least some forms of noncolonial social life and material culture (Farriss 1984; Graham, Pendergast, and Jones 1989; Simmons 1995; Restall 1997). Former Maya rulers and administrators became *casta* elites, who took advantage of their social status, organized labor, and collected taxes in newly founded colonial towns (Quezada 1985; Oland 2014). In later years, those more politically motivated Maya administrators became revolutionaries (Bricker 1981). Systems of collective ownership and centuries-old agricultural practices continued, though in metamorphosed forms (Robin 2012; Alexander and Hernández Álvarez 2018; Dedrick, McAnany, and Batún Alpuche, chapter 2 in this volume). New forms of economic exchange and capitalist expansion began to sink in too as the tensions between Spanish systems of tribute and competition between European imperial powers grew and settled throughout the region (Pezzarossi 2015).

Following trends in ethnohistory and cultural anthropology, recent archaeological models of the European Colonial period in the Americas have moved away from top-down assimilationist and acculturative explanations. These forms of explanation tend to rely too heavily on assumptions of the superiority of European cultural and technological forms and the attempts by surviving Native populations to incorporate them. Instead, researchers are moving toward a more dynamic model emphasizing bidirectional cultural exchange and the agency of colonially subjugated persons (Oland 2012; Gillenwater 2014; Palka 2015; Alexander 2019). This sort of exchange leads to the formation of new cultural practices and new social systems—a process known as "ethnogenesis" (Restall 2004; Restall and Gabbert 2017; see also Voss 2008).

Yet, we see opportunities still to complicate this model further by expanding archaeological notions of ethnogenesis to reflect the realities of a multiethnic colonial society. Such analyses necessitate attention to not only European settlers and Indigenous peoples but also the Afro- and Asian-descendant peoples brought to this region by the capitalist forces of slavery, unfree labor, and maritime life under the colonial project (Cheek 1997; Bennett 2009; Restall 2009; Herrera 2010; Wesp, chapter 3 in this volume). Although there have been recent engagements with this framework across Mesoamerica, archaeologists of the Maya region specifically are only now taking our material understandings of colonial social life in this direction (Victoria Ojeda and Canto Alcocer 2006; Tiesler, Zabala, and Cucina 2010; Wesp, chapter 3 in this volume). Moreover, issues of gender, health, and childhood all remain areas of potential for the archaeological study of colonial Maya society (Danforth, Jacobi, and Cohen 2008).

The chapters in part I augment the even more sparse investigations of the Middle Colonial period (roughly 1620–1780)—a period characterized by a steadily rooting European colonial rule (Pendergast 1993; Pendergast, Jones, and Graham 1993; Sampeck 2014; Awe and Helmke 2015). Our case studies highlight some of the diverse ways in which residents of the region dealt with changing lifeways and varied levels of subjugation. In what follows, we will see that this burgeoning world order created new patterns of movement and migration, alternative food subsistence strategies, new networks of exchange, and concerns for security. We also see that the settler colonial logics set in motion during this period continue to play out in the ways we have traditionally constructed knowledge about "the Maya." We can upset such forms of colonialist knowledge construction by making subtle-but-substantial shifts in the sorts of questions we chose to ask of the historical and archaeological records.

References

Alexander, Rani T., ed. 2019. *Technology and Tradition in Mesoamerica after the Spanish Invasion: Archaeological Perspectives*. Albuquerque: University of New Mexico Press.

Alexander, Rani T., and Héctor Hernández Álvarez. 2018. "Agropastoralism and House-hold Ecology in Yucatán after the Spanish Invasion." *Environmental Archaeology* 23 (1): 69–79.

Alexander, Rani T., and Susan Kepecs, eds. 2018. *Colonial and Postcolonial Change in Mesoamerica: Archaeology as Historical Anthropology.* Albuquerque: University of New Mexico Press.

Awe, Jaime J., and Christophe Helmke. 2015. "The Sword and the Olive Jar: Material Evidence of Seventeenth-Century Maya European Interaction in Central Belize." *Ethnohistory* 62 (2): 333–360.

Bennett, Herman L. 2009. *Colonial Blackness: A History of Afro-Mexico. Blacks in the Diaspora.* Bloomington: Indiana University Press.

Bracamonte y Sosa, Pedro. 2001. *La conquista inconclusa de Yucatán: Los mayas de las montañas, 1560–1680* [The unfinished conquest of Yucatán: The mountain Mayas, 1560–1680]. Mexico City: Centro de Investigaciones y Estudios Superiores en Antropología Social (CIESAS).

Bricker, Victoria Reifler. 1981. *The Indian Christ, the Indian King: The Historical Substrate of Maya Myth and Ritual.* Austin: University of Texas Press.

Bryant, Douglas Donne, ed. 1988. *Archaeology, Ethnohistory, and Ethnoarchaeology in the Maya Highlands of Chiapas, Mexico.* Provo, Utah: New World Archaeological Foundation, Brigham Young University.

Carruthers, Clive. 2003. "Spanish 'Botijas' or Olive Jars from the Santo Domingo Monastery, La Antigua Guatemala." *Historical Archaeology* 37 (4): 40–55.

Chamberlain, Robert S. 1948. *The Conquest and Colonization of Yucatan, 1517–1551.* Washington, DC: Carnegie Institution.

Cheek, Charles. 1997. "Setting an English Table: Black Carib Archaeology on the Caribbean Coast of Honduras." In *Approaches to the Historical Archaeology of Mexico, Central and South America,* edited by Janine Gasco, Greg Smith, and Patricia Fournier-Garcia, 101–109. Los Angeles: Institute of Archaeology, UCLA.

Christensen, Mark Z. 2013. *Nahua and Maya Catholicisms: Texts and Religion in Colonial Central Mexico and Yucatan.* Stanford, CA: Stanford University Press.

Christensen, Mark Z. 2016. *The Teabo Manuscript: Maya Christian Copybooks, Chilam Balams, and Native Text Production in Yucatán.* Austin: University of Texas Press.

Chuchiak, John F., IV. 2010. "Writing as Resistance: Maya Graphic Pluralism and Indigenous Elite Strategies for Survival in Colonial Yucatan, 1550–1750." *Ethnohistory* 57 (1): 87–116.

Clendinnen, Inga. (1987) 2003. *Ambivalent Conquests: Maya and Spaniard in Yucatan, 1517–1570.* Cambridge, UK: Cambridge University Press.

Danforth, Marie Elaine, Keith P. Jacobi, and Mark Nathan Cohen. 2008. "Gender and Health among the Colonial Maya of Tipu, Belize." *Ancient Mesoamerica* 8 (1): 13–22.

Farriss, Nancy M. 1984. *Maya Society under Colonial Rule: The Collective Enterprise of Survival*. Princeton, NJ: Princeton University Press.

Gasco, Janine. 1992. "Material Culture and Indian Society in Southern Mesoamerica: The View from Coastal Chiapas, Mexico." *Historical Archaeology* 26 (1): 67–74.

Gasco, Janine. 2005. "The Consequences of Spanish Colonial Rule for the Indigenous Peoples of Chiapas, Mexico." In *The Postclassic to Spanish-Era Transition in Mesoamerica: Archaeological Perspectives*, edited by Susan Kepecs and Rani T. Alexander. Albuquerque: University of New Mexico Press.

Gillenwater, Collin Roderick. 2013. "Agency at Hacienda Pancota: Early Colonial Daily Consumption of a Contested Age and Material Culture." MA thesis, Illinois State University, Normal.

Golden, Charles W., and Greg Borgstede, eds. 2004. *Continuities and Changes in Maya Archaeology: Perspectives at the Millennium*. New York: Routledge.

Graham, Elizabeth. 1998. "Mission Archaeology." *Annual Reviews of Anthropology* 27: 25–62.

Graham, Elizabeth, David M. Pendergast, and Grant D. Jones. 1989. "On the Fringes of Conquest: Maya-Spanish Contact in Colonial Belize." *Science* 246 (4935): 1254–1259.

Hammond, Norman, and Gordon R. Willey, eds. *Maya Archaeology and Ethnohistory*. Austin: University of Texas Press.

Hanks, William F. 2010. *Converting Words: Maya in the Age of the Cross*. Berkeley: University of California Press.

Herrera, Robinson A. 2010. *Natives, Europeans, and Africans in Sixteenth-Century Santiago de Guatemala*. Austin: University of Texas Press.

Jones, Grant D., ed. 1977. *Anthropology and History in Yucatán*. Austin: University of Texas Press.

Jones, Grant D. 1989. *Maya Resistance to Spanish Rule: Time and History on a Colonial Frontier*. Albuquerque: University of New Mexico Press.

Jones, Grant D. 1998. *The Conquest of the Last Maya Kingdom*. Stanford, CA: Stanford University Press.

Kepecs, Susan. 1999. "The Political Economy of Chikinchel, Yucatan, Mexico: A Diachronic Analysis from the Prehispanic Era through the age of Spanish Administration." PhD diss., University of Wisconsin, Madison.

Kepecs, Susan, and Rani T. Alexander, eds. 2005. *The Postclassic to Spanish-Era Transition in Mesoamerica: Archaeological Perspectives*. Albuquerque: University of New Mexico Press.

Lee, Thomas A., and Sidney D. Markman. 1977. "The Coxoh Colonial Project and Coneta, Chiapas Mexico: A Provincial Maya Village under the Spanish Conquest." *Historical Archaeology* 11 (1): 56–66.

Miles, Suzanne W. 1957. "The Sixteenth-Century Pokom-Maya: A Documentary Analysis of Social Structure and Archaeological Setting." *Transactions of the American Philosophical Society* 47 (4): 733–781.

Miller, Arthur G., and Nancy M. Farriss. 1979. "Religious Syncretism in Colonial Yucatan: The Archaeological and Ethnohistorical Evidence from Tancah, Quintana Roo." In *Maya Archaeology and Ethnohistory*, edited by Norman Hammond and Gordon R. Willey, 223–240. Austin: University of Texas Press.

Oland, Maxine. 2012. "Lost among the Colonial Maya." In *Decolonizing Indigenous Histories: Exploring Prehistoric/Colonial Transitions in Archaeology*, 178–200. Tucson: University of Arizona Press.

Oland, Maxine. 2014. " 'With the Gifts and Good Treatment That He Gave Them': Elite Maya Adoption of Spanish Material Culture at Progresso Lagoon, Belize." *International Journal of Historical Archaeology* 18 (4): 643–667.

Oland, Maxine, and Joel W. Palka. 2016. "The Perduring Maya: New Archaeology on Early Colonial Transitions." *Antiquity* 90 (350): 472–486.

Panich, Lee, and Tsim D. Schneider, eds. 2014. *Indigenous Landscapes and Spanish Missions: New Perspectives from Archaeology and Ethnohistory*. Tucson: University of Arizona Press.

Panich, Lee M., and Tsim D. Schneider. 2015. "Expanding Mission Archaeology: A Landscape Approach to Indigenous Autonomy in Colonial California." *Journal of Anthropological Archaeology* 40: 48–58.

Palka, Joel W. 2015. "Lacandon Maya Culture Change and Survival in the Lowland Frontier of the Expanding Guatemalan and Mexican Republics." In *Studies in Culture Contact: Interaction, Culture Change, and Archaeology*, edited by James G. Cusick, 457–475. Carbondale: Southern Illinois University Press.

Pendergast, David M. 1993. "Worlds in Collision: The Maya/Spanish Encounter in Sixteenth and Seventeenth Century Belize." *Proceedings of the British Academy* 81: 105–143.

Pendergast, David M., Grant D. Jones, and Elizabeth Graham. 1993. "Locating Maya Lowlands Spanish Colonial Towns: A Case Study from Belize." *Latin American Antiquity* 4 (1): 59–73.

Pezzarossi, Guido. 2015. "Tribute, Antimarkets, and Consumption: An Archaeology of Capitalist Effects in Colonial Guatemala." In *Archaeology of Culture Contact and Colonialism in Spanish and Portuguese America*, edited by Pedro Paulo A. Funari and Maria Ximena Senatore, 79–102. New York: Springer.

Pugh, Timothy W., José Rómulo Sánchez, and Yuko Shiratori. 2012. "Contact and Missionization at Tayasal, Petén, Guatemala." *Journal of Field Archaeology* 37 (1): 3–19.

Pugh, Timothy W., Katherine Miller Wolf, Carolyn Freiwald, and Prudence M. Rice. 2016. "Technologies of Domination at Mission San Bernabé, Petén, Guatemala." *Ancient Mesoamerica* 27 (1): 49–70.

Quezada, Sergio. 1985. "Encomienda, cabildo y gubernatura indígena en Yucatán, 1541–1583." *Historia Mexicana*, 34 (4): 662–684.

Restall, Matthew. 1997. *The Maya World: Yucatec Culture and Society, 1550–1850*. Stanford, CA: Stanford University Press.

Restall, Matthew. 2004. "Maya Ethnogenesis." *Journal of Latin American Anthropology* 9 (1): 64–89.

Restall, Matthew. 2009. *The Black Middle: Africans, Mayas, and Spaniards in Colonial Yucatan*. Stanford, CA: Stanford University Press.

Restall, Matthew, and Wolfgang Gabbert. 2017. "Maya Ethnogenesis and Group Identity in Yucatán, 1500–1900." In *"The Only True People": Linking Maya Identities Past and Present*, edited by Bethany J. Beyette and Lisa J. LeCount, 91–130. Boulder: University Press of Colorado.

Rice, Don S., and Prudence M. Rice. 2004. "History in the Future: Historical Data and Investigations in Lowland Maya Studies." In *Continuities and Changes in Maya Archaeology: Perspectives at the Millennium*, edited by Charles W. Golden and Greg Borgstede, 71–87. New York: Routledge.

Rice, Don S., and Prudence M. Rice. 2005. "Sixteenth- and Seventeenth-Century Maya Political Geography in Central Petén, Guatemala." In *The Postclassic to Spanish-Era Transition in Mesoamerica: Archaeological Perspectives*, edited by Susan Kepecs and Rani T. Alexander, 139–160. Albuquerque: University of New Mexico Press.

Rice, Prudence M, and Don S. Rice, eds. 2018. *Historical and Archaeological Perspectives on the Itzas of Petén, Guatemala*. Boulder: University Press of Colorado.

Robin, Cynthia, ed. 2012. *Chan: An Ancient Maya Farming Community*. Gainesville: University Press of Florida.

Sampeck, Kathryn E. 2007. "Late Postclassic to Colonial Landscapes and Political Economy of the Izalcos Region, El Salvador." PhD diss., Tulane University, New Orleans.

Sampeck, Kathryn E. 2010. "Late Postclassic to Colonial Transformations of the Landscape in the Izalcos Region of Western El Salvador." *Ancient Mesoamerica* 21 (2): 261–282.

Sampeck, Kathryn E. 2014. "From Ancient Altepetl to Modern Municipios: Surveying as Power in Colonial Guatemala." *International Journal of Historical Archaeology* 18 (1): 175–203.

Sigal, Pete. 2000. *From Moon Goddesses to Virgins: The Colonization of Yucatecan Maya Sexual Desire*. Austin: University of Texas Press.

Simmons, Scott E. 1995. "Maya Resistance, Maya Resolve: The Tools of Autonomy from Tipu, Belize." *Ancient Mesoamerica* 6 (2): 135–146.

Tiesler, Vera, Aguirre P. Zabala, and Andrea Cucina, eds. 2010. *Natives, Europeans, and Africans in Colonial Campeche: History and Archaeology*. Gainesville: University Press of Florida.

Victoria Ojeda, Jorge, and Jorge Canto Alcocer. 2006. *San Fernando Aké: Microhistoria de una comunidad afroamericana en Yucatán*. Tratados 24. Mérida: Ediciones de la Universidad Autónoma de Yucatán.

Voss, Barbara L. 2008. *The Archaeology of Ethnogenesis: Race and Sexuality in San Francisco*. Berkeley: University of California Press.

2

A Livelihoods Approach to Colonial Period Farming Strategies at Tahcabo, Yucatán

Maia Dedrick, Patricia A. McAnany, and Adolfo Iván Batún Alpuche

Food insecurity threatens populations around the world today, especially as climate change presents special challenges to subsistence farmers. Our research considers how food insecurity developed throughout the Colonial period in Yucatán, Mexico, and how it impacted local livelihoods over the long term. Archaeological investigation of humble residences produces data about the lives of people who may not have been literate and whose voices are accordingly underrepresented in the historical record. Their experiences can highlight the negative legacies of colonialism but can also reveal the ways in which people assert agency and, in some cases, reject colonial policies and practices that threaten their well-being.

Yucatán, where Spaniards first made landfall during the 1510s, is considered to have been conquered by 1547, though rebellions and the presence of unconquered zones continued to interrupt colonial interests for centuries (Farriss 1984, 14). Beginning in the late 1540s, Spaniards exacted tribute from local populations, forcibly resettled them into designated communities, and sought to convert them to Catholicism. Spaniards integrated Yucatecan products into the global

https://doi.org/10.5876/9781646422845.c002

economy by selling them in Europe and elsewhere. The Colonial period ended by 1821, when Mexico officially won Independence from Spain, initiating the Republican period. Research into Yucatecan Colonial and Republican period livelihood strategies can provide useful comparative material for understanding economic activities pursued in rural communities today. The events of these periods set into motion the stark social inequities, global market integration, and technological developments that now characterize the region. While Spaniards and Spanish Creoles benefited from resource extraction and global trade, Yucatecan farmers living in rural communities experienced exploitation and abuse that threatened their lives and food security. Archaeology can provide insights into the economic decisions that farmers made given the circumstances and the outcomes of those decisions in terms of the sustainability of livelihoods, environments, and institutions.

At the site of Tahcabo, Yucatán, we excavated Colonial period houses located around the outskirts of the contemporary community. As a result, we focus not on town elites, who likely lived centrally in the community (Alexander 2012, 17), but on marginalized and mobile populations less well-integrated into the social life and economic underpinnings of the town. In this chapter, we explore the strategies that farming households used to reduce risk and promote household well-being (and particularly food security) throughout the Colonial period at Tahcabo. Notably, our inferences about the evidence recovered from these houses do not align well with descriptions of Spanish expectations for the region based on historical documents or excavation findings from contemporaneous elite residences. However, a livelihood framework (adapted from rural development studies) can help to explain the discrepancies between archaeological data and historical documents.

Livelihoods Approach

Scholars crafting policies for sustainable rural development have advanced and critiqued the livelihoods framework for the study of household decision making (Ellis 2000; Scoones 2009; figure 2.1), which defines the range of contexts, including the historical and political factors as well as macroeconomic conditions that shape local economic activities. This framework proposes that households make economic decisions while considering their assets and the social mediators and institutions that pertain to them. According to the framework, sustainable decisions result in livelihood security and well-being for communities and environments.

Agricultural and livelihood strategies may include the intensification, extensification, and diversification of economic activities, as well as migration or mobility (Messer 1989; Morrison 1996; Ellis 2000, 290–294; Hostettler 2003; Steward 2007). During the Colonial period and beyond in Yucatán, populations used mobility

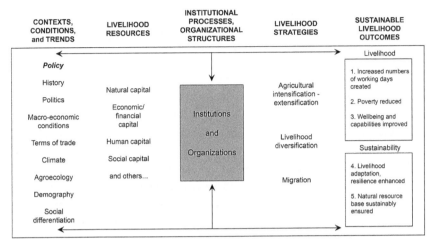

| CONTEXTS, CONDITIONS, and TRENDS | LIVELIHOOD RESOURCES | INSTITUTIONAL PROCESSES, ORGANIZATIONAL STRUCTURES | LIVELIHOOD STRATEGIES | SUSTAINABLE LIVELIHOOD OUTCOMES |

FIGURE 2.1. *Schematic of the sustainable livelihoods framework. Adapted from Scoones 1998,* Sustainable Rural Livelihoods: A Framework for Analysis, IDS working paper, 72 *(Brighton, UK: Institute of Development Studies). Reproduced with permission.*

as a strategy for food and livelihood security in order to distance themselves from harsh tax burdens, droughts, political unrest, and other changing contexts (Farriss 1984, 78; see Badillo Sánchez [chapter 6], Houk and colleagues [chapter 7], Mathews, Gust, and Fedick [chapter 10], and Meierhoff [chapter 8], this volume). This strategy meant that rural populations considered flexibility when evaluating investment in the production of any specific good within a livelihood portfolio (Farris 1984, 73). On the other hand, and especially later in the Colonial period, as people moved to work at private estates such as haciendas and *ranchos*, Yucatec populations grappled with the existential predicament of exchanging autonomy for food and livelihood security against a background of increasing insecurity induced by droughts, associated pestilence, land pressure, and political factors (Peniche Moreno 2009; Hoggarth et al. 2017; see Mathews, Gust, and Fedick, chapter 10 in this volume).

In the following section, we introduce the research site of Tahcabo and provide context for understanding the livelihood strategies of the town's residents. Because mobility played a large role in livelihood strategies throughout the Colonial period, we explore the different types of mobility employed through time and introduce data from surviving population records. Next, we present archaeological evidence that provides insights into livelihood strategies selected in Tahcabo. In particular, we consider the sizes of residences and the range of plant and animal foods consumed within them. We then compare the identified livelihood strategies to expectations based on historical documents and previous archaeological research. These comparisons allow us to highlight the

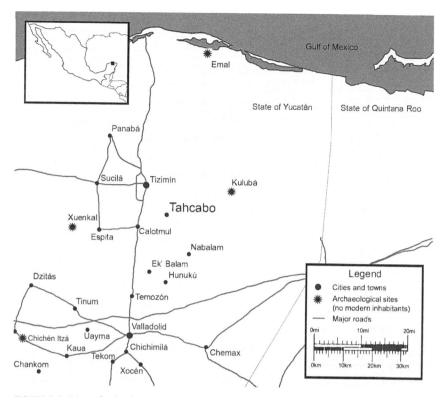

FIGURE 2.2. *Map of Tahcabo in relation to other sites and settlements of northeastern Yucatán. By Maia Dedrick.*

utility of the livelihoods framework for archaeological analysis, and to suggest refinements to the framework that might be explored through additional archaeological study.

Research Site and Historical Context

Adolfo Iván Batún Alpuche of the Universidad de Oriente in Valladolid and Patricia A. McAnany of the University of North Carolina (coauthors) at Chapel Hill codirect the Proyecto Arqueológico Colaborativo del Oriente de Yucatán (PACOY), based in Tahcabo (Batún Alpuche et al. 2017). Maia Dedrick (coauthor) collected the excavation data reported herein as part of her dissertation fieldwork (2019). Tahcabo, situated in northeastern Yucatán, is today a small community of about 500 inhabitants (SEDESOL 2014; figure 2.2). In the distant past, Tahcabo was a minor ceremonial center, as indicated by a central mound with a Preclassic core, next to which sits a Colonial period church dedicated to San Bartolomé and established by 1612 (López de Cogolludo 1688; Fernández

1945; Andrews 1991, 365). Tahcabo was a colonial *visita*, meaning that it was a relatively small community visited by priests from larger population centers. Early on, priests visited Tahcabo from Tizimín, about thirteen kilometers to the northwest (RHGY [1579] 1900, 58). By the seventeenth century, however, priests were dispatched from the municipal seat of Calotmul, just ten kilometers to the southwest (López de Cogolludo 1688, 238; figure 2.2).

Archaeological survey in areas around the town center indicates that Tahcabo sustained a high population from the Middle Preclassic through Early Classic periods (ca. 300 BC–AD 550) and during the Late to Terminal Classic period (ca. AD 550–1100). We found Postclassic artifacts mostly within the central area of the town, where people have lived consistently through time, mixing archaeological contexts as they go about their daily lives. Colonial and Early Republican period artifacts can be found distributed across the site and indicate higher populations during those periods than today, a point we will further explore in the section "Population Mobility."

Historical Context

Historical records indicate Tahcabo's long history as a tributary community, first to the rulers of Ek' Balam, and then to Spaniards. According to an early colonial document, Tahcabo paid tribute to the ruler of Ek' Balam, Namon Cupul, prior to Spanish arrival in products such as maize, turkeys, fish, cotton, and cloth (RHGY [1579] 1900, 53). During the sixteenth century, Spaniards forcefully gathered Maya peoples from dispersed settlements across Yucatán into selected communities (including Tahcabo), through a process known as *reducción* or *congregación* (Patch 1993). By driving people together into fewer, larger towns, Spaniards could more easily convert and extract tribute from a locally controlled and surveilled population. As part of the congregación process, Catholic clergy commanded that people live in nuclear-family dwellings organized along a gridded street plan, prohibited fields and forests within town, and encouraged the adoption of cattle and other European-introduced domesticates (Ancona 1889, 541, 553, 555; Farriss 1984, 169).

Spaniards especially desired valuable trade goods, including cotton cloth and thread as well as honey and beeswax, and enacted many policies to extract these products from Yucatecan communities. By the 1540s, heavy taxes were demanded by encomenderos, Spaniards to whom the Spanish Crown granted rights to the labor and goods of native inhabitants within an encomienda (designated territory). Encomienda territory assignments, which did not respect previously established divisions, contributed substantially to political change over the following century (Farriss 1984, 149; Quezada 1993; Alexander 2004a, 39).

The Spanish Crown gave encomenderos permission to extract goods and labor from the people who lived in their assigned areas, even as populations

FIGURE 2.3. *Coin found at a later colonial house at Tahcabo (see "Late Colonial House 3," figure 2.5). With permission from M. K. Smaby.*

dwindled. Apart from encomienda taxes, church donations called *limosnas* also burdened Maya communities during the Early Colonial period (Farriss 1984). By the late Colonial period if not sooner, *obvenciones* (mandatory church head taxes) and *repartimiento* (the purchase of commodities from communities at low prices) added to the heavy tax burden that people faced from the church and the state (Hunt 1974; Farris 1984, 43; Quezada 2001b). Community taxes eventually contributed to the tax load as well.

By the late 1600s populations began to pay tribute in currency rather than in products (García Bernal 1978, 388–394). At a late colonial house platform on the southeast side of Tahcabo, we found a coin dating to 1775 worth one-half *real* (figure 2.3). This find demonstrates the increasing integration of even small households near the edge of town into Spanish currency exchange, perhaps for tribute payments. Tahcabo residents also may have engaged with markets through involvement in wage labor, repartimiento contracts, or the sale of agricultural products.

An early historical record dating to 1565 ("Residencia de Don Diego de Quijada") mentions that established and newly appointed elites vied for power at Tahcabo as Spaniards attempted to subvert traditional power structures (Quezada 2014, 114). Similarly, Spaniards sought to break apart earlier trade networks and supplant them with their own exchange system. Encomendero Juan de Contreras imposed repartimiento on Tahcabo and other towns in his jurisdiction during the mid-1500s. He forced the sale of cacao on those living in his encomienda territory (Quezada 2014, 93) and obtained cotton from them, which he then sold at high prices to those in areas unable to produce the crop at satisfactory levels (Quezada 2001b, 22). Apart from cotton, thread, and cloth, Spanish authorities

FIGURE 2.4. *Cross-section of rejollada. Drawing by M. K. Smaby.*

sought beeswax from Tahcabo, a place of apiaries, as indicated by the town's ancient name (*tah cab*, which can be translated as honey of the *tajonal* [*Viguiera dentata*] flower; Roys 1933, 26). The demand for wax to produce church candles likely augmented the importance of beekeeping at Tahcabo during the Colonial period. While few documents relating to Tahcabo survive from the seventeenth or eighteenth centuries, a repartimiento list from 1664 indicates that Tahcabo residents collectively fifty 50 *mantas* (cotton cloths), eight *arrobas* (blocks) of beeswax, and eighty bales of raw cotton on three occasions that year (García Bernal 2005, 245).

Assets

Tahcabo and surrounding communities contain abundant cenotes and *rejolladas* (figure 2.4). Both of these landscape features are sinkholes; cenotes are deeper and retain water year-round, while rejolladas do not reach the water table and instead are areas where soil and water collect, providing a rich cultivation medium for almost any plant. The central municipal land of Tahcabo contains eight rejolladas, 60 to 100 meters in diameter and up to 6 meters deep (figure 2.5). Tahcabo residents use those located close to houses for gardening. Rejolladas maintain soil deposits that often are more than two meters in depth (González de la Mata 2006) in an area otherwise characterized by thin soils (0 to 30 centimeters in depth). These landscape features share consistent characteristics across the northern Yucatán peninsula: high humidity, fertile soil, and great utility for growing diverse plant crops. Tahcabo residents easily identify and

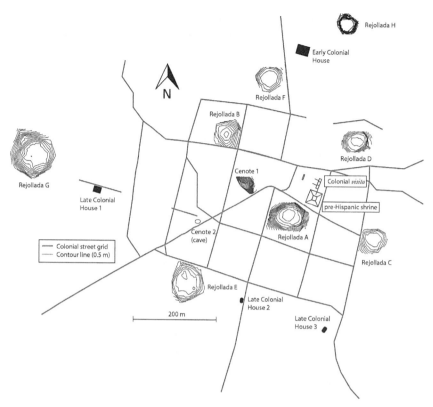

FIGURE 2.5. *Map of Tahcabo with colonial structures and gridded street plan. By Maia Dedrick.*

scientific studies confirm these characteristics (Munro-Stasiuk et al. 2014). Over time, these sinkholes attracted sometimes highly mobile populations who maintained landscape knowledge indispensable for those seeking flexible livelihoods. In Tahcabo, people have used rejolladas for thousands of years despite dramatic population fluctuations, and they continue to make use of them today for both ritual and agricultural purposes (Kanxoc Kumul and Dedrick 2016; Dedrick, Pope, and Russell 2018; Dedrick 2019).

Within rejolladas and gardens in Yucatán, the maintenance of biodiversity produces the highest biomass (del Amo and Ramos 1993; de Clerck and Negreros-Castillo 2000). Today, Tahcabo residents cultivate fruit trees and root crops in rejolladas due to the availability of moist and deep soils (Kanxoc Kumul and Dedrick 2016). Sun-loving crops, however, are generally at a disadvantage in rejolladas, since their ideal environment requires the removal of trees and tall shrubs. Thus, only with considerable motivation would households use rejolladas located near their houses, which are typically biodiverse food sources, for the specialized production of crops such as sun-loving maize and cotton (or crops such as watermelon today). Spaniards demanded both maize and cotton as tribute during the Colonial period, and Jones (2017) identified pollen grains from both crops in soil samples from rejolladas located in Tahcabo, though the cotton pollen grain may date to an earlier period. Historical documents indicate that northeastern Yucatán was an exceptionally productive area for cotton cultivation (Quezada 2001a).

Population Mobility

Throughout the Colonial period, people moved across the landscape in several different ways. During the earliest phase, as already mentioned, Spanish authorities forced populations off their lands and into sanctioned towns. Throughout the Early Colonial period (defined here as ca. 1520–1650), people fled across the frontier to resist Spanish orders to congregate and also to avoid disease (Alexander 2006, 450). Soon after Spaniards drove people into towns, populations left again to escape tax burdens, debt, factionalism, and political unrest (Farriss 1984, 75). They moved to areas beyond the frontier or to another town or city, to which debts from their previous places of residence could not be traced. They also may have joined communities in which family members were already established. Colonial documents indicate that people arriving at new towns would be warmly welcomed by those sharing a surname (de Landa [1566] 1982, 41–42; Restall 1997, 18, 48). There may have been little reason to remain in congregated communities, especially in light of a royal ordinance issued in 1552 prohibiting people from keeping stands of trees within their towns (though a few isolated fruit trees were allowed; Ancona 1889, 541, 553). In many cases, lands to which people held rights were located as far as twenty kilometers away from the towns in which they were resettled, so it made sense for families to relocate closer to their landholdings, even though Spaniards might have burned their previous homes and orchards to force compliance with congregación (Quezada 2014, 57). Entire communities were known to have moved to areas across the frontier (Farriss 1984, 75), and even very late in the Colonial period (1784), a village under the jurisdiction of Nabalam, near Tahcabo, threatened to leave because a local Spanish official made community members produce so much cotton "that they had no time to raise food for themselves" (Farriss 1984, 78). Cyclic nucleation and dispersal characterize population dynamics during the Colonial period throughout Yucatán (Farriss 1978). Rani Alexander (2004b) documented these movements archaeologically and historically for the zone around Yaxcabá in central Yucatán, while Adam Kaeding (2013) and Tiffany C. Cain (2019) studied these shifts in the former province of Beneficios Altos in southeastern Yucatán.

By the late Colonial period (aided especially by the Bourbon Reforms of the late eighteenth century) and into the Early Republican period (1821–1867),

TABLE 2.1. Nineteenth-century population estimates for Tahcabo, the county seat Calotmul, and nearby ranchos and haciendas

Year	Total Population of Calotmul	Total Population of Tahcabo	Population of the Ranchos and Haciendas of Calotmul[a]
1806	2,608	624	290
1828	3,241	750	1,029
1841	1,395	1,543[b]	1,124
1851	298[c]		
1897	3,035	78	1,698

[a] In most cases, this includes the population of ranchos and haciendas located near Tahcabo.

[b] This number includes the population of nearby Hacienda Yokpita, located immediately north of town.

[c] Source indicates the presence of 298 contribuyentes, or taxpayers, in the entire Calotmul municipality at that time.

Spanish Creoles established haciendas for the production of sugarcane, cattle, maize, and other products (Alexander 2006, 456). Ranchos were private lands used similarly but generally had Indigenous owners and mixed subsistence and commercial production (Rugeley 2009, 18; Morgan-Smith 2019). This development created the option of moving to a private estate, which offered consistent food rations. However, haciendas and ranchos often trapped their laborers into debt, forcing them to shop at expensive estate-based stores. In addition, a *hacendado* (hacienda owner) might oblige a laborer to give an upcoming harvest in exchange for needed rations (Peniche Moreno 2009, 203). The migration of pueblo populations to haciendas and ranchos accelerated during famine years of the mid-1700s (specifically 1765–1774) and continued into the next century (Peniche Moreno 2009).

Population Records

According to surviving census documents, the population of Tahcabo (including nearby haciendas and ranchos) fluctuated rapidly during the 1800s ("Padrón general de habitantes del pueblo de Calotmul" n.d.; "Padrón general de habitantes del pueblo de Calotmul" n.d. table 2.1; Dumond and Dumond 1982). Growth in populations living at ranchos and haciendas was a major trend of the nineteenth century. For instance, the population living on these estates within the municipality of Calotmul numbered about 300 people in 1806 and reached almost 1,700 people by 1897. Meanwhile, the population of the town of Tahcabo itself grew to well over 1,000 people prior to the onset of the Caste War, at which point it shrunk considerably and remained low or nonexistent for the remaining portion of the nineteenth century. In 1897, census records indicate that seventy-eight people lived in Tahcabo. Calotmul also suffered population loss during and immediately preceding the Caste War of Yucatán. Terry Rugeley (2009, 1) explains population loss in nearby Tizimín—which began in the mid-1830s—as attributable to Mexican military recruitment for wars with Texas, which prompted many people to leave for the woods—and perhaps for Tahcabo and nearby haciendas (Rugeley 2009, 1). Population loss in Tizimín also followed the 1836 Rebellion of Santiago Imán y Villafaña based in Tizimín, which foreshadowed the Caste War and regional population losses (Rugeley 2009, 2).

Population fluctuations at Tahcabo can also be noted in changing surnames. In 1563, Don Diego de Quijada issued the title of governor to two residents of Tahcabo: Juan Tun and Juan Pantí (Quezada 2014, 161). Neither of these names can be found in the community today, nor in extant historical records dating primarily to the nineteenth century. The 1841 Tahcabo census is populated with many Spanish and Maya surnames that no longer exist in the community today. However, a subset of family surnames found in the 1841 census continues to be found in the community, including Aguayo, Balam, Chimal, Dzul, May, Medina, Poot, Puc, Uh, Un, and Sulu. Despite extreme population drawdowns in the region during the late nineteenth century, it is possible—based on surnames that are consistent through time—that repopulation of the area in the early twentieth century included descendants of families that had lived there previously.

The 1841 census is rich, because apart from listing names of the residents of Tahcabo, Calotmul, and surrounding ranchos, it also includes the age of each person and the professions of adult males, and it separates residents according to household. According to the census, the average residence housed 4.7 people, clearly indicative of a pattern of nuclear family residences. Only eight people named in the census, who resided in three different dwellings, receive *don* or *doña* titles of respect, and they do not correlate with age. Those eight people live in households with merchants or a painter, and all have Spanish surnames. At each of the three residences with inhabitants receiving these titles, there also lived up to seven young people with different surnames. These young individuals had surnames of Indigenous origin and may have served as domestic servants and field hands to wealthier families. The 1841 population of Tahcabo residents included musicians, blacksmiths, painters, muleteers, and merchants, in addition to farmers, called *labradores* (laborers) in the census.

Resource Access

Having considered Tahcabo's historical context and regional assets, we now address access, another component of the livelihoods framework. Larger households have an advantage in access to resources because they can mobilize more labor to pursue diversified and risk-reducing production strategies (Clark 1989; Wilk 1991). Extended family households allow for teamwork, task and tool sharing, and efficiency (Farriss 1984, 133). The formation of nuclear family households in congregated towns, and the demand of tribute from each married male during the early Colonial period, challenged residents' abilities to diversify economic activities and exposed them to greater risk during political instability or droughts (Farriss 1984, 169). For this and other reasons, people often dispersed across the landscape when possible, or otherwise negotiated restrictions to household size. For example, patronymic groups tended to live in the same neighborhood within a settlement (Alexander 2012, 15), facilitating collaboration among adjacent households. Nancy Farriss (1984, 134) found evidence from a 1583 census of Espita, located twenty-five miles west of Tahcabo, which extended family residences continued into colonial times. In the Espita census, the average residence housed 9.4 people (AGN 1583). This figure differs notably from the figure of 4.7 people per average house recorded in the 1841 Tahcabo census.

Yucatec land tenure during pre-Hispanic times varied by location and cannot be understood as strictly public or private (McAnany, Dedrick, and Batún Alpuche 2016). Elites often restricted access to rejolladas, even while communities shared cenotes (Redfield and Villa Rojas [1934] 1962, 67; Smith 1962; Farriss 1984; Hare, Masson, and Russell 2014). Archaeological examples from northeastern Yucatán show that residential structures often surrounded rejolladas (Hanson 2008; Koby 2012; Munro-Stasiuk et al. 2014), and that household social standing correlated with proximity of a residence to a rejollada (Hanson 2002; Barrera Rubio 2015). At the pre-Hispanic coastal site of Emal, north of Tahcabo, Susan Kepecs and Sylviane Boucher (1996) report the presence of walled rejolladas, one of which contained pollen from the plant families of cacao and cotton respectively. This discovery supports the idea that cash crops were cultivated within these features. Valuable crops, and especially trees such as cacao, most likely represent private property held by elites (Farriss 1984, 274).

Apart from cultivation, Tahcabo residents use rejolladas for hunting and for water access and irrigation. Ancient populations often dug into the bases of rejolladas due to their low elevations and proximity to the water table. These wells provided convenient sources of water to irrigate gardens and orchards cultivated within rejolladas. On the other hand, rejolladas with sheer rock walls and overhangs attract wild animals, providing opportunities for hunting, especially at night. Therefore, the distinct characteristics of rejolladas and investments in rejollada improvements, such as wells, impact who can access them. People today restrict entry into rejolladas used for cultivation more than they do for rejolladas used primarily for hunting.

Households that settled an area earlier and had the longest claim to land often grew to be the wealthiest, as they held the parcels most highly valued for cultivation ("principle of first occupancy," McAnany 1995, 96–97). Often, they lived in houses near the town center. During the Colonial period, resettled populations technically maintained rights to land near their previous homes, but the long distance to these agricultural plots resulted in reduced productivity and eventual loss of authority over traditional landholdings (Roys 1939; Alexander 1998, 42). Thus, we expect that families residing in Tahcabo during the Postclassic period would have maintained advantageous access to rejolladas during the Colonial period, while families forced to move to Tahcabo suffered disadvantageous land access.

Archaeological Evidence from Tahcabo

In Tahcabo we conducted excavations at four Colonial period residences located around the edge of the contemporary town: one Early, one Middle, and one Late Colonial period residence, as well as one house with mixed remains that spanned the Colonial period (figure 2.5; Dedrick 2019). Through excavation in and around these Colonial residential areas and in nearby rejolladas, we sought to understand how fairly mobile populations made a living and worked to achieve food security in Tahcabo. Excavation results challenge some of our expectations for how people lived based on historical narratives—specifically, that residents of congregación communities lived in nuclear households in accordance with Spanish orders (an expectation that begins to break down with the study of historical census documents) and that they made use of Spanish-introduced plants and animals soon after conquest.

Extended Family Residences

The excavated early colonial residence can be found north of the colonial street grid and atop a wide platform (20 by 22 meters) dating to the Late Preclassic and Early Classic periods. Excavations around the platform suggest that Colonial period residents made use of the extensive area, as they discarded kitchen trash to the east of the platform, deposited Late Postclassic period censers along the southern edge of the platform, and used the area west of the platform (near the current-day road) as an activity area. This evidence supports the idea that during the Early Colonial period, resettled populations moved in extended family groups and founded residences at the edge of congregated towns.

In contrast, by the Middle to Late Colonial period, the residential platforms that town residents reused were smaller (middle colonial: 10 by 16 meters; late colonial: 8 by 13 meters), suggesting space sufficient only for a nuclear family—an assertion supported by the 1841 Tahcabo census. Later colonial houses, moreover, were more closely aligned to the street grid, indicating possible nuclear-family residences clustered into extended-family neighborhoods, as often occurs in Tahcabo and elsewhere in Yucatán today (e.g., Cabrera Pacheco 2017, 504), or that nuclear families simply cooperated with their relatives across town.

We might expect that Spanish clergy enforced orders that families in congregated towns live in nuclear houses. However, they would have faced difficulties in attempting to impose this residential configuration, especially because they visited rather than resided in Tahcabo. As mentioned earlier, large coresidential groups provided a number of benefits, including risk management through diversified economic activities, shared food production, and child rearing. Drawing on practice theory (Bourdieu 1977; Giddens 1984) and its recent elaborations in the field of archaeology (e.g., Silliman 2001; Houk, Bonorden, and Kilgore, chapter 7 in this volume), we expect that extended family structures continued to shape daily life and activities in communities after conquest. Daily practices and household formation result from various economic and social considerations and resist outside forces. In particular, populations would have sought to preserve risk-reducing strategies when facing the insecurities resulting from conquest. In addition, it would have been especially difficult for Spaniards or others in power to exact change in the behavior of relatively mobile groups of people living near the outskirts of town.

Food Security

Introduced plants and animals spread across the Americas during the Early Colonial period—in fact, in Hispaniola (present-day Dominican Republic and Haiti) and Nueva Galicia (in present-day Mexico) banana plants and citrus trees established themselves so rapidly that early visitors believed they were native to the Americas (Dunmire 2004, 107, 195). A description of Tizimín's convent, based on a friar's visit in 1588, notes the presence of an irrigated garden in which friars cultivated introduced plants, including bananas, citrus, figs, and grapes. The friars also grew local plants, including *zapote colorado* (mamey; *Pouteria sapota*), avocado, guayaba (*Psidium guajava*), and *ciruela de la tierra* (*Spondias purpurea*; de Ciudad Real 1993, 323). Due to the early presence of imported plants and animals across the Mexican landscape, we might expect that rural communities immediately began to experiment with these exotics and incorporate them into the cuisine, rituals, and medicines of Yucatán. Eventually, a hybrid cuisine did develop in Yucatán, as can be seen in the ingredients of innumerable dishes today; some play a significant role in annual events, such as banana-leaf wrapped tamales cooked in the *píib*, or earth oven, and the consumption of pork along with turkey in *relleno negro*, a dish often served at town fairs prior to the *baile de cochino* (dance of the pig's head). Today, banana trees are said to grow quite well within rejolladas, where their leaves are protected from harsh winds and are preserved intact for tamale wrapping.

However, regarding the extent to which experimentation with introduced plants occurred in rural areas during the Early Colonial period, we might consider the pressures that residents at that time faced in terms of tax obligations, drought, population loss, and disease. For some, the threat of food insecurity may have been too pressing to allow for experimentation with unfamiliar plants. In addition, those plants that became most integrated into daily life in Yucatán—citrus and banana—are not annuals and would have required extended periods of care before they fruited. This characteristic may have rendered them irrelevant to populations wishing to preserve a transient, flexible lifestyle that would permit mobility if conditions deteriorated. Likely, early experimentation with introduced plants and animals took place among wealthier populations, while contemporaneous populations living on the margins continued to depend on their vast knowledge of the local forests and on easily transported and quick-growing crops. Experimentation became more widespread during the late Colonial period and likely took place in rejolladas due to their optimal growing conditions. Today, Tahcabo residents favor rejolladas as locations to cultivate more recently introduced fruit trees, two of which are mango (introduced to Mexico in the early 1800s; Popenoe 1974; Dunmire 2004, table 5.1) and noni (*Morinda citrifolia*; recently introduced and currently growing in a Tahcabo rejollada).

Identification of animal bone from a kitchen midden located within the Early Colonial residential area mentioned in "Extended Family Residences" indicates that house residents continued to depend on hunted animals as well as dogs for their food (Jiménez Cano 2018). At this time, the only bone from a domesticated animal introduced from Europe that analyst Nayeli Jiménez Cano has identified in the faunal assemblage associated with the house is a horse (*Equus caballus*) tooth and an unidentified equine (*Equus* sp.) tooth located in a context near the surface that may not have dated to the Early Colonial period. Excavation of the residence yielded fifty projectile points, including finished, in-progress, and broken examples (figure 2.6). The residence is directly southwest of a rejollada that is used today for trapping wild animals (Rejollada H, figure 5), including *tepezcuintle*, or paca (*Cuniculus paca*), which Nayeli Jiménez Cano also identified in the faunal collection. The evidence suggests that inhabitants of this early colonial residence depended heavily on hunted animals for food and may have accessed the adjacent rejollada.

A calibrated AMS date on charcoal from the midden produced a 95 percent confidence calendar age range of 1484 to 1640 CE (Laboratory number AA110664). Colonial ceramics comprise more than 85 percent of the assemblage (by count) from the midden, and consisted primarily of Yuncu Unslipped ceramics, with an additional, low-frequency presence of Sacpokana Red and Columbia Plain types. Additional animal bone was found at the residence, but only the assemblage from the securely dated early colonial midden is included here. Based on the atmospheric curve generated for the IntCal13 AMS date calibration and the ceramic evidence, the midden likely formed during the late 1500s to early 1600s, thus providing a relevant point of comparison with an early colonial settlement at nearby Ek' Balam (which dated to ca. 1540–1620 CE). Susan deFrance and

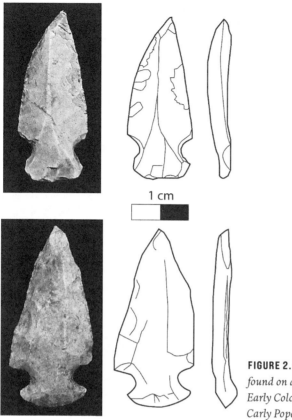

FIGURE 2.6. *Select projectile points found on and around the excavated Early Colonial house. Drawings by Carly Pope.*

Craig Hanson (2008) argued, based on dense faunal refuse from a rectangular shaft feature at the site, that Spaniards had successfully restricted the mobility of the early colonial Ek' Balam population and had stymied their exchange networks, thereby reducing local access to hunted and traded animal foods on which residents had depended during earlier periods.

Table 2.2 compares the number of individual specimens (NISP) and minimum number of individuals (MNI) of vertebrate fauna identified within Tahcabo's early colonial kitchen midden (from a two-by-two-meter unit, excavated to fifty centimeters in depth; 308 grams of bone overall) and Ek' Balam's early colonial cultural stratum (from a two-by-one-meter unit, eighty-centimeter-thick cultural deposit; 4,946 grams of bone overall; deFrance and Hanson 2008, table 2.2). While the Ek' Balam context contained a great deal more animal bone than the best-preserved midden at Tahcabo, we can make some useful observations. Fauna common to both the Tahcabo and Ek' Balam assemblages include peccary (Tayassuidae), brocket, and white-tailed deer (*Mazama* sp., *Odocoileus virginianus*),

TABLE 2.2. Vertebrate fauna by stratum from select Early Colonial contexts at Tahcabo and Ek' Balam.

Common Name	Taxon	Tahcabo		Ek' Balam	
		NISP	MNI	NISP	MNI
horses, mules, burros	*Equus* spp.	–	–	30	3
pig	*Sus scrofa*	–	–	77	3
peccary	Tayassuidae	6	2	2	1
peccary/pig	Tayassuidae/Suidae	–	–	2	1
brocket deer	*Mazama* sp.	1	1	3	2
white-tailed deer	*Odocoileus virginianus*	32	3	25	1
dog/coyote	*Canis* sp.	5	2	705	38
gray fox	*Urocyon cinereoargenteus*	–	–	1	1
weasel	*Mustela frenata*	–	–	1	1
Mexican porcupine	*Coendou mexicanus*	–	–	5	1
raccoons	*Proyonidae*	–	–	1	1
cf. margay	*Felis* cf. *wiedii*	–	–	6	1
opossum	*Didelphis virginiana*	–	–	63	5
armadillo	*Dasypus novemcinctus*	74	2	54	3
rabbit	*Sylvilagus* spp.	2	2	7	3
pocket gopher	*Orthogeomys hispidus*	2	1	2	1
hispid cotton rat	*Sigmodon hispidus*	–	–	12	6
lowland paca	*Cuniculus paca*	4	1	–	–
rats, mice	Muridae	–	–	1	1
macaw	*Ara* spp.	–	–	10	2
macaws, parrots, parakeets	*Psittacidae*	–	–	2	1
chicken	*Gallus gallus*	–	–	4	4
turkey	*Meleagris* spp.	–	–	96	12
unidentified birds	Aves	40	–	172	3
sea brams	Sparidae	1	1	–	–
poisonous snakes	Viperidae	–	–	18	2
snakes	Serpentes	2	–	9	2
mud turtle	*Kinosternon* sp.	9	2	–	–
turtles	Testudines	3	1	–	–
Sample total		181	–	1,308	–

Note: Unidentified mammal bone was not tabulated.

dog (*Canis* sp.), armadillo (*Dasypus novemcinctus*), and rabbit (*Sylvilagus* spp.). Species found at Tahcabo but not at Ek' Balam include paca (*Cuniculus paca*), sea bram (Sparidae), and turtles (including mud turtle [*Kinosternon* sp.]). The lack of these latter species and an overall low frequency and variety of native taxa at Ek' Balam led deFrance and Hanson (2008, 310) to argue that Spaniards had successfully restricted hunting. On the other hand, the Ek' Balam sample contained species that were notably absent from the Tahcabo assemblage, such as equines (apart from the exception noted above in this section), pig, and chicken—European-introduced domesticates.

Some differences exist between the contexts at Tahcabo and Ek' Balam that might help to explain the distinct faunal collections. At Ek' Balam, the refuse pit from which deFrance examined animal remains was located about 120 meters from and possibly within sight of the colonial chapel. The nearest residence to the analyzed pit, called HT-21, exhibited more elaborate architecture than other residences (Hanson 2002, 378) and contained Spanish artifacts including iron knife blades, olive jar sherds, majolica, and porcelain. This assemblage led Hanson to hypothesize that ranking members of the settlement lived there (deFrance and Hanson 2008, 303). Moreover, the pit was located between HT-21 and an updraft kiln (Hanson 2002, 380). Hanson argues that residents of HT-21 controlled production from the kiln and nearby rejolladas. In contrast, the early colonial house at Tahcabo was situated about 240 meters from the church, with numerous houses present along the indirect route connecting them. We found only two majolica sherds (Columbia Plain and Ichtucknee Blue on Blue) at the early colonial residence and no olive jar sherds, suggesting reduced access to Spanish trade networks.

The evidence matches what we might expect for a mobile family, which Farriss (1984, 73) reported would have "lived on game and the same wild fruits and roots that have been identified as 'famine food' until a new milpa could be harvested." From an interview in Tahcabo about what people grow in rejolladas, one person noted, "My grandparents told me they couldn't plant the same things that we do. They moved a lot and couldn't plant like this. There were many wars, and for that reason they couldn't plant much." This statement attests to the relationship between mobility and food security in Yucatán and the importance of knowing how to procure food from the forests when the cultivation of trees and perennial plants becomes unworkable (on Postcolonial period war, see Fryer [chapter 5]; Badillo Sánchez [chapter 6]; Houk, Bonorden, and Kilgore [chapter 7]; and Meierhoff [chapter 8], this volume).

While the data presented here demonstrate the importance of hunting during the Early Colonial period, its significance continued into the late Colonial period and beyond. Oral histories passed down in Tahcabo indicate that not long ago, town residents depended to a large extent on hunted animals—more so than they do today. Animal husbandry also played an increasingly large role in rural economies of Late Colonial and Early Republican period Yucatán, both in ranchos and haciendas, and within town house-lots.

Discussion

Based on historical evidence we might expect that rural populations in early colonial Yucatán abided by Spanish orders—that they quit hunting and accessing local trade networks, divided their extended families to live in nuclear family households, adopted introduced plants and animals, and dutifully paid taxes. While people in early colonial Tahcabo had diverse experiences related to their varying levels of political and economic access, at least one extended family living on the margins of the community used hunting as a primary food procurement strategy, grew and gathered native plants that would allow for economic flexibility (Dedrick 2019), and likely escaped extreme tax burdens and threats of disease by moving on a regular basis. Mobility and economic flexibility continued to serve farmers as they sought to escape debt and secure food for their families throughout the Colonial period.

We can explain most of the disparities between our expectations for how people lived and the inferences we make based on the archaeological evidence from Tahcabo using the sustainable livelihoods framework and its key components: context, assets, and access. For example, demographic change could provide an additional explanation for why hunting played an important role in food security during the Early Colonial period. In addition to the need for livelihood flexibility due to political instabilities and other factors, the demographic collapse that occurred in Yucatán during the sixteenth century (Hoggarth et al. 2017, fig. 4) likely led to an increase in wild animal populations, especially as Spaniards tried to disallow traditional hunting practices (Ancona 1889, 543, 555–556; deFrance and Hanson 2008, 303). Social differentiation, climate, agroecology, and terms of trade also contribute to the livelihoods framework and help to explain the evidence outlined in this chapter.

The livelihoods framework proposes that the outcomes of sustainable livelihoods include improved well-being, enhanced resilience, and conserved natural resources. This aspect of the framework, when compared to trajectories of Colonial period livelihoods, highlights the true costs of colonialism and antimarkets (Pezzarossi 2015) for rural populations. Due to the tumultuous conditions of life during the Early Colonial period (see, e.g., García Lara and Olán, chapter 4 in this volume), the livelihood strategies selected by marginalized populations reduced immediate risk, but did not lead to long-term wealth accumulation or resource sustainability. The forces that compelled populations to maintain economic flexibility undermined the viability of other options, such as investment in orchards, participation in animal husbandry, or development of irrigation systems that could have led to sustainable outcomes. Continued marginalization eventually led to reduced resiliency to drought, disease, and land theft—challenges that continued into the late Colonial period and pushed people to work at haciendas and ranchos.

One man we interviewed in Tahcabo remembered stories his grandparents had told him about how their parents had lived at a sugar hacienda. This was during a period that people call the *tiempo de esclavitud*, or time of slavery, since life at the haciendas was like slavery. He recounted that around the turn of the twentieth century there existed a mule-train system in which the pack animals pulled goods—primarily sugar—along a narrow-gauge track (see Mathews, Gust, and Fedick, chapter 10 in this volume). This system connected haciendas in eastern Yucatán to markets in Tizimín and Mérida. The interviewee's grandparents had recounted to him the harsh living conditions under the hacienda *patrones* (owners), though, luckily, they only lived there for two years. Once they left the hacienda, "they didn't have many things . . . but they had corn, they had everything [they needed], they had food." According to the interviewee, many families lived at the haciendas during that time, and from this account, we surmise that concerns about food security played a large role in keeping an impoverished labor force on the haciendas despite abusive working conditions (see also Gust, chapter 9 in this volume).

While the livelihoods framework addresses the need for a thorough accounting of the contexts, assets, and issues of access that shape household decision making, it may underestimate the influence of environmental knowledge, past livelihood strategies, and the political nature of daily activities—that is, the practices of rural farmers themselves. To lump history into a larger category consisting of the contexts in which people live impedes a full consideration of the relationality of established daily action and inaction within a household, the level at which people negotiate even radical changes that occur in larger political economic systems. In addition, the livelihoods framework may underemphasize the stark power differentials that colonial systems and policies entail. The approach can provide archaeologists with a useful heuristic for thinking about why rural farmers made the decisions they did, and archaeologists can in turn help to strengthen the model as it is applied even today.

Conclusion

By studying Colonial and Republican period landscapes and agriculture in Yucatán, archaeologists can contribute to discussions of contemporary rural livelihoods. In Tahcabo, we have begun to study the economic decisions that people made during the Colonial period, shedding light on how food insecurity developed throughout that time and acted as a kind of violence on the population (see Fryer and Badillo Sánchez, chapters 5 and 6, respectively, in this volume; Dedrick 2019). Migration and flexibility, strategies that marginalized populations used to survive during difficult times, also kept people from building the wealth that they could have achieved by maintaining family orchards and livestock. Land theft, droughts, and lack of social support drove people to haciendas and ranchos throughout the eighteenth and nineteenth centuries until the Mexican Revolution (1910–1920), after which point communities could petition for communal lands (called *ejidos*). Tahcabo residents petitioned for an ejido in 1922 and were granted lands by Yucatán's governor, Felipe Carrillo Puerto, in 1923.

Today in Tahcabo, farmers express the sentiment that the land does not produce as much as it once did. Some people refer to the difficulties posed by climate change, while others point to a lack of capacity and labor as many of their family members have moved to cities or to tourist zones for work. Others mention a loss of traditional knowledge and changes in food preferences associated with migrations to zones of tourism, such as the Maya Riviera. Still others draw attention to the chemical fertilizers and herbicides on which they now depend to attain harvests and which lead to reduced biodiversity. Many of the difficulties farmers face today relate to the consequences of colonialism, in which technologies of multinational corporations hold great sway and markets cater to international interests while rural communities remain impoverished. As government and not-for-profit programs strive to promote sustainability for subsistence farmers, studies of how farming changed throughout the Colonial and Republican periods can provide a foundation for understanding rural livelihoods today.

Acknowledgments. We thank Kasey Diserens Morgan and Tiffany C. Fryer for inviting us to participate in the conference session and edited volume. We express gratitude for the collaboration of Tahcabo community members, many of whom worked as members of the team excavating contexts analyzed in this chapter, and others of whom participated in interviews about rejollada cultivation, as part of a study deemed exempt through IRB #14-3001 at the University of North Carolina at Chapel Hill. Maia Dedrick conducted the rejollada interviews with José Miguel Kanxoc Kumul, then a student and now a graduate of the program in Maya Linguistics and Culture at the Universidad de Oriente in Valladolid, Yucatán. We thank Nayeli Jiménez Cano, who conducted the faunal analysis presented in this chapter. Maia Dedrick also wishes to thank C. Margaret Scarry, Silvia Tomášková, Anna Agbe-Davies, and Rudi Colloredo-Mansfeld for their support and thoughtful comments regarding aspects of this work. Survey and excavation at Tahcabo were permitted by the Instituto Nacional de Antropología e Historia (INAH; National Institute of Anthropology and History). This research was supported by the Society of Ethnobiology, the Wenner-Gren Foundation, and the National Science Foundation, as well as the Royster and Off-Campus Fellowships from UNC–Chapel Hill.

References

Alexander, Rani T. 1998. "Community Organization in the Parroquia de Yaxcabá, Yucatán, México, 1750–1847." *Ancient Mesoamerica* 9 (1): 39–54.

Alexander, Rani T. 2004a. "Archaeological Site Structure before the Caste War." In *Yaxcabá and the Caste War of Yucatán: An Archaeological Perspective*. Albuquerque: University of New Mexico Press.

Alexander, Rani T. 2004b. *Yaxcabá and the Caste War of Yucatán: An Archaeological Perspective*. Albuquerque: University of New Mexico Press.

Alexander, Rani T. 2006. "Maya Settlement Shifts and Agrarian Ecology in Yucatán, 1800–2000." *Journal of Anthropological Research* 62 (4): 449–470.

Alexander, Rani T. 2012. "Prohibido Tocar Este Cenote: The Archaeological Basis for the Titles of Ebtun." *International Journal of Historical Archaeology* 16 (1): 1–24.

Ancona, Eligio. 1889. *Historia de Yucatán desde la época más remota hasta nuestros días*. Vol 2. Barcelona: Jaime Jesús Roviralta.

Andrews, Anthony P. 1991. "The Rural Chapels and Churches of Early Colonial Yucatán and Belize." In *The Spanish Borderlands in Pan-American Perspective*, edited by David Hurst Thomas, 355–374. Washington, DC: Smithsonian Institution Press.

Archivo General del Estado de Yucatán (AGEY). 1841. "Padrón general de habitantes del pueblo de Calotmul." N.d. Poder Ejecutivo, Censos y Padrones. Vol. 1. Exp. 3.

Archivo General del Estado de Yucatán (AGEY). 1841. "Padrón general de habitantes del pueblo de Tahcabo." N.d. Poder Ejecutivo, Censos y Padrones. Vol 5. Exp. 55.

Archivo General de la Nación (AGN). 1583. Tierras 2726, no. 6, Autos de visita del pueblo de Espita.

Barrera Rubio, Alfredo. 2015. "Kulubá: Asentamiento, cosmovisión y desarrollo de un enclave itzá del Nororiente de Yucatán." Mexico City: Escuela Nacional de Antropología e Historia.

Batún Alpuche, Adolfo Iván, Patricia A. McAnany, and Maia Dedrick. 2017. "Tiempo y paisaje en Tahcabo, Yucatán." *Arqueología Mexicana* 25 (145): 66–71.

Bourdieu, Pierre. 1977. *Outline of a Theory of Practice*. Cambridge: Cambridge University Press.

Cabrera Pacheco, Ana Julia. 2017. "Primitive Accumulation in Indigenous Mexico: The Contested Transformations of the Maya *Solar* of Yucatán." *City* 21 (3–4): 503–519.

Cain, Tiffany C. 2019. "Materializing Political Violence: Segregation, War, and Memory in Quintana Roo, Mexico." PhD diss., University of Pennsylvania, Philadelphia.

Clark, Gracia. 1989. "Separation between Trading and Home for Asante Women in Kumasi Central Market, Ghana." In *The Household Economy: Reconsidering the Domestic Mode of Production*, edited by Richard R. Wilk, 91–118. Boulder: Westview Press.

de Ciudad Real, Antonio. 1993. *Tratado curioso y docto de las grandezas de la Nueva España*. Vols. 1 and 2. Mexico City: Universidad Nacional Autónoma de México.

de Clerck, Fabrice A. J., and Patricia Negreros-Castillo. 2000. "Plant Species of Traditional Mayan Homegardens of Mexico as Analogs for Multistrata Agroforests." *Agroforestry Systems* 48 (May): 303–317.

Dedrick, Maia. 2019. "The Archaeology of Colonial Maya Livelihoods at Tahcabo, Yucatán, Mexico." PhD diss., Department of Anthropology, University of North Carolina at Chapel Hill.

Dedrick, Maia, Carly Pope, and Morgan Russell. 2018. "Ritual Use of the Rejolladas of Tahcabo, Yucatán." Paper presented at the Society for American Anthropology Annual Meeting, Washington, DC.

del Amo, R. S., and P. J. Ramos. 1993. "Use and Management of Secondary Vegetation in a Humid-Tropical Area." *Agroforestry Systems* 21 (1): 27–42.

deFrance, Susan D., and Craig A. Hanson. 2008. "Labor, Population Movement, and Food in Sixteenth-Century Ek Balam, Yucatán." *Latin American Antiquity* 19 (3): 299–316.

de Landa, Diego. (1566) 1982. *Relación de las cosas de Yucatan.* Translated and edited with notes by Alfred M. Tozzer, 1941. Papers of the Peabody Museum of Archaeology and Ethnology, Harvard University vol. 18.

Dumond, Carol S., and Don E. Dumond. 1982. "Demography and Parish Affairs in Yucatan 1797–1897: Documents from the Archivo de la Mitra Emeritense Selected by Joaquín de Arrigunaga Peón." Eugene, Oregon: University of Oregon Anthropological Papers No. 27.

Dunmire, William W. 2004. *Gardens of New Spain: How Mediterranean Plants and Foods Changed America.* Austin: University of Texas Press.

Ellis, Frank. 2000. *Rural Livelihoods and Diversity in Developing Countries.* Oxford: Oxford University Press.

Farriss, Nancy M. 1978. "Nucleation versus Dispersal: The Dynamics of Population Movement in Colonial Yucatan." *The Hispanic American Historical Review* 58 (2): 187–216.

Farriss, Nancy M. 1984. *Maya Society under Colonial Rule: The Collective Enterprise of Survival.* Princeton, NJ: Princeton University Press.

Fernández, Justino. 1945. *Catálogo de construcciones religiosas del Estado de Yucatán.* Mexico City: Talleres Gráficos de la Nación.

García Bernal, Manuela Cristina. 1978. *Población y encomienda en Yucatán bajo los Austrias.* Sevilla, España: Escuela de Estudios Hispano Americanos.

García Bernal, Manuela Cristina. 2005. *Economía, política y sociedad en el Yucatán colonial.* Mérida: Ediciones de la Universidad Autónoma de Yucatán.

Giddens, Anthony. 1984. *The Constitution of Society.* Cambridge: Polity Press.

González de la Mata, Rocío. 2006. "Agua, agricultura y mitos: El Caso de tres rejolladas de Chichen Itza." In *XIX Simposio de Investigaciones Arqueológicas en Guatemala, 2005,* edited by Juan Pedro Laporte, Bárbara Arroyo, and Héctor Mejía, 305–318. Guatemala City: Museo Nacional de Arqueología y Etnología.

Hanson, Craig A. 2002. "In Praise of Garbage: Historical Archaeology, Households, and the Maya Political Economy." In *Ancient Maya Political Economies*, edited by Marilyn A. Masson and David A. Freidel, 365–397. Walnut Creek, CA: AltaMira Press.

Hanson, Craig A. 2008. "The Late Mesoamerican Village." PhD diss., Department of Anthropology, Tulane University, New Orleans.

Hare, Timothy, Marilyn Masson, and Bradley Russell. 2014. "High-Density LiDAR Mapping of the Ancient City of Mayapán." *Remote Sensing* 6 (9): 9064–9085.

Hoggarth, Julie A., Matthew Restall, James W. Wood, and Douglas J. Kennett. 2017. "Drought and Its Demographic Effects in the Maya Lowlands." *Current Anthropology* 58 (1): 82–113.

Hostettler, Ueli. 2003. "New Inequalities: Changing Maya Economy and Social Life in Central Quintana Roo, Mexico." In *Anthropological Perspectives on Economic Development and Integration*, edited by Norbert Dannhaeuser and Cynthia Werner, 25–59. Boston: JAI.

Hunt, Marta Espejo-Ponce. 1974. "Colonial Yucatan: Town and Region in the Seventeenth Century." Unpublished PhD diss., University of California, Los Angeles.

Jiménez Cano, Nayeli G. 2018. "Zooarchaeological Report: Faunal Analysis at Units C11 and G15 from Operation 15, Tahcabo, Yucatán." Unpublished report.

Jones, John G. 2017. "Analysis of Pollen Samples from Tahcabo, Yucatan." Unpublished report. Tempe, AZ: Archaeological Consulting Services, Ltd.

Kaeding, Adam. 2013. "Negotiated Survival: An Archaeological and Documentary Investigation of Colonialism in Beneficios de Altos, Yucatan, Mexico." PhD diss., Department of Archaeology, Boston University.

Kanxoc Kumul, José Miguel, and Maia Dedrick. 2016. "Interdisciplinary Views of Gardens Produced through Ethnographic Research in Tahcabo, Yucatán, Mexico, as Part of a Collaborative Archaeological Project." Paper presented at the American Anthropological Association Annual Meeting. Minneapolis.

Kepecs, Susan, and Sylviane Boucher. 1996. "The Pre-Hispanic Cultivation of *Rejolladas* and Stone-Lands: New Evidence from Northeast Yucatán." In *The Managed Mosaic: Ancient Maya Agriculture and Resource Use*, edited by Scott L. Fedick, 69–91. Salt Lake City: University of Utah Press.

Koby, Peter. 2012. "Spatial Analysis of Ancient Maya Settlement Near Karst Sinkholes at Xuenkal, Yucatán, Mexico." Honors thesis, Kent State University, OH.

López de Cogolludo, Diego. 1688. "Historia de Yucatán." Madrid: Juan García Infanzón.

McAnany, Patricia A. 1995. *Living with the Ancestors: Kinship and Kingship in Ancient Maya Society*. New York: Cambridge University Press.

McAnany, Patricia A., Maia Dedrick, and Adolfo Iván Batún Alpuche. 2016. "El control de las tierras y mano de obra a través del tiempo en los Pueblos del Oriente de Yucatán." Presented at the X Congreso Internacional de Mayistas, Izamal, Yucatán.

Messer, Ellen. 1989. "Seasonality in Food Systems: An Anthropological Perspective on Household Food Security." In *Seasonal Variability in Third World Agriculture*, edited by David E. Sahn, 151–175. Baltimore: Johns Hopkins University Press.

Morgan-Smith, Mary Margaret. 2019. *"Caciques* and Community: Historical Maya Archaeology at Rancho Kiuic, Yucatán, México." PhD diss., Department of Anthropology, University of North Carolina at Chapel Hill.

Morrison, Kathleen D. 1996. "Typological Schemes and Agricultural Change: Beyond Boserup in Precolonial South India." *Current Anthropology* 37 (4): 583–608.

Munro-Stasiuk, Mandy J., T. Kam Manahan, Trent Stockton, and Traci Ardren. 2014. "Spatial and Physical Characteristics of *Rejolladas* in Northern Yucatan, Mexico: Implications for Ancient Maya Agriculture and Settlement Patterns." *Geoarchaeology* 29: 156–172.

Patch, Robert W. 1993. *Maya and Spaniard in Yucatan: 1648–1812*. Stanford, CA: Stanford University Press.

Peniche Moreno, Paola. 2009. "Migración y sobrevivencia: Los Mayas ante las hambrunas en el Yucatán Colonial." In *Diásporas, migraciones y exilios en el mundo maya*, edited by Mario Humberto Ruz, Juan García Targa, and Andrés Ciudad Ruiz, 189–206. Mérida: Sociedad Española de Estudios Mayas, Universidad Nacional Autónoma de México.

Pezzarossi, Guido. 2015. "Tribute, Antimarkets, and Consumption: An Archaeology of Capitalist Effects in Colonial Guatemala." In *Archaeology of Culture Contact and Colonialism in Spanish and Portuguese America*, edited by Pedro Paulo A. Funari and Maria Ximena Senatore, 79–102. New York: Springer.

Popenoe, Wilson. 1974. *Manuel of Tropical and Subtropical Fruits*. Facsimile of 1920 ed. New York: Hafner Press.

Quezada, Sergio. 1993. *Pueblos y caciques yucatecos, 1550–1580*. Mexico City: El Colegio de México.

Quezada, Sergio. 2001a. "Tributos, limosnas, y mantas en Yucatán, Siglo XVI." *Ancient Mesoamerica* 12 (1): 73–78.

Quezada, Sergio. 2001b. *Breve historia de Yucatán*. Mexico City: Fondo de Cultura Económica.

Quezada, Sergio. 2014. *Maya Lords and Lordship: The Formation of Colonial Society in Yucatán, 1350–1600*. Norman: University of Oklahoma Press.

Redfield, Robert, and Alfonso Villa Rojas. (1934) 1962. *Chan Kom: A Maya Village*. Chicago: University of Chicago Press.

"Residencia de Don Diego de Quijada (1565)." Justicia. Leg. 245, ff. 1370v–71. Archivo General de Indias (AGI).

Restall, Matthew. 1997. *The Maya World: Yucatec Culture and Society, 1550–1850*. Stanford, CA: Stanford University Press.

RHGY. (1579) 1900. *Relaciones histórico-geográficas de las provincias de Yucatán: Colección de documentos inéditos relativos al descubrimiento: Relaciones de Yucatán.* Vol. 13. Madrid: Real Academia de la Historia.

Roys, Ralph L. 1933. *The Book of Chilam Balam of Chumayel.* Washington, DC: Carnegie Institution.

Roys, Ralph L. 1939. *The Titles of Ebtun.* Washington, DC: Carnegie Institution.

Rugeley, Terry. 2009. *Rebellion Now and Forever: Mayas, Hispanics, and Caste War Violence in Yucatán, 1800–1880.* Stanford, CA: Stanford University Press.

Scoones, Ian. 1998. "Sustainable Rural Livelihoods: A Framework for Analysis." IDS working paper, 72. Brighton, UK: Institute of Development Studies.

SEDESOL, unidad de microrregiones. 2014. "Información de localidad Tahcabo." Accessed September 9, 2014. http://www.microrregiones.gob.mx/catloc/contenido.aspx?refnac=310080013.

Silliman, Stephen W. 2001. "Agency, Practical Politics and the Archaeology of Culture Contact." *Journal of Social Archaeology* 1 (2): 190–209.

Smith, A. Ledyard. 1962. "Residential and Associated Structures at Mayapán." In *Mayapán Yucatan, Mexico.* Vol. 619, edited by H.E.D. Pollock, Ralph L. Roys, Tatiana Proskouriakoff, and A. Ledyard Smith, 165–320. Washington, DC: Carnegie Institution.

Steward, Angela. 2007. "Nobody Farms Here Anymore: Livelihood Diversification in the Amazonian Community of Carvão, a Historical Perspective." *Agriculture and Human Values* 24 (1): 75–92.

Wilk, Richard R. 1991. *Household Ecology: Economic Change and Domestic Life among the Kekchi Maya in Belize.* DeKalb: Northern Illinois University Press.

3

Excavating the Third Root

Constructing Archaeological Narratives That Include Afro-Yucatecans

Julie K. Wesp

While popular and historical perspectives tend to emphasize the colonial populations of Yucatán and New Spain (present-day Mexico) as being Spanish, Indigenous, and the mixed heritage children of unions between these groups, it also included free and enslaved people with African heritage. Various colonial documents depict Juan Garrido, a free Black conquistador who accompanied Hernán Cortés during his conquest of Tenochtitlan in 1519, as among the first Blacks to set foot in Mexico (Gerhard 1978; Restall 2000). Shortly thereafter, enslaved Africans began arriving in New Spain, principally through the ports of Veracruz and Campeche (Slave Voyages Database 2016, for voyages specific to Veracruz and Campeche see https://www.slavevoyages.org/voyages/3wSJk3lU), with an estimated total of 250,000 enslaved Africans arriving from the sixteenth century through the eighteenth (Aguirre Beltrán 1946). This early presence of individuals of African heritage in New Spain demonstrates that it was always a multiethnic society, yet scholars have rarely included this third root of colonial society as a focus of analysis in their research.

Recently, historians have conducted an extensive amount of historical research that specifically highlights the presence of Africans and their descendants within

https://doi.org/10.5876/9781646422845.c003

documentary sources (Vinson III and Restall 2009; de la Serna 2010; Velázquez 2011). Documents associated with the trade of enslaved peoples, such as ship manifests and bills of sale, demonstrate the shift in geographic origins, from the Senegambia region in West Africa to the Congo region of Equatorial Africa, and the changing scale of trade in New Spain from the sixteenth to the eighteenth century (Davidson [1973] 1996; Palmer 1976; Alcántara López 2010; Masferrer León 2011; Seijas and Sierra Silva 2016). Parish records for marriage and baptism serve as another important documentary source that highlights both the presence of Africans in colonial New Spain and the interethnic relationships that developed, and the offspring of these unions (Love 1970; Castillo Palma and Kellogg 2005; Restall 2005; Von Germeten 2009; Schwaller 2012). Similarly, inquisition records often explicitly mention the defendant's or witness's self-identified or perceived racial category and illustrate the varied locations and occupations of Afro-descendants in New Spain (Cope 1994; Vinson III 2001; Velázquez 2006; Bristol and Restall 2009).

These documents not only provide evidence of the presence of Africans and their descendants in colonial society but also help to underline the complexity of daily life in the colonial world beyond the "Spanish/Indian" binary (Carroll 1991; Bennett 2009; Katzew and Deans-Smith 2009; Proctor 2010; Rinaudo 2012). In his analysis of plebian society in colonial Mexico City, Cope notes that the "secret of the colony's stability over some three centuries lay not in government regulations but in the dense thicket of social relationships" (Cope 1994, 48). These social relationships were cemented through the daily interactions in public and private spaces. Vinson (2018, 10) notes that "skin color, lineage, ethnicity, culture, place of residence, place of birth, [and] geographic mobility" all impacted the ability of the colonial government to create a simple and orderly separation between colonial subjects. These historical analyses draw our attention to how this multiethnic society negotiated new conceptions of class, identity, and labor within the bounds of changing social, political, and religious power. At the same time, historians acknowledge that the specific contexts in which these documents were created—such as documenting trade and business transactions, regulations meant to restrict behavior, or court documents of an inquisition trial—ultimately result in an overemphasis on negative behavior and a lack of a broader understanding of Afro-descendant daily life in colonial society (Carroll 2005; Restall 2005; Vinson III and Restall 2009).

Archaeological research, with its focus on the material remains of daily life, has the potential to fill in some of the gaps of the documentary record. In Latin America generally and in Mesoamerica more specifically, however, there has not been as much of an emphasis on incorporating the Afro-descendant population into archaeological research agendas (Fournier-Garcia and Miranda-Flores 1992; Fournier and Charlton 2008; Weik 2004, 2008). As this volume emphasizes, there is an expanding group of scholars now exploring the Colonial and National periods archaeologically, yet there continues to be a noticeable absence of Afro-descendants in archaeological reconstructions of the past. The prevalence of the colonial "Spanish/Indian" binary has resulted in a myopia regarding the actual demographic diversity in both urban and rural environments that is often only cured when there is a clearly visible indicator of an African presence.

In this chapter, I will highlight some of the recent historical archaeology scholarship that focuses on Africans and their descendants throughout New Spain. While some of this research is the result of "finding" an African presence when one was not expected, others have intentionally designed their research to examine the Afro-descendant population. My own research in this area is the result of a broadened analytical focus of skeletal data to explore Afro-descendants within colonial Mexico City. Historical archaeology in the Maya area and beyond must begin from the perspective that a significant portion of colonial society consisted of free and enslaved Blacks from the earliest period of New Spain. This interpretive refocus has the potential to not only create a more accurate representation of the past but also significantly impact the lived experiences of Afro-descendants who continue to form an important part of Mexican society today.

Broadening the Analytical Frame

Archaeological narratives are constructed within the frameworks decided on by the researcher. Any change thus begins with developing new methods of perceiving our data. Historical archaeology in Latin America is still a growing field of study because of a tendency to focus on pre-European archaeological contexts by both Latin American and otherwise-foreign scholars. When historical contexts are examined, scholars continue to focus on how colonial interactions with Europeans transformed the lives of the Indigenous population, unintentionally excluding many other members of colonial society, such as free or enslaved Africans and their descendants. While there has been an extensive focus on the archaeology of the African diaspora in North American contexts (Orser Jr. 1998; Blakey 2001; Fennell 2010), research in Latin America has tended to focus on areas that received the largest number of enslaved people, such as Brazil or islands in the Caribbean, plantations or sites that utilized slave labor, or contexts of rebellion and resistance, such as settlements of people who escaped enslavement and modern communities of their descendants (Orser Jr. 1998; Haviser 1999; Weik 2004; Funari 2006). This focus effectively excludes areas not typically associated with slave labor, such as Mexico and Central America, and significant research about the large free black population that existed throughout the Spanish colonial world.

In Mexico, this lack of attention to individuals with African heritage is the result of a broader societal erasure of Afro-descendants from the national narrative, particularly after the Mexican Revolution in the twentieth century (Hernández Cuevas 2004; Jones 2013). Important national heroes with documented African heritage, such as Vicente Guerrero and José María Morelos, are often whitened in popular visual representations of them, including lighter skin, different hair textures, and narrower noses. This erasure of African heritage also permeates research and modern national narratives about their lives. As part of the bicentennial celebration of Mexican Independence in 2010, the skeletal remains of national heroes were exhumed and analyzed (Rivero Webber and Pompa y Padilla 2012). Guerrero was positively identified through pathological changes to his right arm from a war injury that did not properly heal and resulted in a permanently flexed forearm, yet physical anthropologists dispute his documented African heritage because he did not have "typical African" skeletal features (Pompa y Padilla 2016).[1] If the African heritage of these well-known figures is erased from historical narratives, the rest of the Afro-Mexican population exists within what Arce calls "a stunning paradox that constitutes their simultaneous presence and absence" (Arce 2017, 3).

For archaeological research, active erasure of Afro-Mexican material culture may play a lesser role than its perceived lack of visibility within the archaeological record. While Africans and their descendants were a numerous population within colonial society, they may not leave material traces of daily life discernably different from those of Indigenous or Spanish individuals (Eschbach 2019). Scholars have tended to focus on identifying distinctly "African" cultural features or traces in the archaeological record in order to ensure the presence of members of this population (Orser Jr 1998). Yet, as the historical record shows, these populations were not distinct entities. When thinking about the plebeian majority of colonial society, Daniel Nemser (2017, 104) argues that they are "better understood not as a category that encompasses many races and thus constitutes a 'mixed' group, but as a collective embodiment of 'mixture' itself." This distinct colonial process, of early and continual *mestizaje*, or the mixing of individuals of distinct ethnic origins, further complicates our ability as archaeologists to meaningfully discern differences between African, European, or Indigenous cultural features (Fournier and Charlton 2008). A growing number of researchers are attempting to remedy these explicit and implicit acts of erasure. For instance, the newly established Afro-Latin American Archaeology Interest Group of the Society for American Archaeology brings together a community of scholars whose central concern is to chart a path to address the unique challenges of an archaeology of the African diaspora in Latin America (Sampeck 2018).

As exemplified by my own journey to this area of research, a key factor in constructing archaeological narratives that include Africans and their descendants is a reevaluation of how we approach our data (see also Fryer, chapter 5 in this volume) and a conscious acknowledgment of the multiethnic society that existed across all areas of the Spanish Americas. When I began my research on labor in urban New Spain, I was primarily focused on how gender impacted labor requirements and opportunities (Wesp 2014). I analyzed skeletal indicators of activity and biomechanical stress for a subsample of individuals from the skeletal collection associated with the Hospital Real San José de los Naturales (HSJN) in the historic downtown of Mexico City (Báez Molgado and Meza Peñaloza 1995; Sánchez Vázquez et al. 1996; Cabrera Torres and García Martínez 1998). This hospital was established in 1553 and served as the first royally financed hospital to care specifically for the Indigenous population (Muriel 1956; Zedillo Castillo 1984; Wesp 2016). Due to this specific historical context, my analysis did not initially include ethnic origin as a significant category of analysis. Yet, by changing how I viewed these data, I could identify differences in labor among individuals of the same sex and similarities in labor of individuals of different sexes. I showed that it might be possible to attribute these similarities and differences to other aspects of identity, such as ethnic origin, since in the changing colonial world it was more significant in organizing labor requirements and opportunities, yet we tend not to acknowledge this expanded perspective on colonial life in our initial research questions (Wesp 2020).

For example, a closer inspection of historical documents and visual sources depicting Mexico City, and the hospital itself, reveals a clear and accurate representation of the diversity of urban inhabitants. Paintings that illustrate daily life in the capital from the seventeenth and eighteenth centuries include individuals of African descent among the milieu of urban inhabitants that interacted with each other on a daily basis. The eighteenth-century paintings, *El parián* (The Marketplace) by Nicolás Enríquez and *Plaza Mayor de la Ciudad de México* by Diego García Conde, both depict daily life in the central marketplace in Mexico City and specifically highlight ethnic diversity, either as a method of demonstrating *casta* designations (a system of racialized status marking) in the case of the former or through diverse phenotypic features and jobs in the latter (figure 3.1). In fact, as a codified method of categorizing ethnic mixing, the casta system was enacted in the eighteenth century as an attempt to bring order to the already centuries-long history of mixing in the colonies. Casta paintings were created to demonstrate the different categories of mixing yet also serve as historical evidence of attempts to control the often-complicated ways in which colonial subjects negotiated identity through reputation, occupation, dress, and language (Carrera 2003; Katzew 2004).

While Africans and their descendants were a crucial part of colonial life, they did not always have access to the same legal or institutional resources. Documentary sources underscore how they attempted to navigate these challenges. In 1568, a group of Afro-descendants appealed to the Spanish

FIGURE 3.1. *Representation of the multiethnic colonial society whose members encountered one another in their daily life. Detail of the painting* Plaza Mayor de la Ciudad de Mexico *by Diego García Conde at the Museo Nacional de Historia, Mexico City. Photograph by the author.*

Crown to establish a hospital that would specifically care for Africans and Afro-descendants, but the petition was denied (Von Germeten 2009). It is no surprise then that, when necessary, these individuals likely sought care at other hospitals, despite supposed rules and regulations governing their care for individuals with a specific illness or a specific portion of the urban population at facilities such as the HSJN. In fact, the hospital administrator was officially reprimanded for providing services to a diverse range of ethnicities at a meeting in 1785, documented within the meeting notes for the hospital (Hospital Real de Naturales 1777–1815, 36).

Indeed, the individuals in the skeletal collection associated with the hospital appear to represent an accurate cross-section of the ethnic diversity that existed in colonial populations. Of the approximately 600 individuals recovered during the excavations, approximately 5 percent represent individuals who likely had African ancestry based on cranial morphometric analysis and non-metric dental analysis (Karam Tapia 2012; Ruíz Albarrán 2012; Meza Peñaloza 2013) and have since been further supported with ancient DNA analysis (Barquera et al. 2020; Wesp, Sandoval-Velasco, and Avila-Arcos 2020). Additionally, analysis of nonmetric dental markers also suggests the presence of Europeans, Mestizos (a category from the casta system that is generally used to indicate individuals of mixed heritage), and Asians within the skeletal population (Hernández López and Negrete Gutiérrez 2012).[2] Additionally, four individuals have modified teeth using a percussion method, a common cultural marker found among many different African communities. This method is distinct from the filing method traditionally employed by Mesoamerican populations (Lagunas Rodríguez and Karam Tapia 2003).

My current research builds on these morphological analyses to examine affiliation at the molecular level through a collaborative genomics project. We are analyzing the ancient DNA of a subset of the skeletal population that likely has African heritage. Anthropological genetics is a relatively new field of study that allows scholars to trace migratory relationships through specific changes in DNA that arose after the spread of modern humans across the globe. These data help us answer questions about the specific ethnogeographical origin in Africa of individuals forcibly brought to the Americas as well as the biological admixture of these populations with European and Indigenous American populations. Since documentary sources often only indicate ship embarkation points, ancient DNA analysis can help us better understand cultural practices, such as tooth modification and others, that may have been incorporated into daily colonial life in New Spain.

New archaeological narratives must make use of interdisciplinary research that incorporates historical, archaeological, and biological data to create more realistic reconstructions of the impact of sociopolitical, religious, and demographic changes on daily life of inhabitants of New Spain. The swell of historical research on Afro-descendant populations in Mexico and Central America in recent years has provided important information to supplement current archaeological research, as well as set the stage for incorporating Afro-descendants into our research designs from the beginning.

Incorporating Afro-Yucatecans into Archaeological Narratives

Historical research on Afro-descendants has tended to focus on areas with modern Afro-descendant communities (Aguirre Beltrán [1958] 1985; Correa Duró 2012; de la Serna, Ebergenyi, and Chacón Fregoso 2012); large urban landscapes, such as Mexico City or Puebla (Cope 1994; Sierra Silva 2015; Seijas and Sierra Silva 2016); or port cities where known slave ships landed (Carroll 1991; Alcántara López 2010; de la Serna y Herrera 2013). Yet, Africans and Afro-descendant peoples were critical actors in all corners of colonial life. Perhaps one of the most extensive studies on the Yucatán is Matthew Restall's (2009) *The Black Middle: Africans, Mayas, and Spaniards in Colonial Yucatan*, in which he explores slavery, population demographics, labor, and ethnic mixing throughout the sixteenth, seventeenth, and eighteenth centuries in the Yucatán peninsula—an area often characterized as having very few Afro-descendant communities. This broad historical analysis of the presence of Afro-descendants across various areas of Yucatecan life provides a crucial first step in our ability to create inclusive archaeological narratives.

Similar to the presence of Black conquistadors in Central Mexico, documentary sources suggest that free and enslaved Black conquistadores were a part of Francisco de Montejo's various conquest campaigns of the Yucatán in the early sixteenth century (Restall 2000). Thus, their presence in the Yucatán peninsula began in the Early Colonial period, and while the Afro-descendant population in the Yucatán may not have been as numerous in comparison to other parts of New Spain, especially the capital city, they were still a significant percentage of the local community. Population estimates suggest that they made up approximately 7 percent of the total Yucatecan population in CE 1645 and 14 percent in CE 1725 (Aguirre Beltrán 1946, 219–222; Restall 2009, 28). As Restall notes, however, it is important to remember the distribution of both free and enslaved Afro-Yucatecans was uneven. The majority of the total Afro-Yucatecan population was clustered around Campeche, which served as a debarkation point for various slave ships as well as a significant port for clandestine trade within the Americas (Restall 2009; Voyages Database 2016; Vinson III 2018).

Not all Afro-descendants in Yucatán, however, were enslaved. Historical documents highlight two different free Black towns that were established on the peninsula—San Fernando de Aké in the northeast and San Francisco de Paula in the northwest. Both were established in the late eighteenth and early nineteenth centuries by people who arrived in the Yucatán from Cuba. The former consisted of previously enslaved people who had fought for Spain during the successful slave uprising in Saint Domingue (present-day Haiti) between 1791 and 1804. They were subsequently split up and relocated to different parts of the Spanish Americas because of a fear from the governor of Cuba that they might instigate further insurrections. In 1796, a total of 115 adult men, women, and children were sent to Campeche and granted land to establish a town on the site of a former pre-Hispanic Maya town near Tizimin (Vinson III 2001; Restall 2009). The latter town, designated on historical maps as "Rancho de Negros" in the early 1800s, was located south of the port of Sisal. Documentary evidence indicates that various community members can trace their lineage back to Cuba, though it is also possible that some of the inhabitants may be transplants from the newly established San Fernando Aké (Andrews and Robles Castellanos 2002; Cortés A. 2016).

Despite the lower distribution of Afro-Yucatecans in more rural locales of the peninsula, we must not exclude them from our understanding of life in these areas. Parish records demonstrate that Afro-Yucatecans often intermarried with and lived among ethnically Maya communities. It is also important to note that in 1829, around the time that both of these towns began to flourish, slavery was abolished throughout Mexico and restrictions on Afro-Yucatecans' movement and interaction with nearby Indigenous towns may have been less restrictive. As outlined in this chapter, however, this integration into Indigenous communities, including widespread adoption of corn farming (Collí Collí 2005), may make identifying their presence archaeologically more difficult. Regardless of these challenges, archaeological and bioarchaeological research in each of these places have illustrated how archaeological narratives can successfully incorporate Afro-Yucatecans.

Campeche

Bioarchaeologists analyzed the presence of Afro-descendants in the collection of skeletal remains that were recovered from the sixteenth- and seventeenth-century cemetery in downtown Campeche (Zabala et al. 2004; Tiesler, Zabala, and Cucina 2010). Their analysis of the nearly 200 individuals recovered from the cemetery confirmed that the cemetery was a multiethnic representation of this colonial port and included individuals of European, Indigenous, and African ancestry (Cucina, Rodriguez, and Tiesler 2012; Cucina Ojeda Mas, and Huitz Baquiero 2013). Biological affiliation was estimated using a number of different methods, but due to poor preservation of the crania, nonmetric dental traits form the basis of their analysis (Cucina, Neff, and Tiesler 2004; Cucina, Ojeda Mas, and Huitz Baquiero 2013). Four individuals from the Campeche cemetery also have culturally significant modified teeth (Tiesler Blos 2003). Using radiographs and a scanning electron microscope, Tiesler shows that the modifications were made using a percussion chipping that is similar to the individuals from the HSJN hospital in Mexico City as well as other Afro-descendant skeletal remains excavated in the Americas (Tiesler 2002).

Specialized analyses, such as stable isotope analysis, allow bioarchaeologists to identify where an individual lived during their childhood when their teeth were developing. Analysis of dental enamel from the individuals with culturally significant dental modification had strontium levels that more closely resembled those in West Africa than parts of Mesoamerica, whereas other individuals with likely African heritage instead suggested they were born in the Americas (Price, Tiesler, and Burton 2006; Tiesler and Price 2013). Given that Campeche was one of the main ports, it is quite possible that the people with modified teeth were born in Africa and later transported as part of the Transatlantic Slave Trade to New Spain. While the historical record emphasizes the higher frequency of Afro-descendants in this area of the Yucatán peninsula, these bodies provide material evidence of this ethnic diversity, including the presence of American-born individuals of African heritage, in a way that may not always be as clear in other archaeological data.

Additionally, biological affiliation combined with other skeletal indicators of activity, health, and diet can answer many questions about the daily life of Afro-descendants that are not as clear in historical documents. For example, Andrea Cucina and colleagues found a lower frequency of linear enamel hypoplasia, a skeletal indicator of childhood nutritional stress, for the African-born individuals than for all those born in the Americas, including Indigenous people, Mestizos, and Afro-descendants (Cucina, Rodriguez, and Tiesler 2012). The authors suggest that these data show that in Campeche, social role may not have caused a significant difference in available resources or external stress. This hypothesis provides an interesting avenue for further research into how different aspects of identity influenced daily life. These similarities may also appear across other categories of material culture in the archaeological record.

San Fernando Aké

Archaeological survey at San Fernando Aké recorded ceramics and architectural foundations associated with the Afro-Yucatecan occupation period in the early nineteenth century (Victoria Ojeda and Canto Alcocer 2006). The official regulations for the establishment of the town ordered that households be constructed along a north-south, east-west grid system, but the lack of architectural remains for these structures, which were likely made of wood and straw, made it impossible for the archaeologists to identify whether they followed these rules. They did identify the remains of four masonry structures—one elliptical, two rectangular, and a rectangular structure with a semicircular side toward the east—that were grouped together on the edge of a large plaza. The archaeologists suggest that these may have served as administrative buildings or even a jail, which documentary evidence suggests housed individuals on occasion throughout the town's history. A fifth structure was located some distance away and elevated on a base structure; it primarily consisted of a single wall in ruins (51–53). It is possible that this final masonry structure represents the church—another requirement outlined in the official regulations for the establishment of the town. However, the archaeologists are tentative with this designation because the structure would have been too small to hold the town's population (52). The ceramics Ojeda and Alcocer found on the surface consist of intermixed local pre-Hispanic and colonial types, probably because of later agricultural and cattle-ranching disturbance (Victoria Ojeda and Canto Alcocer 2006). There does not appear to be a cemetery in town; historical research suggests that individuals were instead buried in the nearby town of Kikil. Ultimately, the town was abandoned in 1848 during the Caste War, when the bulk of the inhabitants fled to Belize (89–91). Currently, the site of the former free Black town is a small cattle ranch.

San Francisco de Paula

Archaeological surveys at San Francisco de Paula indicate a more significant set of still-visible architectural remains that are organized along a main street running east-west (Andrews, Cortés A., and Robles C. 2015). Approximately twenty-five house structures with associated lots, a church, and a common meeting house were recorded at the site. Inhabitants constructed these buildings using dry masonry, wood, and thatch roofs. In addition, various areas surrounding this central settlement appear to have been used for active cultivation of plants. Anthony Andrews and colleagues conducted excavations at San Francisco de Paula in 2014. Artifacts recovered include manos and metates (grinding stones and pestles), faunal remains, and glass and metal artifacts. They also encountered a range of ceramics, such as kaolin pipes, likely of English or French origin, pearl white English Transfer ware, and local colonial ceramics such as Yuncu Unslipped and Sakpokana Red (2015). The members of this community likely participated in *palo de tinte*, the logwood trade, which was used to make a dye and was in high demand in the nineteenth century. The site in currently abandoned; however, the archaeologists also conducted oral history interviews with older residents of a nearby town who remember the town residents as corn farmers who would occasionally also sell cane sugar in the market in Sisal (Andrews, Cortés A., and Robles C. 2015; Sampeck 2018).

Summary

While each of these archaeological projects have included Afro-Yucatecans in their reconstructions, the ability to do so is still somewhat dependent on confirmation by historical texts. The detailed historical accounts documenting Campeche as a slave ship port suggest that we should expect the presence of Africans in the colonial Campeche cemetery, yet it was the phenotypic differences in the skeleton and cultural body modifications that allowed scholars to confirm their presence with more confidence. As with my own research, the skeletal remains of these individuals provide important clues for more detailed bioarchaeological research. Isotopic or ancient DNA research would allow us to expand our understanding of the slave trade and cultural origins of these individuals within the African continent. Documentary evidence of origins in Africa often only indicate port of embarkation. More often still, these data may be unavailable because of illicit trade of enslaved individuals born in the Americas—a practice that increased in frequency during the late seventeenth century and early eighteenth (Rout 1976; Seijas and Sierra Silva 2016). Moreover, these specialized studies have the potential to impact our understanding of cultural continuity and change among Afro-Yucatecans as well as other important aspects of their daily lives, such as variations in diet, health, or activity. These specialized analyses, however, are expensive, destructive, and require adequate preservation of skeletal material to yield significant results. As such, these areas of research tend to be carried out only when there is a high likelihood of African heritage among the study populations.

Distinguishing the presence of Afro-Yucatecans in the archaeological survey and excavation of rural settlements may be equally challenging. In addition to being granted land for the establishment of San Fernando Aké, the refugees from Cuba were also given building tools such as axes, machetes, and hoes; enough ceramic plates for each person; two ceramic pots per family; and rations of corn and beef (Victoria Ojeda and Canto Alcocer 2006). These local basic household items, as well as houses built from local materials, would not leave an ethnically distinct trace in the archaeological record. Furthermore, while these residents were prohibited from moving to Indigenous towns, a census of the San Fernando Aké residents in 1841 shows an increase to 853 people, with 44 percent of the residents classified as ethnically Maya (Victoria Ojeda and Canto Alcocer 2006, 57). The intermixing of Afro-Yucatecans and Maya people along with the adoption of corn farming in these rural locations could result in quite similar artifact assemblages.

Similarly, the material recovered from the excavations at San Francisco de Paula may represent the typical range of local and foreign artifacts that you would expect from a historic site. Local ceramics were likely acquired because of easy trade access for everyday-use goods and a similar demand for objects associated with corn processing and consumption. Imported glazed ceramics are common at historic sites in varying quantities and would likely be present in locations with permanent or visiting religious figures, a point suggested as a possible interpretation by the archaeologists. The presence of other foreign items, such as glass bottles, could also be the result of the site's proximity to the port of Sisal and easier access to these foreign trade items through the logwood trade market. Andrews and colleagues suggest that the most ethnically distinct artifacts are the collection of kaolin pipes recovered from in and around house structures, since smoking was not typically practiced by Maya or Mestizos (Andrews, Cortés A., and Fernando Robles C. 2015).

Archaeological explorations of a Black Carib settlement in Honduras (Cheek and Gonzalez 1988) offer a comparative example of a transplanted community of African heritage from the Caribbean, such as the two free Black towns in the Yucatán. Charles Cheek (1997) suggests this community may have attempted to establish a unique identity within its new home by adopting more British ceramic styles, though overall the excavations yielded a mix of ceramic wares, including local Indigenous ceramics, Hispanic ceramics, and other non-Hispanic European ceramics. The authors suggest that participation in the Haitian Revolution may have negatively impacted how this community was perceived, and the adoption of British material culture may have served to distance them from the French revolutionary ideas. Further research among other Afro-descendant historical communities in Belize and the Caribbean coast of Central America could provide additional comparisons for how these communities integrated into daily life.

Conclusion

The inclusion of Africans and their descendants within archaeological narratives is best supported by integrating evidence from multiple different historical and archaeological sources. Historical research of documentary and visual evidence of Afro-descendants in colonial society can provide important clues about the presence of this portion of society in different areas of New Spain. Similarly, these data provide important clues for identifying minute differences in archaeological data that can provide new interpretations of colonial life. For example, at least two other free Black towns were established in Veracruz after separate, successful revolts led by enslaved persons in the early seventeenth and mid-eighteenth centuries. Recent excavations at one of these towns, Nuestra Señora de Guadalupe de los Morenos de Amapa, established in 1765, could further help us understand whether or not daily life of the inhabitants of these towns leave a distinct archaeological trace (Amaral 2015). As with the presence of kaolin pipes at San Francisco de Paula, the presence of certain kinds of archaeological data may indicate the presence of Afro-descendants in these spaces because of distinct cultural practices that they bring with them or develop over time.

It is also important to acknowledge that a distinct Afro-descendant archaeological signature may not exist because of the use of local materials and daily goods. The intermixing across ethnic groups and the adoption of Indigenous subsistence methods may further complicate our ability to distinguish between individuals of different ethnic origins. Despite these challenges, however, we should still make an effort to broaden our perspective when developing our research projects and constructing interpretations of data. The current focus on Indigenous history as a key aspect of Mexican national identity has obscured the importance of colonial life and this long history of intermixing that gave way to the diversity of modern Mexicans. The recent 2015 census by the National

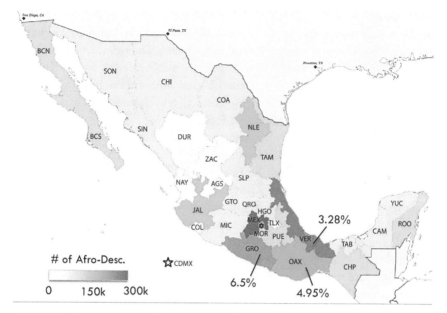

FIGURE 3.2. *Map representing the population of Afro-descendants in Mexico with color shading corresponding to the approximate number of 2015 INEGI census respondents. The states of Guerrero (6.5 percent), Oaxaca (4.95 percent), and Veracruz (3.28 percent) have the highest percentages of self-identified Afro-descendants. Drawn by Julie Wesp.*

Institute of Statistics and Geography (INEGI) recorded 1.38 million Mexicans with African heritage (figure 3.2), approximately 1.16 percent of the total population (INEGI 2015).[3] In addition, recent genomic research has shown that the average amount of African admixture for the general Mexican population is 3–5 percent, further highlighting this long history of a multiethnic society (Magana et al. 2007; Ávila Arcos et al. 2016). The current revisionist national history narrative that focuses on an exalted pre-Hispanic past has resulted in prejudice and discrimination toward current Afro-descendant communities, both nationally and abroad (Hoppenjans and Richardson 2010; Lewis 2012; Velázquez and Iturralde Nieto 2012; on revisionist national histories see also Diserens Morgan, chapter 11 in this volume). A more inclusive colonial past could in fact have an impact on how Mexican society is understood in the present.

Archaeological research has the potential to help commemorate important sites and make Afro-descendant history a more prominent part of Mexican history. There is a collaborative effort by the Instituto Nacional de Antropología e Historia (INAH; National Institute of Anthropology and History), the National Program for Afrodescendant and Cultural Diversity Research, and UNESCO's Slave Route Project to officially recognize heritage sites associated with slavery and African and African-descendant populations. Three sites are currently recognized, each with a freely available published written and visual history: the Historic Downtown of Mexico City; Cuajinicuilapa, Guerrero; and the Port of Veracruz and Yanga (Velázquez et al. 2016; Domínguez et al. 2017; Velázquez and Martínez Maldonado 2017). Archaeological sites and the physical tangible materials recovered in excavations provide further avenues for these histories to be experienced by and showcased for the public.

An exploration of colonial life, and a reckoning with the coloniality of the commemoration process, must start from the perspective that colonial society is not adequately captured by the European/Indigenous binary; people from multiple cultural and phenotypically different groups lived together, worked together, and formed families together, and this intermixing was not unique to urban spaces. This multiethnic society was present from the creation of New Spain in the early sixteenth century and was constant throughout the Colonial, National, and Modern periods. Archaeological narratives that accurately represent this past reality must recognize the contribution of Africans and their descendants—the third root of mestizaje—to colonial life.

Acknowledgments. I would like to thank Tiffany C. Fryer and Kasey Diserens Morgan for inviting me to contribute a chapter to this volume. The bulk of this research was conducted while I was a UC MEXUS/CONACYT Postdoctoral Fellow, and I am indebted to my gracious host María Elisa Velázquez and the members of the Programa Nacional de Investigación Afrodescendiente y Diversidad Cultural at the Coordinación Nacional de Antropología in Mexico City. I would also like to thank Katie Sampeck and the other workshop participants at the Afro-Latin American Research Institute at the Hutchins Center at Harvard who provided insightful comments on my own research and about how we might incorporate Afro–Latin Americans into archaeological research.

Notes

1. The analysis of "race" from skeletal features has its own problematic history within physical anthropology, which these scholars blatantly disregarded. While most anthropologists acknowledge that race is a social construction, biological affiliation may be visible in the skeleton through an analysis of how the frequency of traits differ across geographical boundaries (see Goodman, Moses, and Jones 2012 and Hefner et al. 2016).

2. A related topic is the lack of research on the transpacific slave trade from Manila in the Philippines to the port of Acapulco on the pacific coast of Mexico. Seijas (2014) demonstrates that both enslaved Africans and enslaved Asians were transported along this route.

3. The 2015 Census was the first to include a question about African heritage, though questions about Indigenous heritage and Indigenous language use have been recorded since the mid-twentieth. The question asked for self-identification as an Afro-descendant, and scholars have since suggested that this may have resulted in an undercounting of the actual number of people with African heritage living in Mexico (María Elisa Velázquez, personal communication, June 2016).

References

Aguirre Beltrán, Gonzalo. 1946. *La población negra de México: 1519–1810, Estudio etno-histórico*. 2nd ed. Colección Tierra Firme. Mexico City: Fondo de Cultura Económica.

Aguirre Beltrán, Gonzalo. (1958) 1985. *Cuijla: Esbozo etnográfico de un pueblo negro*. Mexico City: Fondo de Cultura Económica.

Alcántara López, Álvaro. 2010. "Negros y afromestizos del Puerto de Veracruz: Impresiones de lo popular Durante los Siglos XVII y XVIII." In *La Habana / Veracruz Veracruz / La Habana: Las Dos Orillas*, edited by B. García Díaz and S. Guerra Vilaboy, 175–191. Veracruz: Universidad Veracruzana.

Amaral, Adela L. 2015. "The Archaeology of a Maroon Reducción: Colonial Beginnings to Present Day Ruination." PhD diss., University of Chicago.

Andrews, Anthony P., Carlos Cortés A., and Fernando Robles C. 2015. *Proyecto San Francisco de Paula y Kaxek: Final Report to the Committee for Research and Exploration, National Geographic Society*. Washington, DC.

Andrews, Anthony P., and Fernando Robles Castellanos. 2002. "An Archaeological Survey of Northwest Yucatan, Mexico: Final Report of the 2002 Season." Edited by Instituto Nacional de Antropología e Historia.

Arce, B. Christine. 2017. *México's Nobodies: The Cultural Legacy of the Soldadera and Afro-Mexican Women*. Albany: State University of New York Press.

Ávila Arcos, María C., Andrés Moreno Estrada, Karla Sandoval Mendoza, Marcus W. Feldman, and Carlos D. Bustamante. 2016. "The Third Root of Mexico: Genetic Structure of Mexicans of African Descent." Conference Presentation. 85th Annual Meeting of the American Association of Physical Anthropologists. *American Journal of Physical Anthropology* 159 (S62): 84.

Báez Molgado, Socorro, and Abigail Meza Peñaloza. 1995. *Proyecto metro línea 8: Análisis de los restos óseos del Hospital Real de San José de los Naturales*. Mexico City: Dirección de Salvamento Arqueológico, Instituto Nacional de Antropología e Historia.

Barquera, Rodrigo, Thiseas C. Lamnidis, Aditya Kumar Lankapalli, Arthur Kocher, Diana I. Hernández-Zaragoza, Elizabeth A. Nelson, Adriana C. Zamora-Herrera, Patxi Ramallo, Natalia Bernal-Felipe, Alexander Immel, KirstenBos, Victor Acuña-Alonzo, Chiara Barbieri, Patrick Roberts, Alexander Herbig, Denise Kühnert, Lourdes Márquez-Morfin, and Johannes Krause. 2020. "Origin and Health Status of First-Generation Africans from Early Colonial Mexico." *Current Biology* 30 (11): 2078–2091.e2011.

Bennett, Herman L. 2009. *Colonial Blackness: A History of Afro-Mexico*. Bloomington: Indiana University Press.

Blakey, Michael L. 2001. "Bioarchaeology of the African Diaspora in the Americas: Its Origins and Scope." *Annual Review of Anthropology* 30: 387–422.

Bristol, Joan, and Matthew Restall. 2009. "Potions and Perils: Love-Magic in Seventeenth-Century Afro-Mexico and Afro-Yucatan." In *Black Mexico: Race and Society from Colonial to Modern Times*, edited by Ben Vinson III and Matthew Restall, 155–179. Albuquerque: University of New Mexico Press.

Cabrera Torres, José Jorge, and María de los Ángeles García Martínez. 1998. "Utilización, modificación y reuso de los espacios del edificio sede del Hospital Real de San José de los Naturales." Mexico City: Arqueología, Escuela Nacional de Antropología e Historia.

Carrera, Magali Marie. 2003. *Imagining Identity in New Spain: Race, Lineage, and the Colonial Body in Portraiture and Casta Paintings*. Austin: University of Texas Press.

Carroll, Patrick J. 1991. *Blacks in Colonial Veracruz: Race, Ethnicity, and Regional Development*. Austin: University of Texas Press.

Carroll, Patrick J. 2005. "Black-Native Relations and the Historical Record in Colonial Mexico." In *Beyond Black and Red: African-Native Relations in Colonial Latin America*, edited by Matthew Restall, 245–267. Albuquerque: University of New Mexico Press.

Castillo Palma, Norma Angélica, and Susan Kellogg. 2005. "Conflict and Cohabitation between Afro-Mexicans and Nahuas in Central Mexico." In *Beyond Black and Red: African-Native Relations in Colonial Latin America*, edited by Matthew Restall, 115–136. Albuquerque: University of New Mexico Press.

Cheek, Charles D. 1997. "Setting an English Table: Black Carib Archaeology on the Caribbean Coast of Honduras." In *Approaches to the Historical Archaeology of Mexico, Central and South America*, edited by J. Gasco, G. C. Smith and P. Fournier-Garcia, 101–109. Los Angeles: Institute of Archaeology.

Cheek, Charles D., and Nancie L. Gonzalez. 1988. "Black Carib Settlement Patterns in Early Nineteenth-Century Honduras: The Search for a Livelihood." In *Ethnohistory: A Researcher's Guide*, edited by D. Wiedman, 403–429. Williamsburg, VA: College of William and Mary.

Collí Collí, Mario Baltazar. 2005. "Componentes africanos en Quintana Roo." Thesis. Universidad Autónoma de Yucatán, Facultad de Ciencias Antropológicas, Mérida.

Cope, R. Douglas. 1994. *The Limits of Racial Domination: Plebeian Society in Colonial Mexico City, 1660–1720*. Madison: University of Wisconsin Press.

Correa Duró, Ethel. 2012. "Población y familia en el Distrito del Jamiltepec, Costa Chica de Oaxaca, Censo de Población de 1890." In *Raíces y actualidad de la afrodescendencia en Guerrero y Oaxaca*, edited by Luz María Espinosa Cortés and Juan Manuel de la Serna Herrera, 137–168. Mexico City: Plaza y Valdés.

Cortés A., Carlos. 2016. "Investigación arqueológica del Pueblo de San Francisco de Paula, Yucatán." Paper presented at the Estudios de Arqueología y Bioantropología: Africanos y Afrodescendientes en México, Mexico City.

Cucina, Andrea, Hector Neff, and Vera Tiesler. 2004. "Provenance of African-Born Individuals from the Colonial Cemetery of Campeche (Mexico) by Means of Trace Element Analysis." *Dental Anthropology* 17 (3): 65–69.

Cucina, Andrea, Heber Ojeda Mas, and Carlos Huitz Baquiero. 2013. "La población africana en un cementerio multiétnico: La Plaza de Armas de Campeche." *Arqueología Mexicana* 19 (119): 45–51.

Cucina, Andrea, Monica Rodriguez, and Vera Tiesler. 2012. "Physiological Stress in a Multi-ethnic Cemetery Population from Colonial Campeche, Mexico." Conference Presentation. 81st Annual Meeting of the American Association of Physical Anthropologists. *American Journal of Physical Anthropology* 147 (S54): 123.

Davidson, David M. (1973) 1996. "Negro Slave Control and Resistance in Colonial Mexico, 1519–1650." In *Maroon Societies: Rebel Slave Communities in the Americas*, edited by Richard Price, 82–103. Baltimore, MD: Johns Hopkins University Press.

de la Serna, Juan Manuel, ed. 2010. *De la libertad y la abolición: Africanos y afrodescendientes en Iberoamérica*. Mexico City: Instituto Nacional de Antropología e Historia.

de la Serna y Herrera, Juan Manuel. 2013. "Negros, mulatos y pardos en la Historia Veracruz." *Arqueología Mexicana* 19 (119): 52–57.

de la Serna, Juan Manuel, Ingrid Ebergenyi, and Gina Chacón Fregoso. 2012. "El Rostro de una región: Los descendientes de Africanos en la Costa Chica." In *Raíces y actualidad de la afrodescendencia en Guerrero y Oaxaca*, edited by Luz María Espinosa Cortés and Juan Manuel de la Serna Herrera, 197–218. Mexico City: Plaza y Valdés.

Domínguez, Citlalli, Alfredo Delgado, María Elisa Velázquez, and José Luis Martínez Maldonado. 2017. *El Puerto de Veracruz y Yanga: Sitios de memoria de la esclavitud y las poblaciones africanas y afrodescendientes*. Mexico City: Instituto Nacional de Antropología e Historia.

Eschbach, Krista L. 2019. "Ceramic Technology in Afromestizo Neighborhoods of the Colonial Port of Veracruz, Mexico." In *Technology and Tradition in Mesoamerica after the Spanish Invasion: Archaeological Perspectives*, edited by Rani T. Alexander, 53–72. Albuquerque: University of New Mexico Press.

Fennell, Christopher C. 2010. "Early African America: Archaeological Studies of Significance and Diversity." *Journal of Archaeological Research* 19 (1): 1–49.

Fournier, Patricia, and Thomas H. Charlton. 2008. "Negritos y pardos: Hacia una arqueología histórica de la población de origen africano en la Nueva España." In *Perspectivas de la investigación arqueológica III*, edited by Fernando López Aguilar, Walburga Wiesheu, and Patricia Fournier Garcia, 201–234. Mexico City: PROMEP-CONACULTA-ENAH.

Fournier-Garcia, Patricia, and Fernando A. Miranda-Flores. 1992. "Historic Sites Archaeology in Mexico." *Historical Archaeology* 26 (1): 75–83.

Funari, Pedro Paulo A. 2006. "Conquistadors, Plantations, and Quilombo: Latin America in Historical Archaeological Context." In *Historical Archaeology*, edited by Martin Hall and Stephen W. Silliman, 209–229. Malden, MA: Blackwell.

Gerhard, Peter. 1978. "A Black Conquistador in Mexico." *Hispanic American Historical Review* 58 (3): 451–459.

Goodman, Alan H., Yolanda T. Moses, and Joseph L. Jones. 2012. *Race: Are We So Different?* Malden, MA: Wiley-Blackwell.

Haviser, Jay B., ed. 1999. *African Sites: Archaeology in the Caribbean*. Princeton, NJ: Markus Weiner Publishers.

Hefner, Joseph T., Marin A. Pilloud, Jane E. Buikstra, and C.C.M. Vogelsberg. 2016. "A Brief History of Biological Distance Analysis" In *Biological Distance Analysis: Forensic and Bioarchaeological Perspectives*, edited by Marin A. Pilloud and Joseph T. Hefner, 3–22. London: Elsevier.

Hernández Cuevas, Marco Polo. 2004. *African Mexicans and the Discourse on Modern Nation*. Dallas, TX: University Press of America.

Hernández López, Paulina Elizabeth, and Samantha Sharon Negrete Gutiérrez. 2012. "¿Realmente eran indios? Afinidad biológica entre las personas atendidas en el Hospital Real San Jose de los Naturales, Siglos XVI–XVIII." Tesis de Licenciatura. Mexico City: Antropología Física, Escuela Nacional de Antropología e Historia.

Hoppenjans, Lisa, and Ted Richardson. 2010. "Mexican Ways, African Roots." In *The Afro-Latin@ Reader: History and Culture in the United States*, edited by Miriam Jiménez Román and Juan Flores, 512–519. Durham, NC: Duke University Press.

Hospital Real de Naturales. 1777–1815. "Libro de juntas del Hospital Real de Naturales." In *Colección Antigua 03*. Vol. 679. Mexico City: Biblioteca Nacional de Antropología e Historia.

INEGI. 2015. "Principales resultados de la encuesta intercensal 2015: Estados Unidos Mexicanos, 122." Mexico City: Instituto Nacional de Estadística y Geografía.

Jones, Jennifer A. M. 2013. "'Mexicans Will Take the Jobs That Even Blacks Won't Do': An Analysis of Blackness, Regionalism and Invisibility in Contemporary Mexico." *Ethnic and Racial Studies* 36 (10): 1564–1581.

Karam Tapia, Carlos Enrique. 2012. "Estimación del mestizaje mediante la morfología dental en la Ciudad de México (Siglo XVI al XIX)." Tesis de Licenciatura. Mexico City: Antropología Física, Escuela Nacional de Antropología e Historia.

Katzew, Ilona. 2004. *Casta Painting: Images of Race in Eighteenth-Century Mexico*. New Haven, CT: Yale University Press.

Katzew, Ilona, and Susan Deans-Smith. 2009. *Race and Classification: The Case of Mexican America*. Stanford, CA: Stanford University Press.

Lagunas Rodríguez, Zaid, and Carlos E. Karam Tapia. 2003. "Cráneos africanos de la época colonial con mutilación dentaria, procedentes del ex Hospital Real de San José de los Naturales de la Ciudad de México, D.F." *Estudios de Antropología Biológica* 11 (2): 967–981.

La Jornada. 2013. "Gurrero tenía brazo sin mover: Bravo, sífilis y vicario, Sobrepreso." Mexico City, January 16.

Lewis, Laura A. 2012. *Chocolate and Corn Flour: History, Race, and Place in the Making of "Black" Mexico*. Durham, NC: Duke University Press.

Love, Edgar F. 1970. "Legal Restrictions on Afro-Indian Relations in Colonial Mexico." *Journal of Negro History* 55 (2): 131–139.

Magana, M. T., F. J. Perea, J. R. Gonzalez, and B. Ibarra. 2007. "Genetic Relationship of a Mexican Afromestizo Population through the Analysis of the 3' Haplotype of the Beta Globin Gene in Beta(a) Chromosomes." *Blood Cells Molecules and Diseases* 39 (2): 169–177.

Masferrer León, Cristina V. 2011. "Niños y niñas esclavos de origen africano en la capital novohispana (Siglo XVII)." In *Debates históricos Contemporáneos: Africanos y afrodescendientes en México y Centroamérica*, edited by María Elisa Velásquez, 195–242. Mexico City: Instituto Nacional de Antropología e Historia.

Meza Peñaloza, Abigail. 2013. "Presencia africana en el Cementerio del Hospital Real de San José de los Naturales." *Arqueología Mexicana* 19 (119): 40–44.

Muriel, Josefina. 1956. *Hospitales de la Nueva España: Fundaciones del siglo XVI*. Publicaciones del Instituto de Historia. Vol. 1. Mexico City: Instituto de Historia.

Nemser, Daniel. 2017. *Infrastructures of Race: Concentration and Biopolitics in Colonial Mexico*. Austin: University of Texas Press.

Orser, Charles E., Jr. 1998. "The Archaeology of the African Diaspora." *Annual Review of Anthropology* 27: 63–82.

Palmer, Colin A. 1976. *Slaves of the White God: Blacks in Mexico, 1570–1650*. Cambridge, MA: Harvard University Press.

Pompa y Padilla, José Antonio. 2016. "Vicente Guerrero: Noticias a partir del análisis de sus restos." Paper presented at the Estudios de Arqueología y Bioantropología: Africanos y Afrodescendientes en México, Mexico City.

Price, T. Douglas, Vera Tiesler, and James H. Burton. 2006. "Early African Diaspora in Colonial Campeche, Mexico: Strontium Isotopic Evidence." *American Journal of Physical Anthropology* 130 (4): 485–490.

Proctor, Frank T. 2010. *Damned Notions of Liberty: Slavery, Culture, and Power in Colonial Mexico, 1640–1769*. Albuquerque: University of New Mexico Press.

Restall, Matthew. 2000. "Black Conquistadors: Armed Africans in Early Spanish America." *Americas* 57 (2): 171–205.

Restall, Matthew, ed. 2005. *Beyond Black and Red: African-Native Relations in Colonial Latin America*. Albuquerque: University of New Mexico Press.

Restall, Matthew. 2009. *The Black Middle: Africans, Mayas, and Spaniards in Colonial Yucatan*. Stanford, CA: Stanford University Press.

Rinaudo, Christian. 2012. *Afromestizaje y fronteras étnicas: Una mirada desde el Puerto de Veracruz*. Translated by L. Karnoouh. Xalapa, Mexico: Universidad Veracruzana.

Rivero Webber, Lilia, and José Antonio Pompa y Padilla. 2012. *Los restos de los héroes en el Monumento a la Independencia: Conservación y restauración, Análisis de antropología física*, Vol. II. México: Instituto Nacional de Antropología e Historia: Instituto Nacional de Estudios Históricos de las Revoluciones de México.

Rout, Leslie B., Jr. 1976. *The African Experience in Spanish America*. Princeton, NJ: Markus Wiener Publishers.

Ruíz Albarrán, Perla del Carmen. 2012. "Estudio de variabilidad biológica en la Colección Esquelética Hospital Real de San José de los Naturales: Un acercamiento a través de la técnica de morfometría geométrica." Tesis de Licenciatura. Mexico City: Antropología Física, Escuela Nacional de Antropología e Historia.

Sampeck, Kathryn E. 2018. "Insights of Afro-Latin American Archaeology." *International Journal of Historical Archaeology* 22 (1): 167–182.

Sánchez Vázquez, María de Jesús, Cecilia Susana Lam García, Georgina Tenango Salgado, José Jorge Cabrera Torres and Alicia Blanco Padilla. 1996. *Proyecto metro línea 8, informe final*. Mexico City: Instituto Nacional de Antropología e Historia, Dirección de Salvamento Arqueológico.

Schwaller, Robert C. 2012. "The Importance of Mestizos and Mulatos as Bilingual Intermediaries in Sixteenth-Century New Spain." *Ethnohistory* 59 (4): 713–738.

Seijas, Tatiana. 2014. *Asian Slaves in Colonial Mexico: From Chinos to Indians*. New York: Cambridge University Press.

Seijas, Tatiana, and Pablo Miguel Sierra Silva. 2016. "The Persistence of the Slave Market in Seventeenth-Century Central Mexico." *Slavery an Abolition* 37 (2): 1–27.

Sierra Silva, Pablo Miguel. 2015. "From Chains to Chiles: An Elite Afro-Indigenous Couple in Colonial Mexico, 1641–1688." *Ethnohistory* 62 (2): 361–384.

Tiesler, Vera. 2002. "New Cases of an African Tooth Decoration from Colonial Campeche, Mexico." *HOMO-Journal of Comparative Human Biology* 52 (3): 277–282.

Tiesler Blos, Vera. 2003. "La práctica africana de mutilación dental en las Américas: Evidencias coloniales en una población negroide." *Estudios de Antropología Biológica* 11 (2): 951–965.

Tiesler, Vera, and Douglas Price. 2013. "Las primeras generaciones de africanos en las Américas." *Arqueología Mexicana* 19 (119): 58–62.

Tiesler, Vera, Pilar Zabala, and Andrea Cucina, eds. 2010. *Natives, Europeans, and Africans in Colonial Campeche: History and Archaeology*. Gainesville: University Press of Florida.

Velázquez, María Elisa. 2006. *Mujeres de origen africano en la capital novohispana, siglos XVII y XVIII*. Mexico City: Universidad Nacional Autónoma de México.

Velázquez, María Elisa. 2011. *Debates históricos contemporáneos: Africanos y afrodescendientes en México y Centroamérica.* Mexico City: Instituto Nacional de Antropología e Historia.

Velázquez, María Elisa, and Gabriela Iturralde Nieto. 2012. *Afrodescendientes en México: Una historia de silencio y discriminación.* Mexico City: INAH / Consejo Nacional para Prevenir la Discriminación.

Velázquez, María Elisa, and José Luis Martínez Maldonado. 2017. *Cuajinicuilapa, Guerrero: Sitio de memoria de la esclavitud y las poblaciones africanas y afrodescendientes.* Mexico City: Instituto Nacional de Antropología e Historia.

Velázquez, María Elisa, José Luis Martínez Maldonado, Gabriela Iturralde Nieto, and María Camila Díaz Casas. 2016. *El centro histórico de la Ciudad de México: Sitio de memoria de la esclavitud y las poblaciones africanas y afrodescendientes.* Mexico City: Instituto Nacional de Antropología e Historia.

Victoria Ojeda, Jorge, and Jorge Canto Alcocer. 2006. *San Fernando Aké: Microhistoria de una comunidad Afroamericana en Yucatán.* Tratados 24. Mérida: Ediciones de la Universidad Autónoma de Yucatán.

Vinson, Ben, III. 2001. *Bearing Arms for His Majesty: The Free-Colored Militia in Colonial Mexico.* Stanford, CA: Stanford University Press.

Vinson, Ben, III. 2018. *Before Mestizaje: The Frontiers of Race and Caste in Colonial Mexico.* Cambridge Latin American Studies. Cambridge, UK: Cambridge University Press.

Vinson, Ben, III, and Matthew Restall, eds. 2009. *Black Mexico: Race and Society from Colonial to Modern Times.* Albuquerque: University of New Mexico Press.

Von Germeten, Nicole. 2009. "Colonial Middle Men? Mulatto Identity in New Spain's Confraternities." In *Black Mexico: Race and Society from Colonial to Modern Times* edited by Ben Vinson III and Matthew Restall, 136–154. Albuquerque: University of New Mexico Press.

Voyages Database. 2016. Voyages: The Trans-Atlantic Slave Trade Database. https://www.slavevoyages.org.

Weik, Terry. 2004. "Archaeology of the African Diaspora in Latin America." *Historical Archaeology* 38 (1): 32–49.

Weik, Terry. 2008. "Mexico's Cimarron Heritage and Archaeological Record." *African Diaspora Archaeology Newsletter* 11 (2): Article 3.

Wesp, Julie K. 2014. Bodies of Work: Organization of Everyday Life Activities in Urban New Spain. PhD diss., University of California, Berkeley.

Wesp, Julie K. 2016. "Caring for Bodies or Simply Saving Souls: The Emergence of Institutional Care in Spanish Colonial America." In *New Developments in the Bioarchaeology of Care: Case Studies and Extended Theory*, edited by Lorna Tilley and Alecia Schrenk, 253–276. New York: Springer Press.

Wesp, Julie K. 2020. "Working in the City: A Historical Bioarchaeology of Activity in Urban New Spain." *Historical Archaeology* 53 (4): 92–109.

Wesp, Julie K., Marcela Sandoval-Velasco, and María Avila-Arcos. 2020. "Ethno-Geographic Origins and Genomic Diversity of Afro-Descendants in Colonial Mexico City." Conference Presentation. 89th Annual Meeting of the American Association of Physical Anthropologists. *American Journal of Physical Anthropology* 171 (S69): 305.

Zabala, Pilar, Andrea Cucina, Vera Tiesler, and Hector Neff. 2004. "La población africana en la Villa Colonial de Campeche: Un estudio interdisciplinario." *Los Investigadores de la Cultura Maya* 12 (1): 165–172.

Zedillo Castillo, Antonio. 1984. *Historia de un hospital: El Hospital Real de Naturales.* Mexico City: Instituto Mexicano de Seguro Social.

4

Piracy and Smuggling on the Eastern Colonial Frontier of the Yucatán Peninsula during the Eighteenth Century

Fior Daliso García Lara and
Fabián Alberto Olán de la Cruz

In colonial cartography, spaces with no Spanish population were marked on the maps as "depopulated," which made the people settled in those regions invisible. The eastern Yucatán peninsula was often visualized as a place full of danger, and its coasts as spaces used only by illegal subjects such as pirates and "runaway natives." This perceived emptiness made the region and town of Tihosuco important as a frontier, not only because it was the last Spanish settlement at the margin of the colony that could provide protection to the eastern coast but also a vulnerable point for piracy and smuggling. With the Caste War (1847–1901), a negative image of eastern Yucatán was reinforced due to the insurrection of Maya Indigenous persons. The Caste War was a turning point in history: it caused the loss of historical records and the erasure of colonial structures that were covered by the jungle. Although the historical understanding of the earlier period before the Caste War is limited because of the loss of sources, historical archeology—a discipline that studies the past using both documentary and material sources (Little 2016, 42)—opens a window to fill these gaps.

https://doi.org/10.5876/9781646422845.c004

Historical archeology in the Mayan area has diversified into an endless number of topics in recent years. Now more than ever researchers focus on colonial and postcolonial times (as this volume shows). However, most archeologists interested in those periods of history are foreigners who see great potential in the region and continue to exploit it, as the editors mention in the introduction to this volume (chapter 1). This chapter seeks to increase the historical-archaeological literature on the eastern coast of the Yucatán peninsula and show that colonial periods are as fascinating and fruitful as the pre-Spanish era. This research focuses on the Late Colonial period (defined in this volume as ca. 1650–1821), a time of important changes in the Spanish overseas colonies. With this chapter begins the thread of discussion of historical processes marked by violence and one of its most visible and common materialization on the region: the *trincheras*, stone defensive structures. It treats the same geographical area as the two following chapters by Fryer (chapter 5) and Badillo Sánchez (chapter 6).

Piracy and smuggling, essential subjects when approaching the eighteenth-century frontier, triggered the establishment of trincheras as part of the defensive systems, the military reconnaissance of the territory, and the delimitation of spaces. In their historiographic study on borderlands, Jeremy Adelman and Stephen Aron (1999, 815) understand the colonial frontier as "a meeting place of peoples in which geographic and cultural borders were not clearly defined." As Adelman and Aron observe, the frontier, different from the concept of border, includes zones of interactions and negotiation between subjects from different empires and nations. Those interactions led to the creation of subsystems between people who maintained their identities but also added new characteristics (Pohlenz 2005, para. 15). We understand smuggling as a subsystem, the dynamics of which defined the frontier as a point of interaction between colonial inhabitants outside of Spanish control and towns at the margin of the empire, such as Tihosuco.

Tihosuco had a relevant position in the central-eastern Yucatán peninsula. Before the Spanish conquest it was the residence of the Halach Uinic,[1] and it was the center of power for the ancient Maya province of Cochuah (Roys 1957, 137; de la Garza 1983, 198). During the Colonial Period, the region came under the jurisdiction of Valladolid, and, later, in the eighteenth century, it was part of El Partido de los Beneficios Altos (figure 4.1), an Spanish administrative region that included the villages of Celul, Chacsinkín, Chikindzonot, Chunhuhub, Dzonotchel, Ekpedz, Ichmul, Peto, Petulillo, Polyúc, Saban, Sacalaca, Tahdziú, Tela' (Tilá), Tepich, Tiholop, Tihosuco (*cabecera*, or parish seat), Tinum, Tituc, Tixhualantún, Tzucacab, Uaymax (Gerhard 1991, 63). As the cabecera, or parish seat, Tihosuco communicated with peripheral places such as its subject town, Tela', and the Bahía de la Ascensión—located in what is today in the state of Quintana Roo—through a country highway.

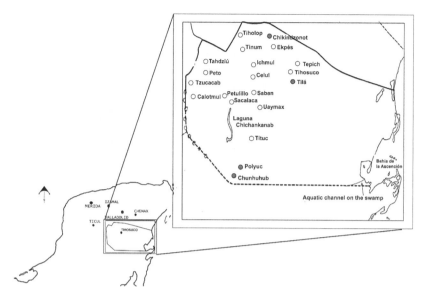

FIGURE 4.1. *The Partido de los Beneficios Altos. After Roys (1957) and Gerhard (1991). Map adapted by María Novelo.*

In the course of our research, we had the opportunity to visit a structure on a disappeared pathway, known today by Tihosuco's community as "El Fuerte." However, its characteristics resemble a trinchera—a defensive structure from which soldiers could protect themselves and at the same time shoot the enemy—rather than a fort. Forts were designed to host the military companies in a permanent way. Trincheras, on the other hand, were initially made from perishable materials such as wood and later changed to masonry. It is probable that they had patrol cycles and that when a watchman gave his warning, the guards from nearby villages moved toward the coast and took their positions in the trincheras (Barrera Rubio and Leyva 1993, 45). Up until now, there has been little documentation of trincheras in the area (except for less-elaborate trinchera forms used during the nineteenth century; see Kaeding 2013, 212; Cain 2019, 100–161).

This chapter argues that piracy and smuggling affected movement throughout the frontier and created a need for defense that went beyond the construction of permanent fort-based residencies. The trinchera at Tela'—possibly erected because of pirates' attacks and used later as a kind of control post—integrates Tihosuco with larger Caribbean histories, economies, and networks of imperially unauthorized exchange. Using primary and secondary sources in conjunction with archeological data, we aim to answer: What events made it necessary to establish a trinchera in this region? What kind of piracy affected the Yucatán peninsula's eastern coast during this century, and what kind of connection did the trinchera have to unauthorized trade networks?

Establishing a Network from Tihosuco to the Coast

The existence of a road that connected Tihosuco to the coast indicates that this space, apparently empty, was transited. Despite a common narrative that describes the eastern peninsula as uninhabited, the jungle and the coast were occupied during the Colonial period by Maya fugitives fleeing forced removal and congregation operations (Bracamonte y Sosa 2004, 56; Cain 2019, 58–71). Also, during the seventeenth and eighteenth centuries, pirates and smugglers settled near places such as Cabo Catoche, Isla Mujeres, Cozumel, Bahía de la Ascensión, Bahía del Espiritu, Zacatán, and the Walix River in the Mayan province of Dzuluinicob, now Belize (Victoria Ojeda 1993, 211; 2003, 100; Andrews and Jones 2001, 26; Buscaglia-Salgado 2011; figure 4.2). These clandestine settlements made it necessary for the colonial administration to establish a defensive system from the coast inland.

In 1588, Friar Antonio de Ciudad Real already mentioned the favorable characteristics that prevailed in the region of the Bahía de la Ascensión as a port and zone for transporting merchandise to the interior. He remarked:

> Twenty-five leagues from Ichmul is Ascensión Bay, in the North Sea, a very good and large port for ships that go to and from Yucatan and Havana, and even for those that come from Spain . . . If it were to be used and frequented, it would be a great refuge for these ships and certainly good enough for the land of Yucatan, because it is no more (as they say) than thirty leagues from the town of Valladolid [and it has a] wiry road which can be walked by mule train, bringing on it the merchandises that are usually brought from Bacalar with great work, risk and danger, for being far away and [because] there are many marshes and lagoons . . . Ships would not be lost, as many of them have already been lost in that place [of Bacalar] and [its] coast because that one is not a frequented port. (Ciudad Real 1993, 2:328–329; our translation)[2]

However, its geographical position also made this bay vulnerable to pirate landing because Havana, the Gulf of Honduras, and the Yucatán peninsula were scenes of geopolitical competition and commercial interests. Rafal Reichert (2012) and Carlos Conover Blancas (2013) have analyzed the importance of the Yucatán peninsula in the economic disputes in the Caribbean. Such studies relate the eastern coast to piracy and smuggling, especially the commerce of *palo de tinte*, or logwood (*Haematoxylum campechianum*), a tree well appreciated in the European textile industry for its properties to dye during the viceroyalty period and part of the nineteenth century (Villegas and Torras 2014, 70).

FIGURE 4.2. *English settlements on the peninsular Caribbean coast during the seventeenth and eighteenth centuries. Adapted from Jones 1989. Map adapted by María Novelo.*

During the Colonial period, it was considered piracy to undertake any action that threatened the economy of the Spanish king, including theft of his wealth in America (Victoria Ojeda 2007, 7–9; Baños Ramírez 2012, 76–77). While on the one hand, Othón Baños Ramírez (2012) uses Immanuel Wallerstein's world-systems theory to analyze how the dyewood extraction transformed pirates' social organization, Jorge Victoria Ojeda (1999), on the other, relies primarily on dendritic model to explain how commodities were introduced through unauthorized channels from the *vigías* (lookouts or watchtowers) to the nearby towns and other centers of distribution. Regardless of the explanation, piracy was a symptom of the global economy. Pirates' presence had a real effect on Spain's policies because refuge zones, production zones, and economic routes created the conditions necessary for the violation of imperial boundaries. Victoria noticed that mercantilism gave rise to the appearance of a pirate class that was integrated into the foreign economy through assault, and, over time, the dividing line between piracy and contraband was blurred (Victoria Ojeda 1994, 134–135). From a global perspective, the political scene and economic models in Europe changed the order in the Caribbean, and vice versa, affecting New Spain's frontiers.

In this chapter, we often use the terms "pirate," "de Ciudad Real bayman,"[3] "woodcutter," or "logwood cutter" interchangeably because this is how they are used in the Spanish historical records. This work aims to analyze the complex relationships behind such words and their impact on the colonial frontier. For example, in the seventeenth century, the attacks on Spanish towns such as Tihosuco forced people to abandon their nearby villages, often predominantly Maya settlements. For example, Bacalar, Cozumel, Ecab, Polé, and Zamá—all founded in the sixteenth century—disappeared as their population relocated inland during the seventeenth century, pulling the frontier back from the coast (Andrews and Jones 2001, 24). Agreements between the European powers in the following century increased English presence in the Caribbean (Orser 2019). Together with the Spanish commercial monopoly, they caused favorable circumstances for pirates to introduce and market merchandise outside the Spanish legal framework.

The remainder of this chapter is divided into three sections. The first describes the structure settled at the outskirts of Tela', a currently uninhabited Maya town located in the present-day ejido of Tihosuco. Our analysis led us to identify it is not a military fort but a trinchera. The second section examines the role of the trinchera within its local context by analyzing the Yucatecan government's actions to counteract pirate attacks, smuggling, and English expansion on the eastern coast. Finally, the last section analyzes the role of the trinchera in terms of a global perspective of piracy and smuggling.

Description of the Trinchera

In 2015 we visited Tela' for the first time. During our exploration we knew about the existence of a structure—called "El Fuerte" by Tihosuco's current residents. We returned a few months later to do a preliminary survey and began to compile the bibliographic and historical work about the site to determine the function of this structure and the role it performed. Since 2013, as part of an archaeological project conducted by the University of Pennsylvania, a regional archaeological survey has been done, including mapping this trinchera (figure 4.3). It was this previous fieldwork that informed us that the structure was there. During our preliminary survey visit, we observed a stone structure settled on a natural elevation that shared a similar form—the dual constructive system, the presence of an internal sidewalk, and the shape of the accesses—with trincheras previously only reported on the northern coast of the Yucatán peninsula in Ixil (Barrera Rubio 1985, 44), Chuburná, and Chelém (Victoria Ojeda 1995, 111). According to Andrews, such defenses "were built at certain locations along the north coast to repel pirate attacks. These are located a short distance inland from the coast, near coastal vigías (lookouts) of the Colonial period" (Andrews 1981, 12). Unlike those northern trincheras located a short kilometer's distance from the north coast, the trinchera at Tela' is located about eighty kilometers inland. And, while the structures on the north coast have an L-shaped base (Barrera and Leyva 1993, 48), This trinchera is an irregular B-Shape base. On the whole, the

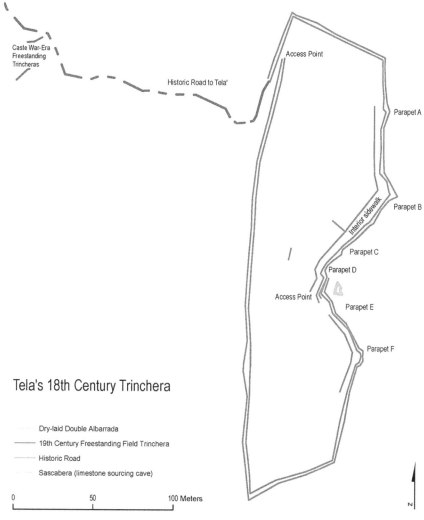

Tela's 18th Century Trinchera

Caste War-Era Freestanding Trincheras

Historic Road to Tela'

Access Point

Parapet A

Parapet B

Interior sidewalk

Parapet C

Parapet D

Access Point

Parapet E

Parapet F

.... Dry-laid Double Albarrada

——— 19th Century Freestanding Field Trinchera

–––– Historic Road

.... Sascabera (limestone sourcing cave)

0   50   100 Meters

N

Map created by Tiffany C. Cain, Secundion Cahum Balam, Elias Chi Poot, and Bartolome Poot Moo as part of the archaeological survey of the Tihosuco Heritage Preservation and Community Development Project

FIGURE 4.3. *Plan map of the eighteenth century trinchera at Tela'. Created by Tiffany C. Fryer, Secundino Cahum Balam, Elias Chi Poot, and Bartolome Poot Moo as part of the archaeological survey of the Tihosuco Heritage Preservation and Community Development Program.*

structure measures approximately 280 meters long, and 87 meters, 48 meters, and 70 meters at its widest points (bearing in mind that these measurements correspond with its "B"-shape), delimiting an interior space with no known surface constructions or artifact assemblages.

The trinchera at Tela' uses a dual construction technique. First, most of the structure is composed of a dry-laid perimeter wall, made of amorphous stones of medium to large sizes. Where this technique is used, the walls stand approximately one meter in height, and 80 centimeters to one meter wide (due to significant collapse and deterioration). We observed that this dry-laid wall opened into two separate walls running parallel to one another on both the eastern and western sides of the structure, creating open spaces that could have been security access points. One access point was located on the west side, facing Tela', and the other on the eastside, leading toward the pathway to Bahía de la Ascensión. Second, there are some masonry walls made from small and medium amorphous stones joined with lime mortar and embedded within the wall that we recognized as the structure's parapets. We documented a total of seven parapets all located along the eastern wall (table 4.1). Six of the parapets we examined have bracket-shaped bases and one an inverted L-shaped base. Most of the parapets still have stucco cover on their inner sides. The wall thickness is not the same for each parapet, varying between twenty and sixty centimeters. The measures of the walls' outer sides suggest that some parapets almost reached a height of 1.80 meters, a good approximation of the overall height of the entire structure at the time of its construction. Due to the uneven ground, though, the walls of the inner sides are sometimes low enough for a person to look over the upper edges. Parapet F is the best preserved and most elaborated (figure 4.4). It had an inscription engraved on its superior section probably when the stucco still was fresh. Although the inscription is a little blurred by mold, the words "'Tela'" and "Año de 178[?]"[4] are still readable. Some of the parapets have round holes of 35 centimeters in diameter in the lower part whose function was probably to serve as embrasures. The diameter was wide enough to allow the placement of artillery or a gunman lying on the ground. Not all the parapets had loopholes, but it is possible that at least two of the other parapets, flanking the access point toward the Bahía de la Ascensión, had rectangular loopholes. Unfortunately, deterioration makes this assertion difficult to confirm. On the interior of the eastern wall, there is a line of irregularly shaped stones that form the sidewalk, linking the parapets and the embrasures system by allowing the movement of soldiers from one parapet to another. In some sections, the sidewalk is as much as two meters wide, enough to hold the artillery. It is also a possibility that the perimeter wall had a palisade on top because it is a bit low.

The current condition of the trinchera is damaged. Most of the walls have collapsed, the parapets are losing their stucco and three of the parapets have lost part of the walls. We hope to conduct additional archaeological studies aimed at understanding the function of the structure better and to potentially arrive at a more precise date.

Our work has been to arrive at a better understanding of Tihosuco's, and by extension Tela' and its trinchera's, role as part of the eastern colonial frontier. The structure allows us to rethink the historical continuity of the region in ways

TABLE 4.1. Details on the parapets of the trincheras at Tela', listed from north to south.

Parapet	Height of internal wall's face	Height of external wall's face	Embrasure or loophole	Base's shape	Internal stucco covering	Comments
A	130 cm	180 cm	Embrasure's 35 cm diameter	"⌐"-shaped	Not conserved	It is in one of the highest parts of the natural elevation.
B	160 cm	180 cm	Embrasure's 33 cm diameter	Inverted "L"-shaped	Good condition	Its wall has a large crack in the middle section from top to bottom.
C	135 cm	145 cm	Loophole not well preserved	"⌐"-shaped	Not conserved	Part of the wall is collapsed at its middle part, and the conserved section has a large crack.
D	150 cm	160 cm	Loophole not well preserved	"⌐"-Shaped	Not conserved	Part of the wall is collapsed at its middle part. It has a zoomorphic figure engraved on its inner wall.
E	150 cm	165 cm.	Embrasure not well preserved	"⌐"-shaped	Not Conserved	The wall is in bad condition.
F	145 cm	160 cm	Embrasure's 35 cm. diameter	"⌐"-shaped	Good condition	It is the best-preserved and most elaborated wall. It has engraved the words "año de 178[?]"
G	150 cm	165 cm	Embrasure's 35 cm diameter	"⌐"-shaped	Not Conserved	It is like parapet F, but it is not in good condition. It is in one of the highest parts of the natural elevation.

that have sometimes seemed impossible because of the circumstances caused by the Caste War. Despite their abandonment, the structure and Tela' are part of the culture of Tihosuco's current inhabitants as well as a witness of the colonial history of this region.

FIGURE 4.4. *Parapet F. Photo taken by Fabián Alberto Olán de la Cruz.*

The Trinchera at Tela': Defensive Strategies on the Eastern Coast of Eighteenth-Century Yucatán

By the eighteenth century, New Spain was struggling to stop the expansion of foreign nations on its northern and southern frontiers. Piracy had been an issue for the Spanish Monarchy since the early sixteenth century (Victoria Ojeda 1993, 210). However, territorial safety also became an issue because neither Spain, France, nor England had the will to give up the American enterprise. Yucatán's military government required its Spanish inhabitants to help protect the territory, including the duty to take up arms, and donate money and horses for the colony's defense.[5] However, the lack of royal support led Yucatecans to look for cheaper solutions, including vigías (Victoria Ojeda 2015c, 9) and trincheras, as minor fortifications that could protect the territory from enemies and counteract illegal trade (Barrera Rubio 1985, 31).

Because of its location and the intense political and economic activity in the Caribbean, it is possible that the eighteenth-century trinchera at Tela' had a double purpose. First, as a defensive structure, its main objective was to protect the surrounding towns and respond to the warning of the watchmen in the vigía of Bahía de la Ascensión. Due to its distance to the coast, Tihosuco's military guard had enough time to take their positions along the main thruway to Tela'. There is still a lack of knowledge about these kinds of structures, especially in the eastern peninsula. The fort of San Felipe de Bacalar and the battery of the Chac River were the only known military structures on the southeastern coast from the Colonial period (Andrews and Jones 2001, 27) until now.

Documentary evidence suggests, however, that eighteenth-century residents of Tihosuco would have had some knowledge of how the trincheras in the north functioned. In 1712, Pedro de Ancona Frías, father of Tihosuco's assistant priest Francisco de Ancona, "went in company of First Sergeant Don Antonio Casanova, to clean, and raise the trincheras from Mérida to the Port of Chuburná, because of the news received from here about the enemies that threatened the Kingdom [Spain] . . ."[6]

Such a precarious situation also affected the eastern coast. For example, as we mentioned early, the Spanish settlement at Bacalar was abandoned at the half of seventeenth century because attacks by pirates and natives, unhealthy conditions, food shortage, the long distance from the center of colonial power in Mérida, and other reasons. But because of ongoing pirates' attacks, in 1727 Governor Antonio de Figueroa y Silva received the order to establish a guard and start the construction of the fort to restore this village as a defense site (Andrews and Jones 2001, 24; Vásquez Barke 2014, 331).

We consider that despite the role of the Bacalar settlement in the defensive system, Tihosuco remained strategic in protecting the eastern coast because it was a middle point between the Caribbean Sea and Mérida.[7] In 1712, before the repopulation of Bacalar, the military company of Tihosuco was founded under the rule of Lieutenant José Coello Gaytán, subordinate to the captain of Valladolid Juan Muñoz. According to Michel Antochiw, in this year the company had 69 Spanish men, 34 firearms, 20 men with pikes, 11 who were sick, and 4 who were absent (2006, 64–65). By 1721, Tihosuco had a captain of war who lived either in the town Tihosuco itself, Ichmul, or Peto (Gerhard 1991, 63).

According to Victoria Ojeda (1994, 140), piracy made it necessary to integrate people from different castes, such as Pardo (Afro-Maya descendants)[8] and natives who were sent to the guards and had to be ready for war. After the military reforms in 1778, whites and Pardos were divided into different companies (Bock 2013, 12). Restall points out that Beneficios Altos (the province within which Tihosuco was situated) had a "urban militia battalion" in 1774, which included around eighty-five whites and Pardo men (2009, 164).

The defensive strategy also required a reconnaissance of the peninsula's territory, especially of the paths that connected to Mérida. In 1733, the cartographer Joseph de Guelle documented the pathway from Tihosuco to Bahía de la Ascensión, which included various locations such as Tela' and water reservoirs called *aguadas* (Antochiw 2004, 25; figure 4.5). Considering that trincheras

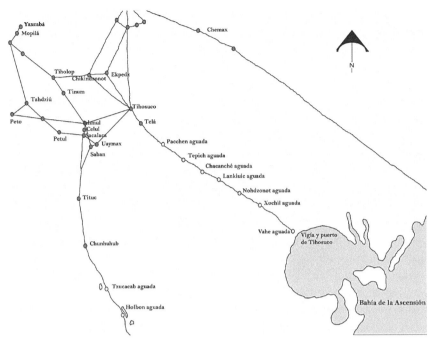

FIGURE 4.5. *Segment adapted from de Guelle's map (1733), showing the pathway between Tihosuco and the Bahía de la Ascensión. Map adapted by María Novelo.*

were military structures to protect the territory from enemies arriving along the coast, counteracting attacks and illegal trade (Barrera Rubio 1985, 45), they were also a symbol of territorial possession.

Second, the trinchera at Tela' might have also operated as a customs or checkpoint for commercial purposes, mainly because its pathway connected the coast with notable inland towns such as Tihosuco and Valladolid. Not only pirates and smugglers utilized this pathway, but also local merchants, muleteers, and Spanish, Maya, Mestizos, and Pardos must have traveled to and from the coast.

Yucatán's Eastern Coast in Global Perspective: Piracy and Smuggling as an Effect of Global Decisions

We understand the Bahía de la Ascensión as a dynamic region of military encounters and trade—both authorized and illicit. The introduction and commercialization of illegal merchandise required the participation of subjects of different social status inside the colonies. In 1784, Bishop Luis Piña y Mazo denounced that "motivated the trade that some of them [men of Tihosuco] have in the Port of Ascensión where they are up to six and eight months, according to the licenses that the captain or their lieutenants grant them, and when I took possession of my parish I found out that there were subjects of more than a year or two who lived in it."[9] Although they tried, Spanish colonial administrators struggled to dictate the terms of trade and travel throughout this southeastern province. For example, in the last decade of the eighteenth century, illicit commerce controlled by Spanish subjects themselves implicated people from Tela'. Don Pedro Gutiérrez, then captain of the urban militia of Beneficios Altos and judge of the town of Chikindzonot, made his executor distribute mules to Indigenous people from Tela' through unauthorized channels. It was a profitable business. Gutiérrez traded mules to eleven muleteers from Tela' who then had to pay five pesos every five months until they paid back the total value of forty pesos (Padilla Pérez 2010, 113). The Maya muleteers, who were usually poor and needed to turn a profit from their own business endeavors, had to repay Gutiérrez either with the agreed amount of cash or with comparable goods (Padilla Pérez 2010, 111).

Victoria Ojeda (1999) shows that illegal trade goods came into Yucatán through the vigías. Its official, also called the vigía or watchman, was responsible for warning of possible dangers from the sea and stopping illegal trade. Unauthorized commodities that made it past the vigía were sent to nearby coastal towns because these towns were the first contact of the contraband network inland, and those who bought illegal commodities got better prices on the coast. Then, merchandise was transported along the rural highway to the next settlement and so on. By understanding the trinchera at Tela' as operating within this complex network, we infer it could have served as a custom's checkpoint to regulate people's transit and their merchandise.

Colonial life was a factor that helped smuggling to proliferate in Yucatán because its society was organized in terms of castes and honor, both marking the access to jobs and privileges not just for an individual but also for all members of his family (Zavala et al. 2015, 30–34). Honor was manifested through cultural and social practices that made it necessary to obtain items linked to the ideas of modernity, civilization, and status but that were not always available in the legal market. Many people therefore chose to buy items illegally for less money in places close to the principal ports (Victoria Ojeda 2003, 21–23). Tihosuco was among the places whose elite residents participated in illegal trade in order to obtain items such as oil, olives, alcohol, wine, cookies, clothes, shoes, soap, lingerie, cheese, tobacco, and arms (Victoria 2015b, 189–190). The complexities of Yucatán's eastern frontier context—which included the continental portion of the eastern coast of Yucatán and Honduras—combined with external factors such as international conflicts, the demand for raw material, and disagreements on rights over the Walix River thus provided ideal conditions for smuggling.

The Treaty of Utrecht in 1713 gave England a monopoly over the Transatlantic Slave Trade, causing more presence of its ships in the Caribbean. According to

Reichert (2012, 26) the English assumed a strategic position because they violated and took advantage of the treaty in several Spanish overseas areas, such as Laguna de Términos and the Hondo, Nuevo, and Walix Rivers. As part of its reforms, the Spanish Monarchy created protective measures, such as only allowing trade between Spain and its colonies through authorized ports. Under those regulations, the Spanish Crown expected to control New Spain's wealth, but the monopoly could not stop contraband, as the metropolis was not able to fully supply its subjects' needs.

On the other hand, the governors were able to order the construction of forts, batteries, coastguards, watchtowers, and trincheras to keep people whom they saw as seafaring and landed pirates alike away from Laguna de Términos in the Gulf of Mexico and the Walix River in the Caribbean (Rubio Mañé 1961). Between the seventeenth century and the nineteenth, the government established forts in Campeche, Laguna de Términos, Bacalar, Sisal, and the citadel of Mérida, as well as towers in Lerma and Champotón. It also built vigías on the coast from Campeche to Bacalar, as well as trincheras on the north and west coasts (Victoria Ojeda 1995, 61, 205). For example, historical documentation reported the first English attack of Tihosuco in 1686 by pirates Lorencillo and Grammont (Molina Solís 1910, 2:317), and probably Tela' was assault that time too. It is more likely that the trinchera did not exist before this attack.

In the second quarter of the eighteenth century, Governor Antonio de Figueroa y Silva may also have ordered the establishment of the vigías of Polé (Xcaret), Zamá (Tulum), the Bahía de la Ascensión, and Tihosuco (Andrews and Jones 2001, 26). Also, Governor Figueroa carried out several military operations by sea and land in order to expel these people who he understood as pirates settled in Walix (Antochiw 2004, 35; Rubio 1961, 339–342). In 1716, baymen dedicated to the extraction of logwood were driven out of Laguna de Términos, a vast lagoon located in the Gulf of Campeche (Contreras Sánchez 1987, 54). The baymen relocated, moving through the depopulated southeastern areas of the Yucatán peninsula, where logwood was abundant. Othón Baños Ramírez (2012, 78), who has typologized piracy in Laguna de Términos and Campeche, characterized their activities as "forest piracy." He explains that such an economic endeavor necessitated organized inland labor, a systemized process to assign logwood an exchange value, and a means of making the economic exchange itself.

Maya people were also part of the economic endeavor and geopolitics of the Caribbean basin. In 1716, pirates disembarked in Bahía de la Ascensión and pillaged the village of Tela', taking Indigenous captives with them: women, men, and children (Conover Blancas 2013, 54). There are reports from early periods about the capture of Yucatecan Indigenous people who were then taken to English colonies such as Jamaica and Turtle Island as a labor force. For example, in 1658 governor of Yucatán Don Francisco de Bazán recounted that:

when I came to the government of this province, it was necessary to stop in Santo Domingo . . . I found on the clear of a hill that falls along the edge of the city and the sea a small village of Indios from this province (Yucatan) that the enemy had taken from different places and made prisoners and were taken to Turtle Island so that they would populate it and help the work of the fortification that they intended to create in that port, and when that place was recovered they brought them to Santo Domingo and gave them the site to which I refer . . . I realized that the enemy had taken them on these beaches of Turtle Island humiliating and disturbing them greatly, having left on their own lands their women, children, and small farms, and that since the day they had been prisoners, they neither confessed nor received any of the holy sacraments because the time they were in Turtle Island they were held by heretics where there was no ecclesiastical minister, and since they were in Santo Domingo where the ecclesiastical ministers did not understand the Mayan language that is the vulgar [language] of the Indigenous provinces nor could they confess or [receive the] doctrine . . . thus committing an immensity of sins, heinous incest with their mothers and sisters, who also bore large numbers of Indias. (as quoted in Baudot 1986, 31)[10]

Attacks on coastal towns or and inland began in the sixteenth century and continued throughout the seventeenth and eighteenth centuries (Victoria Ojeda 2007, 41–43), while ideas of Indigenous inferiority and Spanish imperial superiority were constantly reproduced in reports such as the one quoted. Pirates from France, the Netherlands, and England frequently assaulted and abducted people in the Yucatán peninsula—something we know also happened at Tela' (Victoria Ojeda 1993, 212).

Clearly, the Treaty of Utrecht did not stop hostilities. From 1717 to 1740 there were six Spanish military expeditions to Walix (Rubio 1961, 321–350; Reichert 2012, 28–30), as well as at least two attacks against eastern Spanish villages. During the expeditions, Yucatán's troops burned the English establishments near the Walix River. Some of the settlers were captured and others escaped, but baymen always returned, breaking inland, assaulting, and destroying villages. In 1727, English baymen and their Mosquito-Zambo Indigenous allies looted Chunhuhub and Tela' as an offensive measure against Governor Antonio de Figueroa's plans to attack their settlements (Molina Solís 1913, 3:184; Antochiw 2004, 35; Victoria Ojeda 2007, 50). They also likely attacked Polyuc that year (Bretos 1987, 209). In 1733, Governor Figueroa attacked the English settlement on the Walix. He burned their houses, forcing them to leave the region (Rubio 1961, 342–343; Careaga and Higuera 2016, ix). In 1740, Indigenous Mosquito-Zambo from Walix tried to assault Tela' again, but this time eighty of them died in the attack (Conover Blancas 2013, 55–56). Again in 1758, some pirates reached Tihosuco, but their attack failed: they were trapped and later hanged in Mérida (Carrillo y Ancona 1879, 8).

In an effort to stop a possible expansion of England, in 1763, at the end of the Seven Years' War (1756–1763), Spain gave English baymen in Walix recognized legal status (Shuman 1969, 153), but the conflict for the territory continued. The 1783 Treaty of Versailles defined in more detail the concessions for logwood cutting and the confined area designated between the Hondo and Walix Rivers. However, this area was already fully exploited, leading cutters to break the negotiated limits. Three years later, the Convention of London permitted the extraction of logwood as far south as the Sibun River, and the area between the Walix and Sibun Rivers became the new limit (Shuman 1969, 325). The convention preserved Spanish sovereignty and allowed Spanish commissioners to enter the English settlement twice a year to examine it. It also stipulated that all British settlers in the Mosquito Shore and Roatan should abandon the area (Reichert 2012, 14), which caused new migration to the Walix.

At the end of the eighteenth century, conflicts between Spain and England remained, and an alertness to this fact prevails in the archives.[11] Claims over the territory were negotiated with subsequent agreements, but news about war or peace arrived late to the colonies and as a result the Yucatecan governor sometimes ordered attacks on Walix during periods of peace. In the conflict, Tihosuco played an in-between role that made it an ideal hub on the contraband route. First, its geographical location placed it as a midpoint between the English colonies in the Caribbean and significant inland Spanish settlements such as Valladolid, and baymen were legally allowed to roam its Parish coast. Second, its location near the Caribbean Sea at the margin of the "depopulated" zone but into old Indigenous commercial regions made possible the movement of people out of Spanish administrative control.

Arturo López Ornat (1983, 40–42) talks about the existence of an artificial aquatic channel in the depopulated area that dates from the pre-Spanish era and may have been used in colonial times. It may be the same as that described by Juan Darraygoza, encomendero de Zamá, in his 1579 account in which he reports that "southeast there is a port named the Bahía de la Ascensión; there is 14 leagues, and there is a river that goes inland more than two, it is proper to the navigations of many vessels, its bottom is pristine" (de la Garza 1983, 149; our translation).[12] The 28.5-kilometer-long aquatic channel begins to the southeast of the current village of Chancah, Veracruz, crosses the swamp, and empties into a river that then converges into the Bahía de la Ascensión (see figure 4.1). Possibly in peace times, this aquatic channel provided access to smuggling networks (Victoria Ojeda 1988, 23), while also providing English baymen and Zambo-Mosquitos an access point from which to raid the interior towns.

From a global perspective, Tihosuco found itself inserted into a region economically and geopolitically disputed by multiple powers, often making it vulnerable to piracy. It appears likely that the Tihosuco Parish was vulnerable from both the land-based throughway leading to the Bahía de Ascensión and via the artificial aquatic channel that López Ornat (1983) reports.

Conclusion

This chapter reconsiders the characterization of southeastern Yucatán as "empty" during the Colonial period. We had two primary aims: first, to show the region's intimate connection to international political changes, economic networks, and localized protective measures against illicit trade that triggered the establishment of defensive systems, including forts, batteries, vigías, and trincheras; second, to introduce an important military structure, the inland trinchera located on the rural highway to the Bahía de la Ascensión just outside of the Maya town of Tela', a former subject town of the parish seat, or cabecera, at Tihosuco. We approached the analysis of the trinchera from both a global and a local view that led us to consider its two possible functions: as a defensive structure and a mercantile custom's checkpoint. We propose that it likely served as both, since defensive concerns on this side of the peninsula were so heavily linked to illicit trade and piracy.

We argued that the trinchera at Tela' was erected during the eighteenth century (as opposed to during the Caste War, for instance) after earlier pirates' attacks. The date engraved in parapet F, discussed in the section "Description of the Trinchera," probably corresponds to a remodeling of the Yucatecan defensive system during the 1780s. We believe that the protection of the parish of Tihosuco, the greater province of Beneficios Altos, and the peninsula's central colonial towns such as Valladolid would have depended heavily on the strategic placement of trincheras like the one at Tela' and other defensive technologies along the coast.

We also aimed to fill the gaps about the history of this region before the Caste War, which—even as other chapters in this volume show—has dominated its historical narrative. This chapter sought to rethink the image of Tihosuco as a colonial settlement of minor importance by looking at its insertion into the structure of a global economy. We understand eighteenth-century colonial Tihosuco as a go-between town instead of an isolated place on the Spanish imperial margin. The geographical location of Tihosuco and Tela' made them vulnerable to constant external attacks, but at the same time, their location was beneficial for smuggling's development.

Finally, the trinchera shows us a segment of the materialization of power structures by the Spanish Empire in its struggle for control of a disputed territory during the eighteenth century. Power structures triggered complex dynamics on the different social groups that suffered the violent manifestations of imperial politics such as war, migration, and movement control, as well as exploitation of raw material and people. The trinchera allows us to rethink how Tihosuco's inhabitants developed strategies of resistance and the ways these structures of power remain today.

Acknowledgments. We thank all the professors, colleagues, and friends, especially Dr. José Buscaglia-Salgado and Dr. Victor Hugo Medina Suárez, who shared their knowledge about the Caribbean and colonial Yucatán, and Don Secundino Cahum Balam, for leading us to Tela'. We especially want to recognize the efforts of Tiffany C. Fryer and Kasey Diserens Morgan to guide the construction of this tome; thanks for inviting us to participate with a chapter in this volume.

Notes

1. The name given to the supreme Maya political ruler (Izquierdo 1993, 19).

2. "Veinticinco leguas de Ichmul cae la Bahía de ascensión, en el mar del norte, puerto muy bueno y grande para los navíos que van y vienen de Honduras a Yucatán y a la Habana, y aun para los que vienen de España, y dicen que si se comenzase a usar y frecuentar, sería gran refugio para estos navíos y no pequeño bien para la tierra de Yucatán, porque no está (según dicen) de la villa de Valladolid más de treinta leguas de camino enjuto, que se puede andar en arrias, y traer por él las mercaderías que se traen por bacalar con grande trabajo, riesgo y peligro, por estar lejos y haber muchas ciénagas y lagunas, y no se perderían navíos, como se han perdido ya muchos en aquel paraje y costa por no estar frecuentado aquel puerto."

3. According to Shuman (1969, 10), the first logwood cutters settled on the current Belize's coast called themselves baymen.

4. "Tela'" and "Year of 178[?]" (our translation).

5. In 1795, the Spanish king required Yucatán's priests, their lieutenant captaincy, and all white inhabitants to donate mainly horses and gold as part of their duty as subjects. This order included Tihosuco's white inhabitants (AHAY 1975).

6. "Salió en compañía del Sargento Mayor Don Antonio Casanova, a limpiar, y levantar las Trincheras, que van desde Mérida al Puerto de Chuburná, por la noticia que se recibió de esta aquel Reyno amenazado de los Enemigos en cuya ocasión estuvo por orden del mismo Gobernador toda una noche hasta que amaneció" (our translation; AGI 1752).

7. Bacalar had a swampy pathway that suffered flood during the rainy season, disconnecting the settlement from the outside world. As the priest in charge reported to Bishop Piña y Mazo in 1782, such conditions remained through the century, making it difficult for the detachment settled in Bacalar to protect the interior towns under its jurisdiction (Chunhuhub, Tituc, Polyuc, and Ichmul; AHAY 1784–1785, Chunhuhub).

8. According to Victoria Ojeda (2015a, 31), in colonial Yucatan, "Pardos" were African and Maya descendants, whereas the term "Pardo" may refer to other forms of racial admixture in other regions.

9. "Motivado el comercio que algunos de ellos [hombres de Tihosuco] tienen en el Puerto de la Ascensión en donde se suelen estar hasta seis y ocho meses, según las licencias que los capitanes, o sus tenientes les conceden, y cuando tomé posesión de mi curato me informé que había sujetos de más de un año, o dos que habitaban en él" (AHAY 1784–1785, Luis de Piña y Mazo, 1784, folder 3, box 622).

10. "Cuando vine al gobierno desta provincia fue preciso hazer escala en Santo Domingo . . . hallé en lo eminente de un montecillo que cae frontero de la ciudad y sobre la mar un pueblecito de Indios todos desta provincia (Yucatán) que de diferentes partes había cojido el enemigo y hécholos prisioneros y llevados a la Tortuga para que la poblasen y ayudasen al trabajo de la fortificación que pretendían hazer en aquel puerto, y cuando se recuperó aquel paraje los trajeron a Santo Domingo y los dieron el sitio que refiero . . . me dieron cuenta como los había cojido el enemigo en estas playas y llevado a la Tortuga haziéndoles grandes vejaciones y molestias, habiendo dejado en esta tierra sus mujeres y hijos y su hazenduela y que desde el día que avían sido prisioneros ni se avían confesado ni recibido ninguno de los santos sacramentos porque el tiempo que estuvieron en la Tortuga estovan en poder de herejes y donde no había ministro eclesiástico, y desde que estaban en Santo Domingo como los ministros eclesiásticos no entendían la lengua maya que es la vulgar de los Indios destas provincias ni les podían confesar ni doctrinar . . . cometiendo inmensidad de pecados, atrozísimos incestos con sus madres y hermanas, que también cojieron gran número de Indias" (AGI 1752, as cited by Georges Baudot).

11. See for instance the "Letter to S.M. from the Governor of Yucatán," July 15, 1658, as cited by Georges Baudot.

12. "Al suroeste está un puerto que se dice la Bahía de la Ascensión; hay 14 leguas, y es un río que entra la tierra dentro más de dos leguas y es capaz para muchas naos y de fondo limpio."

References

Adelman, Jeremy, and Stephen Aron. 1999. "From Borderlands to Borders: Empires, Nation-States, and the Peoples in between in North America History." *American Historical Review* 104 (3): 814–841.

Andrews, Anthony. 1981. "Historical Archaeology in Yucatan: A Preliminary Framework." *Historical Archaeology* 15 (1): 1–18.

Andrews, Anthony, and Grant Jones. 2001. "Asentamientos coloniales en la costa de Quintana Roo." *Temas Antropológicos* 23 (1): 20–35.

Antochiw, Michel. 2004. *Alejandro Joseph de Guelle: El Primer cartógrafo de la Península de Yucatán*. Campeche: Instituto de Cultura.

Antochiw Michel. 2006. *Milicia de Yucatán (siglos XVI–XVII): La unión de armas de 1712*. Campeche: CONACULTA-INAH.

Archivo General de Indias (AGI), Sevilla-España. 1752. Indiferente, 237, Méritos: Antonio Francisco de Ancona. January 1.

Archivo General de Indias (AGI), Sevilla-España. 1658. México, 360, carta a S.M. del gobernador de Yucatán, de Mérida de Yucatán. July 15.

Archivo Histórico de la Arquidiócesis de Yucatán (AHAY). 1784–1785. Conkal-Yucatán. Gobierno. Visitas Pastorales. Caja 622. Exp. 3. Santa Visita del Pueblo de Tihosuco hecha por Don Fray Luis de Piña Y Mazo. Yucatán.

Archivo Histórico de la Arquidiócesis de Yucatán. (AHAY). 1795. Conkal-Yucatán. Gobierno. Obispos. Caja 418. Exp. 5. Donativos para la Guerra.

Baños Ramírez, Othón. 2012. "Piratería forestal y economía-mundo: El Caso de la Laguna (1558–1717)." *Relaciones: Estudios de Historia y Sociedad* 33 (132): 75–107.

Barrera Rubio, Alfredo. 1985. "Arquitectura Militar de un Sitio del Yucatán Colonial." *Revista Mexicana de Estudios Antropológicos* 31: 43–47.

Barrera Rubio, Alfredo, and Miguel Leyva. 1993. "Las trincheras: Un sistema colonial de defensa de la Costa Norte de Yucatán." *Cuadernos de Arquitectura Virreinal* 14 (November): 45–56.

Baudot, Georges. 1986. "Dissidences indiennes et complicités libustières dans le Yucatán du XVII siècle." Cahiers du monde hispanique et Luso-Brésilien. *Contre-Cultures: Utopies et Dissidences en Amérique Latine* 46: 21–31.

Bock, Ulrike. 2013. "Entre 'españoles' y 'ciudadanos.' Las milicias de pardos y la transformación de las fronteras culturales en Yucatan, 1790–1821." *Secuencia* 87 (September–December): 9–27.

Bracamonte y Sosa, Pedro. 2004. "El poblamiento de Quintana Roo durante la Colonia." *El vacío imaginario; Geopolítica de la ocupación territorial en el Caribe oriental mexicano*, edited by Gabriel Aarón Macías Zapata, 49–75. Chetumal: CIESAS–Congreso del Estado de Quintana Roo.

Bretos, Miguel. 1987. *Arquitectura y arte sacro en Yucatán*. Mérida: Dante.

Buscaglia-Salgado, José Francisco. 2011. *Infortunios de Alonzo Ramírez (1690), de Carlos Sigüenza y Góngora, edición crítica*. Madrid: Consejo Superior de Investigaciones Científicas.

Cain, Tiffany C. 2019. "Materializing Political Violence: Segregation, War, and Memory in Quintana, Roo, Mexico." PhD diss., Anthropology. Philadelphia: University of Pennsylvania.

Careaga, Lorena, and Antonio Higuera. 2016. *Historia Breve: Quintana Roo*. Mexico City: FCE.

Carrillo y Ancona, Crescencio. 1879. *El origen de Belice*. Mexico City: Imprenta de José Diaz de León.

Conover Blancas, Carlos. 2013. "Llave y custodia de esta provincia: El Presidio de San Felipe de Bacalar ante los asentamientos británicos de la Península de Yucatan (1779–1798)." MA thesis, Universidad Autónoma Nacional de México, Mexico City.

Ciudad Real, Antonio de. 1993. *Tratado curioso y docto de las grandezas de la Nueva España*. Vol2. 1 and 2. Edited by Josefina García Quintana y Víctor M. Castillo Farreras. Mexico City: Universidad Nacional Autónoma de México.

Contreras Sánchez, Alicia. 1987. "El palo de tinte: Motivo de un conflicto entre dos naciones, 1670–1802." *Historia Mexicana* 37 (1): 49–74.

de Guelle, Alejandro Joseph. 1733. "Plano de la Provincia de Yucathan, su capital la Ciud. De Merida con las Villas de Valladolid, Campeche y Vacalar, con los demás pueblos sujetos a su Capitanía General y su Obispado: Tavasco, Laguna de Términos y Petén Itzá." Mapoteca ProHispen. Mérida-Yucatán. Copy made by Michel Antochiw Kolpa from the original in Centro Geográfico del Ejército (CGE), Madrid-España.

de la Garza, Mercedes, ed. 1983. *Relaciones histórico-geográficas de la gobernación de Yucatán: Mérida, Valladolid y Tabasco.* Vol. 2. Mexico City: Universidad Autónoma Nacional de México.

Gerhard, Peter. 1991. *La frontera sureste de la Nueva España.* Mexico City: Universidad Autónoma Nacional de México.

Izquierdo, Ana Luisa. 1993. "El poder y su ejercicio entre los mayas." *Revista de la Universidad de México* 515 (December): 18–22.

Kaeding, Adam R. 2013. "Negotiated Survival: An Archaeological and Documentary Investigation of Colonialism in Beneficios Altos, Yucatan, Mexico." PhD diss., Boston University.

Little, Barbara J. 2016. *Historical Archeology: Why the Past Matters.* London: Routledge.

López Ornat, Arturo. 1983. "Nota que reporta la existencia de un canal artificial en la provincia prehispánica de Vaimil, Bahía de la Ascensión, Quintana Roo." *Boletín de la E.C.A.U.A.D.Y.* 10 (60): 39–43.

Molina Solís, Juan Francisco. 1910. *Historia de Yucatán durante la dominación española.* Vol. 2. Mérida: Imprenta de la Lotería del Estado.

Molina Solís, Juan Francisco. 1913. *Historia de Yucatán durante la dominación española.* Vol. 3. Mérida: Imprenta de la Lotería del Estado.

Orser, Charles, Jr., ed. 2019. *Archaeologies of the British in Latin America.* New York: Springer.

Padilla Pérez, Elvis de Jesús. 2010. "Ámbitos de justicia en Yucatán: La práctica de los procedimientos judiciales de finales del siglo XVIII y las primeras décadas del Siglo XIX." MA thesis, Centro de Investigaciones y Estudios Superiores en Antropología Social, Mexico City.

Pohlenz Cordova, Juan. 2005. "Formación histórica de la frontera México-Guatemala." *En Las fronteras del Istmo: Fronteras y sociedades entre el sur de México y América Central,* edited by Philippe Bovin, 75–81. Mexico City: Centro de Estudios Mexicanos y Centroamericanos. https://doi.org/10.4000/books.cemca.670.

Reichert, Rafal. 2012. "Navegación, comercio y guerra: Rivalidad por el dominio colonial en la Región del Golfo de Honduras, 1713–1763." *Peninsula* 7 (1): 13–37.

Restall, Matthew. 2009. *The Black Middle: Africans, Mayas, and Spaniards in Colonial Yucatan.* Stanford, CA: University Press Stanford.

Roys, Ralph L. 1957. *The Political Geography of the Yucatan Maya*. Washington, DC: Carnegie Institution of Washington.

Rubio Mañé, Ignacio. 1961. *Introducción al estudio de los virreyes de Nueva España, 1535–1746*. Vol. 3. *Expansión y defensa II*. Mexico City: Universidad Nacional Autónoma de México.

Shuman, William. 1969. "The British Superintendency of the Mosquito Shore 1749–1787." PhD diss., University College, London.

Vásquez Barke, Gabriela. 2014. "El Bacalar colonial, una villa española en los confines de Yucatán." *Revista Brasileira do Caribe* 14 (28): 325–348.

Victoria Ojeda, Jorge. 1988 "Arquitectura religiosa en Tihosuco, Quintana Roo: Notas y comentarios sobre este importante conjunto colonial" *Boletín de la E.C.A.U.A.D.Y.* 16 (93): 9–27.

Victoria Ojeda, Jorge. 1993. "La piratería y su relación con los indígenas de la península de Yucatán: Mito y practica social." *Mesoamérica* 14 (26): 209–216.

Victoria Ojeda, Jorge. 1994. "Piratería y estrategia defensiva en Yucatán durante el siglo XVIII." *Revista Complutense de Historia de América* 20: 129–144.

Victoria Ojeda, Jorge. 1995. *Mérida de Yucatán de las Indias: Piratería y estrategia defensiva*. Mérida: Departamento de Comunicación Social del H. Ayuntamiento de Mérida.

Victoria Ojeda, Jorge. 1999. *De la defensa a la clandestinidad: El sistema de vigías en Yucatán (1750–1847)*. Tesis de doctorado en historia, Facultad de Filosofía y Letras, UNAM, Mexico City.

Victoria Ojeda, Jorge. 2003. *La Piratería en la América española: Siglos XVI al XIX. Una transición de intereses*. Campeche: Gobierno del Estado de Campeche.

Victoria Ojeda, Jorge. 2007. *Piratería en Yucatán*. Mérida: Área Maya.

Victoria Ojeda, Jorge. 2015a. "Africanos y afrodescendientes en el mundo de los mayas." In *Yucatecos de otros rumbos*, edited by Jorge Victoria Ojeda and José Juan Cervera, 23–46. Mérida: SEDECULTA, CONACULTA.

Victoria Ojeda, Jorge. 2015b. *"Corrupción y contrabando en la Península de Yucatán: De la colonia a la independencia."* Mérida: SEDECULTA, CONACULTA.

Victoria Ojeda, Jorge. 2015c. "El vigía de la costa: Funcionario olvidado de la historia de Yucatán, siglos XVI al XIX." *Iberoamericana* 15 (59): 7–24.

Villegas, Pascale, and Rosa Torras. 2014. "The Extraction and Exportation of Campeche Wood by Foreign Colonists: The Case of B. Anizan and Co." *Secuencia* 90 (September–December): 79–93.

(POST)COLONIAL LIVES

Tiffany C. Fryer and Kasey Diserens Morgan

If the Early and Middle Colonial periods have been engaged sporadically by archaeologists, the Late Colonial and Postcolonial / Early National Periods (roughly 1780–1910) have received even less attention. Rani Alexander's sustained interest in the investigation of the Yaxcabá Parish in north central Yucatán during this period is of notable exception (Alexander 1998, 1999, 2012; Alexander and Kepecs 2013). Throughout the Americas, this era was peppered with rebellions, revolutions, and periods of immense change. Though Yucatán hardly underwent a war of Independence, it joined Mexico in its separation from Spain between 1821 and 1823. This moment ushered in a tumultuous geopolitical moment whereby Yucatán flip-flopped between federalist and centralist administrations, waged small-scale political uprisings, and intensified many aspects of its unequal society rather than ridding itself of them following the juridical end to colonial rule. Just twenty-five years into its era of Independence, the worst of these uprisings broke out: the Caste War of Yucatán (1847–1901). British Honduras (today, Belize) exploited this tumult, feeding and arming the predominantly Yucatec Maya insurrectionist forces. Meanwhile, raids by and against Lacandon Maya

https://doi.org/10.5876/9781646422845.p002

communities in the Petén and several uprisings in Chiapas and the highlands of Guatemala transpired (Palka 2005; Alexander et al. 2018). The Caste War had a lasting impact on the peninsula, and its origins and outcomes are still hotly debated by scholars across the humanities and social sciences (see, for instance, Rugeley 1996; Dumond 1997; Alexander 2004; Caplan 2010). The underlying political, social, and economic inequalities that were exposed by this rebellion continue to influence the region today.

The following chapters deal with the aftermath and consequences of this war. Before, during, and after colonization, the struggle to control land and labor in the Maya regions of Yucatán and Central America was a constant investment on the part of the imperial powers of Spain and Britain. This struggle can be seen as a long-term, dynamic process that included circumventing specific structures of power, class, economics, and religion through both peaceful and armed resistance (Alexander 2004, 9). Alexander argues that the changes in the agrarian structure of the Yucatán during the late nineteenth century were not based purely on the Caste War itself, but also on the longer-term process of accommodation, survival, and resistance to the structures imposed on Indigenous people, some of which may remain unresolved (Alexander 2004; see also Farriss 1984; Sullivan 1989; Eiss 2010; Kaeding 2013).

The archaeological study of this time period is essential for understanding the modern transformation of geopolitical relationships across southeastern Mexico and Central America. Migration and new patterns of movement as a result of war-induced upheaval drove people beyond the southern border of Mexico and into Belize and Guatemala, creating refugee communities and semiautonomous Maya communities in previously sparsely populated areas (Harrison-Buck et al. 2018; Bonorden and Houk 2019; Church, Yaeger, and Kray 2019; Meierhoff 2019; Houk, Bonorden, and Kilgore, chapter 7; Meierhoff, chapter 8). The everyday lived experiences of the Caste War, and the violence that it inflicted across the region, can be studied archaeologically through processes of abandonment, fortification, and military campaigning that distressed the region in the late nineteenth century (Fryer; Badillo Sánchez, chapters 5 and 6, respectively in this volume).

Beyond the reaches of the war, the remains of colonial systems generated new forms of labor and debt peonage—especially in the form of export-oriented, capitalist, commercial plantations called haciendas—and therefore new racialized hierarchies of wealth access (Pendergast 1982; Millet Cámara 1984; Andrews, Burgos Villanueva, and Millet Cámara 2002; Meyers and Carlson 2002; Nichols 2003; Meyers 2005, 2017; Meyers, Harvey, and Levithol 2008; Olán de la Cruz 2012; Gust, chapter 9 in this volume). These transformations were often deeply tied to technological advances of the late nineteenth century (1877–1911; Hernández Álvarez 2014, 2019; Mayfield 2015; Alexander 2019; Mayfield, Graham, and

Pendergast 2019; Sampeck 2019a, 2019b), which allowed for increased efficiency in production chains and greater reach to both domestic and international markets.

The boundaries of these studies can be pushed deeper into the contemporary era, aiding us in understanding people's current movements, how they adapt, the labor practices they adopt or are forced into, and new experiences of everyday life that nonetheless maintain connections with the postcolonial past. A historical archaeology that considers the contemporary will forces us to imagine a how the past influences the present and can provide new avenues for research into life in the twentieth and twenty-first centuries. In this region, that might mean a consideration of local labor practices related to the growing tourism industry, or the archaeology of past restoration efforts at historic and archaeological sites—a topic to which we return in part III.

References

Alexander, Rani T. 1998. "Community Organization in the Parroquia de Yaxcabá, Yucatan, Mexico, 1750–1847: Implications for Household Adaptation within a Changing Colonial Economy." *Ancient Mesoamerica* 9 (1): 39–54.

Alexander, Rani T. 1999. "The Emerging World System and Colonial Yucatan: The Archaeology of Core-Periphery Integration, 1780–1847." In *Leadership, Production, and Exchange: World Systems Theory in Practice*, edited by P. Nick Kardulias, 103–124. Lanham, MD: Rowman and Littlefield.

Alexander, Rani T. 2004. *Yaxcabá and the Caste War of Yucatán: An Archaeological Perspective*. Albuquerque: University of New Mexico Press.

Alexander, Rani T. 2012. "Prohibido Tocar Este Cenote: The Archaeological Basis for the 'Titles of Ebtun.'" *International Journal of Historical Archaeology* 16 (1): 1–24.

Alexander, Rani T., ed. 2019. *Technology and Tradition in Mesoamerica after the Spanish Invasion: Archaeological Perspectives*. Albuquerque: University of New Mexico Press.

Alexander, Rani T., and Susan Kepecs, eds. *El Pueblo Maya del siglo XIX: Perspectivas arqueológicas e históricas*. Centro de Estudios Mayas, Cuaderno No. 40. Mexico City: Universidad Nacional Autónoma de México.

Alexander, Rani T., Susan Kepecs, Joel W. Palka, and Judith Francis Zeitlin. 2018. "Archaeologies of Resistance." In *Colonial and Postcolonial Change in Mesoamerica: Archaeology as Historical Anthropology*, edited by Rani T. Alexander and Susan Kepecs, 73–96. Albuquerque: University of New Mexico Press.

Andrews, Anthony P., Rafael Burgos Villanueva, and Luis Millet Cámara. 2002. "The Henequen Ports of Yucatan's Gilded Age." *International Journal of Historical Archaeology* 16 (1): 25–46.

Bonorden, Brooke, and Brett A. Houk. "Kaxil Uinic: Archaeology at a San Pedro Maya Village in Belize." In *Archaeologies of the British in Latin America*, edited by Charles E. Orser Jr., 13–35. New York: Springer.

Caplan, Karen D. 2010. *Indigenous Citizens: Local Liberalism in Early National Oaxaca and Yucatán.* Stanford, CA: Stanford University Press.

Church, Minette C., Jason Yaeger, and Christine A. Kray. 2019. "Re-centering the Narrative: British Colonial Memory and the San Pedro Maya." In *Archaeologies of the British in Latin America,* edited by Charles E. Orser Jr., 73–97. New York: Springer.

Dumond, Don E. 1997. *The Machete and the Cross: Campesino Rebellion in Yucatán.* Lincoln: University of Nebraska Press.

Eiss, Paul K. 2010. *In the Name of El Pueblo: Place, Community, and the Politics of History in Yucatán.* Durham, NC: Duke University Press.

Farriss, Nancy M. 1984. *Maya Society under Colonial Rule: The Collective Enterprise of Survival.* Princeton, NJ: Princeton University Press.

Harrison-Buck, Eleanor, Brett A. Houk, Adam R. Kaeding, and Brooke Bonorden. 2018. "The Strange Bedfellows of Northern Belize: British Colonialists, Confederate Dreamers, Creole Loggers, and the Caste War Maya of the Late Nineteenth Century." *International Journal of Historical Archaeology* 23 (1): 172–203.

Hernández Álvarez, Héctor. 2014. "Corrales, chozas y solares: Estructura de sitio residencial de la Hacienda San Pedro Cholul, Yucatán." *Temas Antropológicos* 36 (2): 129–152.

Hernández Álvarez, Héctor. 2019. "Technological Change of Henequen Decorticating Machines during Yucatán's Gilded Age." In *Technology and Tradition in Mesoamerica after the Spanish Invasion,* edited by Rani T. Alexander, 125–146. Albuquerque: University of New Mexico Press.

Kaeding, Adam. 2013. "Negotiated Survival: An Archaeological and Documentary Investigation of Colonialism in Beneficios de Altos, Yucatan, Mexico." PhD diss., Boston University.

Mayfield, Tracie D. 2015. "The Nineteenth-Century British Plantation Settlement at Lamanai, Belize (1837–1868)." PhD diss., University of Arizona, Tucson.

Mayfield, Tracie, Elizabeth Graham, and David Pendergast. 2019. "Cane and Consumerism: Nineteenth-Century Sugar Growing at Lamanai, Belize." In *Technology and Tradition in Mesoamerica after the Spanish Invasion,* edited by Rani T. Alexander, 147–166. Albuquerque: University of New Mexico Press.

Meierhoff, James. 2019. "You Don't Have to Live Like a Refugee: Consumer Culture at the Nineteenth-Century Refugee Village at Tikal, Guatemala." In *Archaeologies of the British in Latin America,* edited by Charles E. Orser Jr., 157–178. New York: Springer.

Meyers, Allan D. 2005. "Material Expressions of Social Inequality on a Porfirian Sugar Hacienda in Yucatán, Mexico." *Historical Archaeology* 39 (4): 112–137.

Meyers, Allan D. 2017. "Prerevolutionary Henequen Landscapes of Northwestern Yucatan." In *The Value of Things: Prehistoric to Contemporary Commodities in the Maya Region,* edited by Jennifer P. Mathews and Thomas Guderjan, 124–143. Tucson: University of Arizona Press.

Meyers, Allan D., and David L. Carlson. 2002. "Peonage, Power Relations, and the Built Environment at Hacienda Tabi, Yucatan, Mexico." *International Journal of Historical Archaeology* 6 (4): 225–252.

Meyers, Allan D., Allison S. Harvey, and Sarah A. Levithol. 2008. "Houselot Refuse Disposal and Geochemistry at a Late Nineteenth-Century Hacienda Village in Yucatán, Mexico." *Journal of Field Archaeology* 33 (4): 371–388.

Millet Cámara, Luis. 1984. "Logwood and Archaeology in Campeche." *Journal of Anthropological Research* 40 (2): 324–328.

Nichols, Christopher M. 2003. "Solares in Tekax: The Impact of the Sugar Industry on a Nineteenth-Century Yucatecan Town." *Ethnohistory* 50 (1): 161–189.

Olán de la Cruz, Fabián Alberto. 2012. "Paisaje, espacio y desigualdad social a través del Patrón de Asentamiento de la Hacienda Henequenera San Pedro Cholul, Yucatán." BA thesis, Universidad Autónoma de Yucatán, Mérida.

Palka, Joel. 2005. "Postcolonial Conquest of the Southern Maya Lowlands, Cross-Cultural Interaction, and Lacandon Maya Culture Change." In *The Postclassic to Spanish-Era Transition in Mesoamerica: Archaeological Perspectives*, edited by Susan Kepecs and Rani T. Alexander, 183–201. Albuquerque: University of New Mexico Press.

Pendergast, David M. 1982. "The Nineteenth-Century Sugar Mill at Indian Church, Belize." *Journal of the Society for Industrial Archeology* 8 (1): 57–66.

Reed, Nelson A. (1964) 2001. *The Caste War of Yucatán*. 2nd ed. Stanford, CA: Stanford University Press.

Rugeley, Terry. 1996. *Yucatan's Maya Peasantry and the Origins of the Caste War*. Austin: University of Texas Press.

Sampeck, Kathryn E. 2019a. "Cacao and Violence: Consequences of Money in Colonial Guatemala." *Historical Archaeology* 53 (3-4): 535–58.

Sampeck, Kathryn E. 2019b. "The Archaeology of Indigo: Changes in Labor and Technology in the Izalcos Region of Western El Salvador." In *Technology and Tradition in Mesoamerica after the Spanish Invasion*, edited by Rani T. Alexander, 167-188. Albuquerque: University of New Mexico Press.

Sullivan, Paul. 1989. *Unfinished Conversations: Mayas and Foreigners between Two Wars*. New York: Knopf.

5

Confronting Violence in the Layered Landscapes of East-Central Quintana Roo

Tiffany C. Fryer

A substantial body of ethnohistorical work focused on the earliest years of contact, colonial domination, and Indigenous resistance exists for New Spain (now, Mexico). Between the 1520s and the 1550s, Spain's colonial project in Yucatán looked more like piecemeal concession than sweeping conquest (Chamberlain 1948; Bracamonte y Sosa 2001; Kaeding 2017). The region changed administrative hands rapidly, passing back and forth between the jurisdictions of the Viceroyalty of New Spain, the Capitancy General of Guatemala, and the Audiencia de los Confines (Honduras). As the eastern areas of what have today been carved into southern Mexico, Honduras, Guatemala, and Belize were brought under colonial control by Spain and Britain, the Yucatán buoyed—an administratively neglected limestone jungle of questionable value—to competing European imperial powers. As such, historians often characterize Yucatán's history of so-called conquest as uneven and contested (Gerhard [1979] 1993; Himmerich y Valencia [1984] 2010). Central to that uneven process of conquest are the several waves of violent reclamation (Jones 1989; Gosner 1992; Patch 2002) and myriad other forms of Indigenous resistance (e.g., Chuchiak 2010;

https://doi.org/10.5876/9781646422845.c005

Matsumoto 2016) that occurred across the Yucatán between the sixteenth century and the eighteenth. The Rebellion of Jacinto Kan Ek,[1] in 1761, is perhaps the most famous of the pre-Independence uprisings, not least because the circumstances surrounding its inception were eccentric and its resultant violence rather spectacular (Bartolomé 1978; Bricker 1981, 70–76, 253–255; Patch 1998, 2014; Bracamonte y Sosa 2004). In an almost serendipitous confluence of events, the Indigenous community of Cisteil joined a man calling himself Jacinto Kan Ek, who they were told was the chosen king, in a rebellion against Spanish colonial authorities. The encounter was brief and the consequences swift. Kan Ek was sentenced to be torn apart by pincers until he died, then to have the remainder of his body burned and ashes thrown. His comrades were sentenced to similarly brutal punishments, including hanging, dismemberment, public lashing, exile, and forced labor (Patch 1998, 78–81).

In this chapter however, I will focus on a less swift yet equally violent instance of anticolonial uprising just two decades following Mexican and Yucatecan Independence from Spain. I present the results of a regional survey, conducted alongside longtime collaborators from a predominately Maya town called Tihosuco. Tihosuco is located in what was the easternmost extent of Spanish inland rule in the peninsular provinces of New Spain and the postcolony of Yucatán—what is today the State of Quintana Roo, Mexico. Our work began as a survey of historic sites, likely constructed between the seventeenth century and the nineteenth, which were abandoned or destroyed because of the uprising often glossed as the "Caste War" of Yucatán (*guerra de castas*, commonly dated to between 1847 and 1901). Our investigations revealed a landscape far more dynamic than historic maps and even the secondary historiography usually present. Although I will offer a glimpse of the many places that made up the late colonial to early Republican landscape of the Tihosuco Parish, the focus of this chapter will be to highlight the ways in which studies of war and everyday life—two areas that Maya archaeology has made significant contributions to—might be brought together to address the experience of prolonged collective violence such as that characterized by the Caste War. Our archaeological investigations allow us to interrogate the organization and structuration of social life in this often-overlooked frontier region. But they also allow us to begin to think through the contexts of violence, apprehension, and oppression that would have qualified social interactions during the transition from Spanish subjecthood to Mexican citizenship on the peninsula.

I will make the case for the value of exploring the period associated with the Caste War and its aftermath archaeologically. I argue this not from a place that privileges the usefulness of archaeological research to the verification or dismissal of historical narratives, but from a recognition that large-scale and prolonged forms of political violence invariably alter human geographies and material culture. Social, cultural, and physical landscapes become draped with the excesses of violence, amplifying, reforming, and erasing human connections across time and space. Drawing on material evidence of localized fortification practice and abandonment conditions, I begin to think through how both actualized violence and the fear of it impacted social life. I move through a brief history of the Caste War and the Tihosuco Parish before arriving at an analysis of two common artifacts of the landscape that we have documented through our collaboration with present-day Tihosuco's *ejido* (communal land organization): limestone rock walls and grinding stones. I close with a consideration of what a materialist approach to the study of the war might offer while advocating for an even wider-reaching reformulation of traditional archaeological approaches to the study of both settler colonialism and political violence.

The Caste War of Yucatán and the Materialities of Political Violence

On July 26, 1847, Maya *batab* (representative leader), Manuel Antonio Ay Tec, was publicly executed by firing squad in the town square of the colonial Yucatecan Creole center, Valladolid. He was charged, tried, sentenced, and executed in fewer than four days on a count of conspiracy to rebel. Following his execution, officials displayed his body in his hometown of Chichimilá as a signal to the community of the repercussions for would-be revolters (Baquiero Preve [1878] 1990, 371–372; Bricker 1981, 95–97). The violent spectacle did nothing to cow Ay's co-conspirators: just four days following Ay's execution, Maya batab Cecilio Chi burned Tepich, his hometown of just under 2,000 inhabitants, to the ground. Within days, the parish seat, Tihosuco, had also been seized by its batab, Jacinto Pat. This multisited rebellion would transform into a full-scale insurrection, then paramilitary action, and finally a long-sustained guerrilla war in which the fluid borders between republican administration and insurrectionist reach would be maintained through targeted raiding on both sides (Reed [1964] 2001; Angel 1993; Rugeley 1996; Dumond 1997; Rugeley 2009). Lasting fifty-four years by conventional periodization, the Caste War is arguably the most successful Indigenous insurrection to have been mounted in the Americas (Bricker 1981, 87).

Even as the war unfolded, deeply racialized propaganda resulted in oversimplified readings of the rebellion as a primitive "race war" whereby so-called Indios were set on annihilating the white race. Early histories of the war propagate this discourse, and it has admittedly been relied on uncritically by scholars of Yucatecan and Maya history as well as popular media outlets (see, Baquiero Preve [1878] 1990; Reed [1964] 2001). The romanticism that results from the overrepresentation of war's spectacularity understandably makes some archaeologists turn their gaze toward what may seem like more deeply entrenched, complex, and long-term processes such as settlement strategy or the onset of global capitalism. Yet collective and sustained violence constitutes one of the most fundamental processes of human social life. Indeed, Rani Alexander's (2004) *Yaxcabá and the Caste War of Yucatán: An Archaeological Perspective* was a vital contribution to the legitimation of historical archaeology in the Yucatán that nonetheless positioned the Caste War as a temporal bracket rather than as a central subject of study. Alexander convincingly argued that the origins of the Caste War have been mischaracterized because the agrarian system and cultural ecology of nineteenth-century Yucatán are misunderstood. Hers is an important corrective. Yet, her aversion to the romanticism surrounding Caste War scholarship resulted in the conflict being situated as little more than a proximate context for more important concerns about the persistence of Maya agricultural forms *through* punctuated events like war. I am arguing that that very romanticism may be reason enough to recharacterize the Caste War as part of a prolonged process of social violence warranting archaeological attention.

When does violence become a thing characterizable as war? Punctuated, watershed, or otherwise spectacular moments often inaugurate events called war. These flashpoints (Kazanjian 2003) or tipping points (Robb and Pauketat 2013) can be used to access not only the slower processes obscured by the discursive dominance of political violence but also the experiences of daily life in the midst of said violence. As the late historian María Elena Martínez (2004) showed in her work on racial hierarchy in Spanish America, spectacular acts of violence—such as that suffered by Manuel Antonio Ay Tec and Jacinto Kan Ek before him—were also expected, and thus mundane, aspects of life for many of Mexico's colonial subjects. As Herman Bennett (2009, 30) put it, commonplace acts of spectacular violence eventually led to violence writ large acquiring an ontological status in New Spain and, later, Mexico. In other words, violence permeated daily life. As such, evidence for such violence, punctuated and recursive, ought to be identifiable in the material record.

If we are to understand the experiences of Maya following the onset of Spanish colonialism in the Yucatán and Maya lowlands generally, we might simply consider that around one-tenth of the postconquest experience of Maya in this region was characterized by the event-process of the Caste War itself.[2] And, a far greater portion of that experience could be described as characterized by the oscillation between and coevalness of structural and expressive violence in this settler colonial space. The Caste War ultimately culminated in the massive loss of life and rapid outflux of people that would leave the region in the very state of being *despoblado* (depopulated) that the colonial administration had so often attributed to it in order to justify the continued expropriation of lands and labor from Maya peoples. The point is, if we are going to spend time thinking about life during this period using data from archaeological contexts and archival resources, maybe we should be paying more explicit attention to the lived experience of political violence.

The history of San Agustín de Tihosuco, the town and parish around which our studies center, aptly illustrates the kinds of political violence in operation across the peninsula following Spanish invasion. Tihosuco began as an encomienda (a land and labor tribute grant made to Spanish conquistadors by the Crown; Clendinnen [1987] 2003, 38–40) in the Spanish province of Beneficios Altos. It was positioned along the easternmost limit separating the reach of Spanish authorities from the colonially unsettled jungle buffer between them and the Caribbean Sea. By the late eighteenth century, the town and parish had expanded into a colonial trade outpost where commercial goods, sanctioned and illicit, entering the province from the eastern seaboard were transported and regulated. Despite constant threat of attack by pirates (see García Lara and Olán, chapter 4 in this volume), and although the Bourbon Reforms (especially from the 1760s onward) would alter Spanish colonial administrative structure and tighten control over smuggling and the trade of contraband in the colonies, this frontier town continued to grow and flourish. Tihosuco's known history extends well into the postclassic period (Menchaca Lobato 1998; Martos López 2006), but its emergence as an entrepreneurial Creole outpost at the end of the eighteenth century signals an important shift in both its localized biography and the regional history to which it contributes. As *cabecera de parroquia* (parish seat), Catholic Spain's colonial rule established Tihosuco as an administrative center from which tribute-paying Maya *visitas* (subject-towns) could be controlled and exploited. Parish records from 1784 show that Tihosuco administered at least two haciendas (plantations), known then as xCabil and Tinoh, and three ranches, Acambalam, Yaxche, and xHanan. It also governed two primary subject towns, one to its north, Tepich (where Cecilio Chi made his first attack), and the other to its south, Tela' (Carvajal 1784).

The aftermath of the invasion of Spain by the French in 1808, the short-lived Spanish Constitution of 1812–1814, and Mexican and Yucatecan Independence from Spain in 1821 ushered in a new social and political system for the peninsula (Caplan 2003, 2010). Key characteristics of this new regime included the temporary abolition of the policy of separate republics that regulated Spanish settler incursion into Indigenous territories and communities. Imperial Spain governed its American colonies through a system of colonial administration that recognized "two republics" beneath its purview in New Spain and throughout Spanish America: the *república de españoles* (including peninsular and American-born Spaniards) and the *república de indios* (referring to the Indigenous peoples they were able to subjugate). Subject towns, such as Tepich and Tela', were almost exclusively repúblicas de indios. Reinstatement of repúblicas for taxation purposes following French invasion both escalated unjust taxation practices (Kazanjian 2016) and ushered in Yucatán's first neocolonial phase, intensifying extant unfree labor practices, squeezing land resources through increased capacity to privatize, and precluding the participation of particular social classes in civic society.

Because of the French invasion and War of Independence, many military-aged men from across the peninsula gained combat experience, including many Maya men from the southeastern frontier whom rivaling political factions enlisted in peninsular skirmishes for political power following Independence (Rugeley 1997, 485–486; Caplan 2010). With an increased period of progressivism afoot, Yucatecan Creoles, who had slowly been trickling toward Tihosuco in pursuit of land and free economy, now arrived at the outpost in rapid masses. Their increased presence during the 1830s and 1840s greatly altered the social landscape of the region. Yet, the presence of structural and punctuated violence remained a critical facet of everyday life. For example, Jacinto Pat (who would later emerge as a leader in the Caste War) and his kin, Cecilio Pat, submitted a formal complaint against the local judge, Perfecto Bolio, for abuse of power and extortion in 1838 (AGEY 1838). Although the document is severely damaged, it allows a glimpse of just one instance in which political authority was used to support an unjust system. It wasn't until those legal routes meant to rectify reported injustice proved ineffective beyond acceptance that the Caste War erupted.

Revising Cartographic Knowledges around Materialized Violences

When I began working with Tihosuqueños, the proposed investigations centered on four primary places: the towns of Tihosuco, Tepich, and Tela', and xCulumpich, the former hacienda of insurrectionist leader and patron of Tihosuco, Jacinto Pat. Tela' and Tepich were formerly repúblicas de indios under the administrative authority of Tihosuco. Today, in postwar Quintana Roo, Tepich is a resettled town of around 3,000 residents that formally separated from Tihosuco by its autonomously operating ejido. Tela', on the other hand, became incorporated into Tihosuco's ejido. Although various families from Tihosuco made attempts to permanently resettle Tela' well into the 1980s, the conveniences of life in the reborn cabecera eventually exceeded the appeal of resettling the town: Tihosuco offered a life with access to primary schools, highways, religious and social communities, small corner shops, water, and electricity. Tela' eventually came to occupy a sacred place of sorts for Tihosuqueños. Many still make pilgrimages to Tela's eighteenth-century church to leave dedications to its patron saint, the Archangel Michael, whose images hover over visitors from the still-frescoed altarpiece. Others gather medicinal plants, rare fruits, and small game, or establish their bee colonies to be nourished by the old growth jungle that has sprung up around the once-sizable town.

As a subset of a broader heritage initiative focused on the history of the Caste War, the aims of the archaeological partnership we created with Tihosuco's ejido members focused on identifying and registering the postcolonial sites believed to have been destroyed or "left fallow"[3] due to the violent undertakings of the war. Seven seasons into our investigations, our map has expanded well beyond the

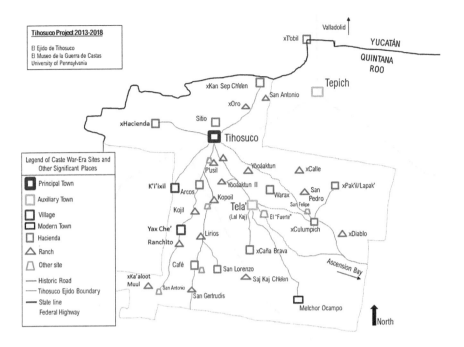

FIGURE 5.1. *Schematic Regional Survey Map, scale omitted for community's privacy. Map drawn by Tiffany C. Fryer.*

four places around which we originally organized our work. Within the ejido, we have located and surveyed 3 towns, 10 haciendas, 16 ranches, 10 full or segmented historic road systems, and 7 other small sites including cenotes, wells, and reappropriated pre-Columbian sites around which significant historic processes have clearly occurred (figure 5.1). Our work complements that of Justine Shaw's (2015) team in the region west of us surrounding Saban, Sacalaca, and Ichmul, as well as the work of Rani Alexander (2004) in the area surrounding Yaxcabá to our north. The survey maps illustrate the proliferating growth of frontier life that occurred between the 1750s and the insurrection in 1847. But the surveys also opened our eyes to the ways in which the Caste War reorganized the landscape and the objects that helped shape it. These changes will be the subject of the remainder of the chapter. I will focus on two key artifacts of the landscape that our work has systematically recovered: *albarradas*—boundary walls made by stacking rough-cut limestone rocks without mortar—and *metates*—the culturally valued, semiportable grinding stones found ubiquitously across Maya households from the Preclassic period well into the twentieth century (Searcy 2011). Both of these artifacts derive from the limestone that dominates the peninsula geologically, and, I argue, can be understood as "core objects" of Maya social life in the region.

Following Ernst Boesch, Alfredo González Ruibal (2014, 36–37) describes core objects as key features of the communal body, those things whose consistent usage is central to the self-identification of a culture. Outside of Tihosuco's historic core, where the smooth walls of its fortified eighteenth-to-nineteenth-century homes replace the albarradas that customarily enclose the Maya *solar* (house plot), albarradas continue to be the most common way of delimiting one family's space from another's—keeping out the uninvited and closing in the claimed. Even after a significant period of depopulation following the Caste War, and the move to resettle Tihosuco in the 1930s, the practice of albarrada building has not ceased in the former frontier hub. Nonetheless, the best example of how albarradas may have been constructed and used during the Colonial and Early Republican periods comes from Tela', where albarradas continue to stand amidst the jungle overgrowth. Metates on the other hand, are increasingly rare. The proliferation of mechanized corn-grinding *molinos* has made the labor-intensive practice of grinding on polished limestone fall out of fashion. Still, these items remain important as heirlooms, often occupying places of honor in the thatched roof kitchens that maintain their position in Tihosuco's architectural practices. While walls and grinding stones make for quite different forms of core objects, they may offer unsuspecting windows into the ways that violence refigures daily life. What happens to core objects during war?

Materializing Punctuated Political Violence

Between 2013 and 2014, our team completed a detailed surface site map of Tela' (figure 5.2). Although its most noteworthy feature is its church, located in the large central plaza near a cenote, Tela's defining feature is its densely interwoven system of albarradas. These walls delimit house compounds and animal/husbandry plots in addition to creating negative spaces that compose roads and plazas. The average house compound contains at least one elliptical house foundation to support a perishable building; one to four garden planters' sometimes a chicken coop or small animal pen; and frequently metates, watering basins, and feeding troughs. There are only six compounds, out of over 600, with standing nonperishable masonry structures—five of which are built in an elliptical style and one of which is cornered (for a detailed description of similar structure forms, see Sweitz 2012). The remaining evidence for structures is limited to those elliptical house platforms that would have supported wood pole and thatch structures that are still visible on the surface in lieu of the heavy jungle debris.

Limestone Barricades: Transforming Albarradas into Trincheras

Dry-laid walls were a defining architectural feature of residential areas throughout the Yucatán peninsula and, in many areas, remain so today. Created from

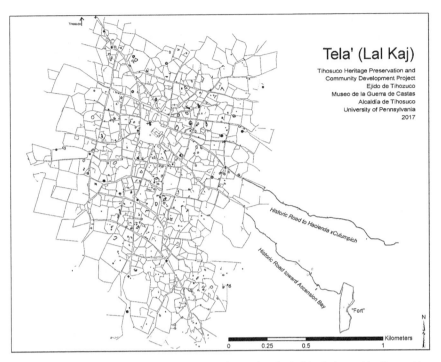

FIGURE 5.2. *Survey map of Tela', also depicting the road to the Bahía de Ascensión (Ascensión Bay) passing through the eighteenth-century trinchera known today as "El Fuerte" (see chapter 4, García Lara and Olán, this volume). Map by Tiffany C. Fryer.*

limestone sourced either from within the delimited house compound itself or from a *sascabera* (sourcing quarry) (Hutson et al. 2007, 464–467; Dahlin et al. 2011, 81–85), these walls are a strong example of core objects. Our survey at Tela' revealed distinct modifications to these core albarradas, though. There are walls that, to the untrained eye, are relatively indistinguishable to the onlooker from the typical albarrada. They are the same general height and width, similarly lack mortar, and are seamlessly integrated into the wall system. With a closer look, however, it becomes clear that these walls are interrupting the negative space, rather than creating it. They run across wide, flowing throughways demarcated by the confluence of compound albarradas, thus functioning to block the roads and disrupt the flow of movement.

War compelled people at Tela' to begin transforming albarradas into *trincheras* (figure 5.3). Contrary to what English speakers might presume, trincheras are not trenches but rather a form of standing field fortification that can be constructed rapidly. Alfredo Barrera Rubio and Miguel Leyba (1993) document a distinct style of trinchera construction north of Mérida that was used between the sixteenth

FIGURE 5.3. *Example of an integrated* trinchera *at Tela'. Notice that this one has been partially deconstructed in the middle to allow for passage—a modification likely made during the mid-twentieth century by Tihosuco's postwar founders. Photo by Tiffany C. Fryer.*

century and the eighteenth to defend against pirates. As García Lara and Olán (chapter 4 in this volume) show, a similar construction is contained within the Tihosuco Ejido on the road leading from Tela' to Ascension Bay. Yet this trinchera, which is partially mortared like those documented by Barrera Rubio and Leyba, is of a far more formal construction style than those that I am highlighting here. The Caste War–era trincheras found scattered across the Tihosuco Ejido measured to between 2 meters and 12 meters long and up to 1.5 meters tall in instances of good preservation. They abut, cross, or reroute roads and in some cases are perched on hills overlooking pathways below them. Across the ejido, our team has mapped 431 trincheras so far. Along the eight-kilometer historic road stretching between Tihosuco and Tela', for instance, we marked forty-five trincheras and an additional ninety-three were marked within Tela' itself. The frequency and magnitude of these trincheras within Tela' make their defensive function clear.

These rapid-construction trincheras are generally classifiable into three typological categories: *bloqueos integrados* (integrated roadblocks), *bloqueos autónomos* (autonomous roadblocks), and *trincheras independientes* (independent breastworks). Integrated roadblocks refer specifically to trincheras found within towns including (but not limited to) Tela'. They abut house-lot boundary walls to create blockades where roads and causeways would have flowed without impediment before their construction. Autonomous roadblocks are trincheras that either cross or abut a road but stand alone because the roads—identified by compacted ruts in the ground that have been caused by many generations of foot, horse, and wagon or cart traffic—are not formed by walls as they are in towns. Finally, the freestanding breastworks are usually strategically elevated or offset from the road to provide views of surrounding compounds and roadways. We found that this form of trinchera most often occurred outside of settlements, but we did occasionally encounter them within both towns and hacienda properties. Within towns such as Tela', trincheras usually take a linear form because they follow the construction logic of the albarradas that are already in place demarcating house lots. Extrasettlement trincheras have a much wider range of forms, including linear, U-shaped, L-shaped, curvilinear, among others. Similarly to Kaeding's (2013, 212–213) observations for the area surrounding Ichmul, however, we found that our preliminary surface clearing and targeted excavations of some of these roadblocks revealed few associated artifacts.

Grinding Stones (Metates), Abandonment, and Gendered Experiences of Violence

In addition to these unique wall features, metates have a high surface occurrence at Tela' (figure 5.4). We might understand metates, like albarradas, as core technologies of daily life. Thick jungle debris at Tela' obscures most of the surface, yet we documented more than sixty-five metates, many near whole, without any surface clearing. Following other studies of violence-induced site abandonment (Schlanger 1991; Inomata et al. 2002), I think there is a likely association between metate presence in the fortified town, the speed of abandonment (often a function of distress), and whether people believed they might ever return. Prior studies suggest that in situations of rapid abandonment, valued items are left behind, whereas in situations of planned abandonment more time is available for removing valued items, making the archaeological assemblages at these locations less plentiful and diverse (Schiffer 1972; Stevenson 1982). In cases of rapid abandonment, multiple whole or broken whole metates are likely to be found within houses or on adjacent patios and in association with other whole objects (Healan 2000). If they are left in habitual-use contexts without packing for safekeeping, rapid abandonment can also be deduced (Simms et al. 2012). The conditions of that abandonment, sudden or anticipated, may be garnered from the subtleties of their in situ positioning.

Thinking about metates with respect to what they can tell us about the conditions under which people left Tela' is enticing because there is little archival documentation speaking to the subject. Metates also remind us that war violence is gendered. Limestone, fashioned as metate, was a core object of Maya communities well into the twentieth century. But metates were culturally valued

FIGURE 5.4. *Example of a three-footed metate found at Tela'. Photo by Tiffany C. Fryer.*

as *women's* core objects, specifically. Metates, like looms (Restall 1997, 126–128), were rural women's technologies of self (González Ruibal 2014)—objects central to making life in their village communities (see, e.g., Hendon's [1997] study at Copán, Honduras). Metates held an esteemed place in the kitchen alongside the centuries-old *k'oben*, or three stone hearth, where women grind corn into meal for making tortillas (Searcy 2011; see also Houk, Bonoren, and Kilgore, chapter 7; Meierhoff, chapter 8). Women's experiences during the Caste War, as with many violent conflicts (see, e.g., Arce 2017) remain insufficiently addressed. Women are ancillary concerns in the historical narrative, mentioned at best when arriving in troves to refugee camps, or at worst when their abuse or rape catalyzes some sort of attack (e.g., Reed [1964] 2001, 66). Attending to these metates allows us a glimpse of both what daily life might have been like prior to the war, and how they figured into women's work and homemaking, but also into the abstract questions of site abandonment and gendered experiences of war. Although we have just begun our systematic study of metates, their potential to elucidate these issues is strong.

Discussion

How did a community-based fortification process impact daily life in the Tihosuco Parish during the early years of the Caste War? What must it have been like to live in a town where you could not walk down the road? Did women and children stay, ready to fight alongside men? The juxtaposition of defense-modified albarradas called trincheras and metates as traces (Joyce 2015) of political violence brings the scalar opposition between overt and structural, punctuated and recursive, violence to the foreground. In some ways, the building of trincheras represents a period of anticipation—a moment when preparation for impending violence was possible. They represent the simultaneous gearing up for and dread of imminent attack. Metates, left behind face-up and unstored, offer a window into other brief moments—flashpoints of a dramatic encounter when the time for preparation had expired. It is difficult to know whether in leaving behind the metates there was hope of return. Yet, it is possible to imagine that life during this period of prolonged violence may have at times acquired a mundaneness, a temporality characterized by waiting through which people, bored with anticipation (Mæland and Brunstad 2009), kept on living until living became impossible.

Archival evidence referencing Tela' is beyond sparse. We do not know the conditions of its abandonment—not when, not under what circumstances. We have recovered articles from early in 1849, originally printed in the *New Orleans Delta*, that recount the advances of Yucatecan and United States volunteer troops against insurrectionary forces between Tihosuco and Tela' (e.g., *Augusta Chronicle* 1849). Based on the accounts of returning wounded US soldiers, these articles claim that Tela' was captured and burned somewhere around the December 28, 1848. Nonetheless, our test excavations returned no evidence of burn lenses or other indicators that the reports might have been true *and* consequential—that is, that this incident led to mass abandonment of the stronghold that had been constructed at Tela'. Neither did we encounter any artifacts that might typically index combat: no artillery shells, no machete fragments, no buttons from soldier's uniforms, no human remains. By February 1852, another article in *El Siglo XIX*, reports that in early February troops under the supervision of Don Manuel Barbachano were advancing south from Tihosuco, spending the night in the "desolate town of Tela" (*El Siglo Diez y Nueve* 1852). Few other reports dealing specifically with the goings-on of the war in the former república de indios were ever made. Did the supposed burning of Tela' force its abandonment? If not, how much longer might it have been occupied? Who stayed? Who fled? When?

Tela' is the first major settlement if one heads south from Tihosuco. We know from 1846 census records—taken less than a year prior to the insurrection—that Tihosuco's population was declining while Tela's was increasing (Quezada 2010, table 12). Did people know the fight was coming? Were there plans in the works to make Tela' a stronghold? Many of these questions may remain unanswered. But, looking at the positioning of core objects, such as metates and albarradas, help us to think through *both* what archaeology can contribute to understanding domestic social life in Maya towns postconquest, and to how communities such as that of Tela' experienced not only living *through* war but attempting to escape it. The motivations for defensive construction are often unavailable through direct materials analysis alone (Winter 1994; Pauketat 2009, 246, 253–254), but made in concert with other interpretative factors, these sorts of landscape and core technology modifications can illuminate people's experiences of violence. For instance, Russell Sheptak, Kira Blaisdell-Sloan, and Rosemary A. Joyce (2012) chose to move beyond describing colonial fortification at a sixteenth-century Honduran town as such, instead questioning the nature of the social subjectivities that fortification engendered. Similarly, I hope to have made space for the serious consideration of the social subjectivity of war as dependent on extant structures of violence in everyday life.

Conclusion: An Archaeology of Violence for the Future

In this chapter, I raised two main issues. First, violence is an important topic of study for archaeologists working in (post)colonial Mexico and Central America. Second, the epistemological divide that has been created between conflict studies and everyday life studies need not be insurmountable. To start, I offered a brief background on the Caste War and colonial violence more generally. Then, in keeping with the notion that any anthropology of political violence "cannot start with violence, or even war itself" (Lubkemann 2008, 30), I offered a snapshot of the historic Tihosuco Parish—the economic hub of our study area at the onset of the Caste War. I then turned to examine two core objects of Maya social life—dry-laid limestone walls called albarradas and grinding stones called metates—in an attempt to organize the analysis of violence as experienced on the Tihosuco Parish during the mid- to late nineteenth century around questions that center nonelites and the lived experiences of violent conflict.

When I consider what a material perspective on a so-called event such as the Caste War might offer, I arrive at its capacity to push us to ask tougher questions about things we often allow to be normalized as representative of certain experiences—for instance, "everyday life"—without recognizing that their mundaneness may in fact offer as rich a record of something deeper. How political violence reshapes lives, and how the act of survival, in itself a material phenomenon, reshapes our understanding of violence become salient. At times I have turned to work emerging from the epistemological shift being called the "new materialisms"—a theoretical movement finding followers across the humanities, social sciences, and material sciences. Some of the leading advocates of the new materialisms in archaeology have argued that we have to begin with the things, the matter, the objects of the archaeological record, taking them as we encounter them, in their own right (Olsen 2010; Witmore 2014). They also argue that to bring our biases and predeterminations to bear on the archaeological record does its own sort of injustice to the potentialities of the past and the life histories of the things that assemble it. That said, acknowledging our intellectual and political agendas may also open important kinds of potentialities in our research. In the case of the work I present in this chapter, our collaboration with members of the Tihosuco Ejido was a key factor in arriving at the questions we came to ask about how violence materializes. Thinking more deeply about past violence and how people persist through times of political upheaval requires recasting the conventional material proxies of violence typically ascribed by archaeology. This is especially true of settler colonial violence, whereby the objective is always to obscure and erase the Indigenous. More than recasting, we must be willing to seek out new categories; we must be willing to ask unasked questions of unsuspecting objects. By illuminating the very ways that people live daily lives, sometimes for entire lifetimes, through war, we might upend its characterization as inherently other than *normal* or *daily*. Such an epistemological shift might more clearly render legible Indigenous experiences of settler colonial violence and the ongoing coloniality of knowledge construction about those experiences.

Acknowledgments. Thank you to my Tihosuco accomplices, especially Bartolome Poot Moo, Secundino Cahum Balam, Elias Chi Poot, Vicente Poot Peña, Sacarías Poot Moo, Lucia Chan Tuz, Tiburcio Caamal Moo, and Marcelina Chan Canche. Also, deepest thanks to Dr. Julio Hoil Gutierrez, without whom my journey into the archives might not have been so fruitful. Finally, to Dr. Richard Leventhal for his sustained commitment to the Tihosuco Project and for thinking and doing archaeological heritage work better.

Notes

1. Also written as Jacinto Canek in some sources.

2. This is not to homogenize the experiences of so-called Maya peoples across time, but to highlight the importance of recognizing continuity and ethnogenesis in the formation of what might today be considered "Maya." Several scholars in history and anthropology have done the work of unsettling the blanket ethnic descriptions normally relied on by scholars, and I certainly recognize that work (Castañeda 2004; Gabbert 2004; Restall 2010).

3. Elsewhere (Cain 2019), I argued that the incompatibility of the concept of "abandonment" with the cultural and discursive practices of Yucatec Maya speakers (and several Indigenous groups throughout the Americas) has caused miscommunications between Maya communities and non-Maya archaeologists at best, and facilitated expropriation and dispossession at worst. What I consistently encountered in my work were two complementary ways of explaining the status of collective versus private land ownership. Under a collective claims framework, land is understood to be in use and thus ascribable to a particular person, family, or subset collective when it has a *representative* who claims responsibility for it. When no one claims such responsibility for care, the land does not default to abandonment. Rather, a notion derived from milpa agriculture, "lying fallow," is used to explain its status as pending or awaiting a future representative caregiver. It is difficult to escape the language of abandonment in archaeological discourse,

but the employment of such terminology has real epistemological consequences and has consistently led to disenfranchisement, discrimination, and the removal of representational power from already-marginalized communities (Colwell-Chanthaphonh and Ferguson 2006).

References

Alexander, Rani T. 2004. *Yaxcabá and the Caste War of Yucatán: An Archaeological Perspective*. Albuquerque: University of New Mexico Press.

Angel, Barbara A. 1993. "The Reconstruction of Rural Society in the Aftermath of the Mayan Rebellion of 1847." *Journal of the Canadian Historical Association* 4 (1): 33–53.

Arce, B. Christine. 2017. *México's Nobodies: The Cultural Legacy of the Soldadera and Afro-Mexican Women*. SUNY series Genders in the Global South. Albany: SUNY Press.

Archivo General del Estado de Yucatán (AGEY). 1838. "Averiguación promovida por los indígenas don Jacinto Pat y Cecilio Pat, vecinos de Tihosuco, contra don Perfecto Bolio, juez del dicho pueblo, por abuso de autoridad." Fondo Justicia. Jugazdo de Primera Estancia de lo Criminal. Serie Penal. Vol. 20, Exp. 2.

Augusta Chronicle. 1849. "From the New Orleans Delta, 25th ult. Important from Yucatan." February 2. Retrieved from Newsbank World Newspaper Archive. Accessed June 25, 2018. www.newsbank.com.

Baquiero Preve, Serapio. (1878) 1990. *Ensayo histórico sobre las revoluciones de Yucatán: El año de 1840 hasta 1864*. Edited by Salvador Rodríguez Losa. 5 vols. Mérida: Universidad Autónoma de Yucatán.

Barrera Rubio, Alfredo, and Miguel Leyba. 1993. "Las trincheras: Un sistema colonial de defensa de la costa norte de Yucatán." *Cuadernos de Arquitectura Virreinal* 14 (November): 44–56.

Bartolomé, Miguel Alberto. 1978. "La Insurrección de Canek: Un movimiento mesiánico en el Yucatán Colonial." Mexico City: Instituto Nacional de Antropología e Historia.

Bennett, Herman L. 2009. *Colonial Blackness: A History of Afro-Mexico*. Blacks in the Diaspora. Bloomington: Indiana University Press.

Bracamonte y Sosa, Pedro. 2001. *La conquista inconclusa de Yucatán: Los mayas de las montañas, 1560–1680*. Mexico City: Centro de Investigaciones y Estudios Superiores en Antropología Social.

Bracamonte y Sosa, Pedro. 2004. *La encarnación de la profecía: Canek en Cisteil*. Mexico City: Centro de Investigaciones y Estudios Superiores en Antropología Social (CIESAS).

Bricker, Victoria Reifler. 1981. *The Indian Christ, the Indian King: The Historical Substrate of Maya Myth and Ritual*. Austin: University of Texas Press.

Cain, Tiffany C. 2019. "Everyday Political Violence: Materiality, War, and Daily Life in Quintana Roo, Mexico (1780–Present)." PhD diss., University of Pennsylvania, Philadelphia.

Caplan, Karen Deborah. 2003. "The Legal Revolution in Town Politics: Oaxaca and Yucatan, 1812–1825." *Hispanic American Historical Review* 83 (2): 255–294.

Caplan, Karen Deborah. 2010. *Indigenous Citizens: Local Liberalism in Early National Oaxaca and Yucatán*. Stanford, CA: Stanford University Press.

Carvajal, Don Antonio. "1784. Santa visita del Pueblo de Tihosuco echa por el ilustrísimo y reverendísimo señor Don Fray Luis de Piña y Mazo." Visitas Pastorales. Caja 622, Exp. 37, Pueblo de Tihosuco, March 22. Archivo Histórico del Arzobispado de Yucatán.

Castañeda, Quetzil E. 2004. " 'We Are Not Indigenous!': An Introduction to the Maya Identity of Yucatan." *Journal of Latin American Anthropology* 9 (1): 36–63.

Chamberlain, Robert S. 1948. *The Conquest and Colonization of Yucatan, 1517–1551*. Washington, DC: Carnegie Institution.

Chuchiak, John F., IV. 2010. "Writing as Resistance: Maya Graphic Pluralism and Indigenous Elite Strategies for Survival in Colonial Yucatan, 1550–1750." *Ethnohistory* 57 (1): 87–116.

Clendinnen, Inga. (1987) 2003. *Ambivalent Conquests: Maya and Spaniard in Yucatan, 1517–1570*. 2nd ed. Cambridge Latin American studies 61. Cambridge, UK: Cambridge University Press.

Colwell-Chanthaphonh, Chip, and Thomas J. Ferguson. 2006. "Rethinking Abandonment in Archaeological Contexts." *SAA Archaeological Record* 6 (1): 37–41.

Dahlin, Bruce, Marjukka Bastamov, Timothy Beach, Zachary X. Hruby, Scott R. Hutson, and Daniel Mazeau. 2011. "Phantom Lithics at Chunchumil, Yucatán, Mexico." In *The Technology of Maya Civilization: Political Economy and Beyond in Lithic Studies*, edited by Zachary X. Hruby, Geoffrey E. Braswell, and Oswaldo Chinchilla Mazariegos, 79–90. London, New York: Routledge.

Dumond, Don E. 1997. *The Machete and the Cross: Campesino Rebellion in Yucatan*. Lincoln: University of Nebraska Press.

El Siglo Diez y Nueve. 1852. "Interior—Yucatan. Sr. Don Manuel Barbachano.—Bacalar, Marzo 23 de 1852." June 17. Newsbank World Newspaper Archive. Accessed June 26, 2018. www.newsbank.com.

Gabbert, Wolfgang. 2004. *Becoming Maya: Ethnicity and Social Inequality in Yucatan since 1500*. Tucson: University of Arizona Press.

Gerhard, Peter. (1979) 1993. *The Southeast Frontier of New Spain*. Rev. ed. Norman: University of Oklahoma Press.

González Ruibal, Alfredo. 2014. *An Archaeology of Resistance: Materiality and Time in an African Borderland*. Lanham, MD: Rowman and Littlefield.

Gosner, Kevin. 1992. *Soldiers of the Virgin: The Moral Economy of a Colonial Maya Rebellion*. Tucson: University of Arizona Press.

Healan, Dan M. 2000. "What a Dump! Rapid Abandonment as Seen from the Perspective of Nonrapid, Impermanent Abandonment at Tula, Hidalgo." *Mayab* 13: 103–107.

Hendon, Julia A. 1997. "Women' Work, Women's Space, and Women's Status among the Classic-Period Maya Elite od the Copán Valley, Honduras." In *Women in Prehistory: North America and Mesoamerica*, edited by Cheryl Claassen and Rosemary A. Joyce, 33–46. Regendering the Past. Philadelphia: University of Pennsylvania Press.

Himmerich y Valencia, Robert. (1984) 2010. *The Encomenderos of New Spain, 1521–1555*. Austin: University of Texas Press.

Hutson, Scott R., Travis W. Stanton, Aline Magnoni, Richard Terry, and Jason Craner. 2007. "Beyond the Buildings: Formation Processes of Ancient Maya Houselots and Methods for the Study of Non-architectural Space." *Journal of Anthropological Archaeology* 26 (3): 442–473.

Inomata, Takeshi, Daniela Triadan, Erick Ponciano, Estela Pinto, Richard E. Terry, and Markus Eberl. 2002. "Domestic and Political Lives of Classic Maya Elites: The Schiffer Excavation of Rapidly Abandoned Structures at Aguateca, Guatemala." *Latin American Antiquity* 13 (03): 305–330.

Jones, Grant D. 1989. *Maya Resistance to Spanish Rule: Time and History on a Colonial Frontier*. Albuquerque: University of New Mexico Press.

Joyce, Rosemary A. 2015. "Transforming Archaeology, Transforming Materiality." *Archeological Papers of the American Anthropological Association* 26 (1): 181–191.

Kaeding, Adam R. 2013. "Negotiated Survival: An Archaeological and Documentary Investigation of Colonialism in Beneficios Altos, Yucatan, Mexico." PhD diss., Boston University.

Kaeding, Adam R. 2017. "Negotiating Colonialism on the Southern Frontier of Spanish Yucatan." In *Frontiers of Colonialism*, edited by Christine D. Beaule, 59–88. Gainesville: University Press of Florida.

Kazanjian, David. 2003. *The Colonizing Trick: National Culture and Imperial Citizenship in Early America*. Minneapolis: University of Minnesota Press.

Lubkemann, Stephen C. 2008. *Culture in Chaos: An Anthropology of the Social Condition in War*. Chicago: University of Chicago Press.

Mæland, Bård, and Paul Otto Brunstad. 2009. *Enduring Military Boredom: From 1750 to the Present*. New York: Palgrave Macmillan.

Martínez, María Elena. 2004. "The Black Blood of New Spain: Limpieza de Sangre, Racial Violence, and Gendered Power in Early Colonial Mexico." *William and Mary Quarterly* 61 (3): 479–520.

Martos López, Luis Alberto. 2006. "Lalcah: Un pueblo olvidado en la selva de Quintana Roo." *Boletín de Monumentos Históricos* 3 (7): 22–20.

Matsumoto, Mallory E. 2016. "Recording Territory, Recording History: Negotiating the Sociopolitical Landscape in Colonial Highland Maya Títulos." *Ethnohistory* 63 (3): 469–495.

Menchaca Lobato, Paula. 1998. "Historia y tenencia de la tierra en Tihosuco." BA thesis, Escuela Nacional de Antropología e Historia, Mexico City.

Olsen, Bjørnar. 2010. *In Defense of Things: Archaeology and the Ontology of Objects*. Lanham, MD: Rowman and Littlefield.

Patch, Robert W. 1998. "Culture, Community, and 'Rebellion' in the Yucatec Maya Uprising of 1761." In *Native Resistance and the Pax Colonial in New Spain*, edited by Susan Schroeder, 67–83. Lincoln: University of Nebraska Press.

Patch, Robert W. 2002. *Maya Revolt and Revolution in the Eighteenth Century*. Armonk, NY: M. E. Sharpe.

Patch, Robert W. 2014. "La Rebelión de Jacinto Canek en Yucatán: Una nueva interpretación." *Desacatos* (13): 46–59.

Pauketat, Timothy R. 2009. "Wars, Rumors of Wars, and the Production of Violence." In *Warfare in Cultural Context: Practice, Agency, and the Archaeology of Violence*, edited by Axel E. Nielsen and William H. Walker, 244–262. Tucson: University of Arizona Press.

Quezada, Sergio, ed. 2010. *Campeche a través de las memorias de los gobernadores: Evolución política y administrativa, 1826–1662*. Campeche: Gobierno del Estado de Campeche.

Reed, Nelson A. (1964) 2001. *The Caste War of Yucatán*. Rev. ed. Stanford, CA: Stanford University Press.

Restall, Matthew. 1997. *The Maya World: Yucatec Culture and Society, 1550–1850*. Stanford, CA: Stanford University Press.

Restall, Matthew. 2010. "The Mysterious and the Invisible: Writing History in and of Colonial Yucatan." *Ancient Mesoamerica* 21 (02): 393–400.

Robb, John, and Timothy R. Pauketat, eds. 2013. *Big Histories, Human Lives: Tackling Problems of Scale in Archaeology*. Santa Fe, NM: School for Advanced Research Press.

Rugeley, Terry. 1996. *Yucatán's Maya Peasantry and the Origins of the Caste War*. Austin: University of Texas Press.

Rugeley, Terry. 1997. "Rural Political Violence and the Origins of the Caste War." *Americas (Washington, 1944)* 53 (04): 469–496.

Rugeley, Terry. 2009. *Rebellion Now and Forever: Mayas, Hispanics, and Caste War Violence in Yucatán, 1800–1880*. Stanford, CA: Stanford University Press.

Schiffer, Michael B. 1972. "Archaeological Context and Systemic Context." *American Antiquity* 37 (2): 156–165.

Schlanger, Sarah H. 1991. "On Manos, Metates, and the History of Site Occupations." *American Antiquity* 56 (3): 460.

Searcy, Michael T. 2011. *The Life-Giving Stone: Ethnoarchaeology of Maya Metates*. Tucson: University of Arizona Press.

Shaw, Justine M., ed. 2015. *The Maya of the Cochuah Region: Archaeological and Ethnographic Perspectives on the Northern Lowlands*. Albuquerque: University of New Mexico Press.

Sheptak, Russell N., Kira Blaisdell-Sloan, and Rosemary A. Joyce. 2012. "In-Between People in Colonial Honduras: Reworking Sexualities at Ticamaya." In *The*

Archaeology of Colonialism: Intimate Encounters and Sexual Effects, edited by Barbara L. Voss and Eleanor C. Casella, 156–172. Cambridge: Cambridge University Press.

Simms, Stephanie R., Evan Parker, George J. Bey, and Tomás Gallareta Negrón. 2012. "Evidence from Escalera al Cielo: Abandonment of a Terminal Classic Puuc Maya Hill Complex in Yucatán, Mexico." *Journal of Field Archaeology* 37 (4): 270–288.

Stevenson, Marc G. 1982. "Toward an Understanding of Site Abandonment Behavior: Evidence from Historic Mining Camps in the Southwest Yukon." *Journal of Anthropological Archaeology* 1 (3): 237–265.

Sweitz, Sam R. 2012. *On the Periphery of the Periphery: Household Archaeology at Hacienda San Juan Bautista Tabi, Yucatan, Mexico.* New York: Springer.

Winter, Susan E. 1994. "Civil War Fortifications and Campgrounds on Maryland Heights, the Citadel of Harpers Ferry." In *Look to the Earth: Historical Archaeology and the American Civil War*, edited by Clarence R. Geier and Susan E. Winter, 101–129. Knoxville: University of Tennessee Press.

Witmore, Christopher. 2014. "Archaeology and the New Materialisms." *Journal of Contemporary Archaeology* 1 (3): 203–246.

6

Traces of Power

An Archaeology of the Porfirian Armed Forces in the Military Campaign against "Rebel" Maya during the Caste War, 1899–1904

Alejandra Badillo Sánchez

The Social War of Yucatán, better known as the "Caste War," began in 1847 and lasted fifty-seven years—the last three of which were dedicated to military campaigns designed to quell any remaining dissention among Maya people perceived as rebels or living in formerly insurrectionist territories. These campaigns did not begin until the last decade of the nineteenth century, when General Porfirio Díaz, then president of Mexico, formulated a plan to regain social control over the Maya movement. Díaz formed his plan beginning in 1895–1896 and, after some mishaps, devised the so-called Campaña Militar de Yucatán contra los mayas rebeldes (Military campaign of Yucatán against the rebel Maya), which began on October 21, 1899 (Bravo 1899). The final objective was to penetrate the central and southern part of the Yucatán peninsula, in order to monitor the displacement of the Maya population and militarily occupy the town of Chan Santa Cruz, founded in 1850. The town was a center of worship and military bastion of the rebellious Maya, self-identified as Maya *cruzo'ob*.

The military actions carried out were violent acts that affected the entire territory and peninsular society. As Terry Rugeley (2018) put it, these actions inform

https://doi.org/10.5876/9781646422845.c006

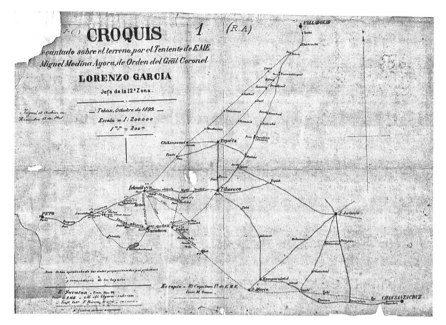

FIGURE 6.1. *Sketch of the "theater of war" at the end of the nineteenth century, created by Lieutenant Miguel Medina Ayora by order of General Lorenzo García, October 1899. Mapoteca Manuel Orozco y Berra-Sagarpa, Alejandra Badillo Sánchez edition.*

an essential part of the social fabric of contemporary Maya society and life. They represent past and ongoing disputes over land and Indigenous rights, bringing to the fore the struggle of an "Indigenous population that is reluctant to comply with the impositions of the Federal Government in matters of territorial domination and exploitation of natural resources" (Ceh Chan 2004; my translation),[1] and in the use of force by the government to achieve that objective.

Acts That Leave a Mark

Following Max Weber ([1921] 1991), I argue that the authorities employed violence to govern; that is, overt violence became an accepted and approved form of governance by the state. During the "Yucatán Military Campaign against the rebellious Maya" violence was used as a political tool to dominate and expand the power of the Mexican government in the rebel zone, a region that for five decades had been under the control of Maya insurrectionists. The type of violence used during the military assault, according to Sarah Ralph (2012), can be considered a "sanctioning violence" because it conditioned the behavior of a group of individuals and transformed the peninsula into a space of war—or better, the "Theater of the War," leaving a clear mark on the landscape (figure 6.1).

Currently, there exist material remnants (moveable and immovable) of the military campaign that lie in the middle of the jungle: vestiges of forts; remains of trenches; foundations of protective walls; water wells protected by walls; traces of railways that connected military stations and ports; or the telegraph lines used by the military to communicate and give notice of the advance of the troops, of the attacks, or of the battles fought. In addition, there are artifacts, such as ammunition, some detonated and others unexploded, and fragments of close combat blades that were used during the final stages of the armed conflict.

These remains are reminders of the government's intentions. This chapter tries to understand the role of violence, in the context of the Military Campaign of Yucatán, by understanding the transformation of the peninsular landscape through military architecture. For this, I rely on various types of information including archaeological evidence—both pertaining to the constructions of the military campaign and to the spaces whose function was modified by the needs of the army—as well as written sources, cartographic documents, and old photographs. The information obtained from fieldwork (through surface reconnaissance and topographic mapping) in some cases compliments and, in others, contrasts data obtained in historical archives. I aim to reconstruct the military advances and elucidate the changes to the landscape produced by the campaign in order to develop a more complete appreciation of the dimensions of this sanctioning violence that socially and politically transformed the peninsular territory.

The Strategy of Control

During the military campaign, the government of Mexico allocated around 2.5 million pesos for the purchase of provisions, war supplies (including the acquisition of warships for the company), and for the payment of "salaries" (i.e., a form of retribution to the military), among other things (Law of Revenues 1901–1904). The Porfirian Federal Army participated in this military enterprise—specifically the 6th, 10th, 13th, 18th, 22nd, and 28th Battalions—alongside members of the National Navy and some battalions of the National Guard of Yucatán: the 1st, 5th, and 7th, to name a few. All of them were supported by an extensive military infrastructure.

In the second decade of the nineteenth century in Mexico, as in other countries of the world, there was a consolidation of the nation-state. This process meant keeping at a distance the groups whose eventual intrusion threatened "the health and integrity of the national body," including (but not limited to) the Indigenous groups whom the nation considered "barbarians" (Traverso 2012, 213). Maya who had taken up arms were considered a "dangerous class," and under the law they were described as "rebels," which made knowing their location and containing them priorities for the government. As an alternative to containment, Yucatecan forces might capture or forcibly move Maya to other geographical areas. The legal connotations of the label "rebel" were important because if, for

FIGURE 6.2. *"Map of the State of Yucatan,"* 1901 *in Memory of War of General Bernardo Reyes 1901–1902. Mapoteca Manuel Orozco y Berra-Sagarpa.*

instance, Maya living in these areas had been called simply "bandits," then the government could not have justified their displacement and other acts of affront.

The state, to put an end to the "rebellious" Maya "problem," proposed that the Porfirian armed forces canvas much of the state of Yucatán following four lines of operation: three fronts by land, which covered the northern part of the peninsula; the central area of the territory; the southern end; and one front by sea that expanded over the entire eastern coast. These are named, respectively, Línea de operación Norte (Northern Line), Línea de operación Central (Central Line), Línea de operación Sur (Southern Line), and Línea de operación del oriente y río Hondo (Eastern Line of Yucatán and the Río Hondo) (figure 6.2). Along each line, the military built a series of fortified architectural works that generated a siege-like atmosphere in the territory.

By analyzing this evidence, I show that the Mexican government relied on a strategy that deployed military architecture as the representation of its power in the peninsular space. That is, it used a system of constructions to limit, fence, contain, and reduce the Maya "rebels." I associate this strategy with the concept of the "panopticon" developed by Jeremy Bentham in 1791 (2000, 33–81)—an architecturally-enabled form of surveillance whose effect on people, though it was proposed for a penitentiary context, closely resembles that of the Yucatecan Military Campaign. The panopticon refers to a physical device of optical architecture, which through the surveillance it facilitates, produces a certain set of behaviors in captives when they know that they are in the authorities' field of vision. This concept was taken up in 1975 by the philosopher Michel Foucault in his work *Discipline and Punish* (Foucault 2009) in which he reflects on the comportment of the individual when they feel like they are being watched. In archaeology there are few studies that take Benthamian concepts to interpret architecture or the landscape. One notable exception is a study by Mark P. Leone (2016), who evaluated the Renaissance Garden of William Paca in Annapolis, Maryland, using landscape archeology.

In my investigation, I use the concept of the panopticon to interpret the military actions that the government of Mexico carried out against the "rebel" Maya (Badillo Sánchez 2019). In this sense, the Military Campaign of Yucatán relied on the formation and distribution of panoptic architectures: military forts, checkpoints, barracks, camps, naval stations, railway stations, ports of embarkation and disembarkation, among others (Badillo Sánchez 2019). All this architecture constituted an "architecture of power" that served as a physical instrument to strengthen the armed forces and generate a system of containment—a surveillance network that covered a wide area with the distribution of its "fortified works." With this system, the Mexican authorities found previously inaccessible places accessible.

This panoptic deployment of armed forces led to a scenario of conscientious and constant visibility, making tangible the power of authority throughout the territory. Those panoptic forces intimidated, limited, and determined the behavior of the people of the villages nearest to military posts and guarded and surveilled those who traveled on the roads and sidewalks. With military reinforcement, the government reestablished control over the population, over the resources, over movement, and over the trade routes by which southern Maya were supplied.

Each of the lines of operation was based on a reduction policy, aimed at causing a demographic decrease of the Indigenous population—a policy whose consequences can be observed in the number of Maya who remained living in each zone (Badillo Sánchez 2019). For example, the so-called Línea del Sur attracted some Indigenous people who were established in small groups on the margin of the Río Hondo. General de la Vega explains that "from the beginning of the advance [we were made] to respect the prisoners and the 'Indians' that remained loitering in some small towns on the banks of the Hondo river, appointing authorities chosen among their indigenous personnel, and even in the first expeditions orders were issued to respect the properties even when the enemy made resistance" (De la Vega 1902, f. 13; my translation).[2] In contrast, the policy that was followed on the Central and Northern Lines was much more aggressive because, continues General De la Vega, "although it was originally intended that we respect the properties and avoid spilling blood as much as possible, we did not persevere in this tactic because retaliation was already the way; to intimidate the rebels we needed to be harsh, bringing extermination to all parts and destruction to the towns and plantings" (De la Vega 1902, f. 13; my translation).[3] The word "extermination" in the military lexicon implies "to desolate, totally eliminate a social group and devastate by means of weapons the places they inhabited" (GTM 1982b, 209). This reduction policy resulted in a rise in migration from the central part of the peninsula, where Maya of Chan Santa Cruz headquartered (Badillo Sánchez 2022), and the north of the peninsula, where there were Maya, like those of Yotzonot, who rejected the authority of the government and who continued attacking the military despite their long established control of the area (Iturralde 1900). Sanctioned acts of extermination advanced as the troops advanced. The persecution that the federal government carried out against eastern Maya was tenacious and rigorous, relying on proclamations "to make the rebels understand the benefits that may result if they submit and promising otherwise the continuation of an *all-out war*" (De la Vega 1902; my translation and emphasis).[4] That is, they threatened a bloodier war in which opponents would not be taken as prisoners but executed if Maya "rebels" did not submit (GTM 1982c, 238). Those who could remain in the territory scattered into the *monte* (forest), among them people who did not consider themselves "rebels" and who were alien to the conflict (under the military's panoptic measures, these people could not meet in groups larger than ten or twelve individuals, because they would be considered suspects and would be punished accordingly). Those Maya who chose to maintain the resistance were known by the Mexican government to organize into groups of forty or fifty, led by their own generals and commanders, making them the main target of the military troop advances. These groups were gradually taken out during the campaign although attacks by Maya forces did not cease—they continued to fight whether from behind trenches, hidden in the forest, or at their own checkpoints—when the end of the war was declared in May 1901. Thus, the Military Campaign of Yucatán was not terminated until June 1904, as ongoing resistance extended the campaign into the first years of the twentieth century (Blanquet n.d.).

Reconstructing the "Theater of War"

Numerous documents in the official historical archives make mention of the posts, forts, and barracks of the time, but they do not specify their locations. Most only indicate actions that were carried out at a named place or offer a glimpse into war architecture: their dimensions or the construction materials the troops used to build them. However, thanks to cartographic evidence, we can begin to locate them on the peninsula. Especially useful is the 1902 map showing the distribution of military establishments, as well as the area they covered (see figure 6.2). With this information, in conjunction with the written testimonies and material remains found in the area, it is possible to compare the historical, archival, and archaeological sources, and reconstruct the extensive punitive panoptic system. After offering some general information about the north, south, and east lines of operation, I will focus on showing the field reconnaissance work that we have done on the central line area, which has made it possible to define the characteristics of its forts.

The panoptic system devised by the military divided the peninsula into zones. In the north, the operation front known as Línea Norte was drawn up under Colonel Ramón Ricoy. This line started from the town of Valladolid and covered the towns of Xcan, Chichimilá, Tekom, Tixcacalcupul, Xpetz and Chiquindzonot, Espita, Tizimín, Chancenote, Chemax, Tepich, Tihosuco and Ichmul (Bravo and De la Vega 1903). In this area several camps and three forts were built: one in Xcan, made of masonry, wood, and stone; another in Mahas; and one more in Carolina. Each of these fortifications was heavily armed, with at least 4 warning bombs, 100 Remingtons (double-barrel shot guns), 100 bayonets, 100 cartridge belts, and 10,000 cartridges (Aguilar 1899). The troops occupied the forts from which they were deployed (Canto Castañeda 1899). From the Fort of Mahas a part of the troops advanced toward the Ichmul camp and later went to Tihosuco (Arce Sosa 1899). The deployment of this operation front managed to cover a radius of fifty to sixty kilometers, corresponding to Valladolid and its connection with Puerto Morelos, from which it was also connected to the Line of the East.

In the south of the peninsula, the operation front was led by General José María de la Vega, who had his base on the coast of the Bay of Ascension—the so-called "General Vega camp" (Arce Sosa 1899). It was an architectural complex where a great variety of operations were housed, including customs, command centers, a school for boys and another for girls, and houses to accommodate the families of the military. In this southern line of operation, the troops moved from the sea to the interior. On the Caribbean Sea, at the head of Chetumal Bay, in 1900, the Mexican Navy founded Xcalak, where the camp known as Xcalak Quebrado was located. This was the site from which the dredging of the so-called Zaragoza Canal was created: it was an artificial seaway through which

Mexican warships could travel freely during the campaign, without the need to navigate through the waters of the English colony.

In the interior of the bay, the San Rafael de Sombrerete camp (Zaragoza) was settled, and together with the *Pontón*—a vessel that had been in place at the mouth of the Hondo River since January 1899—troops protected, monitored, and controlled the illegal trade that Maya "rebels" used to supply themselves with arms and ammunition. They were also able to stop the traffic of precious wood. Inland, a detachment was established at Santa Elena, a border area with the English colony. Then the campaign moved towards Xula (Xulha), located south of the Bacalar lagoon. From there, the troops moved north until they reached Bacalar. In this town the troops adapted the remains of a fort and its surroundings from the sixteenth century to provide for the accommodation of the Fifth and Seventh Battalions.

The military continued skirting the west bank of the lagoon, where they secured at least eight places to control both the road leading north and access to the source of water. This line of operation continued heading north through Santa Cruz Chico, Chuncas, Nohbec, Petacab, and Tzonot, among others. At each point a camp was established and protected by long *trincheras* made of dry-laid stones (defensive walls; see Fryer, chapter 5 in this volume). Trincheras abounded on the landscape at the end of the war: each camp site, fort, or fortified city had many long trincheras that protected their perimeters, a classification of which is also provided by Fryer (chapter 5, this volume).

In total, a radius of fifty to sixty kilometers was covered by the places and points established on this South Line, corresponding to the center-south area of the peninsula. The coastal camps—such as the ones in Vigía, Xcalak, or Sombrerete—connected with the operation line from Oriente de Yucatán to the Río Hondo (Berriozabal F. 1898). The objective of this line was to monitor the peninsular territory from the coast. The National Navy covered this operation front, with Brigadier Angel Ortiz Monasterio as commander in chief. Covering the coast—from the north of Belize and the Bay of Chetumal, to Puerto Morelos—the line reached the north coast in Puerto Progreso, extending into the Laguna de Términos, Campeche, using fluvial navigation to enter the center of the "rebel" territory (Ortiz Monasterio 1898a). The intention was to militarily occupy the Hondo River at its confluence with the Bravo and Arroyo Azul Rivers, as well as the Bacalar Lagoon, Chetumal Bay, and the San Jose River. The Yucatecan forces also sought to block the roads that Maya used to bring contraband into the peninsula from the coast (Ortiz Monasterio 1898b, 1898c). To support navigation, a naval station was installed, and an anchorage was built in the Chinchorro Bank in addition to a port in Cozumel for the exclusive use of the government. This line of operation involved more than thirty boats, which sailed both along the coastal zone and in inland waters (rivers, canals,

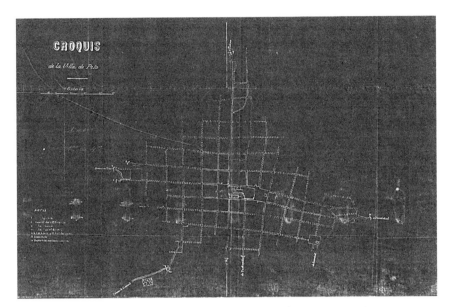

FIGURE 6.3. *Plan of the Villa de Peto, 1900. Mapoteca Manuel Orozco y Berra-Sagarpa, Alejandra Badillo Sánchez edition.*

and lagoons). Among these vessels figured the *Buque Zaragoza*; pilot's boats such as the *Tatiche, Moctezuma*, and *Icaiche*; the *Corbeta Yucatán*, the *Cañonero Independencia*; and vessels such as the *Vapores* and the *Barcazas*, which were part of the "Flotilla del Río Hondo" led by Lieutenant Othón Pompeyo Blanco. Each vessel was armed with guns and gunpowder, in addition to 200 weapons between carbines and Mauser pistols, as well as 20,000 bullets for carbines and another 20,000 for pistols (Castellanos 1900).

Now, returning inland, in the area of Peto, the Línea de operación Central was drawn and directed by General Ignacio A. Bravo, who was also the head of the overall campaign. This line was characterized by major architectural works, including eight forts, four posts, and a variety of camps and barracks, distributed across four sectors located between Peto and Chan Santa Cruz. The first section that the troops traveled was from Peto to Ichmul. The town of Peto was sheltered by a protection wall that blocked access to the central plaza via the main streets at different cardinal points as shown in figure 6.3. From this point heading east, a series of fortifications were built that began in Dzonotchel, where Fort No. 1 was built, in 1895 (Avalos A. 1895). This masonry fortification was irregular in plan and protected the center of the town, with the ability to watch the roads that connected to it (Bravo and de la Vega 1903).

To the southeast was located Fort "Cepeda Peraza," Fort No. 2, which is not described in the sources. However, our observations confirm that the fort was

FIGURE 6.4. *Fort No. 2 Cepeda Peraza, near Calotmul, current state. Photograph by Alejandra Badillo Sánchez, 2016.*

made of masonry, on an elevated area near the old road from Peto to Chan Santa Cruz. Utilizing a cruciform plan, the center had a tall tower (or turret) and three galleys. It was accessed by a wide and long staircase of sinuous steps, flanked by masonry rails and two benches on each side (figure 6.4).

The next point was the Baluarte de Calotmul, or Fort No. 3, which, according to the sources (Bravo and de la Vega 1903), was a construction made of stone, circular in shape. However, we still need to verify this through field investigation. Further along from Calotmul is Ichmul, where the National Guard was housed in Fort No. 4., built on the upper part of a Terminal Classic acropolis located on the south side of the central square of the town, from which the military could have a very broad visual of the area (Flores and Normark 2004, 2005). In addition, a military post was built on top of a pyramidal structure near the Acropolis. There also could have been other fortification works or walls of protection that limited access to the center of the town (figure 6.5).

After Ichmul the second sector began. The first site taken was that of Balché, where Fort No. 5 was erected. The area close to the fort was surrounded by trincheras, points of control and parapets located on the old road that went from Peto to Uaymax (Badillo Sánchez and Flores 2019). In the field we saw a circular construction of approximately fifty centimeters in diameter, which integrated at least four surveillance points and two control points, in addition to a bastion three to four meters high, marking one vigilance points. This group was located 600 meters from the main house of an old colonial ranch that had been

FIGURE 6.5. *Fort No. 4 of Ichmul on a pre-Hispanic acropolis, current state. Photograph by Alejandra Badillo Sánchez, 2018.*

modified by the military to form part of the architecture of Fort No. 5 (Badillo Sánchez and Flores 2018, 2019). Part of the troops settled at Post A in Uaymax (Bravo 1900) to later reach the town of Saban, which had been abandoned in 1859 during the war. In this town the houses were "empty due to lack of inhabitants" (Bravo 1900), so Baluarte No. 6 was built there, finishing construction on January 12, 1900. In this location, different spaces for service and maintenance were integrated, both for the military and the families of generals, officers, and troops who were all attached to the caravan.

Leaving Saban, towards the southeast, was Post B—known as "El Pozo"—and, a few kilometers ahead, Fort No. 7 called Okop. The archival sources make scant mention of these forts, but previous archaeological studies show their architectural configurations (Martos, Rodríguez, and Sánchez 1998; Badillo Sánchez 2015, 223–225). Okop has a set of constructions that included the structure called the "Fort," which is of greater dimensions than the other structures and bastion form with a pit and quadrangular plan, topped in each corner by a polygonal bulwark, united by a thick wall, approximately three meters high, and surrounded by gun ports where the military placed heavy artillery (figure 6.6). In this building the military housed federal battalions and members of the National Guard, in a series of wooden barracks with roof of palm thatch. It also had a well, kitchen areas, and bakery, among other spaces. The accompanying fortification was called Fortín because it was smaller. This construction,

FIGURE 6.6. *Fort No. 7 Okop, current status. Photograph by Alejandra Badillo Sánchez, 2010.*

of irregular plan, had two bastions constructed using the high part of two pre-Hispanic structures, of the site of Yo'okop, which were partially dismantled. These bastions were joined by walls one meter wide that delimited an interior space, which was accessed by an attenuated entrance (Badillo Sánchez 2015). Given the height at which the fort is located, it was a clear position from which the military could monitor the area.

Beyond Fortín was Post C (or Puesto de la Aguada), also built on top of a pre-Hispanic structure belonging to the former site of Yo'okop (Flores and Badillo Sánchez 2014, 228). After this, the troops continued through Soyola (Dzoyolá) until arriving at Chuncab, where Post D was established (Bravo and de la Vega 1903). The National Guard continued toward the southeast until reaching Santa María, a camp that marked the end of the second sector of the Línea de operación Central. Here they established a hospital, among other spaces for the maintenance of the troops. The third sector extended from Hobompich and reached Nohpop. In Hobompich, Fort No. 8 was built, which the written sources mention had a wood and palm thatch building for the troops and a cattle pen. However, it is likely that this fort had even more infrastructure because it was the closest in position to the final objective of the military, Chan Santa Cruz. Meanwhile, another part of the troops took station in the Tabi camp, atop the center of a pre-Hispanic site, in whose highest structures surveillance points were established (figure 6.7). Finally, the last outpost was entrenched in the Nohpop camp, also located in the center of an ancient pre-Hispanic site, where at least three wooden galleys with a palm thatch roof were erected, one of them designated as a barracks. From this point, in April 1901, the advance was made on the Maya stronghold.

A month later, Chan Santa Cruz was occupied. The capture was made without resistance, the Maya forces having abandoned their city and leaving only four inhabited houses (Osorio 1902). At that time the transformation of the landscape was complete: the capital of the Maya insurrectionists was renamed Santa Cruz del Bravo—for General Ignacio Bravo who led the occupying forces—and modified into a military bastion of the Porfirian army. Finally, this Central Line was

FIGURE 6.7. *Tabi Camp 1901 and federal garrison in the "Photographic Album of the memory of the Governor's trip to Santa Cruz, 1901" (Yucatan BY-SEDECULTA, Photo Library Section Alejandra Badillo Sánchez edition).*

connected to the Bay of Ascension, where a railway line was constructed with four stations and camps for the lodging of the troops that traveled to reach the eastern coast. This was the fourth and last sector of the Central Line (Bravo and de la Vega 1903). In total this line managed to cover a radius of sixty to seventy km. It controlled the center of the peninsula and a part of the eastern coast.

In sum, the deployment of the military positions and the establishment of each of the points led to the conformation of the complex panoptic system that was one way in which the government of Mexico appropriated the reclaimed territories of the "rebel" Maya.

Intimidating Territory

As we have seen, the appropriation of peninsular space by the military left a trail both in the jungle and along the coast. There were more than fifty checkpoints: posts, forts, camps, barracks, ports, naval stations, and other fortification works. In addition to those remains of military architecture, there are also spaces whose function was modified by the whims of the campaign. This happened with old churches, some of which served as a refuge for people, as a barracks for the military, as temporary jails for military use, or as a warehouse for military supplies. This conversion happened with towns that during the campaign were transformed into camps and barracks, and pre-Hispanic sites that were partially dismantled to build fortifications. Similarly, new roads and canals were created to enter the territory where Maya lived. These material remains—imposing, armed, aggressive, and dangerous constructions—are testimony to the sanctioned violence practiced by the government of Porfirio Díaz. Some towns and forts were protected by walls, others by long trincheras, others by barriers of barbed wire, and at least one with a pit. All this fortification modified the traffic and daily activities of people. The reconstruction of the theater of war, carried out in the section "Reconstructing the 'Theater of War,'" helps to visualize the military actions and to glimpse the consequences they had on the life of the peninsular society (Badillo Sánchez 2019).

Even after May 1901 the tension of war did not cease. More troops came to the peninsula to reinforce the sites that had previously been taken by the military. For the people who had fled to shelter in *sascaberas* (caves or pits for extracting lime), in the jungle, or in their fields, the presence of more military elements represented imminent harassment and generated an environment of uncertainty. In that moment the Porfirian military forces (which had previously only made linear explorations) began the siege of (self-declared and suspected) Maya insurrectionists, who had retreated to the jungle far from the front lines (de la Vega 1902). In their search soldiers destroyed and burned everything in their path.

The few Maya who remained, among them some "rebels" and others associated with the groups living south of Campeche and recognized as "peaceful" by the authorities since 1853, did not intend to submit to the governments of either Yucatán or Campeche. As a result, the Mexican government formed the Federal Territory of Quintana Roo (Sierra Méndez 1901).

Within this warlike context, the peninsular population lived immersed in a territory that was constantly watched from each of the military and fortified positions. In this territory the punitive panoptic system controlled transit and trade routes, denied access to wells and bodies of water from which the population was supplied, denied the use of fertile lands, and restricted movement to towns that were more populated. With blocked roads and extreme vigilance, the social and traditional ways of obtaining food by subsistence planting were altered, since it was common for the military to destroy crops and set fire to the forests where it was known that Maya people lived (Reyes 1902a). In addition, it was difficult to obtain food through hunting, because if firearms were detonated, even if only to hunt an animal that one wanted to eat, the sound alerted the military who came to the villages and inspected house by house until they found those responsible for the shot (Herrera 1902; on the importance of subsistence hunting to Maya lifeways, see Dedrick, McAnany, and Batún Alpuche, chapter 2 in this volume).

With the forests, roads, and villages under the constant vigilance of the military, these recovering Maya communities could not provide food for themselves. The area became vulnerable, hit with famine. Moreover, newly arrived soldiers brought diseases, such as yellow fever, which caused great stress on the population ("Beneficencia pública" 1901, 187). Without food or provisions many were forced to migrate. Whole families, uninvolved in the war, fled from the violence of the conflict (Badillo Sánchez 2019). Not only did Maya people leave, but a good deal of soldiers also decided to desert the campaign and flee. But the panoptic network of forts and checkpoints facilitated interception of people who fled. Those who did manage to escape took refuge both inside the peninsula and out of it, for example, in the Petén in Guatemala, which is described by James Meierhoff (chapter 8 in this volume). Some refugees went to the districts of northern Belize, such as Orange Walk and Corozal (see Houk, Bonorden, and Kilgore, chapter 7 in this volume), while others went to the island of San Pedro. There were also people who migrated to the border area of Guatemala and to the eastern part of the island of Cuba. There were even those who sailed along the eastern coast and headed toward the south of the continent. Although the path they followed is unclear, some say that they arrived in Argentina, where they live today (Badillo Sánchez 2019).

This military occupation remained until 1904. The center, south, and north of the peninsula became a space of "biopolitical" domination (Traverso 2012, 215): where everyday spaces were changed according to the circumstances of the military enterprise; where power was exercised through architecture to monitor and control people, thereby dictating the behavior of the Maya population to avoid any uprising. Nowadays, the traces of that violence still appear on the peninsula, either in forgotten vestiges in the jungle, or present in the remembrances of the descendants of that fateful time.

Acknowledgments. I would like to thank all of the people of Sacalaca, whom I have known for the last nine years and whom I have had the pleasure of being with in the field, talking, and working. In particular, my gratitude goes to the Noh Chi family, Don Fernando Cocom, and Don Federico Cahum, for the walks in the jungle. A profound thank you to the docents and administrators at CIESAS-Peninsular Unit, where I did my doctoral work, from which came this chapter. Similarly, I want to thank the administrative staff at the Archivo Histórico de la SEDENA; the Armada Nacional de México; the "Género Estrada" de la SRE; the Mapoteca Manuel Orozco y Berra-SAGARPA; and the Biblioteca Francisco Xavier Calvigero, Universidad Internacional de las Américas. And, among others, thanks go to Mexico City and the archives of AGEY and the Biblioteca Yucatanense–Sedeculta of Mérida, Yucatán, for their attention to my work. Finally, I want to thank Dr. Justine Shaw and Dr. Alberto G. Flores of the Cochuah Regional Archaeological Project, for welcoming me to their team and for encouraging archaeological and historical study of this region. In the same vein, I thank Dr. Richard Leventhal, Dr. Tiffany C. Fryer, and Kasey Diserens Morgan for their invitation to join this volume and for their great translation of my chapter. Without their support and company, this investigation would not have been realized.

Notes

1. "Población indígena reacia a acatar las imposiciones del Gobierno Federal en materia de dominación territorial y explotación de recursos naturales."

2. "Se procuró desde el comienzo del avance respetar á los prisioneros y á los indios que permanecían avecinados en algunos pequeños poblados sobre la margen del río Hondo, nombrando autoridades escojidas entre el personal indígena, y aún en las expediciones primeras se dio orden para respetar las propiedades aún cuando el enemigo hiciera resistencia."

3. "Si bien se procuró en un principio respetar las propiedades y evitar en lo posible el derramamiento de sangre, no se perseveró en esa táctica y ya por la vía de represalia, ya para amedrentar á los rebeldes se apeló al rigor extremo, llevando el exterminio á todas partes y la destrucción á los poblados y siembras."

4. "Hacer comprender á los rebeldes los beneficios que pueden resultarles si se someten y prometiéndoles en caso contrario la continuación de una *guerra sin cuartel*."

References

Aguilar, Juan V. (Capitán 1º Comandante). 1899. "Estado que manifiesta el armamento y municiones que tiene la expresada en la fecha. Mahas[,] octubre 9 de 1899." Fondo Municipios, Serie Guerra, Sección Valladolid, Caja 370. Mérida: Archivo General del Estado de Yucatán.

Arce Sosa, José (Capitán Comandante). 1899. "Para el jefe político de Valladolid desde Carolina, agosto 7 de 1899." Fondo Municipios, Serie Guerra, Sección Valladolid, Caja 370. Mérida: Archivo General del Estado de Yucatán.

Avalos, A. (Teniente Coronel de Ingeniería). 1895. "Plano de la Fortificación de Sonotchel, Peto. Octubre de 1895." Colección Porfirio Díaz-, L40/C6/D00031. Mexico City: Universidad Iberoamericana.

Badillo Sánchez, Alejandra. 2015. "Two Places in Time: A Constructed Landscape in the Northwestern Region of Yo'okop." In *The Maya of the Cochuah Region: Archaeological and Ethnographic Perspective on the Northern Lowlands*, edited by Justine M. Shaw, 213–233. Albuquerque: University of New Mexico Press.

Badillo Sánchez, Alejandra. 2019. "Rumbo al corazón de la tierra macehual: La 'Campaña Militar de Yucatán contra los Mayas' 1899–1904." PhD diss. CIESAS Peninsular, Mérida.

Badillo Sánchez, Alejandra. 2022. "Tras las huellas de los militares, el desenlace de la Guerra social de Yucatan 1899–1904." In *U Maayab Ba'ateil: La guerra social maya o de castas, nuevos aportes*. Mexico City: Dirección de Estudios Históricos INAH.

Badillo Sánchez, Alejandra, and Alberto G. Flores, 2018. "Revisiting Xbalche: In Search of 'Fort No. 5 of Balche.'" In *Final Report of the 2018 Field Season: Cochuah Regional Archaeological Survey*, edited by Justine M. Shaw, 103–113. Eureka, CA: College of the Redwoods.

Badillo Sánchez, Alejandra, and Alberto G. Flores. 2019. "Traces of Fuerte No. 5 Xbalche." In *Final Report of the 2019 Field Season, Cochuah Regional Archaeological Survey*, edited by Justine M. Shaw, 110–133. Eureka, CA: College of the Redwoods.

"Beneficencia pública, estado que manifiesta el movimiento de enfermos habidos en el Hospital O'Horán, durante el Mes de agosto de 1901." 1901. *Boletín de Estadística* 7.20 (October 15): 187.

Bentham, Jeremy. (1791) 2000. *O Panóptico*. Translated by Guacira Lopes Louro, M. D. Magno, and Tomaz Tadeu. 2nd ed. Belo Horizonte, Brazil: Editorial Auténtica.

Berriozabal F. 1898. "Consentimiento para vigilar la Costa Oriental emitido al secretario de relaciones exteriores, México, agosto 10 de 1898." Sección Consular, 44-6-4. Mexico City: Archivo Histórico Genaro Estrada–SRE.

Blanquet, Aurelio (General de División). n.d. Bóveda XI/III/1–3. Mexico City: Archivo Histórico–SEDENA.

Bravo, Ignacio A. 1889. "Telegrama al presidente de la república, Mérida 21 de octubre de 1899." Colección Porfirio Díaz, Leg. 58, Caja 8, p.4727. Mexico City: Universidad Iberoamericana.

Bravo, Ignacio A. 1900. "Para el general de división de guerra, Baluarte no. 7. Enero 12 de 1900." Operaciones Militares, Campaña de Yucatán, 1900, XI/481.4/14739. Mexico City: Archivo Histórico–SEDENA.

Bravo, Ignacio A., and José María de la Vega. 1903. "Relación que manifiesta las construcciones hechas por cuenta del gobierno federal en todos los puntos es esta zona ocupados por fuerzas del mismo así como las que se hallan en obra y herramientas que existen: Campamento general vega, diciembre 12 de 1903." Exp. XI/481.4/14738, Quintana Roo 1903, f. 1–18. Mexico City: Archivo Histórico–SEDENA.

Canto Castañeda, P. 1899. "Fuerte Carolina, relación que manifiesta las construcciones hechas en el expresado, así como el tamaño y capacidad de sus alojamientos. Fuerte Carolina. Noviembre 11 de 1899." Fondo Municipios, Serie Guerra, Sección Valladolid, Caja 370. Mérida: Archivo General del Estado de Yucatán.

Castellanos, Manuel. 1900. "Estado que manifiesta el armamento portátil y municiones para el mismo que tienen la Sección de Artillería de la Armada Nacional. Campamento San Rafael de Sombrerete, abril 5 de 1900." Mexico City: Archivo General de la Armada de México–Secretaría de Marina.

Ceh Chan, Dalia Elizabeth. 2004. *Migración, turismo e identidad en la Riviera Maya*. MA thesis. Guadalajara: CIESAS Occidente.

De la Vega, José María. 1902. "Anexo número 14." Certified copy from the secretary of state to the Despacho de Gobernación Pedro Morales, January 1903, Campamento Gral. Vega. In *Informe administrativo rendido a la Secretaría de Gobernación por el Jefe Político Gral. José de la Vega*. Copy from December 24, 1902, Santa Cruz de Bravo. Archivo General de la Nación, México Independiente / Gobernación y Relaciones Exteriores / Gobernación: Sin sección / Caja 2300, 76752625/1/exp. 1.

Flores, Alberto G., and Badillo Sánchez, Alejandra. 2014. "Mapping of the Post of La Aguada (Military Post C)." In *Final Report of the 2005 Field Season, Cochuah Regional Archaeological Survey*, edited by Justine M. Shaw, 228–236. Eureka, CA: College of the Redwoods.

Flores, Alberto G., and Normark Johan. 2004. "Ichmul y sus alrededores." In *Reporte final del Proyecto Arqueológico de la Región de Cochuah: Temporada de Campo 2004*, edited by Justine M. Shaw, 60–77. Eureka, CA: College of the Redwoods.

Flores, Alberto G., and Normark Johan. 2005. "Between Mounds and Sacbeob: Investigations in Ejido of Ichmul." In *Final Report of the 2005 Field Season, Cochuah Regional Archaeological Survey*, edited by Justine M. Shaw, 7–24. Eureka, CA: College of the Redwoods.

Foucault Michel. 2009. "El panoptismo." In *Vigilar y castigar*. [Discipline and Punishment], 180–210. Translated by Aurelio Garzón del Camino. 2nd ed. Mexico City: Siglo XXI Editores.

GTM. 1982b "Exterminio." In *Glosario de términos militares*, edited by Secretaría de la Defensa Nacional, 209. Mexico City: Biblioteca de la Defensa–SEDENA.

GTM. 1982c "Guerra sin Cuartel." In *Glosario de términos militares*, edited by Secretaría de la Defensa Nacional, 238. Mexico City: Biblioteca de la Defensa–SEDENA.

Herrera, Antonio. 1902. "Declaran en la jefatura Teófilo Camil y Susano Cetzal vecinos de Chan Cenote. Informe de Antonio Herrera al gobernador del estado. Junio 17 de 1902." Fondo Poder Ejecutivo, Serie No Clasificados, Sección Guerra y Marina, Caja 374. Mérida: Archivo General del Estado de Yucatán.

Iturralde, José María. 1900. "Los indios de Yodzono se han sublevado. Telegrama para el Sr. Presidente de la República Mexicana. Merida 20 de noviembre de 1900." Colección Porfirio Díaz, L59/C8/4488–91. Mexico City: Universidad Iberoamericana.

Leone, Mark P. 2016. "The William Paca Garden as Ideology, not Taste." Selection from "Interpreting ideology in Historical Archaeology. Using the Rules of Perspective in the Willian Paca Garden in Annapolis, Maryland." In *Critical Historical Archaeology*. 2nd ed. New York: Routledge Taylor and Francis Group.

Martos, Luis Alberto, A. Rodríguez, and Ernesto Sánchez. 1998. *Informe de la Temporada 1998 del Proyecto de Arqueología Histórica. Fortín de Yokob*. Chetumal, Quintana Roo: INAH-DICPA y DSA.

Ortiz Monasterio, Angel. 1898a. "Plan definido el 18 de febrero de 1898 por Monasterio." Exp. I/131/3946, Leg. 3-16-45, Asunto Expediente de Ortiz Monasterio, Angel. Mexico City: Archivo Histórico Genaro Estrada–SRE.

Ortiz Monasterio, Angel. 1898b. "Propone las dimensiones y número de buques necesarios para la ocupación militar del río Hondo, Laguna de Bacalar, Bahía de Chetumal y río San Jose. Al Ministro de Relaciones Exteriores. Belize 21 de Julio de 1898, 4f." Sección Consular, 44-6-4. Mexico City: Archivo Histórico Genaro Estrada–SRE.

Ortiz Monasterio, Angel. 1898c. "Propone compra de dos pequeños cañoneros para el resguardo de la costa oriental de Yucatán. Al Ministro de Relaciones Exteriores. Belize 19 de Julio de 1898." Sección Consular, 44-6-4. Mexico City.: Archivo Histórico Genaro Estrada–SRE.

Osorio, Higinio R. 1902. "Declaración del indígena Zacarías Cian." To the governor of the state of Yucatán, Peto Yucatán, April 16, 1902. Fondo Poder Ejecutivo, Serie No Clasificados, Sección Guerra y Marina, 1902, Caja 365. Mérida: Archivo General del Estado de Yucatán.

Ralph, Sarah. 2012. "Introduction: An Interdisciplinary Approach to the Study of Violence." In *The Archaeology of Violence: Interdisciplinary Approaches*, edited by Sarah Ralph, 1–15. Albany: State University of New York Press.

Reyes, Bernardo. 1902a. "Carta mecanografiada de Bernardo Reyes a José María de la Vega. Noviembre 5 de 1902." Colección Bernardo Reyes, Fondo DLI, Copiador 39, documento 19521. Mexico City: Centro de Estudios de Historia de México.

Rugeley, Terry. 2018. "El amanecer del pasado: Monumentos, museos y memorias de la Guerra de Castas." In *Yucatán en la ruta del liberalismo mexicano*, edited by Sergio Quezada and Inés Ortiz Yam, 245–274. Mérida: Siglo XIX, Ediciones Universidad Autónoma de Yucatán.

Sierra Méndez, Manuel. 1901. "Para el Sr. General Don Porfirio Díaz, México Informe que el que suscribe rinde al Sr. Secretario de Guerra y Marina sobre puntos referentes á la elección del Territorio Federal en Yucatán, 14 de diciembre de 1901." Operaciones Militares Quintana Roo, 1901–1909, f. 1. Mexico City: Archivo Histórico–SEDENA.

Traverso, Enzo. 2012. "Biopoder: Los usos historiográficos de Michel Foucault y Giorgio Agamben." In *La historia como campo de batalla: Interpretar las violencias del siglo XX*, 209–236. Buenos Aires: Fondo de Cultura Económica.

Weber, Max. (1921) 1991. *From Max Weber: Essays in Sociology*, edited by H. H. Gerth and C. Wright Mills, 159–180, 253–265. London: Routledge.

7

Living on the Edge

The San Pedro Maya in British Honduras

Brett A. Houk, Brooke Bonorden, and Gertrude B. Kilgore

Beginning in the 1850s, displaced Maya factions fled the violence of the Caste War (1847–1901) in Mexico and established several villages in the lightly populated forests of western British Honduras (now Belize) and the eastern Petén in what is today northern Guatemala (figure 7.1). Initially this group, collectively known as San Pedro Maya, retained their autonomy in northwestern British Honduras by remaining self-sufficient through milpa, or slash-and-burn, farmers (Ng 2007). However, British logging firms, who depleted mahogany resources along the Belize coast, began to operate farther into the interior of the colony around this same time. Conflicting uses of the landscape eventually led to clashes between San Pedro Maya and the loggers (Bonorden 2016). These clashes culminated in the 1867 Battle of San Pedro and Lieutenant Governor John Gardiner Austin's delegitimization of San Pedro Maya claims to land in the area, which compelled Maya villagers to pay rent to farm the lands they occupied (Church, Yaeger, and Dornan 2011).

For that reason and others related to recognized "ownership" of lands inhabited by Maya, much of San Pedro Maya history in British Honduras is closely

https://doi.org/10.5876/9781646422845.c007

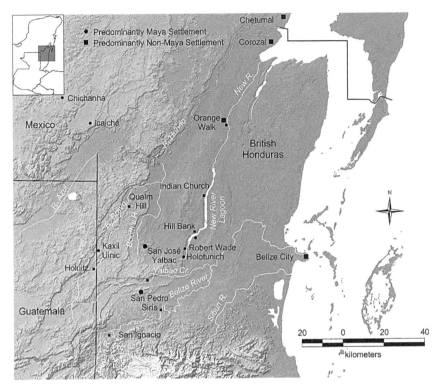

FIGURE 7.1. *Map of selected late-nineteenth-century San Pedro Maya sites and non-Maya camps and towns in northern British Honduras. Base map courtesy NASA/JPL-Caltech, SRTM Mission. Site locations after Church, Yaeger, and Dornan (2011, fig. 9.1) and Jones (1977, map 5-1). Map by Brett A. Houk.*

linked to that of the British Honduras Company (BHC)—a logging firm that owned most of the forested land in British Honduras north of the Belize River and west of Hill Bank Lagoon (figure 7.2). The BHC, which changed its name to the Belize Estate and Produce Company (BEC) in 1875, was a major land-owner, employer, and political force in British Honduras for over a century, and its stranglehold on the rich mahogany forests—as well as the economy and labor force of the colony—still reverberates in Belize today.

As Diserens Morgan and Fryer (chapter 1 in this volume) assert, Maya groups across Central America were not passive recipients of colonialism. Recent archaeological research (Dornan 2004; Ng 2007; Church, Yaeger, and Dornan 2011; Bonorden 2016) further indicates the British did not wholly "incorporate" San Pedro Maya into the colonial economic and social structure of British Honduras following the Battle of San Pedro (cf. Bolland 2003). Rather, Maya communities selectively participated in the colonial cash economy as it suited

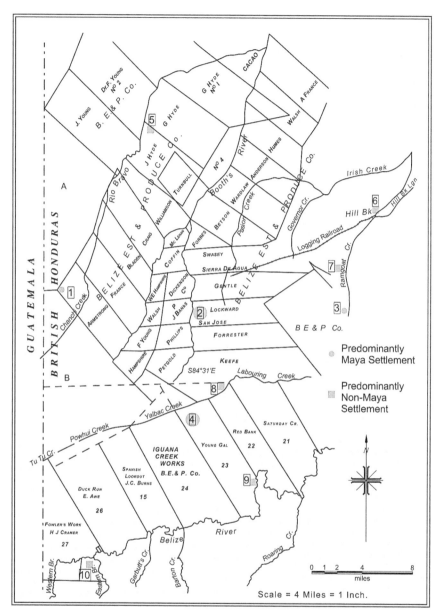

FIGURE 7.2. *Map of Belize Estate and Produce Company Parcels in 1936 (Cook and Lee 1936) with approximate site locations added by authors. (1) Kaxil Uinic, (2) San José Yalbac, (3) Holotunich, (4) San Pedro Siris, (5) Qualm Hill, (6) Hill Bank, (7) Robert Wade, (8) Yalbac, (9) Young Gal, (10) San Ignacio. Redrawn by Brett A. Houk from photograph of original map. The typography has been changed, and a graphical scale has been added; both the spellings and map design are original.*

their needs. Diserens Morgan and Fryer (chapter 1 in this volume) suggest that scholars must examine postcolonialism as a set of long-term, dynamic processes of social, economic, and political control in everyday relationships. This chapter, therefore, presents an examination of everyday life as it can be gleaned from the archaeological record at three San Pedro Maya villages: San Pedro Siris, Holotunich, and Kaxil Uinic. Considerations of the patterns of consumption and materiality observed within each village and the potential motivations for the acquisition of these commodities demonstrate the ways in which these individuals "lived their ethnicity" within and in spite of imposed colonialist systems (Church, Yaeger, and Dornan 2011).

San Pedro Maya occupied about twenty settlements dispersed throughout northwestern British Honduras and Guatemala (Jones 1977). They established San Pedro Siris first, and it grew to be the largest settlement. Although still on land controlled by the BHC, San Pedro Siris was fairly close to colonial settlements in the middle Belize River valley. Holotunich, meanwhile, is the easternmost San Pedro Maya settlement located south of Hill Bank Lagoon near several BHC/BEC facilities. Kaxil Uinic is similarly located on the periphery of the San Pedro Maya settlement cluster, situated near the border between British Honduras and Guatemala. Maya at San Pedro Siris interacted more frequently with colonial agents and colonists, while the residents of Holotunich and Kaxil Uinic had more limited interactions with loggers and BHC/BEC officials. A comparison of archival and archaeological data from these three sites emphasize the similarities and differences in the nature of San Pedro Maya interactions with colonial economic, political, and social structures at the settlement level. The quantity and variety of imported goods and arms, the presence and context of Catholic religious icons, and incorporation of Spanish or British institutions into San Pedro Maya society each reflect how the nature and degree of Maya interactions with their colonial counterparts varied from village to village. These glimpses of late colonial Maya life at the edge of the British Empire illustrate how each village served as a microcosm of the larger San Pedro Maya society.

Agency and Practice

As previously mentioned, recent research (Dornan 2004; Ng 2007; Church, Yaeger, and Dornan 2011; Bonorden 2016) indicates that San Pedro Maya acted strategically and intentionally to further their own agenda while navigating the political landscape of British Honduras during the Late Colonial period (1872–1900),[1] particularly with regard to the manufacture, adoption, and use of local or imported goods (Skibo and Schiffer 2008). The application of agency theory within these studies highlights the dialogic process through which individuals actively used material culture to negotiate cultural identity and status (Diserens Morgan and Fryer, chapter 1 in this volume; Stein 2005). Agency theory frames individuals as "rational actors, maximizing some aspect of economic, political, or symbolic capital" (Silliman 2001, 192). Stephen Silliman (2001), however, suggests that we are not entirely the masters of our fate, as our decisions are only partly of our own making. When contextualized within the historical and social circumstances of a given time and place, social rules and limited access to resources can constrain or give rise to different opportunities (see Dedrick, McAnany, and Batún Alpuche, chapter 2 in this volume). Disjunction in practices is archaeologically visible and can be interpreted as contestations of "correct" representations of knowledge that inevitably arise in colonial contexts when groups are confronted with alternative versions of what they have long considered natural (Joyce and Lopiparo 2005).

Thus, a dialogue occurs between material culture and identity and between structure and agency as well (Giddens 1984). Social agents, Silliman (2001, 192) asserts, "are both constrained and enabled by structure." In Silliman's (2001) nuanced approach to agency theory, social negotiations transform the *doxa* (mundane activities of everyday life) within fluctuating contexts, as individuals attempt to forge residence within their social worlds—oftentimes in the face of oppression and domination (Dobres and Robb 2000; Silliman 2001). Individuals do not blindly follow customs but confront situations that call for conscious choices, like those created by the blurred lines of doxa in shifting colonial contexts (Cowgill 2000). As noted by Rosemary A. Joyce and Jeanne Lopiparo (2005, 371), "*doxa* is an abstraction always made visible either in the form of *heterodoxy* (a knowing break with that which is now viewed as obsolete tradition) or *orthodoxy* (a conscious rearticulation of what is viewed as valued tradition)."

An examination of the varying levels of interaction with the colonial economic, political, and social structures at San Pedro Siris, Holotunich, and Kaxil Uinic illustrates how each group adapted to the breakdown of the doxa of milpa—slash-and-burn—farming (and the autonomy that came with it), forging different alternatives and actively instituting societal change with varying political and economic sovereignty. As noted by Maxine Oland and Joel W. Palka (2016), different zones of colonial contact experience varying structural constraints, resulting in contrasting processes of subjugation, autonomy, and culture change. These varied processes and their effects are evident in the contrasting archaeological assemblages present at San Pedro Siris, Holotunich, and Kaxil Uinic, where requirements to pay land rent in colonial currency catalyzed a shift in Maya labor away from subsistence activities and into commercial production, similar to the Colonial period (ca. 1540 to 1821) *visita* (subject town) of Tahcabo in the Yucatán, where the burden of church and state-imposed taxes precipitated Maya involvement in wage labor to acquire currency (Dedrick, McAnany, and Batún Alpuche, chapter 2 in this volume). Viewing each San Pedro Maya site mentioned at the beginning of this chapter as a microcosm of the larger, shared San Pedro Maya experience and, simultaneously, unique archaeological manifestations of agency and practice, offers an opportunity to reconsider the traditionally monolithic meaning of "the colonial Maya" and the assumption that the dynamics of their relationships with colonists were uniform or their motivations consistent across villages (Oland and Palka 2016). Each village strategically confronted the changing doxa within the parameters of their unique relationship with the colonial system.

A Brief History of Economic, Political, and Social Interactions in Northwestern British Honduras

The scope of this chapter precludes a detailed account of the Caste War (see Reed 1964; Bricker 1981; Rugeley 1996; Sullivan 1989; Alexander 2004, 15; also, Fryer [chapter 5]; Badillo Sánchez [chapter 6]; and Meierhoff [chapter 8], this volume) but warrants a brief summary as it relates to the formation of San Pedro Maya communities. As political turmoil engulfed the Yucatán with the outbreak of the Caste War in 1847, a group of approximately 1,000 Maya splintered from a larger group of "Pacíficos del Sur"—Southern Pacifists who had come to oppose the direction in which the war was going—and moved into territory claimed by Guatemala and British Honduras between 1857 and 1862 (Dumond 1977, 113). Of these initial migrants, 350 resided in the principal village of San Pedro Siris, the largest of the San Pedro Maya settlements (Dumond 1977; Bolland 2003). O. Nigel Bolland (2003) asserts that British authorities and logging firms initially encouraged San Pedro settlement in the remote region, as these entities viewed Maya settlers as a potential source of cheap labor for agricultural development in the face of lagging mahogany exports. Through time, though, conflicts emerged between San Pedro Maya and their colonialist logging counterparts over the two groups' incompatible uses of resources in the forests of northwestern British Honduras. Compounding the situation was widespread disagreement and confusion over the northern and western boundaries of the colony, which led to claims by Maya refugees that the loggers were cutting trees on Mexican territory and subsequent demands for rent by Icaiché Maya, a more belligerent Yucatec Maya faction living in Mexico (see Kray, Church, and Yaeger 2017; for earlier accounts of the logging competition between British settlers, Spanish settlers, and Maya see García Lara and Olán, chapter 4 in this volume). In April 1866, Icaiché factions raided a BHC logging camp called Qualm Hill, taking a number of hostages (Camara 1866).

The raid on Qualm Hill ultimately served as a catalyst for a brief confrontation between British troops and San Pedro Maya on December 21, 1866, which began with the arrival of forty-two men from the Fourth West Indian Regiment, under the command of Major MacKay, at San Pedro Siris. According to Lieutenant Colonel Robert William Harley (1867), the regiment was quietly

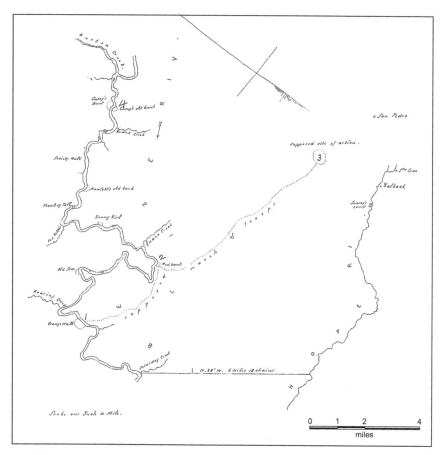

FIGURE 7.3. *Postaction engagement map from the Battle of San Pedro (Austin 1867a), on file at the Jamaica Archives (1B5/56/32). (1) The point at which the troops crossed the river; (2) the route to Red Bank, "where they ought to have crossed"; and (3) "the place (no 3) at which the engagement is believed to have taken place." Redrawn by Brett A. Houk from photograph of the original. The typography has been changed and a graphical scale has been added, but the spellings and map design are true to the original, including the orientation of north.*

marching through the territory to escort a civil commissioner when 400 to 500 "Indians" supposedly ambushed them. After about a half-hour of fighting, during which sixteen British soldiers were wounded, five were killed, and the Civil Commissioner was lost forever, the British troops retreated to Orange Walk on the Belize River (Ng 2007; figure 7.3).

With the arrival of reinforcements from Jamaica in January 1867, Harley led a punitive expedition into San Pedro territory with orders to drive off any "hostile Indians" his troops encountered, ultimately attacking San Pedro Siris, San

José Yalbac, Chunbalche, and other small villages in what became known as the Battle of San Pedro (Jones 1977). Harley's troops burned all the buildings and milpas in these villages, but John Gardiner Austin (1867b) reveals that most Maya living in the settlements had retreated prior to the arrival of British troops and no actual combat occurred. Captain John Carmichael led a final mission to destroy additional San Pedro Maya settlements, ultimately pushing Maya back across the border into the Yucatán in February of 1867 (Carmichael 1867; Jones 1977). It is at this juncture in the narrative of San Pedro Maya–British colonialist relations that we turn our focus specifically to the village of San Pedro Siris and how the Battle of San Pedro transformed the interactions between the residents and the colonial economic, political, and social structures in British Honduras.

San Pedro Siris

Under the direction of Richard Leventhal, Jason Yaeger, and Minette Church, archaeologists working with the San Pedro Maya Project (SPMP) conducted excavations at San Pedro Siris over four field seasons from 2000 to 2003 (Dornan 2004, 13; Yaeger et al. 2004a, 2004b; Church, Yaeger, and Dornan 2011; Kray, Church, and Yaeger 2017;). The village of San Pedro Siris occupied an agriculturally productive and reasonably defensible area with smaller hamlets clustered around its periphery (Dornan 2004). The village center had a church, fiesta house, jail, and other government buildings, and probably contained about fifty residential structures to support a population of 300 to 400 individuals (Dornan 2004; Yaeger et al. 2004a). Archaeological investigations at the village site identified a cobble walkway, a yard, several rock piles, a trash toss zone, and a possible animal pen (Dornan 2004; Yaeger et al. 2005). The archaeological remains at the site, as evidenced by the recovery of incendiary rockets used in the battle (Kray, Church, and Yaeger 2017), most clearly represent the period following the Battle of San Pedro and the reoccupation of San Pedro Siris (Church, Yaeger, and Dornan 2011).

As the head village of the larger San Pedro Maya community, San Pedro Siris was the epicenter of the San Pedro political-military hierarchy and in certain circumstances possessed the authority to dictate the affairs of all twenty villages within the settlement area (Jones 1977; Dornan 2004). As noted by Minette Church et al. (2011), both pre-Columbian political entities and nineteenth-century Mexican militias inspired San Pedro Maya village political organization. Prior to the Battle of San Pedro, the colonial administration in British Honduras officially recognized Asunción Ek, *comandante* (commander) of San Pedro Maya communities, as the *alcalde* (mayor) of San Pedro Siris (Dumond 1997). The alcalde system benefited Maya, who applied the political institution by modifying the traditional Maya position of the *batab*, or town leader. The system also benefited the colonial government, as it made British rule cheaper and more effective in rural areas because these leaders were essentially unpaid officers serving as an extension of the colonial government. The compliance of alcaldes within the administrative hierarchy of British Honduras, therefore, is a point of negotiation within the fractured doxa of Maya political organization during the Late Colonial period. Although San Pedro Maya likely contested any notion of "incorporation" into the social structure of British Honduras due to the implied loss of autonomy and identity associated with the term, the concept of a hierarchical political system was acceptable as a modification of older Maya political structures. Additionally, the alcalde system served as a buffer between Maya and more direct forms of colonial control, allowing the group to maintain a greater sense of autonomy at the village level (Bonorden 2016).

Upon receiving his commission from the colonial administration, Alcalde Ek promptly requested munitions to defend the British territory and the establishment of a school at San Pedro Siris (Dumond 1997). Minette Church, Yaeger, and Dornan (2011) assert that British authorities, though initially reluctant to arm San Pedro Maya, did so with the intention that the group would serve as a buffer between the rest of the colony and other, less amiable Maya factions who were still fighting their war to the north. The SPMP recovered a variety of arms from the site, including flint-lock rifles predating 1850 and British Enfield rifles, which Lieutenant Governor Austin likely supplied to San Pedro Maya in 1866 (Austin 1866; Church, Yaeger, and Dornan 2011, 182). Differential access to such highly coveted imported goods, to which the villages established after the Battle of San Pedro (such as Kaxil Uinic) did not have access, may explain why the residents of San Pedro Siris more readily accepted colonial institutions (like the school) in the village as a leverage point of negotiation.

According to Christine Kray, Church, and Yaeger (2017), the colonial government funded schools in major San Pedro Maya villages, but the Catholic Church actually administered them. While the archives are silent on whether or not the colony ever built Ek's requested school, archaeological evidence suggests that one may have been present. The SPMP discovered toys, including tea sets and dolls, inkwells, and other items possibly associated with a school at San Pedro Siris (Dornan 2004, 215; Church, Yaeger, and Dornan 2011, 190).

The Catholic Church was "fundamental to the extension and establishment of colonial power" in British Honduras (Wainwright 2016, 7). Both the church and the colony sought power over Maya, though their methods of and motivations for achieving this goal greatly varied. The "hidden curriculum" of religious-based education sought to reinforce and justify British control of British Honduras, reifying the social order within the colony (Lewis 2000; Relehan 2008). Even though British Honduras was a Protestant settlement, the Catholic Church had a strong presence in the colony, which was essentially surrounded by countries and colonies rooted in Spanish Catholicism. Jennifer Dornan (2004, 152) reports, "There is archaeological and archival data to support the idea that the inhabitants of San Pedro were catholic [*sic*]." Archaeologically, this evidence is the form of "numerous Catholic religious pendants" and "imported religious icons, specifically crucifixes, in domestic contexts" (Church, Yaeger, and Dornan 2011, 189). Dornan (2004, 152) also notes that San Pedro Maya allowed a Catholic priest to enter the village during the period of armed conflict between Ek's militia and the colonial regiment, indicating "some level of trust in the church." Church, Yaeger, and Dornan (2011, 189) caution that "the exact nature of San Pedro villagers' faith, given their tumultuous Caste War history, is unclear," and Dornan (2004, 153) warns against assumptions that the adoption of certain Catholic symbols equates with "a failure of indigenous agency." As Elizabeth Graham, Scott Simmons, and Christine White (2013) note with regard to Maya religiosity during the Spanish conquest (ca. 1500), changes manifested in the archaeological record reflect the active involvement of Maya in refashioning the cosmos and their place in it. We conversely assert that, though religious innovations (such as adopting aspects of Catholicism after the Spanish conquest) do demonstrate the exercise of agency, the continuation of such practices (i.e., maintaining a Catholic faith within Protestant Belize), when a changing social structure (i.e., the Anglican Church) challenged the religious doxa, also serves as evidence of agency through action.

Dornan (2004) notes that the Late Colonial period following the Battle of San Pedro was a time of increasing ethnic confusion as distinctions between the social categories of "Indian," "Mestizo," and "Ladino" broke down because various groups frequently divided and coalesced in strategic alliances, morphing to adapt to the changing political landscape. Harrison-Buck and colleagues (2019) have recently explored the interactions of colonialists, San Pedro Maya, Creole loggers, and ex-Confederates, whom Lieutenant Governor Austin actively recruited to settle in Belize to spur agriculture and act as an additional buffer against San Pedro Maya following the 1867 battle. Eleanor Harrison-Buck and colleagues' (2019) study concludes that these groups had extremely fluid political and economic agendas, seizing on economic opportunity despite blatantly subverting established protocol, especially with regard to the sale of restricted arms and ammunition. In addition, with British and American technologies widespread, a comingling of "traditional" and colonial goods, beliefs, and practices occurred in the colony.

At San Pedro Siris, challenges to the accepted doxa of foodways precipitated more negotiations of identity. San Pedro Maya found their subsistence practices altered by the prescriptions of colonial institutions, resulting in a reliance on foreign goods that San Pedro Maya could not manufacture. Archaeological evidence from San Pedro Siris indicates the residents served and ate food with bowls and plates imported from England but cooked those same foods in ceramic vessels that were either locally produced or imported from the Yucatán (Dornan 2004; Church, Yaeger, and Dornan 2011). This concurrent use of locally produced and imported vessels is either a reflection of the San Pedro desire to utilize more efficient and effective technologies while maintaining traditional foodways or an effort to consciously manipulate status and identity markers within their local community (Dornan 2004). The inhabitants of San Pedro Siris chose which types of imported vessels to use, selecting types they could incorporate into traditional food preparation and serving techniques (Leventhal, Yaeger, and Church 2001; Church, Yaeger, and Dornan 2011). The lack of flatware found at the site, for example, indicates that San Pedro Maya chose to use tortillas as scoops rather than adopting metal utensils (Yaeger et al. 2004b). It is possible that the inhabitants of San Pedro Siris consciously negotiated food preparation methods while still striving to maintain a distinct Maya identity with regard to what food they actually consumed. Such choices around food consumption and preparation represent active materializations of Native identity in this context, rather than "passive vestiges" of ancient traditions (Silliman 2001, 203). Foodways, as an inherently social phenomenon, solidify group membership and provide distinguishing characteristics between groups (Jaffe, Wei, and Zhao 2018), and the maintenance of group identity via foodways offered a reprieve from the multitude of changing doxa that confronted San Pedro Maya.

While blending traditional foods with imported food-processing techniques and serving goods caused minor changes to San Pedro Maya lifeways and created a new *heterodoxy* of foodways, the necessity of paying rent to BEC more profoundly affected San Pedro doxa for subsistence. Ethnographic accounts collected by the SPMP reveal that, at least in the early twentieth century, village men worked as loggers or as *chicleros* to earn money to pay their rent (Kray et al. 2017, 65). The process of chicle extraction, preparation, and transport is described in detail by Mathews, Gust, and Fedick (chapter 10 in this volume). Several of the "cooking cauldrons" from San Pedro Siris shown in Kray and colleagues (2017, fig. 4.5c) are actually chicle-boiling pots, identical to those we recovered at Kaxil Uinic (discussed in the subsection "Kaxil Uinic"). Villagers also interfaced with the loggers by trading agricultural products for salt pork and wheat flour (Kray et al. 2017, 65). At San Pedro Siris, then, it appears that residents were still able to negotiate their place within the developing colonial system rather successfully, adapting aspects of their social organization and daily practices to "maintain lifeways associated with their lived ethnicity" in the face of constant change (Church et al. 2011, 191), albeit within the somewhat limited realm of possibilities created by the colonial structure.

Holotunich

San Pedro Maya settled the hamlet of Holotunich in the tumultuous political landscape that precipitated the Battle of San Pedro and occupied the site until about 1893. Olivia Ng (2007, 2010; Thornton and Ng Cackler 2013) located and investigated the site in 2006 as part of her dissertation research. With influence from Icaiché, Holotunich initially served as a base camp for Maya to collect rent money from British loggers, helping to maintain the spatial extent of San Pedro Maya control by acting as a boundary marker for their landholdings (Ng 2007, 26). Described by Lieutenant M. B. Salmon in his 1876 reconnaissance report of the village (quoted in Jones 1977; Ng 2007; and Ng 2010), Holotunich consisted of 12 houses that could not contain more than 8 families, or approximately 30 to 50 people. Located on a small and defensible hill near Ramgoat Creek, the settlement occupied a position closer to the British logging works at Hill Bank, Robert Wade Camp, and David O'Brien's Bank, relatively far from the other San Pedro Maya villages in its settlement cluster. Established on the periphery of both San Pedro Maya and British spheres of influence, Holotunich was central to struggles and negotiations of power between these two groups (Ng 2007).

Reoccupation of Holotunich by BEC after San Pedro Maya had abandoned the village complicated Ng's (2007) attempts to isolate the Maya component of the site. However, she did document five features that she interpreted to be Maya architectural remains (Ng 2007, 127), including one that closely resembles a cobble platform and walkway documented at San Pedro Siris (Dornan 2004; Yaeger et al. 2005, 260–261). In general, Ng (2007) identified the structures based on lines of cobbles, which she interpreted as the bases of walls. Artifactual remains clearly associated with San Pedro Maya occupation and these structures, however, could not be isolated. The continuation of traditional construction techniques at Holotunich despite proximity and exposure to alternative methods via the loggers at David O'Brien's Bank indicates the *orthodoxy* of the practice. Constrained by their limited ability to acquire cash, Alyssa Brooke Bonorden (2016) asserts, San Pedro Maya often chose not to purchase items for which they could freely acquire substitutes. The continuation of traditional building practices, therefore, represents an exercise of agency within this context.

The potential for mixing between the two occupational components of Holotunich also hindered Erin Kennedy Thornton and Ng Cackler's (2013, 373) faunal analysis, but their study did conclude that "jute, fish, armadillo, paca, and peccary" occurred more frequently in deposits likely associated with San Pedro Maya occupation. Bird, domestic pig, and deer bones occurred in both the San Pedro Maya and later BEC components (373). While bones from domesticated animals occurred in the San Pedro Maya component of the assemblage, in general the preference appeared to be for wild species and the maintenance of traditional subsistence practices, with the opposite trend characterizing the later BEC occupation (374–375).

The artifactual data from Holotunich is of limited value because of the potential for the mixing of stratigraphic contexts; the long manufacture ranges of most glass, metal, and ceramic objects; and the lag between artifact manufacture and deposition. Ng (2007, 296) proposed that the following materials were likely associated with San Pedro Maya occupation of the site because similar objects were found at San Pedro Siris: "accordion parts, [a] rosary, [a] crucifix, black glass bottles, ceramic doll parts, tobacco pipes, and cast-iron pots."

Ng (2007, 316) suggests that daily life for residents of Holotunich "at the defining edge of San Pedro Maya power appeared to be fraught with tension and negotiation." As she observes, Maya at Holotunich were geographically farther from the closest Maya village than they were from the nearest non-Maya settlement, a logging camp at David O'Brien's mahogany bank, which was less than a mile away. Facing pressures from other San Pedro Maya as well as the Icaiché, the villagers at Holotunich balanced the need to represent Maya interests—including those of the Icaiché who repeatedly claimed that Mexico owned all the territory west of the New River Lagoon (Church et al. 2019)—while coexisting with the nearby logging camps (Ng 2007, 317).

Kaxil Uinic

Of the three sites we are examining, Kaxil Uinic, was situated the farthest from colonial settlements, and as such the residents there likely had the least direct contact with non-Maya actors under normal circumstances. The village was settled in the 1880s and occupied for nearly fifty years until the BEC closed it and forcibly relocated the residents to San José Yalbac in 1931 (Jones 1977, 161–162). Brett A. Houk (2012) first identified the village location based on reports from employees of the nearby Chan Chich Lodge, and Bonorden subsequently conducted survey, mapping, and excavations over the course of two seasons, in 2015 and 2016 (Bonorden and Kilgore 2015, 2016; Bonorden 2016; Bonorden and Houk 2019). Situated 1.85 km east of the border between Belize and Guatemala, the surviving archaeological footprint of the village includes glass bottles, metal objects, and rock clusters scattered around a small *aguada*, or waterhole (figure 7.4, "bottle scatter" and "surface finds"). Contrary to reports by Jones (1977, 161), we found that the site is located approximately two kilometers west of Chan Chich Creek—its aguada is key to confirming the site's location since J. Eric S. Thompson (1963, 233) sketched the village and its "waterhole" in 1931, shortly after it was abandoned.

Based on a handful of archival accounts, we know that Kaxil Uinic had an alcalde, a physical council house (Colonial Secretary [1931] 1991), and approximately twenty "huts" (Thompson 1963, 233), suggesting a population of approximately 120 people (Bonorden 2016, 359). Although distance isolated Kaxil Uinic from the colonial government, footpaths through the forest connected Kaxil Uinic to the outside world: paths ran to Icaiché in the north, San José Yalbac in the southeast (Jones 1977), Yaloch in Guatemala to the southwest, and the Petén region to the west (Miller 1887). The archival record suggests that the village had strong Icaiché

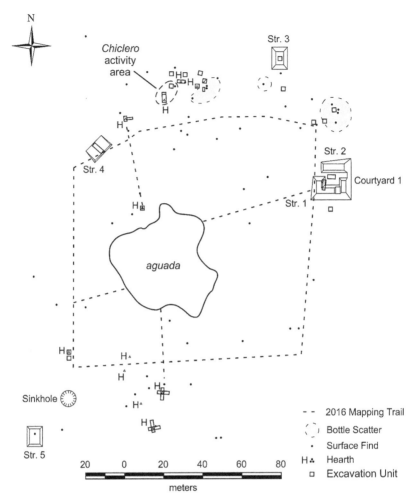

FIGURE 7.4. *Kaxil Uinic site map showing hearths, surface collections, artifact clusters, and structures. Map drawn by Brett A. Houk.*

leanings in the 1880s. J.P.H. Gastrell (1886) wrote to the Earl of Rosebery that the "Ycaiché Indians" "[kept] their power or jurisdiction to nearly as far south as Garbutt's Falls and control . . . Xaxa Venic [Kaxil Uinic] which [was then] supposed to be within [the] Belize frontier." The *alcalde* of the village, Antonio Baños, reportedly considered his village to be in Mexican territory (Bolland 2003) and displayed strong Icaiché sympathies the same year (Jones 1977).

During the 2015 and 2016 field seasons, we identified 10 three-stone hearths similar to those identified by Meierhoff (chapter 8 in this volume) at Tikal, and 66 isolated surface artifacts or artifact scatters at Kaxil Uinic. During this time, we opened thirty excavation units. Over the course of this two-year project, Bonorden and Gertrude Kilgore (2015, 2016) analyzed 5,320 artifacts from the site. We interpret each three-stone hearth to represent the location of a residential structure based on work done at the Caste War Maya village at Tikal by Hattula Moholy-Nagy (2012) and James Meierhoff (2015, 2017, chapter 8, this volume). Several excavated hearths sat on prepared marl floors, and excavations encountered similar marl surfaces associated with dense artifact scatters, but not hearths. We encountered no postholes, which is not surprising given the environmental conditions, but the prepared marl surfaces are likely architectural (Bonorden 2016). Based on the distribution of known hearths (see figure 7.4), Bonorden and Kilgore (2016, 92) proposed that the village may have been divided into two distinct clusters of families, one on the northern side of the aguada and the other on the southern side. The lack of window glass and nails suggests pole and thatch house construction, like the "huts" depicted in Thompson's (1963) sketch.

In the assemblage, Bonorden and Kilgore (2016) found a few shotgun shells, one bullet casing, and one shotgun stock. Because San Pedro Maya first settled Kaxil Uinic in the 1880s, after Lieutenant Governor Austin had restricted the sale of weapons and ammunitions to them, a lack of easy access to firearms explains the relative dearth of such artifacts. This finding stands in stark contrast to the early component at San Pedro Siris (Church, Yaeger, and Dornan 2011) but aligns with the findings at Holotunich, where Ng (2007) found ammunition that postdated San Pedro Maya occupation of the site.

Several artifacts provide glimpses into both daily life at the village and access to European goods: seven clay pipe fragments, a small metal brooch, a metal religious pendant apparently depicting a Catholic saint, a shell comb, shell and bone buttons, and a Guatemalan one-half real coin dated to 1900. Many of the imported items, however, relate to food preparation and/or serving: metal corn grinders, ceramic and metal serving dishes, metal cooking pots, metal cans, and glass bottles. Bonorden and Kilgore (2016, 129) note that the villagers used most of the European items in the perpetuation of local practices, often alongside traditional food preparation methods (such as stone metates). The significance of heirloom "technologies of self," including *metates*, is described in greater detail by Fryer (chapter 5 in this volume). This intentional decision to adopt certain colonial technologies, such as metal corn grinders and pots, to prepare and cook food more efficiently but eschew other things, such as metal forks and spoons, in favor of traditional methods of consuming food, mirrors the pattern seen at San Pedro Siris. In addition, this practice reinforces the notion that as social agents, the villagers chose to perpetuate their traditional foodways despite pressure from and access to colonial technologies (Church, Yaeger, and Dornan 2011, 188).

The faunal assemblage from excavations at the village includes peccary, domesticated pig, deer, turkey, and river turtle bone (Bonorden 2016, 368). These remains align with William Miller's (1887, 422) observations, made while cutting a transect along the border with Guatemala, that Maya villagers here "raise[d] pigs and fowls" in addition to growing "maize, rice, and beans." The lack of cow bones at Kaxil Uinic may reflect either a disdain for cattle among San Pedro Maya—Asunción Ek, alcalde of San Pedro Siris, had once formally complained to the colonial government that the logger's cattle wreaked havoc on their milpas (Cal 1991, 249–250; Dumond 1997, 276; see also Kray, Church, and Yaeger 2017, 59)—or a lack of access to cattle given the village's distance from colonial settlements.

As with San Pedro Siris, the archaeological and archival records suggest that the villagers at Kaxil Uinic engaged in commercial activities to earn cash to pay their rents. Gust (chapter 9 in this volume) asserts that by capturing the means of production (i.e., milpa farmland in this instance), elites, such as the colonial administration in British Honduras, created a workforce "that had no option other than selling their own labor power by working the lands and equipment of others." In the case of Kaxil Uinic, this meant that San Pedro Maya engaged in the colonial economy as chicleros to obtain cash and thus access to the means of production (the land). Bonorden and Kilgore (2016) documented an apparent chiclero activity area at Kaxil Uinic, marked by machetes, chiclero spurs, a shotgun stock, and chicle boiling pots (figure 7.5; see figure 7.4). Harrison-Buck and colleagues (2019) suggest that chicle tapping may have been adopted rather easily into the villagers' normal routine of hunting and gathering in the forests of northwestern Belize and eastern Petén. As Thompson (1963) remarked, however, by the 1930s this shift had a profound effect on San Pedro Maya. Speaking specifically about the village of San José Yalbac, Thompson (1963, 155) noted, "Practically all the beans and much of the maize were brought in from the outside, because so many of the men were away chicle bleeding that they could not make milpa." While the initial move to chicle tapping was a response to the need for cash, it ultimately marked a break in the accepted doxa of milpa farming as the primary means of subsistence. Turning to chicle, as Thompson (163, 155) described, left Maya communities "uprooted." Like the colonial frontier settlement of Tihosuco in the Yucatán (see García Lara and Olán, chapter 4 in this volume), Kaxil Uinic was located on the edge of the colonial empire, which led to the creation of (sometimes illicit) subsystems between peoples from different nations (e.g., chicle smuggling from Guatemala to British Honduras) who maintained facets of their group identities but also adopted new characteristics.

It also appears that perhaps the villagers became overly zealous in their chicle harvesting; Thompson (1963, 6) noted that BEC closed the village in 1931 "because it was believed to be a center of *chicle* smuggling." Combined, the archaeological data and limited archival information depict Kaxil Uinic's residents as largely maintaining traditional Maya lifeways, particularly in terms of

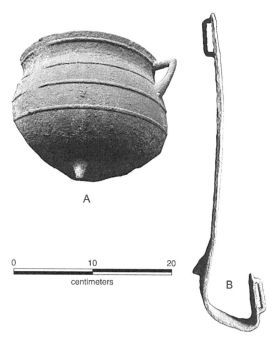

A

0   10   20

centimeters

B

FIGURE 7.5. *Artifacts related to chicle harvesting and processing from Kaxil Uinic. (A) fragment of a chicle pot (Spec. #KUV1497–01), (B) chiclero spur (Spec. #KUV1634-01). Photographs by Brooke Bonorden.*

house construction, subsistence, political organization, and food preparation. They did so despite the pressures of demands for rent payments, which necessitated participation in the chicle industry. Thus, the residents of Kaxil Uinic demonstrated their agency by perpetuating their lived ethnicity in many facets, and when confronted by a *heterodoxy*, they pursued the subsistence strategy most similar to the previously prescribed doxa.

Discussion

The archival and archaeological data from San Pedro Siris, Holotunich, and Kaxil Uinic provide three glimpses into the lived experiences of the communities collectively known as San Pedro Maya following the Battle of San Pedro. The three sites' locations afforded different opportunities for interaction with other Maya groups, English/European colonists, and other subaltern groups including Creole loggers and ex-Confederate immigrants at different chronological intervals (see Harrison-Buck et al. 2019). The archaeological records at the three sites show some compelling similarities while concurrently reflecting different levels of interaction with colonial structures. While Maya at San Pedro Siris and Kaxil Uinic clearly acquired items of personal adornment and religious affiliation—such as European clothing, jewelry, crucifixes and pendants, and modern food preparation tools and techniques—these items do not reflect incorporation of Maya communities into the colonial social structure, but rather denote the adoption of certain technologies and symbols into traditional Maya lifeways. As Church, Yaeger, and Dornan (2011, 194) observe, San Pedro Maya were "free to use the income they obtained . . . to buy goods they desired to enhance life in their chosen place: musical instruments, sewing machines, perfume, toys, decorated ceramics, jewelry, and more." Despite having access to European construction technologies, Maya at Kaxil Uinic, and presumably San Pedro Siris and Holotunich as well, continued to build their houses as they had done for millennia, using marl floors and pole and thatch superstructures centered on three-stone hearths. Domestic pigs may have largely replaced peccaries as a protein source, but Maya residents prepared and consumed them in traditional ways (i.e., *pibil* style), alongside corn, beans, and squash grown in milpas. Machetes eventually replaced stone tools for clearing those milpas, and at San Pedro Siris perforated metal cans replaced baskets or cloth pouches for sowing seeds, but the villagers continued to grow traditional crops of maize, beans, and squash, alongside sweet potato, jicama, spices, fruit trees, and possibly tobacco (Kray, Church, and Yaeger 2017, 61). What is missing from the archaeological record at the three sites—cow bones, large quantities of canned foods, and flatware—also reveals a preference for traditional foods and foodways. In other words, the material record at the three sites reflects the choices made by individuals toward maintaining a common and persistent group identity.

Barnet Pavao-Zuckerman and Diana DiPaolo Loren (2012, 200) note in their study of foodways at a Spanish Colonial presidio on the isolated east Texas frontier that "the power of individuals to express social identity via material means was sometimes limited by the economic parameters of frontier life," and thus "multiethnic communities on colonial frontiers provide an important opportunity to examine the construction and expression of social identities and social difference in a setting in which individuals were both influenced by social hierarchies and limited in their ability to access the material trappings of preferred styles." The same can be said for the three San Pedro Maya villages included in this study, which were located on the frontier of two colonial spheres of influence. Their power (and often lack thereof) to control food production, the extraction of natural resources, and access to preferred goods through exchange moderated their ability to distinguish themselves as a social group through foodways.

The alcalde system, which the British tolerated for reasons mentioned in the subsection "San Pedro Siris," must have had a familiar feel to it for San Pedro Maya, since it had been in use in Mexico since shortly after Spanish conquest as part of the cabildo, or town council, system emplaced by Spanish colonial administrators but adapted by Maya to more closely align with their traditional form of government (Restall 1997, 51). Furthermore, while Asunción Ek served as the alcalde of San Pedro Siris, he was also the acknowledged ruler over the rest of the San Pedro settlements. While this arrangement did not have a formal status in the British colonial system, it may have resonated with Maya who, shortly before Spanish invasion, had a political office called Halach Uinic, a headman who ruled a province from a *hol cahob*, or head town (see Roys 1957; Marcus 1993). While only an alcalde, Ek behaved more like a preinvasion Halach Uinic must have, directing the affairs of smaller settlements from his head town of San Pedro Siris (see Restall 1997, 64).

The quantity and variety of imported goods and arms, Catholic religious icons, domestic animals, and acceptance of colonial political institutions into San Pedro Maya society each reflect how the nature and degree of Maya interactions with their colonial counterparts varied from village to village. These glimpses of late colonial Maya life at the edge of the British Empire illustrate how each village served as a microcosm of the larger San Pedro Maya society. At San Pedro Siris, the residents tolerated a greater colonial presence within the village, including the construction of a school, as a strategic negotiation to acquire firearms. We must consider this break in doxa within the context of the extant structures at the time. Pressured to defend themselves against the Icaiché, the villagers negotiated and forged a new identity through interactions with their colonial counterparts. At Holotunich, however, a greater sense of orthodoxy (in terms of foodways and construction techniques) on the margins of San Pedro society may reflect a desire to maintain group identity in opposition to relative isolation. Finally, Kaxil Uinic presents a microcosm of change at a later juncture in San Pedro Maya history, when the availability of arms decreased, the spread of disease increased, and the colony stripped Maya of their land rights. In more ways than one, we can conclude that the residents of Kaxil Uinic adapted to the requirements of the British colonial system—the need to participate in a cash-generating activity to pay for rents stands out—while at the same time ignoring many elements of colonial control. The villagers adapted to the breakdown of the doxa of milpa farming by forging an alternative economic strategy to retain some sense of autonomy. They added chicle to the list of products they already collected from the forest, they ignored international borders and communicated freely with Maya groups in Petén and Yucatán, and they embraced modern technologies to perpetuate traditional lifeways. In fact, one could argue that the success of San Pedro Maya at adapting to the colonial impositions without embracing European colonial worldviews—despite eighty years of contact with and influence from the colony's political, economic, and social structures—is what ultimately compelled BEC to forcibly move them from their villages and irrevocably alter their lifeways, beginning in 1931 with the closure of Kaxil Uinic. Although the decisions made by San Pedro Maya are evidence of their agency, one is left to consider why they made certain choices over others within the constraints of the colonial system.

Acknowledgments. The authors thank Dr. John Morris and the staff of the Institute of Archaeology, National Institute of Culture and History, in Belize, for issuing a permit to work at Kaxil Uinic village. Mr. Jeff Roberson and Mr. Alex Finkral kindly granted us permission to excavate on Yalbac Ranch. The staff and students on the Belize Estates Archaeological Survey Team were responsible for much of the hard work that made this chapter possible. We also would like to thank James Meierhoff for his helpful collaborations on this shared academic journey. Finally, we extend our deepest gratitude to the Alphawood Foundation for supporting the 2016 fieldwork at Kaxil Uinic village and our archival research in Jamaica and England.

Note

1. The Late Colonial period described here is based on Bolland's (2003) fourth phase of British-Maya interactions during the British occupation of Belize, which begins with the Battle of Orange Walk in 1872 and continues to the twentieth century.

References

Alexander, Rani T. 2004. *Yaxcabá and the Caste War of the Yucatan: An Archaeological Perspective.* Albuquerque: University of New Mexico Press.

Austin, John Gardiner. 1866. Letter to Home Office. December 23. CS 704/34. Jamaica Archives, Spanish Town.

Austin, John Gardiner. 1867a. Letter to Governor J. P. Pleasant. January 12. 1B5/56/32. Jamaica Archives, Spanish Town.

Austin, John Gardiner. 1867b. Letter to Pablo Encalada. March 4. 1B5/56/33. Jamaica Archives, Spanish Town.

Bolland, O. Nigel. 2003. *Colonialism and Resistance in Belize: Essays in Historical Sociology.* Kingston, Jamaica: University of the West Indies Press.

Bonorden, Alyssa Brooke. 2016. "Comparing Colonial Experiences in Northwestern Belize: Archaeological Evidence from Qualm Hill Camp and Kaxil Uinic Village." MA thesis, Texas Tech University.

Bonorden, Alyssa Brooke, and Brett A. Houk. 2019. "Kaxil Uinic: Archaeology at a San Pedro Maya Village in Belize." In *Archaeologies of the British Empire in Latin America*, edited by Charles Orser Jr., 13–35. Cham, Switzerland: Springer International Publishing.

Bonorden, Alyssa Brooke, and Gertrude Kilgore. 2015. "Results of the 2015 Excavations at Kaxil Uinic Village." In *The 2015 Season of the Chan Chich Archaeological Project*, edited by Brett A. Houk, 105–144. Papers of the Chan Chich Archaeological Project, Number 9. Lubbock: Texas Tech University.

Bonorden, Alyssa Brooke, and Gertrude Kilgore. 2016. "Results of the 2016 Excavations at Kaxil Uinic Village." In *The 2016 Season of the Chan Chich Archaeological Project*, edited by Brett A. Houk, 81–134. Papers of the Chan Chich Archaeological Project, Number 10. Lubbock: Texas Tech University.

Bricker, Victoria F. 1981. *The Indian Christ, the Indian King: The Historical Substrate of Maya Myth and Ritual*. Austin: University of Texas Press.

Cal, Angel Eduardo. 1991. "Rural Society and Economic Development: British Mercantile Capital in Nineteenth-Century Belize." PhD diss., University of Arizona, Tucson.

Camara, Felipe. 1866. Letter to Sir Peter Grant. October 13. 1B5/53/13. Jamaica Archives, Spanish Town.

Carmichael, John. 1867. Letter to Lieutenant Governor Austin. March 30. 1B5/56/33. Jamaica Archives, Spanish Town.

Church, Minette C., Jason Yaeger, and Jennifer L. Dornan. 2011. "The San Pedro Maya and the British Colonial Enterprise in British Honduras." In *Enduring Conquests: Rethinking the Archaeology of Resistance to Spanish Colonialism in the Americas*, edited by Matthew Liebmann and Melissa S. Murphy, 173–197. Santa Fe, NM: School for Advanced Research Press.

Church, Minette C., Jason Yaeger, and Christine A. Kray. 2019. "Re-centering the Narrative: British Colonial Memory and the San Pedro Maya." In *Archaeologies of the British Empire in Latin America*, edited by Charles Orser Jr., 73–97. Cham, Switzerland: Springer International Publishing.

Colonial Secretary. (1931) 1991. Letter to Alcalde, Xaxe Venic. March 5. Chicago: Field Museum Archives.

Cook, Hammond, and Ken E. Lee. 1936. Map of Belize Estate and Produce Company Lands in 1936. CO 123/355 2. Public Records Office, Kew, UK.

Cowgill, George L. 2000. "Rationality' and Contexts in Agency Theory." In *Agency in Archaeology*, edited by Marcia-Anne Dobres and John E. Robb, 51–60. New York: Routledge.

Dobres, Marcia-Anne, and John E. Robb. 2000. "Agency in Archaeology: Paradigm or Platitude?" In *Agency in Archaeology*, edited by Marcia-Anne Dobres and John E. Robb, 3–17. New York: Routledge.

Dornan, Jennifer L. 2004. "'Even by Night We Only Become Aware They Are Killing Us': Agency, Identity, and Intentionality at San Pedro Belize (1857–1930)." PhD diss., University of California, Los Angeles.

Dumond, Don E. 1977. "Independent Maya of the Late Nineteenth Century: Chiefdoms and Power Politics." In *Anthropology and History in Yucatan*, edited by Grant D. Jones, 103–138. Austin: University of Texas Press.

Dumond, Don E. 1997. *The Machete and the Cross*. Lincoln: University of Nebraska Press.

Gastrell, J.P.H. 1886. Letter to the Earl of Rosebery. August 18. CO 123/181. Public Records Office, Kew, UK.

Giddens, Anthony. 1984. *The Constitution of Society*. Berkeley: University of California Press.

Graham, Elizabeth, Scott E. Simmons, and Christine D. White. 2013. "The Spanish Conquest and the Maya Collapse: How 'Religious' Is Change?" *World Archaeology* 45 (1): 161–185.

Harley, Robert William.1867. Letter to the Colonial Administration. September 7. CS 704/34. Jamaica Archives, Spanish Town.

Harrison-Buck, Eleanor, Brett A. Houk, Adam R. Kaeding, and Brooke Bonorden. 2019. "The Strange Bedfellows of Northern Belize: British Colonialists, Confederate Dreamers, Creole Loggers, and the Caste War Maya Refugees of the Late Nineteenth Century." *International Journal of Historical Archaeology* 23 (1): 172–203.

Houk, Brett A. 2012. "Kaxil Uinic: A Report on Archival Investigations and Reconnaissance of the Historic Maya Village." In *The 2012 Season of the Chan Chich Archaeological Project*, edited by Brett A. Houk, 31–43. Papers of the Chan Chich Archaeological Project, Number 6. Lubbock: Texas Tech University.

Jaffe, Yitzchak, Qiaowei Wei, and Yichao Zhao. 2018. "Foodways and the Archaeology of Colonial Contact: Rethinking Western Zhou Expansion in Shandong." *American Anthropologist* 120 (1): 55–71.

Jones, Grant D. 1977. "Levels of Settlement Alliance among the San Pedro Maya of Western Belize and Eastern Petén, 1857–1936." In *Anthropology and History of the Yucatan*, edited by Grant D. Jones, 139–190. Austin: University of Texas Press.

Joyce, Rosemary A., and Jeanne Lopiparo. 2005. "PostScript: Doing Agency in Archaeology." *Journal of Archaeological Method and Theory* 12 (4): 365–374.

Kray, Christine A., Minette Church, and Jason Yaeger. 2017. "Designs on/of the Land: Competing Visions, Displacement, and Landscape Memory in British Colonial Honduras." In *Legacies of Space and Intangible Heritage: Archaeology, Ethnohistory, and the Politics of Cultural Continuity in the Americas*, edited by Fernando Armstrong-Fumero and Julio Hoil Gutierrez, 53–77. Boulder: University Press of Colorado.

Leventhal, Richard M., Jason Yaeger, and Minette C. Church. 2001. *San Pedro Maya Project: Preliminary Report of the 2000 Field Season*. Report submitted to the Belize Department of Archaeology, Belmopan.

Lewis, Karla. 2000. "Colonial Education: A History of Education in Belize." Paper presented at the Annual Meeting of the American Educational Research Association, New Orleans.

Marcus, Joyce. 1993. "Ancient Maya Political Organization." In *Lowland Maya Civilization in the Eighth Century A.D.*, edited by Jeremy A. Sabloff and John S. Henderson, 111–183. Washington, DC: Dumbarton Oaks.

Meierhoff, James. 2015. "Maya Refugees, Frontier Exchange and the Reoccupation of Tikal, Guatemala." Paper presented at the 114th American Anthropological Association Annual Meeting, Denver.

Meierhoff, James. 2017. "Consumer Culture at the Nineteenth-Century Maya Refugee Site at Tikal, Guatemala." Paper presented at the 82nd Annual Meeting of the Society for American Archaeology, Vancouver.

Miller, William. 1887. "Notes on a Part of the Western Frontier of British Honduras." *Proceedings of the Royal Geographic Society and Monthly Record of Geography, New Monthly Series* 9 (7): 420–423.

Minute Paper. 1866. Summary of Meeting Regarding Qualm Hill. August 3. 1B5/56/33. Jamaica Archives, Spanish Town.

Moholy-Nagy, Hattula. 2012. *Historical Archaeology at Tikal, Guatemala: Tikal Report No. 37.* Philadelphia: University of Pennsylvania Press.

Ng, Olivia. 2007. "View from the Periphery: A Hermeneutic Approach to the Archaeology of Holotunich (1865–1930), British Honduras." PhD diss., University of Pennsylvania, Philadelphia.

Ng, Olivia. 2010. "Holotunich: A Historic Period Settlement of Northwest Belize." *Mono y Conejo* 5: 3–8.

Oland, Maxine, and Joel W. Palka. 2016. "The Perduring Maya: New Archaeology on Early Colonial Transitions." *Antiquity* 90 (350): 472–486.

Pavao-Zuckerman, Barnet, and Diana DiPaolo Loren. 2012. "Presentation Is Everything: Foodways, Tablewares, and Colonial Identity at Presidio Los Adaes." *International Journal of Historical Archaeology* 16 (1): 199–226.

Reed, Nelson. 1964. *The Caste War of Yucatan.* Stanford, CA: Stanford University Press.

Relehan, Heather Emily. 2008. "Ad/ministering Education: Gender, Colonialism, and Christianity in Belize and Anglophone Caribbean." PhD diss., University of Maryland, College Park.

Restall, Matthew. 1997. *The Maya World: Yucatec Culture and Society, 1550–1850.* Stanford, CA: Stanford University Press.

Roys, Ralph L. 1957. *The Political Geography of the Yucatan Maya.* Washington, DC: Carnegie Institution of Washington.

Rugeley, Terry. 1996. *Yucatan's Maya Peasantry and the Origins of the Caste War.* Austin: University of Texas Press.

Silliman, Stephen. 2001. "Agency, Practical Politics and the Archaeology of Culture Contact." *Journal of Social Archaeology* 1 (2): 190–209.

Skibo, James M., and Michael Brian Schiffer. 2008. *People and Things: A Behavioral Approach to Material Culture.* New York: Springer.

Stein, Gil J. 2005. "Introduction: The Comparative Archaeology of Colonial Encounters." In *The Archaeology of Colonial Encounters,* edited by Gil J. Stein, 3–32. Santa Fe, NM: School of American Research Press.

Sullivan, Paul. 1989. *Unfinished Conversations: Mayas and Foreigners between Two Wars.* Berkeley: University of California Press.

Thompson, J. Eric S. 1963. *Maya Archaeologist.* Norman: University of Oklahoma Press.

Thornton, Erin Kennedy, and Olivia Ng Cackler. 2013. "Late-Nineteenth and Early-Twentieth Century Animal Use by San Pedro Maya and British Populations at

Holotunich, Belize." In *The Archaeology of Mesoamerican Animals*, edited by Christopher M. Götz and Kitty F. Emery, 351–380. Atlanta: Lockwood Press.

Wainwright, Joel. 2016. "The Colonization of the Maya of Southern Belize." *Research Reports in Belize History and Anthropology* 4: 1–14.

Yaeger, Jason, Minette C. Church, Jennifer Dornan, and Richard M. Leventhal. 2005. "Investigating Historic Households: The 2003 Season of the San Pedro Maya Project." *Research Reports in Belizean Archaeology* 2: 257–268.

Yaeger, Jason, Minette C. Church, Richard M. Leventhal, and Jennifer Dornan. 2004a. "Maya Caste War Immigrants in Colonial British Honduras: The San Pedro Maya Project, 2000–2003." *Research Reports in Belizean Archaeology* 1: 103–114.

Yaeger, Jason, Minette C. Church, Richard M. Leventhal, and Jennifer Dornan. 2004b. *San Pedro Maya Project: Preliminary Report of the 2003 Field Season*. Report submitted to the Belize Institute of Archaeology, Belmopan.

8

The Final Frontier

Nineteenth-Century Maya Refugees at Tikal, Guatemala

James Meierhoff

". . . those Indians hope that sometime the authorities will remember them"
— Salvador Valenzuela (1951 [1879], translated in Moholy-Nagy 2012, 47)

Refugees are the primary product of war. This outcome is as true today as it was in nineteenth-century Yucatán. As the furious intensity of the early years of the Caste War of Yucatán shifted into a decades-long standoff between Eastern Maya and Yucatecan-Mexican forces, many communities in the southern zone sought a way out of the violence. Those who remained aligned with the rebel forces known as Santa Cruz Maya viewed the peaceful stance of those seeking refuge as a capitulation with the enemy. Santa Cruz Maya aggressively attacked the region, it became destabilized, and much of the population fled further south into the perceived safety of the vast Petén jungles of Guatemala, or the relative safety of the sparsely occupied forests of British Honduras (now Belize; see Reed 1964; Antochiw 1997; Dumond 1997). This chapter focuses on one such group of refugees who left what would soon be solidified as Mexico during the tumultuous years of the Caste War and

https://doi.org/10.5876/9781646422845.c008

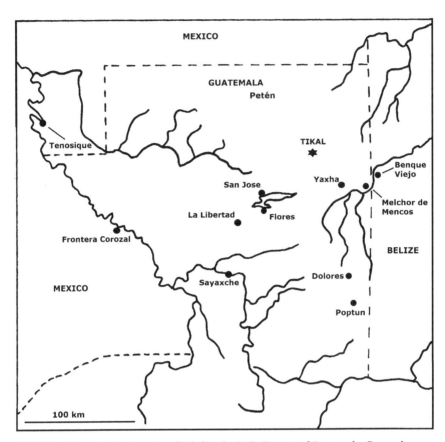

FIGURE 8.1. *Map showing location of Tikal in the Petén District of Guatemala. Drawn by James Meierhoff from Moholy-Nagy (2012, 64). Specifically, I discuss the recent archaeological investigation of the historic refugee village at Tikal and its extensive imported artifact assemblage. In addition, I consider insights from interviews with individuals living near other abandoned refugee villages in the Petén. In this context, I also investigate the materiality of the refugee experience, illuminating aspects of the social construction, and cohesion, of refugee communities in the past. The patterns of consumption of mass-produced consumer goods suggest that different consumer choices were made at Tikal than were made in the eastern Yucatec refugee villages of British Honduras, and may reflect refugee behaviors that are recognized in the modern era.*

established a small, successful (but short-lived), multiethnic community at the ancient ruins of Tikal, Guatemala (figure 8.1).

The investigation of the nineteenth-century refugee village at Tikal is ultimately an archaeology of the refugee experience. However, archaeology's inclusion in the modern field of refugee and forced migration studies is rather new, and its potential role and impact are currently unknown. These unknowns are especially true of what the study of refugee movements from the deeper past might tell us. A major aspect of this problem is that despite historical documentation and research to the contrary, many policy makers believe the refugee is a "particularly modern," post–World War II phenomenon (Elie 2014, 26). However, the archaeologies of past and present refugee experiences and their materialities "are currently in the making, and their constitution will be a collective endeavor" of techniques, applications, and comparative analyses (Hamilakis 2016, 134).

Until recently, there has been a dearth of archaeological perspectives on refugee studies, despite (1) the time depth often associated with refugee movements, (2) the "radical" adaptations to new conditions of materiality, and (3) the social and behavioral change associated with displacement (Harrell-Bond and Voutira 1992; Malkki 1995). These are, in fact, archaeology's specialties. An archaeological perspective on the often-obscured daily lives of refugees and forced migrants is also poised to "understand how these new engagements with spaces and landscapes relate to the long-term human interaction with these features, how perennial paths and routes are shared, and how and whether new knowledges rely on the existing reservoir of human movement through space" (Hamilakis 2016, 128). The historic village at Tikal is rare in that we have documentary evidence contextualizing the material remains of this frontier community as being directly associated with the refugee experience. With this information, we can start to establish what refugee sites look like in the archaeological record. Likewise, the inclusion of an archaeological voice in refugee studies places the outcome of refugee movements in a deep historical context, by exploring how and why refugee groups have adapted, and affected, their new host environments, both socially and materially.

Tikal's historic archaeological assemblage is strikingly similar to nineteenth-century refugee sites excavated in Belize, as well as Lacandon Maya settlements excavated in the western Petén (see Yaeger et al. 2002; Palka 2005). When exactly refugees founded the village at Tikal remains uncertain—as is its direct association, if any, to the Yucatec-speaking refugee village clusters to the east. When Modesto Méndez and Ambrosio Tut officially "discovered" Tikal in 1848, the ruins were completely deserted. Surprisingly, several sources of documentary evidence, such as census records and firsthand accounts, discuss the presence of the village from the years 1875–1879, and the plethora and diversity of nineteenth-century material culture at the site suggest it was founded sometime earlier. However, by the time of Alfred Maudslay's exploration of Tikal in 1881, the ruins had become "absolutely desolate, the nearest Indian village being San Andrés and some other small hamlets on the borders of the lake [Petén Itzá]" (1889–1902, 44). Almost all references to the village in the documentary record mention it being a haven for Yucatec-speaking refugees from Yucatán (see

Morley 1938). Unlike many of the eastern refugee villages in Belize, families of Lacandon Maya and heavily Hispanicized Itza Maya (Ladinos) from Lake Petén Itzá also reportedly inhabited the small village at Tikal (Moholy-Nagy 2012, 4).

How globally produced consumer goods were distributed and consumed by different societies in and around the frontier zone of the nineteenth-century Petén elucidates patterns of economic choice and changing ethnic identities. Even with its apparent remoteness from urban centers, the historic village at Tikal was well provisioned in foreign consumer goods produced in both British and American markets. The presence of metal, glass, and an abundance of refined earthenware pottery, in middens as well as household contexts, demonstrates that this village was participating in local, national, and international economies. The community at Tikal operated on the edge of a frontier shared by three different state societies: Mexico (though Mexico and Yucatán did not officially consolidate until the middle of the Caste War), Guatemala, and British Honduras. These three states viewed and conceptualized this Indigenous zone differently, and the refugees used the frontier to exploit these differences.

By the nineteenth century, the Petén had already been serving as a Maya refuge zone for centuries. Grant Jones (1977) called this native zone the "Last Maya Frontier," the product of Spain's inability to subdue, conquer, and most importantly settle the jungles of Petén and western Belize. This formed a 200-mile frontier that permitted escape from (and resistance to) Spanish institutions and allowed Indigenous life to continue outside of colonial frameworks for some 300 years. Spain would attempt a final domination of this Native zone in 1697, when Martín de Ursúa y Arizmendi conquered the Itza Maya kingdom at Tayasal, deep within the frontier in what is today Flores, Guatemala (see G. Jones 1998). However, Hispanic interest was still not keen on settling the remote jungle, leaving the bulk of the vast Petén jungles to remain a native sphere of interaction (albeit sparsely populated). After the wars of Independence from Spain in the 1820s, the new nations of Mexico, Guatemala, and the British settlement at Belize administratively divided the Last Maya Frontier among themselves. Thus, in the nineteenth century, the vast Petén jungle became these fledgling states' distinct periphery zones, intensifying interest in this area on the part of non-Indigenous people. Still, the greater Petén remained an Indigenous space in practice.

British Honduras and Petén during the Caste War

As the Caste War slowed, villages in southern Yucatán pursued their own agendas for peace, seeking solutions to the conflict that would grant them cessation to the violence along with relative autonomy. In 1851, community leaders at the Yucatec village of Chichanhá entertained a strange envoy from Guatemala. Traveling on foot through the Petén from Flores, Guatemala, and with only the priest Juan de la Cruz Hoil as a traveling companion, the *corregidor* (governor or magistrate) of Guatemala's Petén district, Modesto Méndez, traveled to Chichanhá to mediate a peace treaty on Mexico's behalf (Antochiw 1997; Dumond 1997). Méndez is best known as one of the codiscoverers of Tikal in 1848 (a tantalizing coincidence considering the events that follow). The people of Chichanhá received Méndez's trek through the Petén, with no pomp or comfort of his high office, as an act of contrition, and they solemnly heeded his plea for peace. Soon they signed a treaty that granted the southern villages semiautonomy. When ratified by Mexican authorities, this treaty would give the southern villages the name Los Pacíficos del Sur, the Peaceful Southerners. Peace, however, would not come to the region.

Furious at the notion of peace with Mexico, military leaders at Chan Santa Cruz rejected the south's new-found semi-autonomy and began a vicious campaign to bring the southern region back into the fold of the rebellion (Dumond 1997; Rugeley 2009). Over the next decade, key southern villages would change hands several times, and smaller villages consolidated for protection or fled outright from the Santa Cruz onslaught. In 1857, Santa Cruz insurrectionists utterly destroyed Chichanhá itself. Survivors who did not flee into the Petén or British-held territory in the south responded by founding the village of Icaiché in a more defensible location.

While refugees were trickling south since the onset of the Caste War in 1847, the campaigns initiated by Santa Cruz Mayas against their Pacíficos counterparts in southern Yucatán after 1851 caused mass migrations. In the 1850s, British Honduras was still a coastally focused settlement, whose 10,000-person population comprised primarily enslaved Africans (and their descendants) ruled by a very small white minority. By 1861, the population had soared to over 25,000, just over half of whom British colonial authorities labeled as Spanish, "Indian," or some form of "mixed" race (Yaeger et al. 2002). The largest and best-documented migration occurred after the destruction of Chichanhá, when Asunción Ek led half of the Yucatec-speaking inhabitants of the village over the Hondo River to settle along the eastern edge of the Maya Frontier, straddling the relatively unoccupied Belizean-Petén border zone. Led by Ek, these refugees resettled around the village of San Pedro Siris in west central Belize, becoming known thereafter as San Pedro Maya (G. Jones 1977; Church, Yaeger, and Dornan 2010; Houk, Bonorden, and Kilgore, chapter 7 in this volume; figures 8.2 and 8.3).

Unlike Mexico and Guatemala, the British in mid-nineteenth-century British Honduras saw value in their periphery. The occupation of their western frontier by San Pedro Maya coincided with the shift and intensification of British resource extraction from logwood to mahogany. Logwood, used to make dye, was harvested along the swampy river inlets and marshes close to the shore and did not require extensive capital investment (see García Lara and Olán, chapter 4 in this volume). Mahogany, on the other hand, grew deep inland and

FIGURE 8.2. *Overview of area occupied by San Pedro Maya refugee settlements. Adapted by author from G. Jones (1977, 142).*

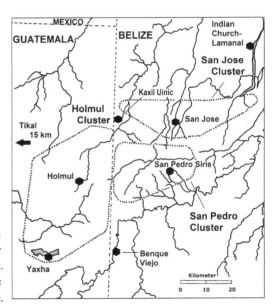

FIGURE 8.3. *San Pedro Maya settlements and approximate locations mentioned in the text. Drawn by author from G. Jones (1977, 142).*

required large "gangs" of woodcutters to cut and transport the massive trees to the coast for shipment to England. The English largely used enslaved, and later indentured, African and Afro-descendant labor for this task rather than the Indigenous populations who, because of their intimate knowledge of the frontier zone in which the British logging industries operated, the British viewed as far less controllable (see Cal 1991). Maya individuals and entire work gangs often disappeared into the frontier when work conditions became too dangerous or uncomfortable, or sometimes after cash advances were handed out. The presence of San Pedro Maya in British Honduras' resource frontier ran counter to the national myth of an unpopulated landscape, rich in timber resources for the British to exploit. This myth would persist well into the twentieth century, easing some of the stigma of colonization and dispossession for the colony. In 1867, British forces burned the San Pedro villages in an attempt to actualize a cleared frontier (Church, Yaeger, and Dornan 2010).

While a large cluster of San Pedro Maya settlements existed over the border in Guatemala, called the Holmul cluster, far less is known about them or the countless other refugee settlements established in the Petén at this time (G. Jones 1977) than is known about those on British Honduras' side. The Austrian explorer Teobert Maler offhandedly mentions different types of refugee habitation sites in nineteenth-century Petén: from ostensibly illicit villages such as the one established at Tikal, to authorized refugee "camps," such as the habitation site located on Laguna Santa Cruz near the village of Chuntuki off the old Camino Real (1911, 34). How these two types of habitation sites were distinguished from one another was not made clear. Even by the late nineteenth century, colonial officials knew little about the Petén—the northernmost third of Guatemala. They knew so little that the president of Guatemala sent an emissary in 1879 to report on the basic geographic, demographic, and economic conditions of the region. The president sent Salvador Valenzuela, the minister of agriculture, on this official assignment.

As part of his exploratory mission Valenzuela traveled along the remnants of the old Camino Real and visited more than a dozen independent refugee villages in northern Petén in 1879. These villages were established without any backing or protection from Guatemala and were inhabited by "restless and war-ridden Indians," who were accustomed to living autonomously in the frontier. According to Valenzuela's report, they "cultivate maize, beans, *yame*, some greens, and tobacco, which are profitably sold in Yucatan and to travelers passing through these communities. They like to raise hogs and domestic fowl, which are abundant, as well as livestock, which is scarce in these places. They maintain some commerce with Belize, where they procure clothing, arms, gunpowder, and hard liquor" (translated in Moholy-Nagy 2012, 47). As I draw out in the opening of this chapter, Valenzuela surmised that "probably those Indians hope that sometime the authorities will remember them" and that approaching these villages with "kindness and common sense, would result in a quick, if not rapid organization" into official Guatemalan political, social, and economic spheres (quoted in Moholy-Nagy 2012, 47). It was on this excursion that Valenzuela reported to the president about the ruins of Tikal—the last-known published visit to the refugee village at the site.

There are indications that Corregidor Méndez, who brokered the Chichanhá treaty in 1851, welcomed this influx of population growth to the district twenty-five years before Valenzuela's writing. If Méndez did so enthusiastically, or if his response was more calculated, is hard to say. What is clear is that refugees poured over the border with or without his blessing, and there was little he could do about it. This wave of refugees represented the first major positive shift in population in the Petén for over a century, and Méndez likely saw it as an opportunity to strengthen the economic potential of his vast territory. As such, the corregidor offered opportunities for these illicit settlements to become incorporated into Guatemalan society, provided they construct a church, a cabildo (council meeting house), and a jail (Rugeley 1997). Some villages complied, including Tikal, which became an *aldea* (subordinate village) to the town of San Jose on Lake Petén Itzá, despite potentially having only two of the three qualifying structures (see the following section "Tikal Village"; Moholy-Nagy 2012, 4). Others remained aloof and attempted de facto autonomy deep in the bush. Some of those who did not comply were located by Guatemalan officials and destroyed. Maler (1911, 34) laments the destruction of the refugee "camp" at Chuntuki by a General Salas but does not state why the camp was razed. According to the explorer John Carmichael, the village of Tulunche, presumably in southeastern Petén, "having in later years proved to be a haunt of smugglers, had been destroyed by order of the Government of Guatemala, and the roads to it closed up" sometime before 1890 (as quoted in Gann 1927, 211).

Tikal Village

The historic village at Tikal was founded sometime after the ruin's discovery by Modesto Méndez and Ambrosio Tut in 1848 and was abandoned by the time of Alfred Maudslay's first archaeological exploration of Tikal in 1881. This makes the longest span of occupation of the village at most thirty-three years. While the plethora of archaeological remains at the site suggests the village may have been occupied for several decades, the documentary records only provide evidence for five years spanning 1875–1879. The earliest-known mention of a village at Tikal comes in 1875 by the English travel writer John Boddam-Whatham (1877), when he received a letter in Flores from Tikal's *alcalde* (mayor). Next, Gustave Bernoulli briefly mentions the village in a letter to Teobert Maler in 1877, where he describes his removal of many of Tikal's ancient wooden lintels (cited in Moholy-Nagy 2012, 2). Amazingly, the ethnographer Ruben Reina discovered census records for the small village in the archives of San Jose, Guatemala, in the 1960s (Moholy-Nagy 2012, 4). The census covers the years 1876–1878, and a final year of demographic documentation was provided by Salvador Valenzuela in 1879. While the village's population was enumerated differently each year, these documents state that over the four years recorded, families of Lacandon Maya as well as several families of Ladinos (individuals of non-Indigenous culture, in this case likely heavily Hispanicized Itza Maya) from San Jose lived among the Yucateco refugees. The Tikal village reached an apex of fifteen households in 1878. The following year Valenzuela reported the village had only ten families of Yucatecos and Lacandones. By 1881 the village was gone.

Although he recorded a population decline from fifteen to ten families between 1878 to 1879, Valenzuela's report made no mention of any problems or intentions to abandon the village (see Moholy-Nagy 2012, 53–55). Many of the explorers and archaeologists who visited Tikal after 1881 mention the village in past tense and often relate the tale of plagues of bats or vermin, or outbreaks in fevers or other maladies as the cause of the village's demise (see Maudslay 1889–1902; Maler 1911; Gann 1927; Reina as quoted in Moholy-Nagy 2012). A passing comment in the early twentieth century from Professor Walter Wolfe of Brigham Young University states that Guatemalan soldiers came to Tikal "against the Indians" in 1879—though there is little evidence to corroborate this claim (as quoted in Moholy-Nagy 2012, 37). Perhaps the most compelling reason for the abandonment of Tikal was the lack of water at the site. Méndez trucked in water during his explorations in 1848 when little was found at the site, and since then nearly every published account of visits to Tikal mentioned the serious water conditions at the site. Conditions seemed to worsen and were so bad in the 1920s that Eric Thompson's (1963, 200) exploration of Tikal had to be cut short, and Thomas Gann procured his expedition's water needs from the *aguada* (water hole) in Uaxactun, some twelve miles further north (Gann 1927, 217).

Likewise, Maler (1911) mentions that the inhabitants became irked by the distance to markets where they could acquire the foreign consumer items that they apparently had become accustomed to. In 2016, archaeologist Sergio Garzona and I conducted interviews among the inhabitants living near the site of the abandoned Caste War refugee village of Yaxjá, on the Yaxha-Sacnab lake system in eastern Petén. While they mentioned attacks of malaria and chiclero disease (leishmaniasis) as annoyances, the prime motivator for the abandonment of Yaxjá was to be closer to the markets in Flores and Melchor de Mencos along the Belizean border. The vast and diverse quantities of globally produced consumer goods found archaeologically at Tikal suggests the market motivation may have been a major factor in Tikal's eventual abandonment.

In summer 2014, I directed the Proyecto Arqueológico Tikal Histórico (PATH), which investigated the nineteenth-century occupation of Tikal. My project added to a body of historic archaeological research at Tikal that Hattula Moholy-Nagy began as part of the Tikal Project in the 1960s. This research was continued by Joel Palka in the 1990s, who led the Lacandon Archaeology Project (LAP) seeking the material remains and confirmation of the historical record of Lacandon habitation at Tikal (see Palka 2005). Understandably, the village was located near the Tikal Aguada, which, with all its faults, was the only year-round water source at Tikal. The bulk of the extant village is located several hundred meters southwest of the aguada, in an area dubbed La Palmera by Palka, due to the presence of exotic palm plants, planted by the inhabitants, still growing at Tikal today (Palka 2005; figure 8.4). The village location is well preserved, and to date a minimum of eight households have been identified at La Palmera (figure 8.5). In 1960 a scatter of historic artifacts approximately 1.5 kilometers north of the La Palmera cluster was discovered by the team mapping the ancient site (Moholy-Nagy 2012, 8). In 2014 the corresponding hearth of this location was discovered, making a total of nine known households at historic Tikal. This northernmost household may represent a milpa (cornfield) house. According to Maler, additional milpas were located between the Great Temples in the Great Plaza (Maler 1911).

We could identify individual households by locating their dis-

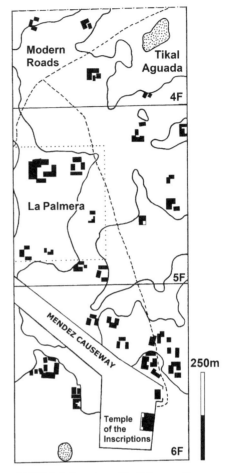

FIGURE 8.4. *Location of La Palmera village cluster at Tikal, in grid square 5F on the Robert Carr and James Hazard map of Tikal (1961). Drawn by author from Palka (2005, 152).*

tinctive three-stone hearths, still visible on the modern surface. These hearths have deep antiquity among the Maya (see O'Connor and Anderson 2016) and are seen at other contemporary Caste War villages such as Kaxil Uinic (Bonorden and Houk 2018, 21). Only one structure at Tikal was constructed with a basal course of stones, thus making its floor plan visible to archaeologists. This relatively large structure, approximately 9.25 by 4.75 meters, may have held the community's church and cabildo, which were required for incorporation into a Guatemalan municipality as decreed by Modesto Méndez (see section "British Honduras and Petén during the Caste War"). It may have also housed a

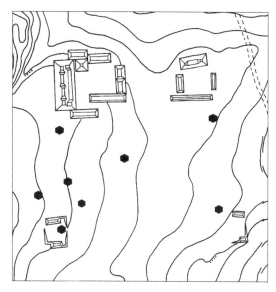

FIGURE 8.5. *Detail of La Palmera, Tikal, with locations of historic households. Note a ninth historic household was located 1.5 km north, and only one household disturbs any ancient architecture, and may have acted as the village church and cabildo. Modified by author from Meierhoff (2018, 169).*

prominent village inhabitant (see Moholy-Nagy 2012, 78). A bronze bell found by workmen in 1950 while constructing the Tikal airstrip likely came from this structure (78). This structure was both the only one to contain a basal course of masonry and the only historic construction to have a (partial) plaster floor and to be located on an ancient mound, thus highlighting its importance to the community. The floor plan of this structure was roughly rectangular, but it does appear that it had curved corners (see Moholy-Nagy 2012, fig. 15). This style of wall design, called "flattened ends," was noted by Robert Wauchope (1938, 18) as being the process of building a rectangular house around the roof framework of an apsidal (rounded ends) house. Neither the apsidal nor flattened ends house was observed in Guatemala during Wauchope's study, and this design may be an amalgamation of Guatemalan and Yucateco labor and engineering.

During our investigations, the Tikal Project, LAP, and PATH identified archaeological evidence associated with the cultural practices of all three documented ethnic groups at Tikal: from Yucatec-style ceramics (likely made in Yucatán), Ladino-style two-room house structures, and highly distinctive Lacandon god pot fragments (see Meierhoff 2018). However, no ethnic markers were exclusive to any one household. Material culture, and likely the people themselves at Tikal, were intermixing as distinctions between ethnic identities were easing within the Last Maya Frontier.

Archaeological information was collected both from within these houses and in historic middens, elucidating the nature of trade, exchange, and consumerism in this frontier setting. Foreign artifacts of glass, metal, imported refined earthenware ("whiteware") ceramics, and Petén-made clay ceramics clearly demonstrate the interconnectedness of this village to outside markets and their corresponding societies. These items were augmented by locally produced or acquired material such as animal products and lithic objects. The lithic component to the village was largely in the form of expedient flakes and simple crude tools (metal trade items likely performed better and were ostensibly easily acquired). All food remains found at La Palmera are obtainable in the surrounding environment, including large turtles, peccary, and brocket deer (Caleb Kestle 2015, personal communication).

The most prominent artifact type at the Tikal village (66 percent by count, similar by weight) was a local ceramic ware, of which just under 2,000 sherds were identified and cataloged. These ceramics were not slipped and contained a crushed calcite temper. Of note, several whole shells are visible in the paste, helping to identify the raw material to the shores of Lake Petén Itzá, twenty-five miles to the south. This clay source with its snail inclusions is similar to the Paxcamán ceramics associated with the much older inhabitants of the area around Lake Petén Itzá.

In the 1970s, Reina and Robert Hill studied the only center of ceramic manufacture known to them in the Petén. This location was none other than San Jose, the same town that incorporated and conducted the census of the Tikal village 100 years earlier. Around this time Reina purchased several vessels from San Jose that are today part of the ceramic type collection in the laboratories at Tikal. The material collected by Reina was very similar, if not an exact match, for many of the whole ceramic vessels (and their pastes) located on the surface during the initial survey of Tikal (see Reina and Hill 1978; Moholy-Nagy 2012). Excavations by Moholy-Nagy in the 1960s, Palka in the 1990s, and myself in 2014 found an abundance of this material as sherds in archaeological contexts. The most common forms were large water ollas, large-mouth cooking vessels, small pitchers, and small rounded bowls.

In addition to the locally made ceramics, excavations by the LAP and PATH recovered over 100 sherds ($N = 118$) of whiteware ceramics from the La Palmera cluster in 1990 and 2014 respectfully. There are no maker's marks visible on any of the whiteware ceramics found in the assemblage at Tikal, but they all highly resemble pottery that was mass-produced in Great Britain during the early and late nineteenth century; the proximity to Belize as the probable point of trade origin is hard to ignore. A wide variety of designs are present from the La Palmera assemblage, including annual dipped (25.5 percent), painted (18.5 percent), sponged (2 percent), cut sponge (33 percent), salt glazed (7 percent) and transfer wares (14 percent).[1] Tikal's imported ceramic assemblage closely resembles those found in Belizean logging and sugar camps, such as at Lamanai (Mayfield 2015), as well as surface deposits at northern Belizean Caste War–era villages such as those near Aventura (M. Jones 2015) and in the main plaza of the ancient site of Cerros. The ceramic assemblage from Tikal is also strikingly similar to the Caste War refugee village of San Pedro Siris (Yaeger et al. 2002) as well as Lacandon villages farther west in Guatemala (Palka 2005).

The minimum number of vessels (MNV) was calculated for the whitewares based on decoration and style (see Brooks 2015, 34). Thirteen sherds were void of decoration and are excluded from this calculation. The remaining sherds ($N = 105$) form a MNV of forty-three. To date, only small portions of any one vessel are represented in the excavated sample; in fact, 56 percent of the MNV are represented by a single sherd. While there are dozens of complete (or restorable) vessels of local manufacture from the Tikal village (Moholy-Nagy 2012), no complete vessels of foreign whiteware have been observed or recovered archaeologically at Tikal, despite the high number of vessels represented from archaeological excavations. This absence suggests that villagers may have taken whole vessels of imported make with them when they abandoned Tikal. Likewise, the vast quantities of European sherds discarded and strewn about the Tikal village demonstrate the readily available nature of these ceramics.

While there is little comparative data, the high MNV of imported ceramics at the Tikal village was surprising. The distribution per household of nonlocal ceramics was even higher when considering these vessels were recovered from house floors and midden contexts in only five of the eight households in La Palmera (the ninth historic household 1.5 kilometers north of the aguada likewise did not contain any imported refined ceramics). It is interesting to note that the unique household with basal masonry, partial plaster flooring, and the only structure that disturbs ancient architecture contained none of these refined ceramics, while a nearby household contained a whopping twenty-two of the forty-three vessels (51 percent). Access to globally mass-produced consumer goods deep within the frontier does not seem to have been completely restricted, however. The other La Palmera households that contained no refined earthenware were provisioned with other consumer materials, including glass and metal implements such as knives, cooking pots, and jewelry items that were found in the households' middens and house floors. There seems to be elements of consumer choice happening on household levels at La Palmera, perhaps only limited by the household's desire to obtain such items.

The colony of British Honduras, and by extension England's trade networks, was likely the source of much of this material. With other imperial settlements surrounding the colony only a few days' walk east through the jungle, several studies have shown the colony's success at expanding its commercialism (see G. Jones 1977; Cal 1991). Related to the imported ceramics found at Tikal are eight fragments of white clay pipes. We recovered both bowl and stem fragments, and three maker's marks (one McDougal and two E. Roach) clearly demarcating the point of origin as the British Isles, Glasgow, and London, respectively. These pipes have production ranges of 1848–1891 and 1859–1899. They are found throughout the historic sites of British Honduras: the infamous Qualm Hill Lumber camp (Bonorden and Smith 2015), the San Pedro Maya village site (and later British lumber camp) Holotunich (Ng 2007), and the colony's original capital on St. George's Caye (Elverson 2014). While maker's marks were preserved on only two other artifacts, many of the consumer goods are extremely similar to known name brands found in nineteenth-century archaeological deposits in Belize, including Kaxil Uinic, and San Pedro Siris (see Houk, Bonorden, and Kilgore [chapter 7]; Gust, chapter 9 in this volume). We also found many fragments of what appear to be Cannon Industries metal clothes irons, small cauldrons and "chicle" pots from Staffordshire, and Martindale *"lagarto"* machetes made in Birmingham (see Moholy-Nagy 2012, 19–20). Staffordshire transferware ceramics by Thomas Bevington, and J. F. Wileman at the Foley Works may also be present based upon identification of distinct "Neva" and "Rhine" transfer patterns (see Meierhoff 2018). Glass bottles from New York were also recovered at Tikal, though these too were most likely introduced to the region via the port at Belize City. The bottles once contained "Agua de la Reina" and "Barry's Tricopherous." Also prolific at the site were fragments of what resemble Collins machetes and distinct Collins axe heads, manufactured in Connecticut.

Trade was especially vigorous during the Caste War, when British settlers were supplying Santa Cruz insurrectionists with guns and gunpowder, much to Mexico's chagrin (see Reed [1964] 2001; Dumond 1997). However, detailed information on small portable objects such as ceramics is lacking. Angel Cal (1991, 94) suggested that the *cabeceras* (major villages) of Belize were sources of a "full array of imported merchandise." Jason Yaeger et al. (2004) have also suggested this, hypothesizing that the San Pedro Maya may have acted as a trading hub of globally produced goods for other San Pedro and Lacandon Maya communities further to the west and into Guatemala. The exact match of several artifacts between Tikal and San Pedro—including metal goods such as clothes irons, pots, cauldrons, religious pendants, glass bottles, and even the firearms discovered in Tikal's middens—strengthens this possibility. However, the imported ceramic assemblages illustrate the major difference between the material culture at the two sites: while both assemblages contained similar decoration styles and patterns, the vessel forms obtained at these two locations were distinct.

Yaeger et al. (2004) concluded that the majority of vessels at San Pedro Siris conform to Yucatec-style foodways, and imported wares that were conducive to serving Yucatec-style cuisine replaced traditional Maya ceramics. At San Pedro Siris, 66 percent of their imported ceramics (by count) represented large bowls, tureens, and deep plates typical of Yucatec foodways, while only 3 percent of their assemblage comprised plates and flat serving ware. Likewise, despite San

Pedro Siris being amid an English diaspora, no teapots or teacups were present there. At Tikal, where three different ethnicities (and correspondent food ways) coexisted, cups and perhaps very small bowls were in fact the bulk of the assemblage, making up some 53 percent of the MNV count; plates were 20 percent of the total. In addition, we recovered the remains of at least one, possibly two, teapots. Thus, imported wares complemented, rather than duplicated, the locally made ceramic material at Tikal. It is possible that San Pedro Maya were pushing unwanted wares west to tertiary markets in Guatemala. However, the plethora of consumer goods flooding Central American markets at this time suggests that even for remote villages such as Tikal, consumer choice may have been a major factor to the assemblages we find today.

Refugees

Even though some nineteenth-century sources describe Yucatecos at Tikal as refugees, anthropologists should be careful when comparing or judging the past by present conditions or concepts. The definition of who constitutes a refugee today is a post–World War II convention that is highly politicized and has critical legal ramifications for millions of people around the world. Succinctly, the United Nations High Commissioner for Refugees (UNHCR) defines refugees as those persons forced to flee their country because of violence or persecution (Article 1A[2] of the 1951 "Refugee Convention"; UNHCR 2010). The emphasis on fleeing one's *country* can, when applied historically, bias researchers' conception of who counts as a refugee, resulting in the exclusion of Indigenous peoples fleeing zones such as the Last Maya Frontier during the nineteenth century from the narrative (see Church, Yaeger, and Kray 2018). However, displaced Yucatec Maya in the nineteenth century knew they were moving out of one political zone into another. When they fled the sustained violence of the Caste War and crossed over the border into neighboring Petén, Guatemala, they acted in such a way as to fulfill the modern definition of a refugee.

Surviving documents between Santa Cruz Maya leaders and Guatemalan officials clearly demonstrate an understanding of the international border separating the two countries (Rugeley 2001, 57–58). Likewise, when Modesto Méndez mediated the peace treaty at Chichanhá, which would later establish the Pacífico Maya faction, people recognized that he had arrived from a different political entity (Antochiw 1997). Soon after fleeing Mexico, the breakaway population of San Pedro Maya approached the British government in Belize City, made their presence known, and requested and received (albeit temporarily) inclusion in local authority (Church, Yaeger, and Dornan 2010). Pacíficos, of which the San Pedro were a splinter group, present a slightly more difficult case because in establishing their refuges they often did not acknowledge or respect the Anglo settlement's borders, charged rents for land usage, and in many ways ruled de facto in the southern frontier. This disregard for internationally recognized borders makes their status as "refugees" under modern definition more difficult to establish.

There is a present and pressing need to identify where and how archaeology contributes to refugee and forced migration studies. There seems to be a consensus that there can be no "justification for conducting research into situations of extreme human suffering if one does not have the alleviation of suffering as an explicit objective of one's research" (Turton 1996, 96, as quoted in Fiddian-Qasmiyeh et al. 2014, 3). This "dual-imperative" (Jacobsen and Landau 2003)—the need to simultaneously advance academic knowledge while performing ethical action—is difficult to establish explicitly in some historical (and archaeological) research, especially when the events, movements, peoples, and experiences of refugees themselves occurred in the relatively deep past. However, the examination of the experiences and outcomes of past refugee movements may elucidate patterns associated with this behavior type, linking past situations with modern, ongoing refugee crises around the world.

There is an interesting parallel between the two refugee communities discussed in the preceding section (if we accept them as such), and modern refugee camps, such as those studied in Tanzania by Liisa Malkki. Malkki (1990) documented refugees who settled in distinct camps, showing that they often have the ability to maintain, and strive to retain, their ethnic identities in both material and social ways. On the other hand, those refugees who settle in cities, or are otherwise dispersed within and among a new dominate culture, are often less pressured or inclined to do the same (Malkki 1990). The refugee villages of the nineteenth-century Petén follow this pattern. The inhabitants of San Pedro Siris were strictly Yucatec Maya. Their material culture seems to point to a reluctance to enter into the cultural pathways of the new land they settled in (e.g., the English tea ceremony), and newly incorporated material culture forms mimic or replace traditional cultural patterns (Yaeger et al. 2004). In fact, the reluctance to adopt many English cultural and economic patterns contributed in a major way to the British burning San Pedro villages in 1867 (G. Jones 1977; Dumond 1997; Church, Yaeger, and Dornan 2010). Meanwhile, at the Tikal village, a different scenario seemed to be occurring. There were three distinct ethnicities cohabitating, presenting a different assemblage of material culture. As discussed, teacups are prevalent, and the foreign trade goods present show that they complement locally made materials. While ethnically marked materials are present at Tikal, they are dispersed and share contexts with materials bearing other ethnic markers. Thus, the households, and perhaps the houses themselves, at the historic village at Tikal suggest a blending of the three ethnic groups in this place.

Multiethnic frontier societies have been documented in other parts of the world as being crucibles of ethnogenesis, the process through which new ethnic identities form (see White 1991 and Hill 1996; part I, this volume). The combined lifeways and traditions become collectively shared experiences and often forge with new forms of materiality. The archaeological evidence at the short-lived Tikal village is a snapshot of ethnogenesis in progress at the household level, where the materiality of daily life on the frontier demonstrates the blending of cultural identities and the acceptance, and later reliance, on new shared material culture that complements traditional practice. Group identity becomes the new shared experiences, which manifests archaeologically in the late nineteenth-century Petén in what a group consumes, rather than what it produces. The inhabitants of Tikal left no known records, and there are no records of where they settled after they left the Last Maya Frontier. It is likely that they merged into the state societies around the frontier, their descendants today identifying as Guatemalans or Belizeans.

The pattern of procuring consumer products identified at Tikal likely reflects the ability of its nineteenth-century inhabitants to exploit the various markets and societies that surround the Petén frontier. This process includes economic relationships with formal municipalities in Guatemala, such as San Jose, where the bulk of the village's ceramic assemblage derives from, to informal interactions with smaller groups in the frontier zones, such as logging gangs and sugar plantations. Here Tikal's residents may have bartered forest products such as tobacco and agricultural produce for the cheaply made British consumer goods such as ceramics and metal wares. As mentioned in the section "Tikal Village," Maler (1911) even went as far to suggest that the refugees' desire to be closer to markets and European goods was the primary reason for the settlement's abandonment. This was also the primary reason given to me for the abandonment of the Caste War–era village of Yaxjá by individuals who live on Lake Yaxha today.

What seems clear is that in the late nineteenth century, the relative remoteness of the Tikal village did not hinder the provisioning of the small multiethnic community. While product availability may have been hampered by a selection of secondary market goods, consumer choice played a key role in the introduction of a plethora of mass-produced products from the world over into the homes of Yucatec refugees, and Lacandon Mayas from the forest regions, as well as heavily Hispanized Itza Maya who all collectively made Tikal their home. The archaeological evidence at Tikal demonstrates the fusing of cultural identities, as seen through changes in the patterns of material culture encountered archaeologically, in the Petén frontier. This fusing occurred in architectural elements at the site as well as in the absorption of British ceramics into the cooking-and-serving ceramic assemblage at historic Tikal. With all likelihood, a much different group of people left Tikal from those who reoccupied the ancient site during the turmoil of war.

Conclusion

The archaeology of the historic Caste War refugee village at the ancient ruins of Tikal, Guatemala, is ultimately the archaeology of the refugee experience in a multiethnic frontier context. Historical and archaeological evidence demonstrate the presence of three culturally distinct ethnic groups in the village. However, the context of this evidence shows a blending of the ethnic markers between the individual households at Tikal, suggesting an easing and eventual merging of cultural identities in the frontier. The Tikal villagers were tapped into regional and international markets that brought cheaply made, mass-produced consumer goods from around the world into their homes. Useful parallels can be drawn between twentieth-century refugee strategies in Tanzania and nineteenth-century refugee villages at Tikal and in British Honduras. In both scenarios, when smaller groups were forced or chose to live among the families of the new societies to which they relocated, they more quickly adapted to new patterns of cultural and material practices, while those who remained in more homogeneous refugee diasporas more often strove to hold on to their previous cultural practices. Thus, the archaeologies of past refugee experiences reveal connections to modern refugee situations, exposing the *longue durée*, or deep historical structure, of many refugee behaviors and movements.

Acknowledgments. I would like to thank everyone who works within the Tikal National Park, with special recognition to Jorge Chocón, Elizabeth Marroquin, Oswaldo Chi (RIP), and Tony Ortiz. This project could not have happened without the expertise of Lorena Paiz and Sergio Garzona. I am continually grateful for the insights of Hattula Moholy-Nagy and Joel Palka. I thank Minette Church and Jason Yaeger of the San Pedro Maya Project, and Brett A. Houk of the Chan Chich Archaeological Project for their collaboration. Last, a special thanks to John Michels and April Cunningham for their tireless editing skills, along with Tiffany Fryer and Kasey Diserens Morgan for their encouragement and advice on this chapter. Thank you all. This project was funded in part by the Wenner-Gren Foundation, and the University of Illinois at Chicago.

Note

1. Percentages are based on minimum number of vessels (MNV).

References

Antochiw, Michel. 1997. "The Peace Treaties of Chichanha." *Saastun* 2 (August): 83–112.

Boddam-Watham, John. 1877. *Across Central America*. South Yarra, Australia: Leopold Classic Library.

Bonorden, Alyssa Brooke, and Bret Houk. 2018. "Kaxil Uinic: Archaeology at a San Pedro Maya Village in Belize." In *Archaeologies of the British in Latin America*, edited by Charles Orser Jr., 13–36. New York: Springer.

Bonorden, Alyssa Brooke, and Briana Smith. 2015. "Results of the 2015 Excavations at Qualm Hill Camp." In *The 2015 Season of the Chan Chich Archaeological Project*, edited by Brett Houk, 67–104. Papers of the Chan Chich Archaeological Project, Number 10. Lubbock: Texas Tech University.

Brooks, Alasdair. 2015. *The Importance of British Material Culture to Historical Archaeologies of the Nineteenth Century*. Lincoln: University of Nebraska Press.

Cal, Angel. 1991. "Capital-Labor Relations on a Colonial Frontier: Nineteenth-Century Northern Belize." In *Land, Labor, and Capital in Modern Yucatan: Essays in Regional History and Political Economy*, edited by Jeffrey Brannon and Gilbert Joseph, 83–106. Tuscaloosa: University of Alabama Press.

Church, Minette, Jason Yaeger, Jennifer Dornan. 2010. "The San Pedro Maya and the British Colonial Enterprise in British Honduras." In *Enduring Conquests*, edited by Matthew Liebmann and Melissa S. Murphy, 173–198. Santa Fe, NM: SAR Press.

Church, Minette, Jason Yaeger, Christine Kray. 2018. "Re-centering the Narrative: British Colonial Memory and the San Pedro Maya." In *Archaeologies of the British in Latin America*, edited by Charles Orser Jr., 73–98. New York: Springer.

Dumond, Don. 1997. *The Machete and the Cross: Campesino Rebellion in Yucatan*. Lincoln: University of Nebraska Press.

Elie, Jerome. 2014. "Histories of Refugee and Forced Migration Studies." In *The Oxford Handbook of Refugee and Forced Migration Studies*, edited by Elena Fiddean-Qasmiyeh, Gil Loescher, Katy Long, and Nando Sigona, 23–35. Oxford: Oxford University Press.

Elverson, Matthew. 2014. "A Smoker's Delight: An Analysis of English Tobacco Pipe Bowls from St. Georges Caye, Belize." In *The St. George's Caye Archaeology Project: Results of the 2013 Field Season*, edited by Jim Garber. Report. Institute of Archaeology, Belmopan, Belize. http://www.stgeorgescayebelize.org/archaeology-project.html.

Fiddian-Qasmiyeh, Elena, Gil Loescher, Katy Long, and Nando Sigona. 2014. "Introduction: Refugee and Forced Migration Studies in Transition." In *The Oxford Handbook of Refugee and Forced Migration Studies*, edited by Elena Fiddean-Qasmiyeh, Gil Loescher, Katy Long, Nando Sigona, 30–35. Oxford: Oxford University Press.

Gann, Thomas. 1927. *Maya Cities*. London: Duckworth.

Hamilakis, Yannis. 2016. "Archaeologies of Forced and Undocumented Migration." *Journal of Contemporary Archaeology* 3 (2): 121–139.

Harrell-Bond, Barbara, and Eftihia Voutira. 1992. "Anthropology and the Study of Refugees." *Anthropology Today* 8 (4): 6–10.

Hill, Jonathan. 1996. *History, Power, and Identity; Ethnogenesis in the Americas, 1492–1992*. Iowa City: University of Iowa Press.

Jacobsen, Karen, and Loren B. Landau. 2003. "The Dual Imperative in Refugee Research: Some Methodological and Ethical Considerations in Social Science Research on Forced Migration." *Disasters* 27 (3): 185–206.

Jones, Grant. 1977. "Levels of Settlement Alliance among the San Pedro Maya of Western Belize and Eastern Petén, 1857–1936." In *Anthropology and History in Yucatan*, edited by Grant Jones, 139–190. Austin: University of Texas Press.

Jones, Grant. 1998. *The Conquest of the Last Maya Kingdom*. Stanford, CA: Stanford University Press.

Jones, Melissa. 2015. "Survey of Historic Sites at and Near Aventura." In *Aventura Archaeology Project: 2015 Season*, edited by Cynthia Robin, 73–91. Report on file at the Institute of Archaeology, Belmopan, Belize.

Maler, Teobert. 1911. *Explorations in the Department of Petén, Guatemala, Tikal*. Cambridge. MA: Peabody Museum of American Archaeology and Ethnology.

Malkki, Liisa. 1990. "Context and Consciousness: Local Conditions for the Production of Historical and National Thought among Hutu Refugees in Tanzania." In *Nationalist Ideologies and the Production of Natural of Cultures*, no. 2, edited by Richard Fox, 32–62. Washington, DC: American Ethnological Society Monograph series.

Malkki, Liisa. 1995. "Refugees and Exile: From 'Refugee Studies' to the National Order of Things." *Annual Review of Anthropology* 24: 495–523.

Maudslay, Alfred. (1902) 1974. "Archaeology, Volume 3." In *Biologia Centrali-Americana*. Vol. 3, edited by F. DuCane Godman and Osbert Salvin. London: R. H. Porter.

Mayfield, Tracie. 2015. *The Nineteenth-Century British Plantation Settlement at Lamanai, Belize (1837–1868)*. PhD diss., University of Arizona. Tucson.

Meierhoff, James. 2018. "You Don't Have to Live Like a Refugee: Consumer Culture at the Nineteenth-Century Refugee Village at Tikal, Guatemala." In *Archaeologies of the British in Latin America*, edited by Charles Orser Jr., 157–178. New York: Springer.

Moholy-Nagy, Hattula. 2012. *Historical Archaeology at Tikal, Guatemala. Tikal Report 37*. Philadelphia: University of Pennsylvania Museum of Archaeology and Anthropology.

Morley, Sylvanus. 1938. *Inscriptions from Petén*. Washington, DC: Carnegie Institution.

Ng, Olivia. 2007. *View from the Periphery: A Hermeneutic approach to the Archaeology of Holotunich (1865–1930), British Honduras*. PhD diss., University of Pennsylvania, Philadelphia.

O'Connor, Amber, and Eugene Anderson. 2016. *K'oben: 3,000 Years of the Maya Hearth*. Lanham, MD: Rowman and Littlefield.

Palka, Joel. 2005. *Unconquered Lacandon Maya*. Gainesville: University Press of Florida.

Reed, Nelson. (1964) 2001. *The Caste War of Yucatan. Revised Edition*. Stanford, CA: Stanford University Press.

Reina, Ruben, and Robert Hill. 1978. *The Traditional Pottery of Guatemala*. Austin: University of Texas Press.

Rugeley, Terry. 1997. "The Caste War in Guatemala." *Saastun* 3 (December): 67–96.

Rugeley, Terry. 2001. *Maya Wars*. Norman: University of Oklahoma Press.

Rugeley, Terry. 2009. *Rebellion Now and Forever: Mayas, Hispanics, and Caste War Violence in Yucatán, 1800–1880*. Stanford, CA: Stanford University Press.

Thompson, J. Eric S. 1963. *Maya Archaeologist*. Norman: University of Oklahoma Press.

United Nations High Commissioner for Refugees. 2010. Convention and Protocol Relating to the Status of Refugees. UNHCR Communications and Public Information Service, Geneva.

Valenzuela, Salvador. (1879) 1951. Informe sobre el departemento del Petén, dirigido al Ministerio de Fomento el 1o. de junio de 1879. *Anales de la Sociedad de Geografía e Historia*. 25: 379–410. Guatemala City, Guatemala.

Wauchope, Robert. 1938. *Modern Maya Houses; A Study of Their Archaeological Significance*. Washington, DC: Carnegie Institution of Washington.

White, Richard. 1991. *The Middle Ground; Indians, Empires, and Republics in the Great Lakes Region, 1650–1815*. Cambridge: Cambridge University Press.

Yaeger, Jason, Minette Church, Jennifer Dornan, and Richard Leventhal. 2002. *San Pedro Maya Report: Preliminary Report of the 2001 Field Season*. Report on file at the Institute of Archaeology, Belmopan, Belize.

Yaeger, Jason, Minette Church, Richard Leventhal, and Jennifer Dornan. 2004. "Maya Caste War Immigrants in Colonial British Honduras: The San Pedro Maya Project, 2000–2003." *Research Reports in Belizean Archaeology* 1: 101–112.

9

Landed and Landless

Comparing Labor Regimes in Northeastern Yucatán and British Honduras

John R. Gust

In Part 8 of *Capital*, Karl Marx ([1867] 1886) discusses in depth the process by which the elite of Europe wrested the land of Europe, and with it the means of production, away from the peasantry.[1] By capturing the means of production, these elites created a workforce that had no option other than selling their own labor power by working the lands and equipment of others. In Mexico's Yucatán peninsula, European-introduced diseases and violent resistance to colonial incursions resulted in decreased Maya populations in the sixteenth and seventeenth centuries. It was not until Maya numbers rebounded circa 1750 (Patch 1985, 30–31) that land became scarce, and even later that access to land was manipulated as a tool of social control. Expropriations of village land started before the onset of the Caste War of Yucatán in 1847 and accelerated after the Maya were defeated in this conflict in all but the southeastern corner of the region. Many in the lower socioeconomic classes accepted debt peonage,[2] in part, to access land to farm. This access to land shored up the subsistence base but at a steep cost. Once accepted, debt peonage was permanent for most workers and de facto hereditary for their children as well.[3]

https://doi.org/10.5876/9781646422845.c009

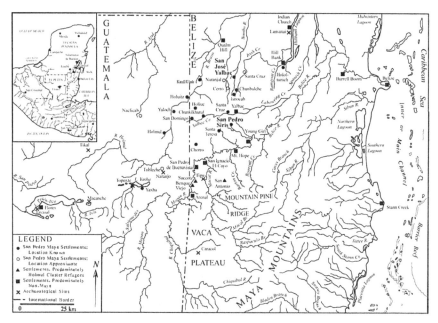

FIGURE 9.1. *Map of northwest British Honduras and adjacent areas in the nineteenth century. Map courtesy of Jason Yaeger.*

In this chapter, I discuss the results of research conducted at three late-nineteenth- / early-twentieth-century sites in two regions of the Yucatán peninsula. The importance of Indigenous land tenure to the autonomy of the working population is striking. The first of these sites is San Pedro Siris, the largest and head village of an independent group of mostly Maya who had immigrated south into British Honduras from Mexico (see figure 9.1). The people of San Pedro Siris worked for the British Honduras Company extracting mahogany (see Houk, Bonorden, and Kilgore, chapter 7 in this volume; Meierhoff, chapter 8 in this volume). The second and third sites are sugar and rum production sites in the northeastern Yucatán peninsula, near the north coast of present-day Quintana Roo, Mexico: San Antonio Xuxub (hereafter, Xuxub), and San Eusebio (Gust and Mathews 2011; Gust 2016; Mathews and Gust 2017). Both sites are haciendas, factory farms where agricultural products are grown and processed to some degree before leaving the operation.

Infrastructure typical of sugar production haciendas in northeastern Yucatán includes a cane grinding mill, a sugar-boiling building, a fermentation tank, and distilling equipment. San Eusebio has a sturdily constructed stone building with a cellar. I believe that this building functioned as a storehouse and that it may have been the distillery building and the company store as well. Due to the uneven need for labor, most sugar haciendas in central Yucatán had few resident workers. Instead, most lived off the hacienda and commuted to the hacienda for work when needed. At San Eusebio, only one possible house has been identified on the hacienda grounds. Local residents report that the current landowner demolished ruins of a house structure with stone walls approximately a half story tall. If this was a house, the upper walls and the roof would have been vegetal. The type of construction and the structure's placement near both the sugar-boiling building and the storehouse imply that this was where the site manager lived. Labor records (table 9.1) for thirty-two weeks at San Eusebio include small payments to workers for (re)constructing houses, indicating that there was some company-owned housing for workers. These minimal financial outlays for company housing, and the fact that few domestic artifacts were found except near the storehouse, suggest that few workers were living on-site. At Xuxub, the site manager Robert L. Stephens (see more about him in the section on Xuxub) did not allow workers to cut paths to the site through the forest, restricting access solely to travel by boat. This implies that most or all of Xuxub's workers lived on-site.

Eric Wolf and Sidney Mintz (1957, 380) define a hacienda based on the social relations surrounding production. For them, a hacienda consists of "an agricultural estate, operated by a dominant land-owner and a dependent labour force, organized to supply a small-scale market by means of scarce capital, in which the factors of production are employed not only for capital accumulation but also to support the status aspirations of the owner." The henequen haciendas of northwestern Yucatán typically contain infrastructure such as a manor house or large wall encircling the main grounds. The sugar production sites in northeastern Yucatán lack this showy monumentality and instead fit the pattern of reduced infrastructure found in haciendas in eastern and southern Yucatán. Site infrastructure is utilitarian. There is no hacienda wall, and the site managers' homes required greater outlay of money and labor than a traditional Maya home but were modest in comparison to the manor houses of henequen haciendas. Thus the "status aspiration" component is the most tenuous part of Wolf and Mintz's definition when it is applied to haciendas in northeastern Yucatán.

San Pedro Siris

Multiple Maya groups ventured south into western British Honduras in response to hostilities from the Caste War of Yucatán (Badillo Sánchez, chapter 6 in this volume; Houk, Bonorden, and Kilgore, chapter 7 in this volume). One group, the San Pedro Maya, settled in the Yalbac Hills by 1862 and soon after founded their largest village, San Pedro Siris (Kray, Church, and Yaeger 2017, 53, 56).[4] In British Honduras, the political position of the San Pedro Maya was always tenuous, but they deftly positioned themselves politically between the colonial

TABLE 9.1. AGEY provenance for the San Eusebio labor records. All records are from the Ramo de Justicia (Judicial Branch) are arranged by box (caja), volume (vol), and folder (exp).

Year, Week	Caja, Vol, Exp	Notes
1909, 24	1289, 216, 26	
1909, 25	1289, 216, 26	
1909, 26	1289, 216, 26	
1909, 34	1289, 216, 26	
1909, 35	1289, 216, 26	
1909, 14	1290, 217, 1	
1909, 16	1290, 217, 1	
1909, 17	1290, 217, 1	
1909, 27	1297, 224, 8	
1909, 28	1297, 224, 8	
1909, 36	1314, 241, 4	
1909, 38	1314, 241, 4	only partially legible
1909, 39	1314, 241, 4	
1909, 49	1314, 241, 4	
1909, 51	1314, 241, 4	
1909, 52	1317, 244, 8	
1909, 53	1317, 244, 8	
1910, 35	1328, 255, 13	
1910, 26	1334, 261, 1	only partially legible
1910, 28	1334, 261, 1	
1910, 29	1334, 261, 1	
1910, 30	1334, 261, 1	
1909, 06	1339, 266, 18	
1910, 13	1347, 274, 3	
1910, 14	1347, 274, 3	
1910, 15	1347, 274, 3	
1910, 16	1347, 274, 3	
1910, 17	1347, 274, 3	
1910, 05	1354, 281, 18	
1910, 06	1354, 281, 18	only partially legible
1910, 07	1354, 281, 18	
1910, 08	1354, 281, 18	

government and the Icaiché, a Maya group hostile to the colonial government (see Houk, Bonorden, and Kilgore, chapter 7, this volume). The San Pedro Maya claimed and defended a large swath of land on which they lived and grew subsistence crops.

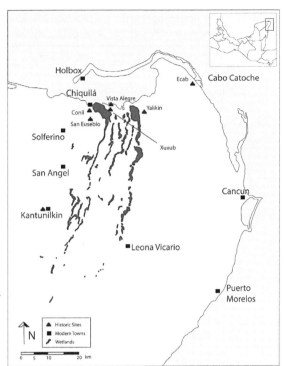

FIGURE 9.2. *Map showing the locations of sites discussed in the text, including the sites of Xuxub and San Eusebio, and the towns of Kantunilkin and Puerto Morelos. Map courtesy of Jeffery B. Glover.*

The British Honduras Company held official title to land to San Pedro Maya land and demanded they cease their traditional swidden agriculture, known in Maya as milpa. The stated reason was the British Honduras Company feared that Maya farmers would do damage when they burned their fields (Dornan 2004, see Houk, Bonorden, and Kilgore, this volume). Had the San Pedro Maya complied and abandoned milpa agriculture, the San Pedro Maya would have become dependent on the company's stores for their basic subsistence. In 1867, the San Pedro Maya villages were eventually burned after a series of altercations between the San Pedro Maya and colonial representatives, including a detachment of the British military (Houk, Bonorden, and Kilgore, this volume). Jennifer Dornan (2004, 119) believes that the underlying rumors of San Pedro Maya disloyalty were spread by the British Honduras Company.

Xuxub

Xuxub is located on the northeast coast of the Yucatán peninsula approximately 7.1 km east-southeast of the modern fishing and tourism-focused village of Chiquilá. Today, the site sits on San Angel–Chiquilá ejido land and is only accessible by small-draft boat through the Laguna de Yalahau (figures 9.2 and 9.3). Travel

FIGURE 9.3. *Guide gauging water depts as boat travels to Xuxub through Laguna de Yalahau. Photograph by Scott L. Fedick.*

time from Chiquilá through the mangrove swamp to Xuxub ranges from one to one and one-half hours depending on the tide, would have been much greater in the past (before small outboard engines were available), and the trip would only have been available to those with a boat. Xuxub (figure 9.4) was founded by Mauricio Palmero circa 1870, and Ramón Aznar purchased the operation in 1872.[5] An American engineer Robert L. Stephens wanted to purchase Xuxub himself but lacked the necessary capital. He convinced Ramón Aznar to partner with him. Aznar purchased the hacienda, and Stephens managed the operation. After ten years they were to sell it and split the proceeds (Sullivan 2004, 21). The thirty or so families that lived at the site and worked for Palmero stayed and worked for Stephens. Whether the families stayed voluntarily or because Aznar and Stephens purchased their debts when they bought Xuxub is unknown.[6]

Stephens's time at Xuxub was cut short. The Maya in the northeastern corner of the Yucatán Peninsula had made peace with the government of Yucatán in the early 1850s, ending Caste War hostilities in the region, but the southeast rebels had declared a free Maya state. These rebels, known as *cruceros* for their worship of a cross that spoke to them (Dumond 1985), considered both whites and Maya who had settled with the government to be their enemies. In 1875, Bernardino Cen, a general from Chan Santa Cruz, and his loyalists fled the town after an internal disagreement. Cen and his fighters attacked Xuxub on October 12, 1875,

FIGURE 9.4. *The sugar boiling house at Xuxub. Photograph by John R. Gust.*

killing Stephens, many of his workers, and their families (Sullivan 2004, 55, 99). Cen followed a road (or walking path) cut by an agent of one of Stephens's political enemies, Balthazar Montilla (Sullivan 2004, 27, 29, 41).

San Eusebio

The largest and war-capitalized of the Mexican sugar ventures to operate in the region was San Eusebio (figure 9.5), owned by La Compañía Agrícola del Cuyo y Anexas (henceforth, El Cuyo). In 1896, El Cuyo was granted control over 1,800 square kilometers of land, including tracts along the southern shore of Laguna de Yalahau (Wells and Joseph 1996; Glover 2006, 239; Glover, Rissolo, and Mathews 2011).[7] El Cuyo operated many related ventures along the north coast

that included harvesting *palo tinto* (logwood prized for its durability and also used to produce dyes), honey production, salt production, and making sugar at San Eusebio. The ruined sugar works for the then-modern San Eusebio are located three kilometers south of Chiquilá. Cubans managed San Eusebio, employing Koreans, Chinese, Afro-Caribbeans, and Mexicans (from throughout Mexico) (Edwards 1957, 174–175; Reed [1964] 2001, 288; Careaga Viliesid 1990, 126–127; Gust 2016, 151). San Eusebio was founded in the early twentieth century and abandoned when fighting connected to the Mexican Revolution reached the area (Sullivan 2004, 1).

Control of the Land

Chattel slavery ended in British Honduras by 1838,[8] as it did in the rest of the British Empire except in territories held by the East India Company, Ceylon (Sri Lanka), and Saint Helena.

FIGURE 9.5. *The smokestack at San Eusebio. Photograph by Scott L. Fedick.*

As in other parts of the British Empire, in place of slavery the owner class in British Honduras instituted a contract labor system. O. Nigel Bolland discusses Black workers, including many formerly enslaved persons, laboring there under such contracts (2003, 163–164; See Wesp, chapter 3 in this volume for discussion of Afro-Yucatecans). Officially, workers entered into these contracts by choice, but lacking access to farmland or capital, most had no other option. Once signed, these contracts legally bound the worker to their employer for the term of the agreement, most often one year. An unofficial system of debt peonage, affecting Maya and Creole alike, emerged in British Honduras (Christine Kray, personal communication, 2018) and further restricted workers' options by limiting their ability to change employers. Whether a worker was indebted to their employer or not, it was rare that their financial position improved over the course of a contract. Few had any better options at expiration of a contract and had no choice but to sign a similar contract binding them to an employer for another year. In this context, free and enslaved are ends of a continuum that includes coercive labor systems in addition to binaries.

Unlike landless workers, the San Pedro Maya were able to negotiate their terms of employment with the British Honduras Company on more even footing as they were not dependent on the company for basic needs (Houk, Bonorden, and Kilgore, chapter 7 in this volume). The wages earned harvesting lumber and rents they reportedly charged the lumber company accessing the land (Dornan 2004, 120) allowed residents of San Pedro Siris to live comfortably compared to their contemporaries in other places.[9] Based on his findings in the highlands of Guatemala, archaeologist Joel Palka has also speculated that the San Pedro Maya were trading imported items purchased in Belize City for profit with more inland groups (Palka 2009; Minette Church, personal communication, 2016; see also Kray, Church, and Yaeger 2017, 62).

The patterns of land tenure for the workers and their families at San Eusebio and Xuxub stand in sharp contrast to that of the people at San Pedro Siris. Many Maya elsewhere on the Yucatán peninsula had been forced to accept debt peonage to access to farmland (Rivero 2003, 572; Alston, Mattiace, and Nonnenmacher 2009, 110; Sweitz 2012, 241). This situation was onerous to the laborers, usually trapping them into work on the hacienda for the rest of their lives (Meyers and Carlson 2002, 229). Wages were low and as debts grew over time, worker movement became more restricted. Indebted peons were legally in the custody of the hacienda owner and their agents and could be beaten or confined for infractions on the hacienda and were sometimes returned to the hacienda for punishment for crimes committed in town (Wells and Joseph 1996, 212).

As mentioned earlier, at Xuxub, Stephens controlled the land and only allowed entrance and exit by boat through Laguna de Yalahau. Stephens had feared the very type of attack in which he was eventually killed.[10] Thus, either the workers were subsistence farming around Xuxub or purchasing food from outside. The latter seems unlikely. Any farming by workers was on Aznar and Stephens's land, and access would end with termination of employment. Some hacienda workers or their families elsewhere performed side work to supplement their meager earnings (Sweitz 2012, 247). Inability to come and go freely had to inhibit worker's families' ability to earn this extra income.

How many of San Eusebio's workers were bound to the operation by debt is currently unknown (Gust 2016, 135–157). Extant labor records from the El Cuyo company found in the Archivo General del Estado de Yucatán (AGEY; Yucatán State Archives) in Mérida tell an incomplete story. Records mention debts but only for a minority of the workforce, and debts are not entered consistently, making it impossible to determine whether the debts are short term and paid off quickly or long-term debts that resulted in peonage (Gust 2016, 149; see also Mathews, Gust, and Fedick, chapter 10 in this volume). Most laborers at

Yucatecan haciendas previously were divided into three types. The first type is full-time *jornaleros*, indebted, usually Indigenous, men who worked at piece rates (for example, weeding a twenty-meter-by-twenty-meter area or cutting 300 stalks of sugarcane). The second type of worker is salaried employees who worked at daily or weekly rates. At San Eusebio, instead of relying primarily on workers who were rigidly classed into one of these two types, the split in the workforce was between workers who were permanent versus those who worked there for a short time. Over one-third (81 of 236) of workers labored at both piece and day rates, often switching back and forth, blurring the line between piecework and salary and indicating that the change in work type was not due to permanent promotion to salaried employee. This shift represented greater reliance the company on the third type of employee, part-time jornaleros. Such workers had long been used in Yucatán to some degree but by 1907 represented the majority of workers at not only San Eusebio but other El Cuyo worksites, known as *fincas*, which had more constant labor needs (González 2014, 291). Some workers appear to have worked at San Eusebio for as short as a single day. As difficult as life as a debt peon could be, life for a free-but-landless part-time jornalero could be even more difficult.[11] One such "part-timer" told muckraker John Kenneth Turner, "They work us until we are ready to fall, and then they throw us away to get strong again. If they worked the full-timers like they work us they would die" (Knight 1986, 103, see also Gust 2016, 69). Further, older full-time jornaleros no longer capable of working a full day were made *reservados*, or reserve workers. This status included lighter duties at reduced pay (Rivero 2003, 572). No such system is documented for old part-timers. Full-time jornaleros also received medical care and subsidized maize for purchase; if they died meager rations were provided for their widows.

While it appears that debt peonage was waning across the board, and wage labor was increasingly more common even before the Mexican Revolution, these changes do not mean that El Cuyo had abandoned trying to control its workers. The precursor company of San Eusebio's owner, "Cuyo del Ancona," is known to have paid wages not in cash but company scrip (figure 9.6). This certainly contributed to the bottom line for the company, as it could buy items at wholesale prices for sale at or near retail prices to a captive clientele and keep the markup itself. Company stores operated at both the company's headquarters in the town of El Cuyo and at San Eusebio (González 2014). There is no reason to believe that El Cuyo discontinued the practice of paying in scrip.

Ambiguity in the documents means that it is unknown whether the group, or some part of the group, of permanent workers were compelled to stay at San Eusebio due to debt. Regardless, payment in scrip was a limiting factor as having money that can only be spent at a company store makes any but the shortest trip hard to complete. So, while the San Pedro Maya made regular trips to Belize City

FIGURE 9.6. *Hacienda token from Cuyo de Ancona, the precursor company to La Compañía Agrícola El Cuyo y Anexas. Photograph by John Gust.*

markets (Rath 2000), the permanent workforce at San Eusebio may not have had even the right to leave without management's permission. Regardless, payment in scrip only usable at the company store, impeding travel and purchase of goods for resale.

The San Pedro Maya and the workers at Xuxub and San Eusebio lived quite differently. Land tenure is the base reason for this difference. By controlling their land, the San Pedro Maya kept freedom of movement and other liberties while the lives of workers at Xuxub and San Eusebio were constrained.

The Artifacts

At first, the artifact assemblages from San Eusebio, Xuxub, and San Pedro Siris seem quite similar. Upon closer inspection, however, the artifacts show important differences. Assemblages from all three sites contain a lot of bottle glass from large bottles that once held alcoholic drinks, Florida water—a type of cologne—and mineral water. For Xuxub, however, the meaning of this is misleading, as most of these alcohol bottles postdate the operation of the site as a sugar mill and rum distillery. All of the conclusively identified and dateable bottle closures (or finishes) are of the crown cap style not introduced until 1892 (Lorrain 1968, 42; Newman 1970, 75; Fike 1987, 8–9; see also Gust 2016, 266). Most undatable finishes are aqua-colored glass,[12] a color usually not used to store alcoholic beverages. Aqua bottle glass usually held either mineral water or Florida water (Lanman and Kemp-Barclay 2017). Thus, in comparison to other sites, Xuxub has remarkably little glass from alcohol bottles dating to when it operated as a sugar hacienda. One possibility is that Stephens limited the bottles on-site to discourage pilferage of the rum produced there (Gust 2016, 267).

San Eusebio yielded bottle glass in a similar range as found at Xuxub, but San Eusebio's later date (1870s to ca. 1914) means that the bottles could have been deposited while the site was producing sugar and rum (Lorrain 1968, 42; Sullivan 2004, 1). Glass from alcoholic beverage bottles accounted for 20 percent to 25 percent of the total site assemblages from both San Eusebio and San Pedro Siris (Gust 2016, 235, 292), but San Pedro Siris has a much larger total assemblage by weight. San Pedro Siris also had a greater variety of glass bottles including more condiment and perfume bottles and more styles of patent medicine bottles (Gust 2016; Kray, Church, and Yaeger 2017, 61–62).

One of the enduring questions at Xuxub and San Eusebio is what were the people eating off? It is possible that the housing areas at San Eusebio have yet to be identified, but Xuxub is a self-contained encampment. All normally dry areas at Xuxub have been surveyed, and all normally dry areas with surface artifacts were investigated with shovel probes. The limited amount of improved white earthenware ceramics found at neither Xuxub nor San Eusebio would account for breakage and disposal of ceramic plates and dishes for everyone living there, and there are not significant quantities of locally produced ceramics. Further, at both sites there were managers living nearby who could account for what little ceramic is found. Why are there so few ceramics? Allen Wells (1985, 138; see also Meyers 2005, 131) indicates that some hacienda owners on the west side of the Yucatán peninsula who owned hacienda stores would sometimes not stock ceramic dinnerware. Your access to such goods is diminished if the one store that accepts your scrip refuses to stock certain items.[13] This may be the case at Xuxub and San Eusebio, or wages could have simply been too low to pay for this type of luxury item.[14]

Metal corn grinder parts were found at all three sites, but whereas San Pedro Siris had a minimum of 18.1 kilogram of manos and well over 50 kilograms of metates,[15] only a single broken, two-handed mano (430 grams) was found at San Eusebio and no groundstone has been recovered from Xuxub. Today, residents near Xuxub and San Eusebio still prefer corn ground with manos and metates. I suspect that the people at sugar production sites simply did not have the time to grind corn by hand, even if that method was preferred.

The San Pedro Maya continued their traditional Maya foodways at great expense in time and money. They used imported ceramics but still ate soups and stews with tortillas made from hand-ground corn (Leventhal, Yaeger, and Church 2001; Yaeger et al. 2004; Church, Yaeger, and Dornan 2011; see Houk, Bonorden, and Kilgore, chapter 7 in this volume). Keeping this aspect of traditional Maya life may have been impossible at Xuxub.

In comparison to the approximately nineteen pairs of scissors represented in the San Pedro Siris assemblage, only one-half of one pair was found at San Eusebio and none at Xuxub. The San Pedro Maya Project found ink wells, sewing machine oil bottles, shoe polish bottles, Jamaica ginger bottles, pepper sauce bottles, numerous patent medicine bottles, and a clothes iron. Excluding large beverage bottles, bottles at the Mexican sites consisted of a few patent medicine bottles, and a machine oil bottle. Current population estimates at San Pedro Siris range from about 350 people to 400 people, and at Xuxub about 100 people. Although Xuxub had one-fourth the population of San Pedro Siris, it had far less than one-fourth the material culture by weight. Whether by weight or breadth of artifacts, the assemblage at Xuxub pales in comparison to San Pedro Siris (Gust 2016, 235, 269).

Land tenure is the key variable affecting the autonomy of these workers. By guarding their lands with force when necessary, San Pedro Maya ensured that they had a protected subsistence base. They could meet their basic needs without the lumber company. For the landless in the Mexican Yucatán, accepting peonage and attaching themselves to a hacienda was often the only way to access land for growing milpa. They had to sell themselves into servitude to meet their basic needs. In British Honduras land was "intentionally kept from the former slaves after 1838 in order to keep these people dependent on the landowners" (Bolland 2003, 163). Despite being freed from chattel enslavement, landowners developed a contract system that ensured most freed Blacks could only make a living at the expense of their freedom of movement. Similarly, for a peon in Yucatán who managed to pay off their debt, remaining unbeholden to the hacienda also meant that their basic subsistence was in doubt as land access was dependent on accepting peonage.

For day laborers in the Mexican Yucatán with land, the hacienda represented a way to earn a little money, including to pay taxes if payment in cash could be negotiated, buy some finished goods, and act as a source of credit in case of crop loss. However, accepting loans entailed risk of eventually falling into peonage. For landless and foreign workers unattached to haciendas, day labor was the only option for most. For them the labor was necessary for basic subsistence.

Changing Fortunes

The importance of land tenure to the largely Maya workforces at these three sites can be seen through the effects change to land tenure had on the workforce. Within a few years after San Pedro Siris was attacked, the site was rebuilt and reoccupied. The San Pedro Maya were, however, eventually displaced from their lands around 1920–1936 (Yaeger et al. 2002, 15; Kray, Church, and Yaeger 2017, 68), and they settled in various places throughout British Honduras. Once removed, the San Pedro Maya lost their political clout and with it much of their autonomy. Eventually, some went to work in the sugarcane fields of northern British Honduras (Kray, Church, and Yaeger 2017, 71).

The reforms of postrevolutionary Yucatán did not create a panacea for the working class, but debt peonage was abolished, and two cycles of land reform expropriated lands from haciendas. The effects of the first round of expropriation on haciendas were minor, but the second, the Reforma Agricultural, initiated in 1934, limited hacienda lands to 300 acres and gave this land to towns and villages, adding to the communal lands, known as *ejidos*, they controlled. This reform negatively affected the operation of haciendas and provided land to Yucatán's poor on which they could grow subsistence crops and collect forest resources in exchange for performing labor for the community.

When the San Pedro Maya were eventually pushed from their land, the people became lower-class wage laborers and were stripped of their political influence. The postrevolutionary reforms in Mexico were not perfect but did result in the repeal of the peonage system and redistribution of hacienda lands to cities and towns. With these changes, the common people gained their freedom and access to land needed for basic subsistence.

Conclusion

In this chapter I have argued that the defining difference between the lived experience workers in northeastern Yucatán and lumber cutters at San Pedro Siris was whether they controlled their own land. In northeastern Yucatán those workers with no land or inadequate land were forced to perform wage work on haciendas or exchange their freedom for loans, attaching themselves to haciendas and gaining access to farmland as part of the bargain.

In British Honduras, by controlling their lands, the San Pedro Maya retained their autonomy even as others had little option other than restrictive and coercive labor contracts. Once finally removed from their lands, San Pedro Maya saw their power diminish as they fell under the purview of governmental authorities. Conversely, in the Mexican Yucatán, the Mexican Revolution eventually resulted in reforms that provided the poor Mexicans a stable subsistence base and diminished the power of the hacienda owners.

Acknowledgments. This research could not have been completed without the aid of many wonderful people and institutions. I thank my dissertation advisor Scott L. Fedick for all his help and commitment to my success, Jennifer P. Mathews for being a great collaborator, Paul Sullivan for generously sharing his research materials, the people of Quintana Roo, and everyone listed in the acknowledgments in the Mathews, Gust, and Fedick chapter (chapter 10 in this volume).

I had my first archaeological field experience with Minette Church in Colorado, and my first foreign field experience when she brought me down to Belize to help with the San Pedro Maya Project. I thank her, Jason Yaeger, and Richard Leventhal for that opportunity. I learned much from then-graduate students Bernadette Cap and Jennifer Dornan. I thank the late John Yaeger, Judy Yaeger, Tino Penados, and the rest of the Trek Stop staff for taking such good care of us. The people of Belize, especially the village of Succotz, have always made my visits enjoyable and memorable.

Portions of this research was funded by UC Mexus; the UC Riverside College of Humanities, Arts, and Social Sciences; and the Alice Hamilton Scholarship. Permits were issued to Jennifer Mathews (2010 and 2011) and me (2014) by the Instituto Nacional de Antropología e Historia (INAH; National Institute of Anthropology and History) for all work conducted in Mexico. Access to the San Pedro Siris artifact collection was granted to me by the Belizean Institute of Archaeology (2012).

Notes

1. Portions of this chapter have been adapted from Gust (2016).

2. Under debt peonage workers accept loans from their employers and are bound to work for that employer until the loan is repaid. The debt system functions so that few workers can ever repay their loans and regain their freedom.

3. Debts of hacienda workers were generally not passed down at the death of indebted workers, but indebted families did not have resources to help their children get married or otherwise start their adult lives (Gust 2016, 73).

4. Jones (1977) assigned the name San Pedro Maya. It is derived from the name of their largest village. See also Kray, Church, and Yaeger (2017).

Jones (1977, 141) has argued that San Pedro Maya lands were depopulated prior to their arrival. However, Scholes and Thompson (1977, 67), as pointed out by Minette Church (personal communication, 2018), note that if an informal census was completed by the military, hamlets of a few houses may be skipped as they are not places that could provide food or lodging for soldiers.

5. After Stephens's death, his widow, Mary Stephens, sought payment for her husband's portion of the business from Ramón Aznar. Aznar acknowledged the partnership but said that it died with Stephens and no payment would be made (Sullivan 2004, 154).

6. Sullivan (2004, 132) argues that indebted peons were a necessary part of an operation such as Xuxub.

7. Laguna de Yalahau is also known as Laguna Escondido and Laguna Holbox.

8. This includes the period of apprenticeship that followed abolition in 1834 resulting from the Slavery Abolition Act of 1833 (Bolland 1981, 592).

9. That the San Pedro Maya made yearly trips to Belize City to purchase goods from the markets (Rath 2000; Yaeger et al. 2002) suggests that wages were paid in cash rather than company scrip.

Later rents were charged by the company for use of the land by the British Honduras Company (Kray, Church, and Yaeger 2017, 64)

10. This rationale became clear in US Consul Alphonso Lapinasse's protestations to the US minister in Mexico City over Montilla opening the path to Xuxub (Sullivan 2004, 45).

11. This difficulty refers to greater precarity with respect to material conditions of life but does not consider the psychological effects of the coercions associated with peonage.

12. Aqua-colored glass is sun-affected glass that was originally colorless, and colorless glass was not commonly used for storing alcoholic beverages.

13. Meyers (2005, 131) also says that *hacendados* sometimes encouraged a minority of the workforce to acquire these goods in other ways. This implies that the hacendados were using access to the goods to bestow social status on certain workers, while denying it to others.

14. I use the term "luxury" advisedly: while I think it applies at the Mexican sites, Minette Church of the San Pedro Maya Project objects to the use of the term for San Pedro Siris' ceramic tableware as it seems that the ceramics found there were used daily (personal communication, 2016).

15. A bedrock metate is also present at San Pedro Siris.

References

Alston, Lee J., Shannan Mattiace, and Tomas Nonnenmacher. 2009. "Coercion, Culture, and Contracts: Labor and Debt on Henequen Haciendas in Yucatán, Mexico, 1870–1915." *Journal of Economic History* 69 (1): 104–137.

Bolland, O. Nigel. 1977. "The Maya and the Colonization of Belize in the Nineteenth Century." In *Anthropology and History in Yucatán*, edited by Grant D. Jones, 69–99. Austin: University of Texas Press.

Bolland, O. Nigel. 1981. "Systems of Domination after Slavery: The Control of Land and Labor in the British West Indies after 1838." *Comparative Studies in Society and History* 23 (4): 591–619.

Bolland, O. Nigel. 2003. "Labour Control and Resistance in Belize in the Century after 1838." In *Colonialism and Resistance in Belize: Essays in Historical Sociology*, 159–167. Kingston, Jamaica: University of West Indies Press.

Careaga Viliesid, Lorena. 1990. *Quintana Roo: Una historia compartida*. Mexico City: Instituto de Investigaciones.

Church, Minette C., Jason Yaeger, and Jennifer L. Dornan. 2011. "The San Pedro Maya and the British Colonial Enterprise in British Honduras." In *Enduring Conquests: Rethinking the Archaeology of Resistance to Spanish Colonialism in the Americas*, edited by Matthew Liebman and Melissa S. Murphy, 173–197. Santa Fe, NM: School for American Research Press.

Dornan, Jennifer L. 2004. "'Even by Night We Only Become Aware They Are Killing Us': Agency, Identity, and Intentionality at San Pedro Belize (1857–1930)." PhD diss., University of California, Los Angeles.

Dumond, Don E. 1985. "The Talking Crosses of Yucatan: A New Look at Their History." *Ethnohistory* 32 (4): 291–308.

Edwards, Clinton R. 1957. "Quintana Roo, Mexico's Empty Quarter." MA thesis, University of California, Berkeley.

Fike, Richard E. 1987. *The Bottle Book: A Comprehensive Guide to Historic, Embossed, Medicine Bottles*. Salt Lake City, UT: Peregrine Smith Books.

Glover, Jeffrey B. 2006. "The Yalahau Regional Settlement Pattern Survey: A Study of Ancient Maya Social Organization in Northern Quintana Roo, México." PhD diss., University of California, Riverside.

Glover, Jeffrey B., Dominique Rissolo, and Jennifer P. Mathews. 2011. "The Hidden World of the Maritime Maya: Lost Landscapes Along the North Coast of Quintana Roo, Mexico." In *The Archaeology of Maritime Landscapes*, edited by Ben Ford, 195–216. New York: Springer.

González, Edgar Joel Rangel. 2014. "Compañías deslindadoras y sociedades forestales: Empresariado en el entorno fronterizo de la Costa Oriental y creación de un borde en las márgenes del Río Hondo, 1876–1935." PhD diss., Centro de Investigaciones y Estudios Superiores en Antropología Social, Mexico City.

Gust, John R. 2016. "Bittersweet: Porfirian Sugar and Rum Production in Northeastern Yucatán." PhD diss., University of California, Riverside.

Gust, John R., and Jennifer P. Mathews. 2011. "Dyewood, Sugar, Rum, and Piracy: The Historic Period of the Costa Esondida, Quintana Roo Mexico." Paper presented at the 110th Meeting of the American Anthropological Association, Montreal.

Jones, Grant D. 1977. "Levels of Settlement Alliance among the San Pedro Maya of Western Belize and Eastern Petén, 1857–1936." In *Anthropology and History in Yucatán*, edited by Grant D. Jones, 139–189. Austin: University of Texas Press.

Knight, Alan. 1986. "Mexican Peonage: What Was It and Why Was It?" *Journal of Latin American Studies* 18 (1): 41–74.

Kray, Christine, Minette Church, and Jason Yaeger. 2017. "Designs on/of the Land." In *Legacies of Space and Intangible Heritage: Archaeology, Ethnohistory, and the Politics of Cultural Continuity in the Americas*, edited by Fernando Armstrong-Fumero and Julio Hoil Gutierrez, 53–78. Boulder: University Press of Colorado.

Lanman and Kemp-Barclay. 2017. "Famous for Its Many Uses." Accessed June 27, 2018. http://floridawater1808.com/index.php?route=pavblog/blog&id=10.

Leventhal, Richard M., Jason Yaeger, and Minette C. Church. 2001. "San Pedro Maya Project: 2000 Field Season Report." Submitted to the Belize Department of Archaeology, Belmopan, Belize.

Lorrain, Dessamae. 1968. "An Archaeologist's Guide to Nineteenth-Century American Glass." *Historical Archaeology* 2 (1): 35–44.

Marx, Karl. (1867) 1886. *Capital: A Critique of Political Economy*. Vol. 1. New York: Humboldt Publishing Company.

Mathews, Jennifer P., and John R. Gust. 2017. "Cosmopolitan Living? Examining the Sugar and Rum Industry of the Costa Escondida, Quintana Roo Mexico." In *The Value of Things: Commodities in the Maya Region from Prehistoric to Contemporary*, edited by Jennifer P. Mathews and Thomas Guderjan, 144–162. Tucson: University of Arizona Press.

Meyers, Allan D., and David L. Carlson. 2002. "Peonage, Power Relations, and the Built Environment at Hacienda Tabi, Yucatan, Mexico." *International Journal of Historical Archaeology* 6 (4): 225–252.

Meyers, Allan D. 2005. "Material Expressions of Social Inequality on a Porfirian Sugar Hacienda in Yucatan, Mexico." *Historical Archaeology* 39 (4): 112–137.

Newman, T. Stell. 1970. "A Dating Key for Post-Eighteenth-Century Bottles." *Historical Archaeology* 4: 70–75.

Palka, Joel W. 2009. "Historical Archaeology of Indigenous Culture Change in Mesoamerica." *Journal of Archaeological Research* 17 (4): 297–346.

Patch, Robert W. 1985. "Agrarian Change in Eighteenth-Century Yucatan." *Hispanic American Historical Review* 65 (1): 21–49.

Rath, Therese. 2000. *A History of Belize: A Nation in the Making*. Dangriga, Belize: Naturalight Productions, Ltd.

Reed, Nelson. (1964) 2001. *The Caste War of Yucatan*. Stanford, CA: Stanford University Press.

Rivero, Piedad Peniche. 2003. "From Milpero and Lunero to Henequenero: A Transition to Capitalism in Yucatán, Mexico." In *The Lowland Maya Area: Three Millennia at the Human Wildlife Interface*, edited by Arturo Gomez-Pompa, Michael F. Allen, Scott L. Fedick, and Juan J. Jimenez-Osornio, 571–584. New York: Food Products Press.

Scholes, France V., and Eric Thompson. 1977. "The Francisco Pérez Probanza of 1654–1656 and the Matrícula of Tipu (Belize)." In *Anthropology and History in Yucatán*, edited by Grant D. Jones, 43–68. Austin: University of Texas Press.

Sullivan, Paul R. 2004. *Xuxub Must Die: The Lost Histories of a Murder on the Yucatan*. Pittsburgh, PA: University of Pittsburgh Press.

Sweitz, Sam R. 2012. "Total History: The Meaning of Hacienda Tabi." In *On the Periphery of the Periphery*, 239–251. New York: Springer.

Wells, Allen. 1985. *Yucatan's Gilded Age: Haciendas, Henequen, and International Harvester*. Albuquerque: University of New Mexico Press.

Wells, Allen, and Gilbert M. Joseph. 1996. *Summer of Discontent, Seasons of Upheaval: Elite Politics and Rural Insurgency in Yucatan, 1876–1915*. Stanford, CA: Stanford University Press.

Wolf, Eric R., and Sidney W. Mintz. 1957. "Haciendas and Plantations in Middle America and the Antilles." *Social and Economic Studies* 6 (3): 380–412.

Yaeger, Jason, Minette C. Church, Richard M. Leventhal, and Jennifer L. Dornan. 2002. "The San Pedro Maya Project: Preliminary Report of the 2001 Field Season." Submitted to the Belize Department of Archaeology, Belmopan, Belize.

Yaeger, Jason, Minette C. Church, Richard M. Leventhal, and Jennifer Dornan. 2004. "Maya Caste War Immigrants in Colonial British Honduras: The San Pedro Maya Project, 2000–2003." In *Archaeological Investigations in the Eastern Maya Lowlands: Papers of the 2003 Belize Archaeology Symposium*, edited by Jaime Awe, John Morris, and Sherilyne Jones, 103–114. Belmopan, Belize: Institute of Archaeology, National Institute of Culture and History.

FUTURES FOR RECENT MAYA HISTORY

Kasey Diserens Morgan and Tiffany C. Fryer

Investigating the histories of the past three centuries necessitates understanding the impacts of past and present archaeological work on the region. Part III shifts focus to the consequences of archaeological work in the Maya region today. Such consequences extend to how the legacies of colonialism are lived, remembered, and recast by living Maya people. This volume seeks to change how we bridge the past, present, and future through archaeological practices—and to examine what is at stake specifically in reinterpreting and reexamining colonialism's history and ongoing nature in Yucatán.

The following chapters invoke heritage, archaeological ethnography, and engaged anthropologies as key conceptual frames and practices. In turn, these frames and practices can cultivate archaeologies that create space for innovative research agendas that seek to better understand the impacts of colonialism, modernism, nationalism, and the constructs of race and Indigeneity on the communities in which/with whom we work. In their piece defining the practice of archaeological ethnography, Yannis Hamilakis and Aris Anagnostopoulos (2009) argue that ethnography should not just be something added to conventional

https://doi.org/10.5876/9781646422845.p003

archeological practices but is in fact a novel frame through which to create projects that foreground the relationships and interaction of the scholar and public, giving up claims to absolute authority over the interpretation of the past. Similarly, heritage can provide a useful frame through which we can study the past because it allows for a multiplicity of fields, opinions, and conceptions of the past to come together through conversation, discussion, and remembering of recent events. The incorporation of broader heritage practices can address gaps in archaeological practices that may not align well with the goals of local actors. For example, the restoration or reuse of certain sites or places may be desired by some, but not by others. By approaching these topics through a heritage lens—that is, by incorporating data and ideas that are beyond the material, by actively engaging with local people who have knowledge of the topics, by reflexively thinking about the impact of our work, and by acknowledging that the work will be inherently political—archaeologists and other heritage practitioners might produce "engaged anthropologies," or anthropological practices that have an impact on social justice and the economic well-being of the communities within which we work.

Ethnographic studies of archaeological sites in the Maya world have produced substantial evidence of the interdependency of archaeological sites and their local communities, but these works are largely tempered by a parallel concern for how tourism (and expectations of tourists) impact these relationships (Castañeda 1996; Breglia 2006). The rise of heritage tourism (Ely 2013; Córdoba Azcárate 2020) has placed increased pressure on archeologists and communities near archaeological sites to provide services to tourists, leaving the social and economic needs of local communities undervalued and usually unmet. On the one hand, archaeological tourism in the Maya world is an economic driver and the source of opportunities for infrastructural, social, and economic development. On the other hand, ethnographers have shown how it is often complicit in the continued disenfranchisement of Maya communities from their lands and natural resources, rapid ecological and archaeological site degradation, increased scarcity of stable employment opportunities, and the exploitative marketing of a past appropriated for corporate gain to the exclusion of the very peoples it seeks to glorify (Castañeda 1996; Juárez 2002; Breglia 2006). Archaeologists themselves are complicit in this, as we continue to grapple with the unbreakable connections between archaeology and tourism, often without truly engaging the communities in which such resources exist (Castañeda and Mathews 2013). Archaeological tourism at grand, "ancient" Maya sites fashions Mayaness as consumable (Pyburn 1998): to the benefit of both international and domestic tourists, a discursive homogenization of "the Maya" is marketed, commodified, and eventually sold by both those producing the narratives at sites, museums, or hotels, and those who have learned they can profit from directly selling a standardized suite of goods related to Maya culture (Castañeda 2004; Little 2004; Taylor 2009). As such, the industry seems perfectly content to misrepresent Maya as a lost culture (Ardren 2004; Torres and Momsen 2005). This perspective is problematic not only because various Maya groups still very much live throughout southeastern Mexico and Central America but because the characterization of the whole of Maya culture prior to the incursion of the Spanish as "ancient" or "exotic" draws a distinct boundary between the archaeologically reconstructed cultures of pre-Columbian Maya and present-day Maya communities (Evans 2004). This form of contradistinction facilitates the supremacy of archaeological characterizations of Mayaness (intentionally or otherwise), creating a rhetoric of stasis that necessarily opposes the dynamism—and modernity—of contemporary Maya cultural practices (Berger 2006). Attention to these misalignments can help archaeologists understand and mitigate our roles in the continued disenfranchisement of Maya peoples. In so doing, we will be more attuned to how Maya today construct their identities while negotiating their recognition and what that may mean for how we chose to practice archaeology for the future.

A deeper ethnographic method is one way to broaden the scope of archaeological practices. Setha Low's (2011) useful characterization of engaged anthropology demonstrates how practicing anthropology toward social justice outcomes can simultaneously uncover systems of exclusion that are hidden, naturalized, or otherwise rendered invisible when practices are not oriented toward this end. She highlights how mixed methods can create professional space for engagement with real world problems. By using post-colonially oriented practices, ethnography, localized studies, participatory methods, creating relationships with communities, and working collectively rather than hierarchically, we create a form of engaged anthropology that directly and actively addresses modern-day issues of dispossession, social inequality, poverty, and disengagement from identity and history.

The following chapters touch on the themes of engagement to argue for blended archaeological heritage practices that focus on understanding the events of the past alongside their contemporary relevance including as the basis of claims over landscapes and the material remains of the past in the present (Meskell 2005; Hamilakis 2007; Castañeda and Matthews 2008). Archaeology of this type calls for constant reimagining and negotiating of our relationships with the communities in which we work and for balancing our expectations as researchers with theirs as communities tied to specific heritage sites and practices (Rissolo and Mathews 2006). It also calls for understanding that material culture continuity may have ruptured but that oral histories can maintain the memory of those practices and the forms of identity that stemmed from them (Kray, Church, and Yeager 2017). We hope to demonstrate that archaeologists can push these temporal boundaries: fully integrating projects into the places where they are being conducted and creating an archaeology of the present as a means of engaging local communities (González-Ruibal 2016). Adding an ethnographic, contemporary, or archival study to a traditional archaeological project can offset the arbitrary divisions of time often present in those studies and can provide avenues for using archaeological research to analyze not only the mysteries of the past but modern-day issues.

References

Ardren, Traci. 2004. "Where Are the Maya in Ancient Maya Archaeological Tourism? Advertising and the Appropriation of Culture." In *Marketing Heritage: Archaeology and the Consumption of the Past*, edited by Yorke M. Rowan and Uzi Baram, 103–113. Walnut Creek, CA: Rowman Altamira.

Berger, Dina. 2006. *The Development of Mexico's Tourism Industry: Pyramids by Day, Martinis by Night*. New York: Palgrave Macmillan.

Breglia, Lisa. 2006. *Monumental Ambivalence: The Politics of Heritage*. Austin: University of Texas Press.

Castañeda, Quetzil E. 1996. *In the Museum of Maya Culture: Touring Chichén Itzá*. Minneapolis: University of Minnesota Press.

Castañeda, Quetzil E. 2004. "'We Are Not Indigenous!': An Introduction to the Maya Identity of Yucatan." *Journal of Latin American Anthropology* 9 (1): 36–63.

Castañeda, Quetzil E, and Christopher N. Matthews. 2008. *Ethnographic Archaeologies: Reflections on Stakeholders and Archaeological Practices*. Lanham, MD: AltaMira Press.

Castañeda, Quetzil E., and Jennifer P. Mathews. 2013. "Archaeology Meccas of Tourism: Exploration, Protection, and Exploitation." In *Tourism and Archaeology: Sustainable Meeting Grounds*, edited by Cameron Walker and Neil Carr, 37–64. Walnut Creek: Left Coast Press.

Córdoba Azcárate, Matilde. 2020. *Stuck with Tourism: Space, Power, and Labor in Contemporary Yucatan*. Berkeley: University of California Press.

Ely, Paula A. 2013. "Selling Mexico: Marketing and Tourism Values." *Tourism Management Perspectives* 8 (0): 80–89.

Evans, R. Tripp. 2004. *Romancing the Maya: Mexican Antiquity in the American Imagination, 1820–1915*. Austin: University of Texas Press.

González-Ruibal, Alfredo. 2016. "Ethnoarchaeology or Simply Archaeology?" *World Archaeology* 48 (5): 687–692.

Hamilakis, Yannis. 2007. *The Nation and Its Ruins: Antiquity, Archaeology, and National Imagination in Greece*. Oxford: Oxford University Press.

Hamilakis, Yannis, and Aris Anagnostopoulos. 2009. "What Is Archaeological Ethnography?" *Public Archaeology* Special Issue: Archaeological Ethnographies 8 (2–3): 65–87.

Juárez, Ana M. 2002. "Ecological Degradation, Global Tourism, and Inequality: Maya Interpretations of the Changing Environment in Quintana Roo, Mexico." *Human Organization* 61 (2): 113–124.

Kray, Christine, Minette Church, and Jason Yaeger. 2017. "Designs on/of the Land: Competing Visions, Displacement, and Landscape Memory in British Colonial Honduras." In *Legacies of Space and Intangible Heritage: Archaeology, Ethnohistory, and the Politics of Cultural Continuity in the Americas*, edited by Fernando Armstrong-Fumero and Julio Hoil Gutierrez, 53–78. Boulder: University Press of Colorado.

Little, Walter E. 2004. *Mayas in the Marketplace: Tourism, Globalization, and Cultural Identity*. Austin: University of Texas Press.

Low, Setha. 2011. "Claiming Space for an Engaged Anthropology: Spatial Inequality and Social Exclusion." *American Anthropologist* 113 (3): 389–407.

Meskell, Lynn. 2005. "Sites of Violence: Terrorism, Tourism, and Heritage in the Archaeological Present." In *Embedding Ethics: Shifting Boundaries of the Anthropological Profession*, edited by Lynn Meskell and Peter Pels, 123–146. London: Berg Publishers.

Pyburn, K. Anne. 1998. "Consuming the Maya." *Dialectical Anthropology* 23 (2): 111–129.

Rissolo, Dominique, and Jennifer P. Mathews. 2006. "Archaeologists Working with the Contemporary Yucatec Maya." *Lifeways in the Northern Maya Lowlands: New Approaches to Archaeology in the Yucatán Peninsula*, edited by Jennifer P. Mathews and Bethany A. Morrison 198–209. Tucson, University of Arizona Press.

Taylor, Analisa. 2009. *Indigeneity in the Mexican Cultural Imagination: Thresholds of Belonging*. Tucson: University of Arizona Press.

Torres, Rebecca Maria, and Janet D. Momsen. 2005. "Gringolandia: The Construction of a New Tourist Space in Mexico." *Annals of the Association of American Geographers* 95 (2): 314–335.

10

Preserving the Nineteenth Century in the Throes of Twenty-First-Century Development

Twenty Years of Historical Archaeology in the Yalahau and Costa Escondida Regions of Quintana Roo, Mexico

Jennifer P. Mathews, John R. Gust, and Scott L. Fedick

Since the mid-1990s, members of the Yalahau and Costa Escondida projects have focused on historical archaeology in northern Quintana Roo, Mexico. Although most of the project research has focused on the ancient Maya (i.e., Fedick and Mathews 2005; Glover, Rissolo, and Mathews 2011; Glover 2012), this chapter will highlight a twenty-year diversion into studying the historic era of the nineteenth century, focusing on the commodities of chicle, or chewing gum latex, sugarcane, and rum production. Our initial trajectory into the historic realm was more by happenstance than intention, as we often came across the infrastructure and artifacts left from the chicle, surgarcane and small-batch rum industries from the late 1800s while we were documenting ancient sites. As Diserens Morgan and Fryer point out in the introduction (chapter 1) to this volume, it is a typical approach to study the historic periods as an addendum for accounting for the discovery of historic materials while focusing on the ancient Maya. In the last decade, however, we have intentionally sought out historic sites for study. Despite their relatively recent occupation period, the production equipment and other artifacts have been picked through by later residents, making it

https://doi.org/10.5876/9781646422845.c010

challenging to be able to reconstruct the historic record. In an attempt to overcome this obstacle, we have combined on-the-ground archaeology with archival research and ethnographic interviews with local peoples as well as experts in commodity production. Through these combined methods, we have attempted to better understand the living and working conditions of postcolonial Maya laborers, and their foreign managers, as well as the production process for making chicle, sugar, and rum in this remote region.

Background on the Nationalist Period in Northern Quintana Roo

Although Mexico's war for Independence in the early nineteenth century emphasized the recoup of Indigenous land rights, in Yucatán Indigenous labor rights and land ownership were in fact further degraded following Independence in 1810. Although there was a desire to modernize the economy through entrepreneurship, this movement did not include the Maya population except as physical laborers (Cline 1947, 32–34). Haciendas —plantation estates—continued to expand, producing products such as corn, beans, beef, sugar, cotton, and, later, henequen for the urban centers of Mérida and Campeche City (Rugeley 1996, 16; Andrews, Burgos Villanueva, and Millet Cámara 2006, 179–180). By 1840, hacienda owners were buying up property, which isolated Maya villages and limited their ability to sustainably grow food, develop infrastructure, or have access to education (Rugeley 1996, xiv, xvi–xvii). The Maya revolted, initiating the Caste War in 1847. The war raged on for several years, resulting in massive casualty losses of approximately 40 percent on both sides. As discussed by Houk, Bonorden, and Kilgore (chapter 7) and by Meierhoff (chapter 8), some Maya fled to western British Honduras (now Belize) and the eastern Petén in northern Guatemala. By 1850 the Spanish had secured the western part of the Yucatán peninsula, and the remaining Maya retreated to the remote "uncontrollable wilds" of the east in today's Quintana Roo (Reed [1964] 2001, 177). As Badillo Sánchez discusses (chapter 6 in this volume), the government dictated that those Maya who retreated into the forest were restricted from gathering in groups of more than ten to twelve people.

In the Yalahau region (of northern Quintana Roo), the small populations that remained in the larger towns had tired of the war, and the sizable population in Kantunilkin (figure 10.1) signed a treaty in 1855 declaring their autonomy and calling for cessation of hostilities in the area (Sullivan 2004, 36). As the focus of the Caste War became concentrated in what is today south-central Quintana Roo, the Mexican government gave two major land grants (to entities known as El Cuyo and La Compañía Colonizadora) in northern Quintana Roo in an attempt to regain political and economic control over the area (Reed [1964] 2001, 288). Yucatecan political leaders attempted to lure whites from Europe and North America to establish themselves on the peninsula as colonists by

FIGURE 10.1. *Map showing the locations of sites discussed in the text, including the sites of Xuxub and San Eusebio, and the towns of Kantunilkin and Puerto Morelos. Map courtesy of Jeffrey B. Glover.*

providing land grants (Sullivan 2004, 19). These land grants led to the development of small-scale commodity industries, including the chicle or chewing gum industry and the sugarcane and rum industry. The soils and climate of the eastern region provided ideal conditions for growing the chicozapote or sapodilla tree (*Manilkara sapota*), which produces the latex used in making chewing gum from the 1870s–1950s (Mathews with Schultz 2009; see also Houk, Bonorden and Kilgore, chapter 7 in this volume for further discussion on the chicle industry of Belize). This region was also well suited for growing sugarcane, particularly along the east coast, which has moist soils with high levels of lime and salts (de Portas 1872, 13–14). Both industries developed small-scale infrastructure such as processing areas and narrow-gauge railroads, as well as housing for workers and managers.

These industries should have left a large footprint in the archaeological record. However, over the last two decades, whenever we began to locate and clear features related to the chicle and sugarcane/rum industries for mapping, we noticed a recurring pattern: while much of the stone features were still standing, there was almost no metal left from the machinery and tools that had been in place at the sites. We believe that this absence reflects the "mining" of any metal that was not removed at abandonment during economic hard times later in the twentieth century. In some cases, it may have been sold for scrap, or repurposed and used around the household. In other cases, the distilling equipment may have been moved to clandestine locations after the government passed "dry laws" prohibiting production and drinking of alcohol following the Mexican Revolution of 1910. The lack of these artifacts has been a severe impediment to our understanding of the productive capacity and operation of these sites.

Our study area is considered a "text free" zone: there are no precolonial stone monuments or texts, and, unfortunately, we have found this to be mostly true for the Postcolonial period as well. While we have found documents pertaining to the forestry concessions in the area, the Catholic Church had a reduced presence in the area compared to the rest of the peninsula because the area had low population density and members of the clergy considered it "dangerous." This has meant that the usual documents such as bills of lading (shipment accounts) or birth, death, and marriage records for the area have been unavailable to us. As stated in the introduction to this volume (chapter 1), many historical archaeologists are combining archaeological research with ethnographic methods by engaging with contemporary descendant communities, and we are no exception. Our limited access to archival and archaeological materials at these sites has increased our reliance on ethnographic interviews in Mexico. However, we have also expanded these sources to include ethnographic sources in the United States to fill gaps in our understanding.[1]

The Role of Ethnographic Interviews in Understanding the Archaeological Record

Starting in the late 1990s, we began documenting chicle camps along a forty-kilometer-long narrow-gauge railroad built in the 1870s that connected the towns of Leona Vicario and Puerto Morelos in Quintana Roo. We soon realized that the chicle industry had existed on a modest scale here until the 1970s, and thus many of the older residents were wonderful sources of information as they had grown up around the railway or worked in the chicle industry until it was abandoned. Although these consultants were skeptical that anyone would have interest in this period of history, we attempted to convey to them how important it was to document their stories about the fascinating but brutal history of life as a *chiclero* (chicle extractor). The low-paid work was dirty, hot, physically taxing, and often dangerous for the men who ran and maintained the rail lines. Alberto Sánchez, who arrived in Puerto Morelos in 1941 at the age of 7 and worked the chicle lines for fourteen years, between the ages of 15 and 29, provided insight into the working conditions during that time period. He said that in addition to tapping and collecting chicle from the chicozapote trees, workers from the different camps were responsible for maintaining about twenty-kilometer segments of the railway, including replacing rails, wooden ties, and nails, as well as repairing the railbed itself. In addition, they cleared an approximately two-meter section of the vegetation on either side of the rail and cut trees to make the wooden ties. Often, workers were told to use black chechem (spp. *Metopium brownei*) trees for the ties, which contain a nasty black sap that produces painful blisters upon contact with skin. Mr. Sánchez reported that this was uncomfortable for laborers, since they often worked shirtless in the heat and humidity. They also usually did maintenance during the wet season, when it was difficult to run the railroad trucks (freight carts) due to the rising water levels (Alberto Sánchez, personal communication, 2002).

We also learned from Sánchez that the railroad trucks were designed to fit the narrow-gauge rails and consisted of low, flat wooden beds, with two metal axles and four metal wheels. This fact was confirmed archaeologically, as we located a segment of railroad tracks, the occasional wooden ties, a handful of spikes, a horseshoe and horseshoe nails, and even a rail truck that was on display in front of one of our consultant's homes. Mr. Sánchez told us that a single horse or mule fitted with a harness pulled each truck, usually running in front, except on the curves, where it would run along the side. One animal could carry about 120 kilograms of chicle on its back and pull one truck, weighing a total maximum of one ton. In addition to carrying bricks of chicle, the trucks were weighed down with construction materials for repairing the rail line, and merchandise such as food that could be brought between the inland camp of Leona Vicario, the coastal camp at Puerto Morelos, and the four chicle camps in between. The camps were spaced out about every ten kilometers, and each animal was usually traded out at the next chicle camp until they reached the coast (Alberto Sánchez, personal communication, 2002). From there, up to eighteen tons of chicle could be loaded on to small sailboats (measuring about eight meters long) and transported to Cozumel Island (Alberto Sánchez, personal communication, 2002). Larger boats, such as steamlines for the United Fruit Company in New Orleans, came to Cozumel once a month and could carry supplies back and forth between Mexico and the United States (Shattuck 1933, 163).

Florentino Chacón, who started working chicle in 1947 at the age of sixteen, described the actual process of collecting the resin in the forest. First, the chiclero would tie metal spikes onto their shoes and use ropes to climb a mature chicozapote tree, as older trees produced more resin. Starting from the base of the tree, they would use a machete to slash zigzagging cuts along the length of the trunk. After rappelling back to the ground, they placed a large cloth bag below the cuts on the base of the trunk, allowing the resin to flow into the collection receptacle. They allowed the resin to flow overnight and would return the next day to collect the full bags and take them back to camp. They then strained the latex resin into a large metal *olla*, or pot and stirred it continuously with a long wooden paddle to remove excess moisture (figure 10.2). They heated

FIGURE 10.2. *Chiclero Pablo Canche Balam stirs the chicle latex to remove excess moisture. Photo courtesy of Macduff Everton.*

the resin until the material coagulated and, then, during the cooling process, whipped it like cake batter and poured it into rectangular wooden molds. Once they removed it from the mold, the chicle formed a hard brick, which would then be weighed and loaded onto the railroad truck and transported to its final destination (Florentino Chacón, personal communication, 2002).

In the summer 2010, we started our investigation of the rum and sugar production sites along the coast of Quintana Roo at the historic site of San Antonio Xuxub (see figure 10.1; see also, Gust, chapter 9 in this volume, and Gust and Mathews in press). Xuxub had been founded by Mauricio Palmero in the late 1860s but was sold to a partnership between an engineer from New Jersey, Robert L. Stephens, and a wealthy Mexican from Mérida named Ramón Aznar. They developed infrastructure for small-scale sugarcane and rum-production, including a sugar mill and a cookhouse for boiling down the cane juice into syrup.

FIGURE 10.3. *Paul Sullivan's photograph of the smokestack at the site of Xuxub before it was destroyed in 2005 by Hurricane Wilma. Photo courtesy of Paul Sullivan.*

Based on Paul Sullivan's (2004) detailed research (figure 10.3) presented in *Xuxub Must Die*, we know that a dissident group of holdout rebel Maya from the sanctuary and military center, Chan Santa Cruz, attacked Xuxub in October of 1875. During this raid they murdered Stephens and several of the workmen; however, we do not know if this is when the site was abandoned. While we have no information that would lead us to believe that the machinery was destroyed, we also do not know how much intact machinery was removed from the site at the time. Another site in our study region, known as San Eusebio (see figure 10.1), is even less clear in terms of what happened after its abandonment. Although Sullivan's interlocutors told him that San Eusebio's "slaves"[2] were freed when the Mexican Revolution reached the area in 1914 (2004, 1), we have found no information regarding the site after that period. This disjuncture of the inhabitants during the time of operation coupled with few identified documents and missing equipment left us with some major gaps in the archaeological record. Although we encountered few documents at the archives around the Yucatán peninsula, we sought out residents who could provide us with knowledge for understanding how this equipment worked.

For example, we know that El Cuyo and La Compañía Colonizadora (the two land grant recipients mentioned in the section "Background on the Nationalist Period") had once each operated an extensive network of Decauville railways like the ones we studied at the chicle camps (figure 10.4; see also discussion of El Cuyo in chapter 9). Unfortunately, these rails had either been removed or deteriorated in situ and some of the railbeds have been victim to tourism expansion projects in the area as railbeds were bulldozed to widen roads, build houses, or put in garbage dumps (see Mathews and Lizama-Aranda 2005). During an online search Mathews identified a small roadside tourist attraction near the town of Cuzama in Yucatán State, where local Maya have put the Decauville tracks back together, added seats to the railcars, and are selling rides through old henequen fields to visit a series of *cenotes*, or water-filled karstic sinkholes. When we visited, we informed our guide Carlos (figure 10.5) that we were more interested in him teaching us how the railway worked than seeing the cenotes. He was very knowledgeable about the trucks and rails and patiently stopped to let us photograph and take notes on various features of the tracks. We were also able to see the trucks and tracks in action and were able to assess generally how much weight they could have piled on the cars based on the small pony that pulled the three of us, confirming what Alberto Sánchez had told us fifteen years earlier in interviews. A side benefit of our attention to the operational details was that we caused a traffic jam when the next group of tourists came up behind us or in front of us. It was then that we understood the flexibility of the small-scale rails. Carlos and the other guides were easily able to move our truck off the tracks, advance the other group beyond us, and reposition our trucks back on the track (figure 10.6). While we had understood that in the past workers would move sections of the narrow-gauge rails to be near the harvesting areas, it had not occurred to us that the trucks themselves were so maneuverable.

Our most important set of ethnographic interviews occurred in March 2015 in two small towns about two hours south of Atlanta, Georgia. We first visited the Richland Rum Distillery, owned and operated by Karin and Erik Vonk, in the small town of Richland. This company uses modern sterilization methods and new machinery, but they are updated versions of the same simple equipment used to make rum from the 1800s. We met with master distiller Roger Zimmerman and owners Karin and Erik to discuss their distillation process and were able to ask their opinions about what we are seeing at our sites in Mexico

FIGURE 10.4. *Stock certificate from la Colonizadora de Yucatán, one of the companies that operated several of the sugar works in our study region. Photo by John R. Gust.*

to confirm some of our research questions. For example, Erik confirmed information from the literature (i.e., Rogoziński 1999, 118; Meyers and Carlson 2002, 230) that says that once cut, sugarcane must be processed within twenty-four hours or it will lose its moisture, become hard to extract, and start to ferment on its own giving the final product off flavors. We were also able to get insight into the raw ingredients that they may have been using in the 1800s. At Richland Rum the process starts with cane syrup. Although 97 percent of modern rum is made from molasses, this requires a lot of bleaching and processing to be able to produce drinkable rum. Instead, Richland models its process from the 1800s, producing *rhum agricole*, which starts with cane syrup or juice. The Vonks informed us that for a time, many producers viewed molasses as a virtually worthless byproduct and would have required a lot more processing, producing an inferior product (Karin Vonk, personal communication, 2015). In the nineteenth century, French distillers in the colonies, to name a common example, preferred to use cane syrup (Williams 2005, 265), while Jamaican rums known for their harsh flavor and high-alcohol content relied on molasses (Barty-King and Massel 1983, 89).

FIGURE 10.5. *Our guide Carlos sitting on a repurposed truck for transporting tourists along the Decauville rails at Cuzamá in Yucatán State. Photo by Jennifer P. Matthews.*

FIGURE 10.6. *Guides removing one of the trucks from the tracks when they came up against each other. This demonstrated the mobility of this equipment. Photo by John R. Gust.*

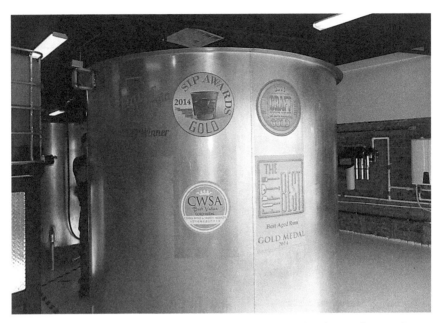

FIGURE 10.7. *Open vat for distilling at Richland Rum in Georgia. Photo by Jennifer P. Mathews.*

We also learned that at Richland the distiller pours the cane syrup into a large and open stainless-steel fermenting vat to which water and yeast are added (figure 10.7). Fermentation takes four to seven hours, depending on the temperature in the distillery, as Richland's facility is not temperature controlled and can get quite warm during Georgia summers. This variance implies that even with a rudimentary set-up in the middle of the jungles of Yucatán, an experienced distiller would have known how to adjust the process accordingly. Seeing the fermenting vat with no lid on it also led us to ask the Richland distillers about the use of large open stone tanks at sites such as Xuxub (figure 10.8), Rancho Aznar, and San Eusebio. We had thought that these might be water cisterns, which have been identified as such elsewhere in Yucatán; however, they are located immediately adjacent to a water well. When we showed owner Erik Vonk photos and drawings of the feature from Xuxub, he noted that the structure has thick stone walls and that the interior appears to have been plastered, making it quite possibly a fermentation tank. He also said that if they had a large quantity of cane syrup available, it was possible for the tanks to be used continuously instead of on a batch-by-batch basis (Erik Vonk, personal communication, 2015).

Roger, the master distiller, went on to explain that after the cane syrup liquid has fermented, it is pumped into one of their copper stills. The still heats its contents slowly, and eventually the high-proof liquid evaporates and condenses. The

FIGURE 10.8. *Interior of a structure at the site of Xuxub with cement on the interior of the walls, used as a possible fermentation tank for rum distillation. Photo by Scott L. Fedick.*

first of this liquid is known as the "heads" and is a potentially poisonous mix of ethyl alcohol, various nonethyl alcohols, and other chemicals produced during fermentation. Roger said that with experience, the distiller knows by smell and taste when the best of the distilling rum is being produced and diverts the flow into the specially prepared wooden barrels of American white oak. The heads are saved and added to the next batch, as much of it is ethyl alcohol. Once most of the alcohol has been evaporated from the tank, the distiller diverts the flow of the evaporating liquid again and continues to condense what he calls the "tails." This liquid is a mix of a little ethyl alcohol but is more noxious, with unflavorful chemicals. Richland retains this mixture for use in its other nonconsumable products such as fuel. This part of the distillation run at sites in our study area could have similarly been used for cleaning products, fuel, and so on.

Although Roger had modern gauges and equipment at his disposal, he seemed not to trust them and said that he really made the rum by experience and taste. This convinces us of how important the human element was in the process. The difference between profitability and ruin for an operation, even if everything else is done right, is and was in the hands of the distiller. The literature on rum production often focuses on the harshness of the work and the large number of people needed to perform monotonous tasks, but it is easy to forget that in order to produce a good product an operation needs a number of highly skilled

FIGURE 10.9. *Rock outline showing the original mill at Xuxub. Photo and illustration by John R. Gust.*

artisans in key positions. Another aspect that has been elusive in the literature is the yield produced from cane juice. Erik Vonk told us that one acre produces 2,500 gallons of cane juice, which produces 250 gallons of cane syrup, which produces 3 barrels, or 750–900 bottles of the final product (Erik Vonk, personal communication, 2015). While we understand that yields will vary based on different sugarcane varieties, these statistics for high-quality, simply produced rum give us a general starting point.

Finally, we benefited from a visit in 2015 to historic Westville near Columbia, Georgia, which is a living museum made up of old regional buildings saved from destruction and relocated. Westville has a nineteenth-century sugar-milling machine that still turns and is used to extract juice from small amounts of cane produced on site. As all we have at Xuxub is a ring of rocks outlining the location of the former mill (figure 10.9), it was helpful to see the actual process of feeding sugarcane stocks into the mill and photograph the various parts that made up the machine to help us identify anything that we do come across archaeologically.

The Role of Archival Research in Understanding the Archaeological Record

Although the archival resources for this study area are limited, we have benefited from a few helpful records that have allowed insight into the laborer-manager relationship. We believe that during the 1800s, ranch managers in the Yucatán viewed laborers within the debt peonage system as fungible, meaning that "any quantity of a specified commodity is considered to be equivalent to another, regardless of its point of origin or producer" (Meyers 2005, 118; quote from ETORO 2014). Debt peonage as an institution of social and labor control was introduced early in the colonial history of the Yucatán peninsula but did not gain traction until around 1840. The Maya were made dependent when hacienda owners forced them off their communally held lands. Prior to the 1840s many Maya became *luneros*, people who worked Mondays for landholders in exchange for access to farmland. These landholders also offered loans for festivals such as weddings, as well as other incentives, for example, freedom from governmental demands like military service and taxes. Robert Patch (1985) indicates that by the 1840s, there was little difference between luneros and debt peons. The landed elite then made it virtually impossible to ever repay debts by paying wages in company scrip that was only usable at the company-owned store (Alston, Mattiace, and Nonnenmacher 2009; see also Gust, chapter 9 in this volume; Gust and Mathews 2020, 43–57).

Although there is debate surrounding the nature of the *hacendado*-peon relationship (Alston, Mattiace, and Nonnenmacher 2009), most scholars agree that there was a paternalistic component in which the wealthy landowner "took care" of the poor peons, making sure that they had their basic minimum needs met. This is evidenced by the fact that hacendados commonly made additional loans to peons who could not repay their current indebtedness. An alternative explanation for this was that greater indebtedness resulted in further restrictions on movement, culminating in the most indebted peons needing permission to leave the hacienda. Allan Meyers and David Carlson (2002, 229) indicate that this was the situation at Hacienda Tabi and other haciendas in Yucatán State (see also Rejón Patrón 1993, 84; Gust 2016, 68; Gust, this volume; Gust and Mathews 2020, 44).

Generally, haciendas had two major classifications of workers: *empleado / trabajador asalariado*, or those who worked on salary for daily or weekly rates, and *jornaleros* (laborers), who worked primarily at piece rates task by task. The salaried employees tended to be Mestizo, while most jornaleros were Maya. However, as Wesp (chapter 3 in this volume) argues, we must recognize that colonial society was multiethnic and not simply an opposition between Indigenous and Spanish peoples. Although workers of other ethnicities are difficult to find in the archaeological record, we recognize that haciendas during the Nationalist period included them. Hacendados saw nonwhite foreigners, such as Koreans and Chinese, as suspect because of their lack of durable connection to the area, and thus they were denied loans and access to hacienda land to farm (Alston, Mattiace, and Nonnenmacher 2009, 119, 126; see also Gust and Mathews 2020,

83). Although there were exceptions, this put nonwhite foreigners on the bottom rung of hacendado society and results in them being mostly invisible in the archaeological and archival record.

Although we do not have labor records for San Antonio Xuxub, Gust (chapter 9 in this volume) uncovered labor records and other receipts from San Eusebio (another site in our study area) in the archives Ramo de Justicia (AGEY n.d.). These records include thirty-two weeks of usable pay data during the years 1909 and 1910, usually in three- to four-week periods. Following the pattern seen elsewhere in the Yucatán, at San Eusebio the salaried workers were paid the best. The *mecánico*, a senior millwright whose equivalent position in Yucatán state was a plant supervisor, was paid two pesos per day and, because he was on call, was paid seven days a week. Most other salaried workers worked five to six days a week. While some positions, such as the capataz (foreman), earned up to 1.5 pesos per day, most positions—such as animal herders, workers who loaded mule-driven railcars, fire tenders, and tenders of the sugar cauldrons—usually made less, most commonly one peso per day. A small number of workers known as *reservados* earned .25 to .375 pesos per day. These were older men who were unable to complete a full day of work and were given lighter duties or were expected to help during time-sensitive parts of the sugar- and rum-making processes (Peniche Rivero 2003, 572). Of the 236 workers on labor rolls at San Eusebio, 61 (25.8 percent) worked only at salaried (per-day or per-week) rates during the period the data cover. Salaried workers averaged a five-day workweek and earned an average of 5.24 pesos per week (Gust 2016, 139–141; Gust and Mathews 2020, 51, 57, 81–83).

Jornaleros were paid per task, such as weeding sugarcane fields, cutting paths in the fields, or cutting sugarcane for harvest. These tasks were compensated at a set rate that usually corresponded to completing the task within an area of twenty by twenty meters (a mecate). A normal daily assignment was completion of a task for one to two mecates. Often the jornalero was unable to complete this task by himself and had to bring family members to help, though they were not directly compensated (Peniche Rivero 1994, 78). In Yucatán, women and girls were usually expected to complete various uncompensated tasks at the hacienda. This uncompensated work, along with the fact that only heads of households (and older boys, who worked at half-rates) were paid, is probably why there are no women on the labor rolls for San Eusebio.

Although jornaleros earned an average of 4.65 pesos per week, assuming a five-day workweek means that they averaged only 88.7 percent of the earnings of salaried employees. When we take into consideration the use of family members to complete tasks, this reduces the earnings per unit time per person considerably. Of the 236 workers at San Eusebio, 88 (37.2 percent) worked at task rates only, and 87 (36.8 percent) worked for salary and at task rates. Thus, nearly

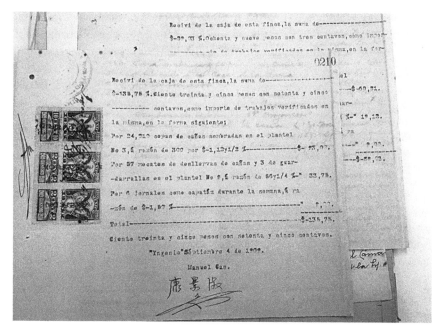

FIGURE 10.10. *Labor receipts from San Eusebio from 1909. Photo by John R. Gust.*

75 percent of the workers worked at task rates sometime during their tenure (Gust 2016, 139; Gust and Mathews 2020, 57).

The amount of time that workers labored at San Eusebio varied widely, but regardless of how workers were grouped, a majority appeared on four or fewer of the weekly labor rolls over the thirty-two weeks for which there are data. For all workers (salaried, task rated, and mixed rated), 64.8 percent worked for four or fewer weeks; for salaried workers, 55.2 percent of them worked for four weeks or fewer; and for task rate workers, 71.2 percent of them worked for four weeks or fewer. When these data are expanded to cover the entire two-year period (104 weeks in 2 years divided by 32 weeks, yielding a multiplying factor of 3.31), the four or fewer weeks of work become 13.25 weeks in total. This means that most workers worked in aggregate less than one calendar season. When similarly calculated over all worker categories (all, 72.5 percent; salaried, 69.0 percent; task rate, 78.2 percent), two-thirds of laborers worked half of one year or less (26.50 weeks) in aggregate over the two-year period.

Gust also found six typewritten receipts (one per foreman per day for September 4, 11, and 18, 1909) signed by two of the foremen named Manuel Can and Hilario Son at San Eusebio (figure 10.10). While Can and Son were paid a total of 455.15 pesos and 383.72 pesos, respectively. Three rates were listed: 1.25 pesos per 300 pieces of sugarcane (presumably cut, cleaned, and stacked for processing, versus one peso usually), 0.5625 pesos per mecate for weeding (versus 0.5 pesos usually), and 0.4375 pesos per mecate for other types of weeding. (The reason for this differential is unknown but may be the amount of vegetation to be cut in a particular mecate.) This means that in these cases, the company paid a premium of 0.125 pesos per 300 pieces of prepared sugarcane. The company also paid an additional amount for most weeding tasks at a rate of 0.0625 pesos per mecate weeded.

Interestingly, these receipts stick out because Manuel Can signed his name in Chinese (Dr. Shyh-wei Yang, personal communication, September 2015), and Hilario Son signed his name in Korean (Dr. Sang-Hee Lee, personal communication, September 2015). Drs. Yang and Lee also indicated that the names typed on the receipt represent a rough transliteration of the sound of the names in the languages of the signatures. We interpret the receipts signed in Chinese and Korean to mean that these two men, Manuel Can and Hilario Son, were labor contractors (see Gust and Mathews 2020, 35). The premiums that were paid on top of the usual rates may have been their contractor fees. Alternatively, these were amounts that went directly to the workers instead of getting the fringe "benefits" (such as access to loans and farmland) of peonage. It is questionable whether the term *jornalero* means anything when there is no real difference between those who worked at a mix of salaried and task rates. Instead, it seems that there was a core group of workers who may or may not have been resident workers; free laborers who worked occasionally and may or may not have been indebted; and a final group (often of ethnicities other than Maya) who worked as subcontractors and were not even paid directly. Thus, managers placed a value hierarchy on the various classes of laborers, and, in some cases, they didn't even warrant an identity in the work log.

Conclusion

When we started a research project in northern Quintana Roo more than two decades ago, it was not our intention to study the nineteenth century. However, as we came across postcolonial sites associated with the precolonial sites that we focused upon, we realized the richness of their history and the opportunity to speak with living people who could provide insight into understanding them. Unfortunately, however, postcolonial archaeology is not the focus of Mexico's tourism industry in the Maya Riviera, and thus resources are not committed to developing these sites. There is also so much rapid development going on that the Instituto Nacional de Antropología e Historia (INAH; National Institute of Anthropology and History) is not always able to keep up with the protection of these historic sites. Thus, they are frequently subjected to obliteration as tourist areas are further developed. On more than one occasion, we returned to visit sites that we spent multiple seasons documenting, only to find that they had been bulldozed for the widening of a road, for the creation of grazing land for cattle, or to clear the way for the building a housing development or hotel. Thus, it has become a race to document what we can before this history is permanently erased by modern development and those who have knowledge of these sites pass on.

Through the documentation of architecture, artifacts, and archival analysis at historic sites related to the chicle and sugarcane and rum industry, we believe that we are gaining insight into these small-scale commodity industries and the daily lives of their workers during the nineteenth century. Documents from San Eusebio allow for investigation into the segmentation of the workforce, and the relative value that management placed on different labor classes. Comparisons from elsewhere on the Yucatán peninsula imply the continuation of a durable but not completely rigid ethnic hierarchy that afforded more mobility to Mestizos, and significantly less to Maya workers and that took advantage of nonwhite foreigners. The short-term nature of the employment for so many of the workers implies their interchangeability and, for the women, children, and foreign workers, the company did not even record their names. In addition, through creative use of ethnographic interviews and visits to a wide variety of sites, we have been able to augment the data on the ground and gain new insights into the use of features, and fill in information about missing equipment, as well as give us insight into the processes of making chicle and rum. Through these interviews with local people, we are also now better acquainted with their understanding of the past, reminding us that the importance of these sites and the equipment that used to make them work did not stop when they were originally abandoned.

Acknowledgments. This work results from the assistance of a number of dedicated individuals and supportive institutions, without which this work would have never happened. We would like to thank several of the local inhabitants of Puerto Morelos and Central Vallarta, including Charles Bush, Florentino Chacón, Juana María Chacón, Gail Drauden, Jesús Hernández, José Luis Montoya, Luis Montoya, Severiano Martínez Canti, Goyo Morgan, Tomás Nuñez, Rosa María Poot Pool, Bill Rogers, Alberto Sánchez, Jorge Sánchez, and Noel Zisa. Thank you to Jorge and Alberto Sánchez for use of their family photos, and to photographer Macduff Everton for his generous use of his beautiful photographs in our work. Additionally, gracious thanks go out to the archaeologists, historians, biologists, and students who assisted us in this process over the last twenty years: Jorge Ceja-Acosta, Bente Juhl-Andersen, María José Con-Uribe, Matthew DesLaurier, Amy Dillon, Fabio Esteban-Amador, Olivia Farr, Claudia Garcia-Des Laurier, Jeffrey Glover, Danielle Haley, Kurt Heidelberg, Mario Hernández Lorenzo, Anna Hoover, Tamzin Howerton, Jordan Kindiger, Carole Leezer, Lilia Lizama-Aranda, Maggie Moore, Katherine Moore-McAllen, Kasey

Moreland-Alley, Shanti Morell-Hart, Helen Neylan, Jana Perser, Holly Prosser, Dominique Rissolo, Kathy Sorensen, Dennis Taylor, and Silvia Torres Pech. In particular, we would like to thank Paul Sullivan for his generosity in sharing photos, documents, data, and his insights into the site of Xuxub. Portions of this research have been generously funded by the Foundation for the Advancement of Mesoamerican Studies, Inc. (FAMSI), Mr. Michael Baker and the Baker Family Foundation, Charles Bush and Gail Drauden, UC MEXUS, and Trinity University. Permits were issued to Scott L. Fedick (1995 and 1997 seasons), Jennifer P. Mathews (1999, 2000, 2001 2002, 2010, and 2011 seasons), and John R. Gust (2014) by the Instituto Nacional de Antropología e Historia (INAH; National Institute of Anthropology and History) for all work conducted.

Notes

1. The authors conducted all ethnographic interviews with the permission of the Institutional Review Boards at Trinity University and the University of California at Riverside. As the information that consultants provided was low risk, all requested that we use their actual names, rather than pseudonyms.

2. "Slaves" is the term used by the interlocutor, but legally they would have been debt peons.

References

Alston, Lee J., Shannan Mattiace, and Tomas Nonnenmacher. 2009. "Coercion, Culture, and Contracts: Labor and Debt on Henequen Haciendas in Yucatán, Mexico, 1870–1915." *Journal of Economic History* 69 (1): 104–137.

Andrews, Anthony, Rafael Burgos Villanueva, and Luis Millet Cámara. 2006. "The Historic Port of El Real de Salinas in Campeche, and the Role of Coastal Resources in the Emergence of Capitalism in Yucatán, México." *International Journal of Historic Archaeology* 10 (2): 179–205.

Archivo General de Yucatán (AGEY). n.d. Caja 1314, Vol. 241, Exp. 4.

Barty-King, Hugh, and Anton Massel. 1983. *Rum, Yesterday and Today*. London: Heinemann.

Cline, Howard F. 1947. "The 'Aurora Yucateca' and the Spirit of Enterprise in Yucatan, 1821–1847." *Hispanic American Historical Review* 27 (1): 30–60.

de Portas, Rafael. 1872. *Tratado sobre el cultivo de la caña y elaboración de azúcar*. Mérida: Imprenta del Gobierno.

ETORO. 2014. "What Are Agricultural Commodities?" Accessed March 26. www.etoro.com/education/what-are-agricultural-commodities.aspxwww.etoro.com/education/what-are-agricultural-commodities.aspx.

Fedick, Scott L., and Jennifer P. Mathews. 2005. "The Yalahau Regional Human Ecology Project: An Introduction and Summary of Recent Research." In *Quintana Roo*

Archaeology: A New Era of Research, edited by Justine Shaw and Jennifer P. Mathews, 33–50. Tucson: University of Arizona Press.

Glover, Jeffrey B. 2012. "The Yalahau Region: A Study of Ancient Maya Socio-Political Organization." *Ancient Mesoamerica* 23 (2): 271–295.

Glover, Jeffrey B., Dominique Rissolo, and Jennifer P. Mathews. 2011. "The Hidden World of the Maritime Maya: Lost Landscapes along the North Coast of Quintana Roo, Mexico." In *The Archaeology of Maritime Landscapes*, edited by Ben Ford, 195–216. New York: Springer.

Gust, John R. 2016. "Bittersweet: Porfirian Sugar and Rum Production in Northeastern Yucatán." PhD diss., University of California, Riverside.

Gust, John R., and Jennifer P. Mathews. 2020. *Sugarcane and Rum: The Bittersweet History of Labor and Life on the Yucatán Peninsula* Tucson: University of Arizona Press.

Mathews, Jennifer P., and Lilia Lizama-Aranda. 2005. "Jungle Rails: A Narrow-Gauge Railway in Quintana Roo, Mexico." In *Quintana Roo Archaeology*, edited by Justine Shaw and Jennifer Mathews, 112–126. Tucson: University of Arizona Press.

Mathews, Jennifer P. with Gillian P. Schultz. 2009. *Chicle: The Chewing Gum of the Americas: From the Ancient Maya to William Wrigley*. Tucson: University of Arizona Press.

Meyers, Allan D. 2005. "Material Expressions of Social Inequality on a Porfirian Sugar Hacienda in Yucatan, Mexico." *Historical Archaeology* 39 (4): 112–137.

Meyers, Allan D., and David L. Carlson. 2002. "Peonage, Power Relations, and the Built Environment at Hacienda Tabi, Yucatan, Mexico." *International Journal of Historical Archaeology* 6 (4): 225–252.

Patch, Robert W. 1985. "Agrarian Change in Eighteenth-Century Yucatan." *Hispanic American Historical Review* 65 (1): 21–49.

Peniche Rivero, Piedad. 1994. "Gender, Bridewealth, Marriage: Social Reproduction of Peons on Henequen Haciendas in Yucatan, 1870–1901." In *Women of the Mexican Countryside, 1850–1990: Creating Spaces, Shaping Transitions*, edited by Heather Fowler-Salamini and Mary K. Vaughan, 74–89. Tucson: University of Arizona Press.

Peniche Rivero, Piedad. 2003. "From Milpero and Lunero to Henequenero: A Transition to Capitalism in Yucatán, Mexico." In *The Lowland Maya Area: Three Millennia at the Human Wildlife Interface*, edited by Arturo Gomez-Pompa, Michael F. Allen, Scott L. Fedick, and Juan J. Jimenez-Osornio, 571–584. New York: Food Products Press.

Reed, Nelson. (1964) 2001. *The Caste War of Yucatan*. Stanford, CA: Stanford University Press.

Rejón Patrón, Lourdes. 1993. "Hacienda Tabi: Un Capítulo en la Historia de Yucatán." Cuadernos de Cultura Yucateca 3. Mérida: Gobierno del Estado de Yucatán.

Rogoziński, Jan. 1999. *A Brief History of the Caribbean: From the Arawak and the Carib to the Present*. New York: Facts on File, Inc.

Rugeley, Terry. 1996. *Yucatán's Maya Peasantry and the Origins of the Caste War*. Austin: University of Texas Press.

Shattuck George C. 1933. "Life in the Forests of Quintana Roo." In *The Peninsula of Yucatan: Medical, Biological, Meteorological and Sociological Studies*, 157–179. Washington, DC: Carnegie Institution.

Sullivan, Paul. 2004. *Xuxub Must Die: The Lost Histories of a Murder on the Yucatan*. Pittsburgh, PA: University of Pittsburgh Press.

Williams, Ian. 2005. *Rum: A Social and Sociable History of the Real Spirit of 1776*. New York: Nation Books.

11

The Cycle of the Living Dead

Ruins, Loss, and Preservation in Tihosuco, Quintana Roo

Kasey Diserens Morgan

The fear of loss is second nature in the fields of heritage preservation and anthropology: the loss of cultural practices, the loss of historic buildings or objects, the loss of information, the loss of what makes us unique. It is these types of losses that we task ourselves with combatting through documentation and study, yet we often become part of the cycle that preserves cultural objects in a manner that results in a view of the past unyielding to new interpretation. The loss, abandonment, or change of cultural practices is part and parcel of being human. Loss does not oppose heritage but is in fact an integral part of the process (Holtorf 2006); change that includes some loss is constant and inevitable. By shifting the discourse surrounding loss in heritage, we can embrace it as a process of culture that will inspire hope rather than fear. That is not to say that we should embrace the loss of historic resources but that we should temper our reactions to change. The heritage community reacted with fury and disbelief at the destruction of the Temple of Bel in Palmyra, Syria, yet very little was discussed about the contexts within which ISIL grew to understand that the destruction of heritage is a powerful tool of war, one that gets noticed on a

https://doi.org/10.5876/9781646422845.c011

national stage. This was a terrible event, but the backlash that it engendered was exactly the desired outcome by ISIL. Had those writing about the destruction clearly placed it within the context of common negative uses of heritage, and the long history of such types of destruction as an act of war, the sensationalism could have been partially avoided.

Anthropologists and preservationists need to continue to interrogate how different conceptions of loss, particularly with regard to the history of contentious events, can influence ways in which preservation of heritage will occur. In fact, by creating closer contact between these disciplines, scholars can create deeper understandings of how loss occurs and how it can impact the telling of history in the present. I argue that we need to accept a certain level of loss, but also manage it through community activism and discussion over what amount is allowable or desired with regard to historic resources. We cannot save every structure or artifact, nor should we. Although in the United States, preservation debates have long focused on legal frameworks for the preservation of resources (see King, Hickman, and Berg 1977; King and Lyneis 1978), the field remains fragmented. In the United States, despite that the creation of Traditional Cultural Properties (Parker and King 1990) has moved the needle, it still is concerned with experts listing the places on a register as a means of avoiding loss; it has the potential, however, to go further toward being a dynamic protection of heritage that includes discussions with local communities. While in Mexico, the Instituto Nacional de Antropología e Historia (INAH; National Institute for Anthropology and History) has high levels of legal control over resources, and community discussion in my experience has been more of a lecture about the legal ramifications of damaging or altering historic resources, this debate has shifted. More local communities and Indigenous groups there are fighting for a seat at the table in debates about the uses of heritage for decades, and a handful of heritage practitioners have responded with a community-oriented approach to the study of heritage (see Smith 1994; Marshall 2002; Colwell-Chanthaphonh and Ferguson 2007; Atalay 2012; McAnany 2016).

In this chapter I address a cycle in heritage preservation that creates a "living dead," whereby both government protections and professional activities confine heritage assets, especially historic buildings and archaeological ruins, to a carefully curated and static past, rendering them essentially extinct. The confinement of historic sites to a specific place and time serves to further the distancing (McAnany and Parks 2012) between communities and their heritage, and it excludes buildings or sites from an active future as a part of a cultural ecosystem. As a cycle, it can hide in plain sight, like the façade of a building preserved to maintain a historic streetscape with a large mall behind it (Hurley 2010, 20), or the creation of a national park or corridor that limits access, physically and psychologically, simply by placing an arbitrary boundary.

I propose that a community-focused and open model of what heritage preservation entails can break the cycle of the living dead in heritage practice. This model bridges anthropology and historic preservation studies, to develop methods and theories that can more deeply explore connections between people and places. To do so, I use the case study of a community-based heritage preservation project in Tihosuco, Mexico. This project employs a model that goes beyond the traditional methods of preserving buildings or archaeological sites, and includes things such as language preservation, oral histories, and historic photographs to document a larger swath of a place's past. This approach works to bridge the historic preservation and archaeological models by focusing on the place, the artifacts, and the people as part and parcel of a larger system of cultural creation and adaptation to loss or change. Broadening our methods in archaeological practice to include ethnography and formal interviews can not only provide deeper insights into the past but also provide very real benefits for the communities within which we work. However, many government protections do not allow for change and adaptation that comes from the inclusion of intangible heritage data and multiple perspectives on the past and, therefore, confine heritage to a static and one-sided story. In the Maya region, this model of heritage preservation is relevant in large part given that many of the heritage assets, and particularly those related to archaeology, have been frozen in time to meet the perceived needs of another group: the tourists (Berger 2006). The increase in the tourist industry and the forces of globalization have created a Maya imaginary (Castañeda 2004) that homogenizes and effectively freezes the Maya identity into something commodifiable (Little 2004; Magnoni, Ardren, and Hutson 2007).

The Creation of a Living Dead

In order to find constructive ways to comprehend and combat the fear surrounding the loss of historic materials and the potential risks associated with that fear (Lowenthal 2005; McCarthy 2012; Holtorf 2015), I want to interrogate the concept of living dead raised by Daniel Janzen (2001) in his environmental preservation work in the Americas and apply it to heritage assets. In his framing, the living dead are individual beings who, because of their context or circumstances, have been removed from the ecosystem and can no longer reproduce or be contributing members of the gene pool. The living dead are essentially extinct, and just because they exist doesn't mean they are active or even that they can in some way be restored back to their former selves or population levels. The clearest example of this is a singular large tree that remains in an agricultural field, a great distance from any others like it, with no hope of receiving pollen or spreading seeds. He argues that due to their continued existence, the living dead lull us into a sense of complacency about their potential loss, as they cannot be extinct if they can be seen living. However, these solitary exemplars in the middle of a field are not a good sign and in fact represent a latent extinction, something that has already ceased to be a part of the ecosystem but is finishing out its material life.

Foregrounding Janzen's ecological concept of the living dead in archaeological preservation work, I liken it to the historic structures and archaeological sites that are left, by either natural or human processes, to live out their lives on the margins, no longer able to contribute to a greater cultural ecosystem. I see the living dead in built heritage, where aging architectural and archaeological resources are not being used to their full potential. Instead, they are left to deteriorate with no thought to their present or future value as historical objects. In many cases, these resources have lost their perceived use value and are relegated to the sideline as relics. Or, they become static. They exist as house museums left to age, no new research or interpretation being done, no allowance for adaptation to modern ideals or openness to the creation of layered histories—a selected, curated, and ancient memorial frozen in time. Once frozen, a space is created between the structures and the communities within which they exist: the bridge between the tangible remains, the intangible traditions, and the memory of the past is broken. Here, anthropologists and preservationists can help to restore these bridges through conversation, collaboration, and research. This concept also resonates with Orlando Patterson's concept of the social death, a being that is not physically dead, but either treated as such, or has been pushed the margins of society such that they are treated differently than others (Patterson 1982; Borgstrom 2017).

There are many reasons historic structures may become the living dead: economic resources are not always available to enable their conservation; they represent a time period that has fallen out of the favor of scholars or students; the government has arbitrarily frozen them for use as a historic site, thereby restricting access; or they have been swallowed up by the processes of globalization and technological advancement to the point that they are no longer deemed relevant. This argument can also apply to artifacts after they are excavated and are kept in storage: they exist, but not as a part of the cultural system that allows them to contribute to knowledge production, income generation, or the history of a place.

Of course, built heritage and artifacts are not generally recognized as living things themselves (cf. Zuni war gods), yet they have ties into larger ecosystems and cultural systems. They were created by living things, *people*, and are depended upon by living things, which makes them integral to life as it has been lived for centuries. Buildings and other cultural objects shape our daily lives in ways both seen and unseen. They provide shelter and comfort; they are imbued with memories and meaning. Structures and spaces can have impacts on the environment and cultural identity through new use, misuse, or disuse (Hayden 1997; Abel 2000; Low 2016). The "living dead" of buildings often exist outside of the realm of memory and history; they are markers of a past that struggles to be relevant, one that was forgotten and needs to be reinvigorated, to be brought back from the dead.

My focus is on buildings that are considered ruins, both because of the nature of my research and because they offer a more romanticized view of built heritage that often attracts interest in preserving them. Ruins, while picturesque, are prime examples of the latent extinction described in Janzen's work: just because they exist or can give us information about the past does not mean they can rejoin the ecosystem. They are set apart from a living city or town and, outside of those ruins that have a large tourism following, contribute very little to the livelihood of a town. Ruins, and, I would argue, any built heritage that is at risk of structural decline or disuse can be considered living dead. Without both being used and allowing for change, they will never regain their status as a functioning part of the cultural "ecosystem." A building that becomes a ruin has ceased to function for the purpose for which it was designed and created. Some ruins, like ancient Maya sites or the Colosseum in Rome, can actively function as tourist sites, their ruined state adding to their allure. However, the ruins of a colonial town, one that is still lived in, cannot take on these functions alone; they are needed to provide shelter and an active dwelling space for many families. Therefore, they must be allowed to change and be restored for use as a house. The alternative would be to create a ghost town where no one lives, which is not in any way desired.

When discussing loss, especially in terms of cultural heritage, the focus tends to be on averting loss rather than acquiring gains of the same value, or more value through change (Holtorf 2015). Buildings are constantly created and remade, and yes, there is some degree of loss in their evolution, but these changes should be celebrated and not avoided or feared. Historic preservation is predicated on the idea of loss, and it seeks to combat the threat of the potential "extinction" of particular types of built heritage and social memory (Holtorf and Kristensen 2015). It is often reactionary and inflexible in terms of acceptance of any type of loss or change. Because of this aversion to change and the constant threat of new development in areas where there are historic resources, we end up with historical markers or static house museums that lack dynamic interpretations or acknowledgment and receptivity toward beneficial changes.

Stuart Brand (1995) describes buildings as part of a cycle of mutual shaping that continues for their lifespan: we shape them, they shape us, then we shape them again, and so on. He attributes these changes to the ability of a building to "learn" and adapt to cultural needs. Following that, why not allow adaptation to continue and allow for new meanings and values to develop over time? We are constantly reinterpreting the past through history; why can the same not be done with historic buildings? Structures often have lifespans that last generations, so the creation of a theoretical framework that allows for and privileges this type of change as an object of study can help bridge temporal gaps and add new meaning to historical studies of sites and structures. Each era is as real and meaningful to those who lived it. While some will perhaps be more eventful than others, the allowance for multiple viewpoints and narratives through active and collaborative approaches to heritage preservation is an important step.

The Politics of Preservation

A traditional means of combating the loss of historic structures, heritage laws and governmental activities can conserve and protect historic resources on legal and political levels. These protections include national and local laws that create registers of historic places, the protection zones for wider areas deemed historically significant, and parks or sites that control access to historic places by visitors and development interests. Some heritage protection practices are considered strict because they do not allow for change, hindering the ability for people who care for or live within historic structures to make changes or maintain them, often due to expensive or arduous bureaucratic processes. As such, preservation policies—intentionally or collaterally—often consign these structures to a continuous state of ruin and disuse, or demolition by neglect.

The process of heritage management is hierarchically structured in Mexico, with many agencies and government programs overseeing all aspects of sites and landscapes. The complexity and top-down approach of these systems offers a glimpse into how well-intentioned protections can impede progress or conservation. There are separate bodies for management and ownership of sites; for the transport and organization of tourists and tour groups; for colonial versus pre-Columbian sites; and for ecotourism, archaeological sites, and museums. The recent moves by the Mexican government toward a more "responsible tourism" (Ely 2013) has created more public awareness about the benefits of the heritage protections but has also served to highlight some of the more negative impacts. As with the benefits of tourism, it is still unclear whether the protections placed by government agencies to guard sites have any impact on the ground. Also, because of the dependence on tourism at the federal level, there is little room for opposition to the practices or for extensive local involvement (Ardren 2004). Despite the focus on infrastructure creation of and economic development through cultural sites, the top-down management style of the federal government keeps only 173 out of 31,887 recognized sites regularly open to public (Ardren 2004). The reasons cited for keeping the greater portion of the archaeological areas closed to the public is lack of resources. Owners of historic properties who are reliant on government interventions for maintenance often wait in vain for resources. When they do come, it is often with little dialogue or input by local groups. The Instituto Nacional de Antropología e Historia, as the experts in Mexico, often make the final decisions. Preservation can be a means of oppression, and the importance placed on it can often create a value on the object being preserved that paradoxically hinders its protection (Pyburn 2007). These frameworks of governmental protection or ownership often instill fears in the local owners that the properties will be reclaimed by government officials for new uses or closed entirely without providing any social, political, or economic benefit to the local community (Castañeda 1996).

An Example: Seeking Resources in Tihosuco, Quintana Roo

Tihosuco, a small town in the in the Mexican state of Quintana Roo, has recently become the focus of various government entities due to its large quantity of historic resources. Tihosuco was a key city during the outbreak of the Caste War of Yucatán in 1847, an Indigenous rebellion that lasted over fifty years (Rugeley 1996; see part II, this volume). During the war, the town was abandoned and not repopulated until the early 1930s. In plan, it is a Colonial era town, with a central plaza and a large church. Some buildings potentially date from as early as the late 1600s, though most are late eighteenth and early nineteenth century. Because of its relative geographical isolation and its lengthy abandonment, over sixty structures from the Colonial era survive into the present. Thirty-three of these structures are listed on the National Register by INAH. Even more survive in the surrounding ejido land: the remains of haciendas and ranches pepper the landscape (see Fryer, chapter 5 in this volume; García Lara and Olán, chapter 4 in this volume). In the center of Tihosuco, the representational figures of the living dead are these Colonial era buildings. They are owned by a variety of families, and yet many are in a partially ruined state, not fully meeting their potential as livable houses. And since they are lived in, they are also not fully the picturesque ruins desired by tourism companies or the government seeking full control over heritage assets and their surroundings.

Historic preservation movements often start with a concern over potential loss of historic resources to development. In Tihosuco, a desire to understand and preserve the colonial structures started less as a fear of loss from development, and more from a fear of loss from disuse or lack of ability to maintain the massive and costly structures. Given the increased interest from local and regional stakeholders, the national and regional government agencies have begun to wield their power over historic resources in a variety of ways. The promises of progress, funding, and benefits of the historic buildings are discussed frequently, but they remain promises, with very little tangible result. As such, the main church in the center of town remains painted halfway, INAH focuses on restoring a painted fresco in a church in the abandoned town of Tela', while Colonial era structures on the main plaza of Tihosuco are at risk of falling down; INAH promises work for restoration in the community that comes in pieces, slowly and incompletely . . . the list of skewed priorities is long.

Further distancing of this narrative occurs with the treatment of these historic sites on the National Register and in the proposed declarations of patrimony at the national and state level in 2018. Both on the government documents, and in conversations with the owners, there is little discussion of the Caste War with regard to the buildings. I believe that this tactic of identifying them as Colonial era houses has created a distancing of the Caste War story from the importance of the buildings in the mind of the government, and therefore the town. They are not spoken about as witness to the start of the rebellion, nor abandoned because of the great turmoil in the region. The declarations have also been imposed on the community, and there was some discussion of historic designation as a benefit for tourism for the town, but there was no communication of what in fact the regulations over the property would entail, and how it would impact ownership rights.

A Cycle of the Living Dead

Returning to the idea of the living dead, it is apparent that this fear of loss and separation from the past has contributed to what I am calling "a cycle of the living dead" in heritage preservation work (figure 11.1). In Tihosuco, the government protections and preservation contribute to this cycle, instead of combating it. The cycle is illustrated here, but the basic mechanics are as follows: Starting with a historic building or site, a threat appears in the form of deterioration, development, or imminent change to its use. Due to the threat, the building and therefore an important piece of history will be lost or become extinct, and no longer useful to community members or outside actors, without immediate intervention. The action then taken by preservationists comes as a move to stabilize or combat the perceived threat through conservation work, a stoppage of demolition, or a claim of eminent domain. These actions often result in freezing the building at a given point, one that is deemed historically or culturally significant, or is re-created as an appropriate approximation of the time period. The buildings are often only interpreted or restored for that moment, erasing any patina, which contributes to further loss of the complete narrative. The outcome of this action is the creation of the building as "living dead," a static memorial to the past. Without allowing for change or continued use as part of a larger cultural ecosystem, this result begins the cycle anew, allowing for the building to become vulnerable to the threats of loss and extinction all over again, through decay, forgetting, and disuse.

This cycle is currently playing out in Tihosuco. Our project through the University of Pennsylvania to better understand the Caste War and the conditions that led to its start has renewed interest in all of the built heritage of the

FIGURE 11.1. *The cycle of preservation that leads to the living dead. Chart by Kasey Diserens Morgan.*

town, from the community itself, the government, and INAH. While not all government intervention is useful or productive when it comes to patrimony in Mexico, the push by INAH to become more involved has created an action-oriented committee in the town focused solely on serving as a go-between for homeowners and the regional INAH office. Through meetings and interactions with the local INAH architects, we have learned a great deal more about the National Register, the proposals for the historic zone, and permitting for restoration projects. The town is being rightfully cautious in these interactions, as there is a history of government interference regarding ownership and use of the colonial structures. The two large houses that have been restored and repurposed for the library and the museum are said to have been taken somewhat forcibly from the previous owners. Despite the long and contentious relationship between INAH and the people of Tihosuco, the current government's interest provides an underlying current of hope in the town that perhaps some of the buildings can be further restored and that, with enough interest, they can be brought back as fully functional dwellings.

The fear of loss comes not from the community, but instead from the governing bodies that impede change in the structures. In fact, on a recent tour given to me by a young man who grew up in Tihosuco, local legend has it that if the church façade was to be fully restored to what it looked like before the Maya rebels bombed it, people would rise up and the Caste War would begin anew. Excluding the now iconic symbol of the church, there is a sense that the protection or restoration of the buildings would be beneficial for future use. In Tihosuco, the fear of loss actually relates to a loss of the future, economically, and socially if there is increased deterioration, as these buildings are considered inheritance for many owners, and an important piece in the story of the repopulation of Tihosuco in the 1930s. Many owners, when asked what should be done to the houses, request a new roof or a floor, to make the space livable, rather than the government response of refurbishing the façade to create a more historically accurate or beautiful streetscape, as seen in other historic cities in the region. The concept of inheritance immediately sets them apart from the "park-ified" or "Disney-fied" archaeological parks that represent the ancient Maya (Castañeda 2009). The Maya are still here, and there is a further obligation to make the town both livable and viable as a historic site. Things will be added, and changes made, and while those adaptations might change the original "authentic" character professionals so often seek, it will allow for continued existence, and avoid placing them on the outskirts of the ecosystem.

Conclusion: Collaboration for the Living

Given that the cycle of the living dead can ultimately lead to a paralysis that doesn't benefit anyone, what can be done to combat its persistence? Community-based heritage preservation work is just one way to combat this cycle, offering new roads forward when we think about the preservation of heritage on a more encompassing scale.

Heritage professionals continue to grapple with ways in which to integrate heritage assets (both tangible and intangible) into living communities. A collaborative heritage project is at an advantage because it invites new relationships and conversations surrounding different conceptions of heritage. The goal of such a project should be to actively challenge the prevailing notion in much of the Mexican preservation work that conservation necessitates freezing the past in perpetuity at a given and arbitrary state and standardizing a narrative to meet the needs of tourist consumption. This is not a new debate, but the fact is that on the ground, the scholarly debate is moving very slowly into practical applications. There is still a fear of relinquishing some of the power of expertise in determining how and what to preserve. If we do not allow for change, we will continue to create examples of buildings and sites that are confined to one time period, or one meaning. Instead, we need to focus on how change validates and contributes to understanding the past, with an eye to the future. The history of Tihosuco continues to evolve and be used in different ways today than it was in the past. The building of meaning over time can be layered so that the newer does not obscure the latter but enhances it.

In our community heritage project, it is not just the buildings that have become the living dead, but also the pieces of heritage such as language, photographs, and intangible cultural practices associated with the history of the Caste War. This fear of loss colors all the preservation work being done, making it a race against time instead of a space for dialogue about what should be preserved. If we take away the stigma associated with loss and acknowledge it as part of the human historical process, then positive change can be made, and protections updated to reflect current cultural values as well as historical values. Tihosuco and the Maya are not on the brink of extinction, nor will they be in the long term.

Our work requires a knowledge of what heritage the community desires to be presented, and what it can do in the present to both recall the past while looking forward to the future. The community of Tihosuco has come together to attempt to preserve these buildings, and now new conceptions of use and identity are created in the face of potential loss of that heritage. Subsequently, revised histories combat perceived loss by reviving the "living dead." As a means to provide a basis for activism and development, the heritage resources once considered dead can come back to life in new forms. Notably, this focus forces us away from the concepts of authenticity and freezing the past as it once was that can be seen in the tourism industry and that requires a set of goods to be sold to potential visitors. By encouraging an already-active community who is interested in understanding its past to explore ways in which the past can continue to change without a sense of losing pieces of it, we can help adapt the preservation and heritage fields to become more open to diverse uses and interpretations of history.

Integrated archaeological and heritage preservation projects can also help to combat some of the cultural heritage façadism that is being put in place by top-down protections. This involves open dialogue, careful listening and watching. It can mean using the story of the Caste War and our relationships within the community to focus on what is important, while understanding the laws and significance of the protections: breathing life back into these structures without whitewashing their powerful story. Repossession of the narrative has the power to help combat poverty and unequal control of access in places that have important heritage resources. However, that is not to say that breaking the cycle alone is the answer; rather, it is just one of the many ways in which the town of Tihosuco can resist the loss of its archaeological and built heritage and avoid the creation of a more static narrative to attract tourists.

References

Abel, Chris. 2000. *Architecture and identity: Responses to Cultural and Technological Change.* 3rd ed. New York: Routledge.

Ardren, Traci. 2004. "Where Are the Maya in Ancient Maya Archaeological Tourism? Advertising and the Appropriation of Culture." *In Marketing Heritage: Archaeology and the Consumption of the Past*, edited by Yorke M. Rowan and Uzi Baram, 103–113. Walnut Creek, CA: AltaMira Press.

Atalay, Sonya. 2012. *Community-Based Archaeology: Research with, by, and for Indigenous and Local Communities*. Berkeley: University of California Press.

Berger, Dina. 2006. *The Development of Mexico's Tourism industry: Pyramids by Day, Martinis by Night*. New York: Palgrave Macmillan.

Borgstrom, Erica. 2017. "Social Death." *QJM: An International Journal of Medicine* 110 (1): 5–7.

Brand, Stewart. 1995. *How Buildings Learn: What Happens after They're Built*. New York: Penguin.

Castañeda, Quetzil E. 1996. *In the Museum of Maya Culture*. Minneapolis: University of Minnesota Press.

Castañeda, Quetzil E. 2004. "'We Are Not Indigenous!': An Introduction to the Maya Identity of Yucatán." *Journal of Latin American and Caribbean Anthropology* 9 (1): 36–63.

Castañeda, Quetzil E. 2009. "Heritage and Indigeneity: Transformations in the Politics of Tourism." In *Cultural Tourism in Latin America: The Politics of Space and Imaginary*, edited by Michiel Baud and Anelou Ipeij, 263–296. Boston: Brill.

Colwell-Chanthaphonh, Chip, and T. J. Ferguson, eds. 2007. *Collaboration in Archaeological Practice: Engaging Descendant Communities*. Lanham, MD: AltaMira Press.

Ely, Paula A. 2013. "Selling Mexico: Marketing and Tourism Values." *Tourism Management Perspectives* 8 (October): 80–89.

Hayden, Dolores. 1997. *The Power of Place: Urban Landscapes as Public History*. Boston: MIT Press.

Holtorf, Cornelius. 2006. "Can Less Be More? Heritage in the Age of Terrorism." *Public Archaeology* 5 (2): 101–109.

Holtorf, Cornelius. 2015. "Averting Loss Aversion in Cultural Heritage." *International Journal of Heritage Studies* 21 (4): 405–421.

Holtorf Cornelius, and Troels Myrup Kristensen. 2015. "Heritage Erasure: Rethinking 'Protection' and 'Preservation.'" *International Journal of Heritage Studies* 21 (4): 313–317.

Hurley, Andrew. 2010. *Beyond Preservation: Using Public History to Revitalize Inner Cities*. Philadelphia: Temple University Press.

Janzen, Daniel. 2001. "Latent Extinctions: The Living Dead." *Encyclopedia of Biodiversity*. Vol. 3, edited by Simon Levine, 689–699. San Diego: Academic Press.

King, Thomas F., Patricia Parker Hickman, and Gary Berg. 1997. *Anthropology in Historic Preservation: Caring for Culture's Clutter*. New York: Academic Press.

King, Thomas F., and Margaret M. Lyneis. 1978. "Preservation: A Developing Focus of American Archaeology." *American Anthropologist* 80 (4): 873–893.

Little, Walter E. 2004. *Mayas in the Marketplace: Tourism, Globalization, and Cultural Identity*. Austin: University of Texas Press.

Low, Setha. 2016. *Spatializing Culture: The Ethnography of Space and Place*. New York: Routledge.

Lowenthal, David. 2005. "Natural and Cultural Heritage." *International Journal of Heritage Studies* 11 (1): 81–92.

Magnoni, Aline, Traci Ardren, and Scott Hutson. 2007. "Tourism in the Mundo Maya: Inventions and (Mis)representations of Maya Identities and Heritage." *Archaeologies* 3 (3): 353–383.

Marshall, Yvonne. 2002. "What Is Community Archaeology?" *World Archaeology* 34 (2): 211–219.

McAnany, Patricia A. 2016. *Maya Cultural Heritage: How Archaeologists and Indigenous Communities Engage the Past*. Lanham, MD: Rowman and Littlefield.

McAnany, Patricia A., and Shoshaunna Parks. 2012. "Casualties of Heritage Distancing: Children, Ch'orti' Indigeneity, and the Copán Archaeoscape." *Current Anthropology* 53 (1): 80–107.

McCarthy, Christine. 2012. "Re-thinking Threats to Architectural Heritage." *International Journal of Heritage Studies* 18 (6): 624–636.

Patterson, Orlando. 1982. *Slavery and Social Death*. Boston: Harvard University Press.

Parker, Patricia L., and Thomas F. King. 1998. "National Register Bulletin 38: Guidelines for the Evaluation and Documentation of Traditional Cultural Properties." Washington, DC: US National Park Service.

Pyburn, K. Anne. 2007. "Archeology as Activism." In *Cultural Heritage and Human Rights*, edited by Helaine Silverman and D. Fairchild Ruggles, 172–183. New York: Springer.

Rugeley, Terry. 1996. *Yucatan's Maya Peasantry and the Origins of the Caste War*. Austin: University of Texas Press.

Smith, Linda Tuhiwai. 1994. *Decolonizing Methodologies: Research and Indigenous Peoples*. New York: Zed Books.

12

Histories for the Maya Present

Archaeology of the Colonial and Recent Past

Rosemary A. Joyce

The contributions to this volume show that archaeological research on the most recent five centuries of Maya history is flourishing and that we are approaching a point at which theoretical issues raised by this history can be considered on a regional scale. Archaeological research on these centuries, which witnessed extraordinary ethnogenesis through which Maya ways of being that were without precedent were created as means of persistence under colonial rule, has already contributed much to understanding global processes. The notable and well-rehearsed example of the emergence of Lacandon ethnicity, as outlined by Joel Palka (2005) is an example that parallels Barbara Voss's (2008) widely recognized contributions to understanding the emergence of Californio identity in Alta California, and the equally powerful, if less often cited by archaeologists, work on Miskito ethnogenesis by historian Eugenia Ibarra (2011, 2012).

Following Palka's lead, we need to examine other situations in which new ways of being Maya emerged, not to measure their authenticity but to understand how Indigenous peoples creatively engaged with changing governmental, economic, and religious structures. In conducting our archaeologies

https://doi.org/10.5876/9781646422845.c012

of the centuries between Maya dominance over the territory stretching from Chiapas to Honduras and the present, we need to remember that this period saw nationalist projects intended to de-Indigenize populations. Particularly beginning with Independence from Spain, when *pueblos de indios* were seen as backward by new governments, these policies included land dispossession, and discouragement of traditional and colonial hybrid practices through which religious observances remained in local control and of use of Indigenous languages. All of the historical forces that were designed to disrupt Indigenous identity and replace it with new peasant identities make it especially important that explorations of the remains of the more recent past by archaeologists take place guided by contemporary understandings of the active and emergent nature of cultural identity.

As we develop a specifically Maya archaeology of the recent past, we might consider the value of concepts developed in understanding Indigenous experiences elsewhere in the world, notably those employed by scholars of Native American and Indigenous identity in North America. As one example, during the early part of the Colonial period, Indigenous communities that survived the demographic crash of the sixteenth century maintained a degree of autonomy and were able to persist in a manner that Anishinaabe scholar Gerald Vizenor (1994, 2008) defined as survivance, the reproduction of historical consciousness through sustained and changing daily practice. Vizenor (1994, vii) writes that "survivance stories are renunciations of dominance, tragedy and victimry," which foreground "an active resistance and repudiation of dominance." Drawing on this analysis, historical anthropologist Russell Sheptak (2019) transformed investigation of the linked Indigenous towns of Masca and Ticamaya into a study of survivance instead of a story of assimilation. For the people of Masca, moving their town was a tactic of survivance that created a history that crossed space, not a loss of authenticity of origin in place. For the people of Ticamaya, bringing in African-descendant spouses contributed to the continuation of meals that were recognizably traditional, yet produced in new ways (Sheptak, Joyce, and Blaisdell-Sloan 2011). For the people of Ticamaya and Masca, shifting from speaking Indigenous languages to Spanish was a means to gain protection from a legal system not created for their purposes (Sheptak 2013). We could easily read each of these changes as endings, rather than as connections that allowed continued histories, survivance stories. In our archaeologies of the colonial and recent past, it is important for us to maintain a focus on the moments when people whose new social position was supposed to force them into compliance with a changed order found ways to occupy that order tactically.

Documentary research shows that due to policies of deliberate assimilation, it is in the most recent two centuries of the 500 at issue when many Indigenous communities lost their purchase and found their survivance in greatest jeopardy. Yet in many cases, as contributions to this volume demonstrate, there are still people alive who maintain personal memory or oral tradition from their not-too-distant predecessors that can assist in the interpretation of material remains as part of survivance stories. Ultimately, these are the people whose stakes in our work matter the most, and to whom we need to be responsible in our representations of the past.

Populating Survivance Stories: Commodities and Places

The question is, How can we conduct an archaeology of the colonial and recent past in which the capacity of colonized people to act is consistently foregrounded? In a review of archaeology dealing with the 500 period from sixteenth-century colonization to post-Independence governance in Central America, my coauthors and I proposed that we think about these periods not in terms of the categories of culture history, but through the places, people, and things that have occupied the attention of archaeologists. We wrote that

> the places where institutions of Spanish colonial administration developed are sites of creative strategic action through which indigenous people persisted under initial violent incorporation in empire, and subsequent exploitative economic relations. They are also the locations where African descendant peoples entered the region, as conquistadors, as enslaved laborers, and as freed people.
>
> The emerging colonial peoples employed things produced outside the Americas, those made in the Americas using new techniques or introduced materials, and other things produced through existing traditions of manufacture. None of these things, however, can be easily equated to specific groups of people. Historical archaeological research suggests instead that we need to understand things as mobilized in strategies by people who were actively constituting new social relations made possible by colonization, but with the primary goal of coping with sometimes dramatic change and persisting in meaningful lives. (Joyce, Gomez, and Sheptak 2015)

The chapters in this volume contribute to achieving the goals we called for in this programmatic statement. People are understood as creatively, or tactically, using both locally available and imported goods to create new ways of living in places that were always structured by the cosmopolitan nature of economic, political, and social relations that joined Yucatán to a global world, even when the places we explore appear to be refuge sites or landscapes of Indigenous "refusal" (after Simpson 2014).

In this, Maya archaeology of this period parallels broader approaches in global archaeology. A mainstay of the archaeology of the recent past elsewhere—the nineteenth to twentieth centuries, a period essentially equivalent with the republican administrations of Mexico and Central America—has been the study of patterns of acquisition of commodities imported from European and US sources. In their discussion of the sites of Kaxil Uinic, Belize, in chapter 7 Houk, Bonorden, and Kilgore bring together official documents and analysis of excavated object assemblages to understand a previously poorly described set of experiences in the nineteenth century and early twentieth. Like many contributions to the broader field of historical archaeology, the case is simultaneously both understood as a particularistic account of one place in the world and offered as illuminating a broader historical event or process. Examining practices of consumption, Houk, Bonorden, and Kilgore show that the Maya of this settlement used market commodities to maintain a locally meaningful way of life. This finding, they note, echoes the conclusion reached by Minette Church and her collaborators in earlier research at the historically related village of San Pedro Siris (Church, Yaeger, and Dornan 2011).

Much global historical archaeology has taken place through precisely this kind of careful dissection of a singular place. In a striking example of a wider regional analysis, Gust, in chapter 9, demonstrates variation in the nature and sources of commodities present at three settlements with very different labor regimes. He shows how political networks (with US goods coming through some but not others) and control of distribution (through company scrip and company stores) can structure the availability of goods. Similar commodity studies, rooted in normative historical archaeology, usually treat settlements as the consumer population. It is thus noteworthy that Meierhoff, in his study of the nineteenth-century population at the location of the Classic Maya Tikal archaeological site in chapter 8, examines differences between households.

There is potential to align these analyses with others from the Caribbean and from Central America that show that even highly marginalized populations exercised selection of commodities in ways that reinforced community and household-level distinction. Examples include the work of Laurie Wilkie in the Bahamas, demonstrating how within a plantation, selection of consumer goods by enslaved Africans varied in ways that can be interpreted as related to asserted identities (Wilkie and Farnsworth 2005). Closer to the Maya area, Charles Cheek (1997) demonstrated variation in use of English tablewares by three different free African-descendant populations located near Trujillo, Honduras, with the Garifuna, resettled from Saint Vincent Island in the 1790s, using different commercial goods than used by refugees from Haiti, in what Cheek argues was a deliberate move to align themselves with British practices. The same kind of link between consumption practices and identity production within settlements was noted at Ticamaya, Honduras, where one household in the late eighteenth century selectively consumed Spanish colonial pottery and Spanish-introduced animals, at a time that documents for the first time described some residents in terms affiliating them more with the non-Indigenous population than with the majority native citizenry (Sheptak, Blaisdell-Sloan, and Joyce 2011).

The glass bottles Houk, Bonorden, and Kilgore (chapter 7) discuss from Kaxil Uinic, and those from Tikal enumerated by Meierhoff, which come predominantly from US sources, reflect the way that even marginal settlements in the Republican period were engaged in a transatlantic world, independent of political structures. Such international engagement of what might be assumed to be marginalized communities mediated through consumption is equally evident in earlier eighteenth-century colonial contexts, such as those of Omoa, Ticamaya, and Masca, in Honduras (Sheptak, Blaisdell-Sloan, and Joyce 2011; Sheptak, Joyce, and Blaisdell-Sloan 2011). Participation in what is called "contraband" trade by Kaxil Uinic's population is thus part of long-established patterns of engagement with broader spheres to provision communities often presented with few official resources for sanctioned consumption. Similarly, in her research on colonial western El Salvador, Kathryn Sampeck (2007) found evidence of unauthorized distribution of Chinese porcelain to both urban and hinterland sites. Such unsanctioned access to goods, available in part because marginal locations were open to economic relations meant to be constrained by political structures that exercised little direct control, cries out for reassessment from the perspective of residents of the settlements involved, to replace the top-down administrative perspective that is signaled by our use of the term "contraband." Without what today we call contraband, the colonial occupation of Caribbean Central America would have collapsed. Importation of unauthorized goods was a major part of the experience in eastern Yucatán that García Lara and Olán discuss as well (chapter 4). Here, they argue that local experiences of illicit economic activity accompanied by violence were effects of the global economy into which the apparently remote coast of Yucatán was integrated. Contraband and piracy were part of the system, not an antisystem, and it reveals a landscape created from the ground up through the coping tactics of local people.

In many parts of the area, shifting perspective in this way might be made difficult by the scarcity or normativity of available documentary sources. In chapter 10, on the Yalahau area, Mathews, Gust, and Fedick show the importance of dialogue with living descendants for whom the nineteenth-century sites of labor are still alive in memory. The detailed engagement with the installations that these authors describe allows them to begin to paint a rich picture of challenging labor conditions, creatively approached by the Indigenous population. The role of women and children in labor is of strong interest, as these are actors about whom most archives and too many anthropological accounts are silent.

Given how productive analyses such as this are, it would be easy to invest all our efforts in understanding the activities of everyday life that materials discarded imply, and the political and economic structures that textual documents often allow us to link to these commodities. Yet focusing exclusively on consumption and everyday life would risk reducing our vision of survivance to an economic account. The maintenance of communities also relied on creative reformulation of beliefs that gave meaning to life. Our archaeological access to these domains comes through multiple channels.

In the Spanish colonial world, every Indigenous town required a Catholic church. Churches quickly became the focus of Indigenous practices, including the kind that William Hanks (2010) has shown generated both new understandings of the political and social landscape and, among Yucatec Maya, the language to talk about them. In Honduras, Catholic churches and *cofradías*, the communal associations formed to sponsor saint's feasts, were central to the continued identity of Indigenous towns, constituting arenas where most activities were controlled by the local population, not the church hierarchy (Sheptak, Joyce, and Blaisdell-Sloan 2011; Joyce and Sheptak 2014).

The presence or absence of religious buildings and the way religious observation was organized thus present a second domain for our interpretation of the last five hundred years. Even the late refugee village at Tikal includes a building identified as likely a church, the only structure with a "basal course of stones" and "(partial) proper plaster flooring." While Meierhoff (chapter 8) cites the need for such a building to attain municipal status, this administrative justification does not erase the importance of such buildings as community centers for town residents. We can compare this example with the eighteenth-century Honduran coastal town of Omoa, which grew up around a military fort and so lacked a formal church (outside the fort chapel) that could be used by the town residents. Despite the lack of such a building, documents tell us that religious veneration, using images owned by a wealthy town resident, united the people of the community (Joyce and Sheptak 2015). We need to take explicit notice of such things as the conversion of churches into warehouses that Badillo Sánchez comments on (chapter 6 in this volume), or the lack of religious structures on haciendas that usually goes unremarked, perhaps considering them as forms of structural violence.

Maya archaeologies of the most recent 500 years are just beginning to link the newly recognized particularities that are being described at scales from household to landscape to broader interpretive frameworks. Yet they have great potential to contribute to global discussions of such processes and structures. Whether it is through illuminating familiar ideas drawn from anthropology—such as ethnogenesis, consumption, and structural violence—or less familiar concepts from Native American and Indigenous studies—such as survivance and refusal—the complexity of the social situations that emerged in this region has great promise to contribute to broader theoretical debates.

Theoretical Contributions

This raises the question, What theoretical approaches might the specificities of colonial and Republican histories of the Maya area demand or allow? Contributions to this volume exemplify two different ways to answer to this question. First, it is clear from projects such as that of Maia Dedrick, Patricia A, McAnany, and Adolfo Iván Batún Alpuche at Tahcabo that classic approaches from political economy, developed to understand agricultural habitation in this zone, can be brought to bear in these more recent periods. In this vein, Gust's analysis (in chapter 9) of San Pedro Siris, San Antonio Xuxub, and San Eusebio, though firmly rooted in a rich body of historical documents and artifacts that are products of global networks of exchange, applies a framework of labor organization that equally could be used in any archaeological analysis.

In other words, we do not need to abandon the kinds of questions that have occupied archaeology of the pre-Columbian Maya in examining the most recent five centuries of history in the same area. In fact, it is urgent for us to address more recent sites with the pre-Columbian in mind, because many of our pre-Columbian models are based on presumed continuities between deeper past and present. Addressing the question of how such continuity could have been generated through a period of colonial and Republican relocations, novel administrative moves, and economic demands is urgently needed.

Other chapters in this volume consider topics that have not emerged in archaeology of the pre-Columbian Maya yet but might push us to ask different questions about that deeper past. Meierhoff's work in chapter 8 on the nineteenth-century village at Tikal is offered explicitly as a contribution to the anthropology of refugees, giving an unusual structure to an analysis of imported materials obtained, as was the case at Kaxil Uinic, from a cosmopolitan network. What might be considered novel experiences of violence and dislocation clearly have historical precedents in the earlier history of the Maya region. Fryer's discussion of political violence (chapter 5) in everyday life in the area affected by the *guerra de castas* is another example. She argues for a reconsideration of "conventional material proxies of violence," fortification and abandonment, in a way that will "center nonelites and the lived experiences of violent conflict." Fryer's work offers an important critique of conflict archaeology as it is currently developing, by insisting on examining how civilian spaces adapt in times of political conflict. Complementing Fryer's examination of the physical organization of villages in the landscape of the guerra de castas, Badillo Sáchez (chapter 6) provides an excellent illustration of how the administrative architectures of militarization were self-consciously designed to contain and limit the actions of a feared Indigenous population. The interplay of the strategies of the state and the tactics of local people has seldom been so evident in a single archaeological setting.

These chapters offer to other archaeologies, including those of the ancestral Maya past, an alternative to standard ways of talking about warfare (such as response to demographic change, or as a strategy of power).

Fryer links her analysis to the urgent archaeology of structural violence, work theoretically explored as well by bioarchaeologists such as Debra Martin (Martin and Harrod 2016). Fryer's discussion of the reworking of the town of Tela' through the production of road-blocking *albarradas* and *trincheras* demonstrates the importance of asking about the productive effects of conflict on identities within and between communities. Generalizing from this example, we can explore the nature of subjectivities, especially gendered subjectivities, produced in newly fortified towns that circumscribed the movement of people not engaged actively in battles. For example, in sixteenth-century Ticamaya, the unprecedented imposition of defensive fortifications built against Spanish invasion had the additional effect of creating spaces shaping new masculinities based on violence, separated from newly constrained spheres of activities for those residents not part of the defense efforts, including all or most women and many men (Sheptak, Blaisdell-Sloan, and Joyce 2011). García Lara and Olán (chapter 4 in this volume) extend the same kind of consideration of the emergence of fortifications along the east coast of Yucatán, also called trincheras during the eighteenth century, as marine-based commercial enterprises loosely grouped together as "piracy" threatened the existence of local political control. Experiential questions such as those that Fryer asks are precisely what we need to bring to bear to make more real the impact of political violence in everyday life, not just in these five centuries in this one area, but globally.

Challenges and Opportunities

There remain challenges in doing this kind of archaeology. Some of these are methodological. Archaeologists trained to examine pre-Columbian societies treated as having ended with the "collapse," or with "the Spanish conquest," almost never consider the possible impoverishing effects of the continued circulation of material culture within descendant communities. Mathews, Gust, and Fedick, in chapter 10, note that the sites they documented have been picked over by successors, who have removed useful materials, in this case, metals. In Honduras, we found a lively presence of religious objects in textual documents that are completely absent in excavated contexts corresponding to these documents (Joyce and Sheptak 2015). In this case, the materiality of religion still exists—but it has moved into new churches or museum collections, requiring us to expand the scope of our analysis from the excavated site to the living landscape. In recent sites to which descendants maintain historic connections, even in radically new social formations, it is essential to remember that what we see in the ground is not the whole picture. Creative uses of documents and oral testimony are not separate lines of evidence for the archaeology of the recent past; they are part of the same analysis.

As we enter into the archaeology of this more recent period, we also need to be aware of the danger of reifying concepts of Spanish administration without regard to the actual unruliness of colonial and (to a lesser extent) Republican life. Gust (chapter 9) explicitly noted the lack of agreement in his analyses between a normative concept of the hacienda and the actual details of the sites he is studying in northern Yucatán. Rather than considering this discrepancy an exception, we might want to consider this violation of normative expectations as a potential common aspect of locally organized life during these periods in all but the most centrally located settlements. When we began our work on colonial Honduras, we were informed about the Spanish practices of *repartimiento*, *encomienda*, and *intendencia* (different forms of officially permitted exploitation of Indigenous labor). What we have found, however, is that each of these words was used in Honduras to label practices that diverged markedly from Spanish legal norms. Indigenous subjects sometimes exploited these divergences to resist forms of exploitation through legal cases drawing attention to local divergence from legal precedents, cases that usually succeeded in the cosmopolitan capital that was invested in asserting these norms (Sheptak 2013). We came to understand that there was an interplay of capital and hinterland, in which what the capital commanded was not always or even usually what the hinterland did, that needed always to be taken into account in our understanding of local life and history (Joyce and Sheptak 2015).

Similarly, we have found that Spanish colonial language of racialized identity, particularly the highly codified form called *casta*, needs to be approached critically. This consideration goes beyond the often-observed fact that there may be contradictions in the way someone self-identified and how they were identified by administrators. Rather, as noted by theorists of new emergent identities in the Americas such as Stephan Palmié (2007), these terms are signals of a broader concern with the unruly ways in which people engaged in intimate, domestic, relations creating populations that could be divided internally by civil status and economic class in ways that the racialized categories did not predict. We can point to extraordinary instances of what we have called "in-between people" who emerged in the processes of colonial life, such as Blás Cuculí, who wrote a petition on behalf of an Indigenous community with which he alternatively identified and disidentified, based on his actual movement between the pueblo de indios of Masca and the colonial *corte* (center of administration) in Guatemala (Sheptak, Blaisdell-Sloan, and Joyce 2011).

To the extent that we transcend the idea that we are describing a specifically "Maya" history, we will end up better understanding global forces that Maya-speaking people negotiated over the centuries since Spanish adventurers and missionaries entered their lands. For this reason, as research continues, archaeology of the colonial and recent Maya past must engage with the archaeologies of neighboring regions that shared experiences of colonization or national administration, as these comparisons will help to throw light on features that either are unique to the Maya region or in need of further reflection, to escape the traps of culture-historical scholarship that contributed until recently to archaeological inattention to the last five centuries. I have offered examples drawn from the archaeology of Central America, the Caribbean, and Alta California. The scope of comparison could and should be even wider, as the colonial histories of the Maya area are among the longest endured in any part of the world and potentially offer points of comparison for every kind of settler society that emerged after the initial colonization of the Americas began.

Our greatest challenges will be detecting and addressing the silences in our archives, to avoid extending and reproducing them as objective realities. Reading these chapters, I wondered about the rarity of African-descendant people in these narratives. The discussion of haciendas in coastal Yucatán by Mathews, Gust, and Fedick (chapter 10) describes a racialized labor force in which there is no mention of African-descendant people. Gust (chapter 9), in his overlapping discussion of the sugar plantation at San Eusebio, explicitly mentions Caribbean Black labor, in addition to Korean and Chinese laborers. This contrasts sharply with neighboring Belize, where Gust describes indentured Black labor, including formerly enslaved people working on contracts after the formal end of British slavery. Gust's description of Black labor in Belize resonates with the situation in Honduras, where the eighteenth-century fort of Omoa was occupied by a majority African-descendant population, including enslaved and free people (Sheptak 2013; Joyce and Sheptak 2015).

The lesser visibility of African-descendant people in Yucatán and the Petén may reflect a real historical pattern of persistence of exploitation of the Indigenous population for the kinds of labor that in neighboring areas shifted to African-descendant people for a variety of reasons. In Honduras this shift happened in the sixteenth century, with the development of gold and silver mining that inflicted high mortality on Indigenous laborers (Sherman 1979). Meierhoff (chapter 8) and Gust (chapter 9) both describe the reliance of the British in Belize on African-descendant labor in place of Indigenous labor, in this case, Meierhoff says, because the Maya were apt to exploit local knowledge and disappear. Research by Matthew Restall (2010) suggests that there may have been a degree of hostility and suspicion of African-descendant people on the part of the Yucatecan Maya. Documents about free Black communities, composed of people who escaped slavery in Belize, provide evidence for their acceptance in Central America, contrasting with the situation they endured in Yucatán and Petén (Russell Sheptak, personal communication 2008).

Wesp provides the major counterpoint, in chapter 3, with an important discussion focused on the African-descendant presence as the "third root" of the Yucatecan present. She notes the need to "broaden the analytical frame" to understand the invisibility of people who were a major component of the colonial and recent past, citing among other reasons for this absence the discourse of Mexican nationalism. She starts with a comparison between advances in understanding the complexity of the urban population in Mexico City and means to address the same questions in Yucatán. While advising caution in projecting simplistic racial categories onto biological remains, Wesp notes that bioarchaeologists have led the way archaeologically in identifying African-descendant people in places like Campeche. In contrast, new settlements established to house free Blacks from the Caribbean at San Fernando Aké and San Francisco de Paula provide no simple indicators of the presence of these populations. She cites census data showing that these towns saw population growth through in-migration of Yucatec Maya in the nineteenth century. Here, as with the Lacandon, we are dealing with ethnogenesis, processes through which new colonial situations allowed the emergence of unprecedented ways of existing—in other words, processes of survivance on the part of both Maya and descendants of formerly enslaved Africans.

Women also make only incidental appearance in most of these chapters. There is no archaeological signature of these actors that distinguishes them in the materials of households, but we would be remiss if we did not consider their specific experiences. Fryer's discussion (chapter 5) of metates as indices of abandonment, even distress, provides a unique and powerful material-based examination of gendered experiences. This is not generalized distress, nor is it likely that the structural violence that was part of the political violence she mentions engaged all members of the population evenly—regrettably, women suffer specific vulnerabilities in situations of military conflicts. Mathews, Gust, and Fedick, in chapter 10, note that women may not be visible in the hacienda work records to which they have access, due to patterns of compensation that took the household and its male head as the unit. Here, as in Fryer's example, we can venture that women required to work, for compensation that was at best relayed through a male household head, experienced kinds of structural domination that are worth our attention.

In our studies of colonial and Republican Honduras, the documentary record forcefully presents women as active agents from the sixteenth century to the nineteenth (Sheptak, Blaisdell-Sloan, and Joyce 2011; Sheptak, Joyce, and Blaisdell-Sloan 2011). Documents created as part of legal cases show us that enslaved women suffered from sexual exploitation, and free working women could be deprived of wages owed them, while free, wealthy women could engage in a wide variety of cosmopolitan exchanges. Taking this complexity into account, our excavations of building foundations from eighteenth-century

Omoa, yielding fragments of imported ceramics and jewelry from a tile-roofed, brick-floored house, become the basis for understanding the way a wealthy woman could manage business in a heterogeneous port town where her African ancestry did not preclude her becoming a community leader (Joyce and Sheptak 2015). Half of the people in all of our case studies are women, and we need to be responsible for accounting for them, and their variation.

Finally, I want to echo Diserens Morgan in her plea (see chapter 11) to rethink our archaeological fetishism of loss of material remains. As she notes, the heritage industry has to be approached critically as it is invested, increasingly, in artificially freezing heritage properties. "Reactionary" and "inflexible" methods are not useful in understanding the complexity of what historian Darío Euraque (2009) calls "textured histories," composed of differences, distinctions, and changes. Euraque notes that the histories preferred by national governments do not equally value all these textures and may in fact suppress histories critical to communities and marginalized populations.

When we are dealing with the relatively recent past, we need to be committed as fully as possible to the tenets of community-engaged scholarship. This focus will require us to cede more control to local populations and to resist being co-opted as agents of national and international commodification of history. We need to acknowledge that some of the ways we archaeologists think knowledge should be created are not seen as useful by local people. If we want to pursue them, we need to do so more humbly, accepting that our epistemological structures are not superior, and may sometimes be seen as (or even be) destructive, to critical work of survivance that these people have managed for centuries, often despite state strategies that traditional archaeological approaches may be better situated to foreground than the tactics used in everyday life. It is up to us to make sure our archaeological work on the recent history of living people is decolonized, to avoid simply being part of a new colonial imposition. Such work will also provide us with partners who can help us understand what we do not see, who can fill the silences we might otherwise perpetuate.

References

Cheek, Charles. 1997. "Setting an English Table: Black Carib Archaeology on the Caribbean Coast of Honduras." In *Approaches to the Historical Archaeology of Mexico, Central and South America*, edited by Janine Gasco, Greg Smith, and Patricia Fournier-Garcia, 101–109. Los Angeles: Institute of Archaeology, UCLA.

Church, Minette C., Jason Yaeger, and Jennifer L. Dornan. 2011. "The San Pedro Maya and the British Colonial Enterprise in British Honduras." In *Enduring Conquests: Rethinking the Archaeology of Resistance to Spanish Colonialism in the Americas*, edited by Matthew Liebmann and Melissa S. Murphy, 173–197. Santa Fe, NM: School for Advanced Research Press.

Euraque, Darío. 2009. "Archaeology, National Identity, and the Coup in Honduras: The Role of the Ancient Maya." A public lecture sponsored by the Center for Latin American Studies, University of California, Berkeley, November 3.

Hanks, William F. 2010. *Converting Words: Maya in the Age of the Cross.* Berkeley: University of California Press.

Ibarra Rojas, Eugenia. 2011. *Del arco y la flecha a las armas de fuego: Los indios mosquitos y la historia centroamericana 1633–1786.* San José, Costa Rica: Editorial UCR.

Ibarra Rojas, Eugenia. 2012. *Pueblos que capturan: Esclavitud indígena al sur de América central del siglo XVI al XIX.* San José, Costa Rica: Editorial UCR.

Joyce, Rosemary A., Esteban Gomez, and Russell N. Sheptak. 2015. "Historical Archaeology in Central America." In *Oxford Handbook of Historical Archaeology,* edited by James Symonds and Vesa-Pekka Herva. Oxford: Oxford University Press. DOI 10.1093/oxfordhb/9780199562350.013.20.

Joyce, Rosemary A., and Russell N. Sheptak. 2014. "History Interrupted: Doing 'Historical Archaeology' in Central America." In *The Death of Prehistory,* edited by Peter Schmidt and Steve Mrozowski, 161–182. Oxford: Oxford University Press.

Joyce, Rosemary A., and Russell N. Sheptak. 2015. "Queering Being in the Colonial Pueblo de San Fernando de Omoa, Honduras."

Martin, Debra L., and Ryan Harrod. 2016. "The Bioarchaeology of Pain and Suffering: Human Adaptation and Survival during Troubled Times." In *Archaeology of the Human Experience,* edited by Michelle Hegmon, 161–174. Archaeological Papers of the American Anthropological Association, vol. 27. Arlington, VA: American Anthropological Association.

Palka, Joel W. 2005. *Unconquered Lacandon Maya: Ethnohistory and Archaeology of Indigenous Culture Change.* Gainesville: University of Florida Press.

Palmié, Stephan. 2007. "The 'C-word' Again: From Colonial to Postcolonial Semantics." In *Creolization: History, Ethnography, Theory,* edited by Charles Stewart, 63–83. Walnut Creek, CA: Left Coast Press.

Restall, Matthew. 2010. *The Black Middle: Africans, Mayas, and Spaniards in Colonial Yucatan.* Stanford, CA: Stanford University Press.

Sampeck, Kathryn. 2007. "Late Postclassic to Colonial Landscapes and Political Economy of the Izalcos Region, El Salvador." PhD diss., Tulane University, New Orleans.

Sheptak, Russell N. 2013. "Colonial Masca in Motion: Tactics of Persistence of a Honduran Indigenous Community." PhD diss., Universiteit Leiden, Netherlands.

Sheptak, Russell N. 2019. "Moving Masca: Persistent Indigenous Communities in Spanish Colonial Honduras." In *Indigenous Persistence in the Colonized Americas,* edited by Heather Law Pezzarossi and Russell N. Sheptak, 19–38. Albuquerque: University of New Mexico Press.

Sheptak, Russell, Kira Blaisdell-Sloan, and Rosemary A. Joyce. 2011. "In-Between People in Colonial Honduras: Reworking Sexualities at Ticamaya." In *The Archaeology of*

Colonialism: Intimate Encounters and Sexual Effects, edited by Barbara L. Voss and Eleanor Casella, 157–172. Cambridge: Cambridge University Press.

Sheptak, Russell N., Rosemary A. Joyce, and Kira Blaisdell-Sloan. 2011. "Pragmatic Choices, Colonial Lives: Resistance, Ambivalence, and Appropriation in Northern Honduras." In *Enduring Conquests*, edited by Matt Liebmann and Melissa Murphy, 149–172. Santa Fe, NM: SAR Press.

Sherman, William. 1979. *Forced Native Labor in Sixteenth Century Central America*. Lincoln: University of Nebraska Press.

Simpson, Audra. 2014. *Mohawk Interruptus: Political Life across the Borders of Settler States*. Durham, NC: Duke University Press.

Vizenor, Gerald. 1994. *Manifest Manners: Narratives on Postindian Survivance*. Lincoln: University of Nebraska Press.

Vizenor, Gerald. 2008. "Aesthetics of Survivance." In *Survivance: Narratives of Native Presence*, edited by Gerald Vizenor, 1–24. Lincoln: University of Nebraska Press.

Voss, Barbara L. 2008. *The Archaeology of Ethnogenesis: Race and Sexuality in Colonial San Francisco*. Berkeley: University of California Press.

Wilkie, Laurie A., and Paul Farnsworth. 2005. *Sampling Many Pots: An Archaeology of Memory and Tradition at a Bahamian Plantation*. Gainesville: University Press of Florida.

13

Engaging Archaeology with the Histories, Cultures, and Political Legacies of the Lowland Maya

Fernando Armstrong-Fumero

As an ethnographer who studies the politics of cultural heritage, I have had many occasions to engage with the work of archaeologists. Often, these engagements focus on broad theoretical discussions of the legal frameworks governing the stewardship of archaeological sites and artifacts. In the case of the essays presented in this volume, my point of engagement speaks to a different shared investment, this time with the histories, cultures, and political legacies of the Maya lowlands. The temporality of historical archaeology grounds this volume in a period that is of great importance for ethnographers and historians of modern Mexico and Central America. Most of the chapters focus on the second half of the nineteenth century and provide snapshots of a period separated by just a few generations from what could be termed the "classic" era of Mayanist anthropology, between the 1920s and 1940s. This period, and the ways it has shaped subsequent generations of scholarship, is a good point of entry for the ethnographically inspired commentary that I offer here.

For ethnographers, the 1920s to 1940s are a period associated with Robert Redfield and his conception of the "folk-urban continuum." This is a foundational

https://doi.org/10.5876/9781646422845.c013

body of work that is subject to generations of academic critiques but that nevertheless left deep traces in vernacular notions of modernity in the Maya area. For archaeology, this same period is significant as the "Carnegie Age," a reference to the wide-ranging project of research and restoration that began at Chichén Itzá. Far from occurring in a political vacuum, the modernizing vision promoted by Redfield and the images of pre-Hispanic Indigeneity that emerged from the Carnegie projects shaped public culture during a pivotal period in the history of Mexico and Central America. For the rural Maya speakers who were Redfield's informants and laborers in the restoration of Chichén Itzá, these decades saw the consolidation of the postrevolutionary state in Mexico, as well as a series of key developments in the complex diplomatic relationship between Mexico, Guatemala, and Belize.

This intersection of anthropological research and political change accounts for why the period captured in Redfield's ethnography seems to hold a special place in the celebration of the distinct cultures of the Maya lowlands. In Mexico, the period between the 1920s and 1930s saw the rise of populist regionalism that linked Maya Indigeneity to the revolutionary "martyr" Felipe Carrillo Puerto. The conflation of Maya heritage and revolutionary nationalism was celebrated in public pageantry and architecture. It was the subject of a flourishing of *indigenista* literature and a regional theater that celebrated rural life. It is evident in the state's appropriation of newly excavated and restored Maya archaeological sites as nationalist symbols. These distinctly modernist and nationalist uses of Mayan identity would find echoes throughout Central America as well.

Because this confluence of canonical anthropological writings and emergent nationalist visions, ethnographers like me often revisit the Age of Redfield and the Carnegie. The 1920s and 1930s are a perennial point of reference in the oral history of the communities where I have conducted research, and ethnographies written during that period are now a valuable record of events, agricultural practices, and rituals that have faded from living memory. The vision of Indigeneity and modernization that was popularized by Redfield also has a powerful hold on the popular and policy imagination, even after half a century of theoretical critiques.

The chapters in this book offer valuable insights into local lifeways that existed just a generation or two before the Age of Redfield, and just beyond the limits of living memory in these communities. It is also striking that the authors seem to reframe a number of classic debates from cultural anthropology through the distinctive lens of material culture studies and social archaeology. The commentary that I offer in this chapter is organized into four broad, but overlapping rubrics, which I hope will offer some lines for future engagement between the research agendas of historical archaeology and the work of those of us engaged in ethnography and documentary historiography.

The first of these rubrics is the question of ethnicity and its relationship to different legacies of colonization and modernity. The complexities of ethnic categories have long been a central theme in Mayanist ethnography, and in the lowlands they are closely tied to different critiques of the "folk–urban" continuum popularized by Redfield. Several chapters in this volume make especially compelling contributions to this discussion.

The second broad theme of my comments will be the relationship of maize agriculture to different colonial and postcolonial labor regimes. One important element of early anthropological critiques of Redfield was a more nuanced historical analysis of different ways in which subsistence was integrated into colonial tribute regimes and capitalist labor markets. Several essays in this volume show how these themes are well represented in historical archaeology, which is also contributing new insights into how these different regimes of labor are manifested in the material life of rural communities.

In a third section, I will look closely at the evolution of the political geography of the Yucatán peninsula in the late nineteenth century and early twentieth. During the first decades of the twentieth century, a range of political actors struggled to define the ultimate fate of the territory that had been "reclaimed" from rebel groups by state and federal forces. The establishment of Quintana Roo as a federal territory and ultimately an independent state would have deep and lasting impacts on the politics and economy of the Mexican Yucatán. During this same period, the diverse society of British Honduras negotiated a tense border relationship with Guatemala and an equally complex relationship to Great Britain, ultimately initiating the process that led to the national Independence of Belize. Several chapters in this volume provide important insights into eighteenth- and nineteenth-century events that preceded this process and that provide important context for local experiences of the emergence of the region's modern political geography.

A fourth section will focus on a series of historical migrations that were fundamental to the development of modern Belize and which tie the former British colony to the long-term legacies of the Caste War. Interestingly, the migration of Spanish and Maya speakers from the Mexican Yucatán into British Honduras is a process that has garnered more recent interest in historical archaeology than it has in ethnographic studies or documentary historiography. This research is providing valuable insight into some of the most understudied elements of the modern social and cultural history of the Maya lowlands.

I will close my commentary with a discussion of what I consider to be the relevance of these four broad themes to understanding the larger question of the cultural heritage, both tangible and intangible, of the Maya lowlands. As I will argue, and as several of the chapters in this volume demonstrate, the historical legacies of the nineteenth century challenge many assumptions about the preservation of cultural heritage that have been central to modern archaeology and the management of sites. These challenges have important implications for thinking about ways in which historical archaeology—along with ethnography and historiography—can become more relevant to local stakeholders and broader publics.

Ethnicity

In his classic *Folk Culture of Yucatan* (1941), Redfield articulated a fairly simplistic and unidirectional process of modernization in which cultural forms diffused eastward from the city of Mérida to areas reigned by more primordial types of subsistence, social organization, and culture. Thus, modernity flowed from Mérida to the sleepy town of Dzitás, from where it continued to trickle eastward to the "folk" village of Chan Kom and finally dripped into the "tribal" village of Tuzik (see also Redfield and Villa Rojas 1934). As Marxist scholars in the 1950s to 1970s would point out, the differences between these communities owed more to the particular and interdependent roles that they played in the globally oriented industries that emerged in the wake of the Caste War. Later authors have observed how the unique structure of ethnic categories in the Yucatán peninsula—where the word "Mestizo" refers to people that other Mexicans would consider "Indigenous," and where boundaries of "Ladinoization" are far more porous than in the highlands—reflects the complexities of the post–Caste War social and political landscape (see Hervik 1999; Gabbert 2004).

In reading the chapters in this book, it is striking how the some of the critiques emerging from contemporary historical archaeology mirror the substance of critiques that emerged earlier in the ethnographic and ethnohistorical literature. Wesp's (chapter 3) analysis of different means of identifying members of historically understudied Afro-descendant populations in the archaeological record of the Yucatán peninsula parallels a problematization of ethnicity that has been a recurrent theme in the ethnographic literature. Afro-descendants are doubly invisible in classic analyses of Mesoamerica, first as a result of the general erasure of individuals of African descent from the history of the region and then through the heritage of theoretical models that focus on unidirectional spectrums of folk-urban transformation or Indigenous-to-Ladino acculturation.

Other chapters in this volume approach ethnicity more obliquely but nevertheless make important contributions to the ongoing discussions about the historical emergence of different social categories in the Maya lowlands. Specifically, the authors document the specific investments of energy, economic exchanges, and social networks that went into reproducing certain material markers of Indigeneity over time. In chapter 9, Gust notes that the practice of subsistence agriculture by San Pedro Maya reflected the relatively flexible arrangement that they negotiated with the Belize Estate and Produce Company

(BEC) in the generation after their migration to British Honduras, a sharp contrast to the dependent wage labor arrangements into which many communities in the northeast of Yucatán were absorbed during the same period. By extension, it becomes evident that the maintenance of older foodways and material culture complexes by the San Pedro Maya was not a simple passive cultural conservatism, but the outcome of conscious spending decisions and labor negotiations that took place within a capitalist forestry economy. The next section will focus more closely on this sort of critical analysis of labor and material culture, and the implications that it has for ethnographers and historians.

Agriculture

As I've hinted early in the chapter, one of the primary shortcomings of Redfield's "folk–urban" continuum was the assumption that the maize agriculture of the 1920s and 1930s represented a primordial pattern with fairly uncomplicated pre-Hispanic roots. But, as Arnold Strickon observed in the 1960s, the subsistence maize agriculturalists of Chan Kom represented a relatively recent settler population that had moved into vast tracts of land that had been abandoned in the wake of the Caste War. The relative autonomous agricultural production of communities such as Chan Kom was not primordial or external to global capital. The "maize zone" of southern and eastern Yucatán played an essential role in the henequen economy by feeding dependent workers in the region dominated by export-oriented monoculture and reflected a series of social and political features with roots in the state-sponsored agrarian reform of the 1920s. Likewise, the autonomy of "tribal" populations in south and central Quintana Roo was maintained by the exploitation of chicle, timber, and other forest resources that were sold on global capitalist markets (Strickon 1964).

Today, this emphasis on developing a more critical understanding of the subsistence techniques that that Redfield reduced to primordial "tradition" has expanded from studies of nineteenth-century globalization to more nuanced analyses of colonial and pre-Hispanic agricultural regimes. This is an important thread linking several of the other chapters here. Studies such as those summarized in Annabelle Ford and Ronald Nigh's *Maya Forest Garden* (2015) have shown that the "classic" swidden field of maize, beans, and squash represents a single tile in a larger ethnobotanical mosaic in which lands that are undergoing various degrees of "fallowing" are exploited for a much broader range of intentionally placed cultivars. What emerges is a diet that was far more varied than the older anthropological portrait of maize subsistence and that involved a more varied series of strategies of land use. The "traditional" maize agriculture that Redfield associated as the dominant means of subsistence among "folk" and "tribal" populations represents a subset of these strategies that proved most advantageous amid the realities of the regional economy that coalesced in the second half of the nineteenth century.

Dedrick, McAnany and Batún's piece in this volume (chapter 2) is a welcome contribution to this expansion of our understanding of the deeper colonial histories of present-day patterns of agriculture. As the authors show, residents of Tahcabo were able to push back against Spanish attempts to control their labor and residence patterns during the early Colonial period by adopting a mobile strategy that made extensive use of "in town" resources such as *rejolladas*, incorporated new Spanish cultivars, and also maintained links to hunting and other forms of resource exploitation that moved people outside of the zones of immediate colonial control. At different points in history, coercive pressures that limited mobility, such as the precarization of key subsistence resources, created conditions in which rural agriculturalists were forced to adapt strategies that brought them closer to dependent labor on haciendas in the eighteenth and early nineteenth centuries.

Taking a broader look at the Yucatán peninsula, we find that one of the long-term catalysts of the increasing dependence of some rural agriculturalists on private estates was the development of the sugar industry. This industry was ravaged by the immediate aftermath of the Caste War, though the henequen industry that emerged in the northwest of the peninsula in the second half of the nineteenth century assumed many similar traits. The contrast between the lifeways of relatively autonomous communities who produced their own food and plantation workers who were transformed into "rural proletarians" has deep roots in the ethnography and historiography of the Yucatán peninsula (see Baños Ramírez 1989).

The fact that Gust in chapter 9—along with Mathews, Gust, and Fedick in chapter 10—trace the transformation of peasant agriculturalists into rural proletarians through the somewhat older regime of sugar production is interesting for a number of reasons. Most histories of Yucatán treat the sugar industry as a phenomenon of the first half of the nineteenth century, which led to the greater elite control over lands in the south and east of the peninsula. Subsistence pressures associated with the expansion of the mid-nineteenth-century sugar industry are often interpreted as one of several catalysts for the outbreak of the Caste War (see Rugeley 1996), and the subsequent eradication of this industry tends to be framed as a stimulus for the rise of henequen monoculture in the northwest.

Something that this narrative tends to downplay or miss entirely, and which Mathews, Gust, and Fedick ably document, was the resurgence of the sugar industry in the northeast of the peninsula in the late nineteenth century (see Sullivan 2004), as well as to the eventual rise of a sizable sugar industry in the south of the state of Yucatán. This industry collapsed after a failed parastatalization in the 1960s, but as late as the 1940s it was seen as a potential substitute for the flagging henequen industry (Fabila 1941). Given its early origins and later revival, it is interesting to see sugar production as a complex that anticipated many of the labor arrangements and infrastructural developments associated with henequen and continued to develop alongside the better-known "green gold."

Geopolitics

The diverse strategies of subsistence and commercial agriculture that are illustrated by the chapters that I have described in the preceding section did not develop in a geopolitical vacuum. Besides its influence on demographic and agricultural patterns, the Caste War had long-term impacts on the contemporary geopolitical layout of the Yucatán peninsula. In addition to leading to the separation of Quintana Roo as a federal territory and eventually independent state, it complicated diplomatic relations between Mexico and the British settlement of Belize. The displacement of large numbers of Hispanic and Maya-speaking people across Mexico's southern border would also have significant resonances in the settlement and makeup of the porous border region between Mexico, Guatemala, and Belize.

The revolutionary-era intellectual and Indigenist poet Antonio Mediz Bolio (1974) characterized the British occupation of Belize and the creation of Campeche and Quintana Roo as separate states as a series of traumatic historical events that led to the historical disintegration of the "authentic" land of Yucatán. For Mediz, as for many elite Yucatecans, the idea of the "Mayab" as the historical territory of Yucatec Maya–speaking people embodied traditional claims to the original Captaincy General of Yucatán. Contemporary historical and ethnohistorical literature has established that the (post)colonial elite's myth of a territorially integral Mayab belied the myriad more localized political and ethnic identities that marked the quotidian experience of rural Yucatec speakers (see Restall 1997; Gabbert 2004). Chapters 4, 5, and 6 provide an intimate portrait of the different ways in which the process that urban elites such as Mediz Bolio saw as a territorial "disintegration" was experienced by these local Indigenous communities.

Turning to the eighteenth century, García Lara and Olán and (chapter 4) demonstrate how the presence of British settlers in what would become Belize was far from an abstract territorial excision for people like the residents of Tela', whose daily lives were disrupted by ongoing piratical raids. The *trincheras* discussed by Fryer (chapter 5) represent a reorientation of these lines of defense after the Caste War, as the same communities that had been preyed upon by the baymen were transformed into a "dangerous" population that was targeted for suppression and control by Yucatecan and Mexican troops. The transformation of a population of the residents of Tela' and Tihosuco from people who were "inside" state-sanctioned defenses to people who were on the "outside" embodies the often-ambivalent relationship between the collective political agency of Maya communities and the states into which they are at least nominally integrated.

Seen within a longer historical perspective, these acts of violence and exclusion laid the foundation for the emergence of new political and economic structures that shaped the twentieth- and twenty-first-century destinies of the peninsula. The late nineteenth-century military campaign against the *cruzo'ob* and other autonomous groups set the state for the emergence of Quintana Roo as a distinct entity within the Mexican. Organized through an increased federal investment in the campaign against rebel Maya during the late *porfiriato*, the architecture of vigilance, control, and intimidation described by Badillo Sánchez (chapter 6) laid the groundwork for the intensive investment of the central government in the development of Quintana Roo. This activity ranged from the vast and controversial territorial concessions that were initially granted to Justo Sierra Méndez and other cronies of Don Porfirio's (Porfirio Díaz's), to the "civilizing" educational projects that came in the wake of the revolutionary state's diplomatic successes with formerly rebel groups. And, of course, there is the foundation of Cancún through the intervention of Mexico City–based technocrats from the Banco de México, which laid the foundation for the modern tourism economy. Traces of the military infrastructure described by Badillo Sánchez (chapter 6) can be glimpsed in later iterations of this federal intervention. The Northern, Central and Southern military lines that she describes bear an eerie resemblance to the three transpeninsular highway routes (running from Mérida to Puerto Juárez, Peto to Chetumal and Escarcega to Chetumal respectively) that were formally chartered by the Lázaro Cárdenas government in 1936 and that established the basic footprint for the network of transpeninsular federal highways that is still in use today and that formed the foundation for the origins of the tourism industry in the Mexican Caribbean (see Armstrong-Fumero 2018b). In this sense, a focus on the history of military infrastructure suggests the geography of state intervention that was consolidated in the second half of the twentieth century might have far deeper and more violent historical roots.

Migration

One common assertion about the agriculturalists of the Maya lowlands is that the ecological context of swidden agriculture necessitates a "mobile" or even "seminomadic" lifestyle. This characterization encapsulates a combination of the realities of rural subsistence and the ideological baggage of colonial and postcolonial states that sought to limit the autonomy of Indigenous communities. But in either case, it is undeniable that the Caste War set in motion waves of migration with few precedents in the preceding or succeeding centuries. The abandonment of broad swaths of the south, east, and center of the peninsula in the mid-nineteenth century triggered the waves of migration that would lead to the emergence of the modern maize zone (see section on agriculture). Just as important was an earlier wave of migration into the north and east of what is now the nation of Belize. Chapters 7, 8, and 9 of this volume contribute to the growing literature on this migration by historical archaeologists.

Refugee populations that moved south of the Río Hondo in the second half of the nineteenth century would play a central role in the economic development of British Honduras and in shaping the social makeup of the often-contentious territorial boundaries with Guatemala. By the mid-nineteenth century, the economy and population of British Honduras were focused on an extractive timber industry. The influx of Maya- and Spanish-speaking refugees in the wake of the Caste War established new bases of labor for subsistence agriculture in the north and west of the colony, transforming the colony's ethnic and linguistic makeup. It also established the complex relationship between the Afro-Creole and Garifuna populations of the coast and the largely Indigenous and Hispanic interior that would define party politics through the twentieth century, especially as the emergent nation-state of Belize negotiated diverse relationships with the West Indies and its inland Central American neighbors (Grant 2008).

Chapters 7, 8, and 9, which deal with the descendants of Caste War refugees living in Belize and Northern Guatemala, provide insight into how the experiences of these local groups continued to play a role in defining the borders of this modern political geography. They demonstrate the dual processes of accommodation and resilience that marked the late nineteenth- and early twentieth-century histories of these refugee communities. First, Caste War migrants and their descendants continued in the centuries-long striving for a socially and culturally coherent practice of subsistence agriculture within the boundaries of modern nation-states. But they also faced a second series of challenges as they adapted to the new limits and possibilities of the forestry-centered extractive economy and a colonial state that were radically distinct from their ancestor's experience under Hispanic domination. As I noted in the section on agriculture, Gust's comparison in chapter 9—between artifact assemblages at San Pedro Maya sites and in sugar hacienda sites in northeastern Yucatán—demonstrates that this new geographic and economic context provided considerable means for both economic autonomy and the reproduction of traditional lifeways.

In chapter 7, Houk, Bonorden, and Kilgore further elaborate on how these adaptations evolved at different settlements within the larger San Pedro cluster, as settlers created different arrangements with neighbors, ranging from BEC logging works to the autonomous Icaiché Maya polity. What I find especially striking in this case is a contrast between two key forms of cultural resilience: local leadership, and subsistence agriculture. While Houk, Bonorden, and Kilgore see continuity in the local leadership offices that were alternately titled *batab*, *comandante*, or *alcalde*, they note that communities such as Kaxil Uinic periodically abandoned maize production to focus on market-oriented chicle extraction, even as they "imported" maize to preserve traditional foodways. This pursuit attests to the degree that the different elements of economic and political life that Redfield associated with "tribal" Maya had fairly independent historical trajectories within different Maya communities. And, more important, this work implies that the ability to maintain some degree of political autonomy at the community level facilitated the preservation of the collective identities expressed through shared foodways amid significant transformations in actual subsistence strategies.

Meierhoff's (chapter 8) analysis of the nineteenth-century settlement at Tikal offers tantalizing clues regarding the origins and organizations of communities at the extreme western extension of these migrations, which left only the barest of traces in the archival record. Drawing ethnographic analogies to multiethnic refugee communities in the more recent past, he notes that displaced people who settle in ethnically diverse areas are often less motivated to preserve distinctive ethnic markers. Assuming that settlers in the isolated settlement of Tikal still enjoyed a degree of choice in the foreign ceramics that they purchased and consumed, the preponderance of "nontraditional" cups and small bowls hints at a parallel homogenization of Yucatec, Ladino, and Lacandon neighbors into a shared and innovated lifeway. I can't help but see parallels today in the contrast between the relatively homogeneous rural communities in the north of the Yucatán peninsula and the ethnically diverse communities of rural Mexicans and Central American immigrants in the sparsely populated south of Campeche, just north of the border with Guatemala's Petén.

How Do these Legacies Relate to Cultural Heritage Politics?

In the previous sections, I have discussed four distinct historical legacies that have shaped the social and cultural world of the Maya lowlands today. Each of these represents a combination of sociohistorical phenomena and theoretical questions that are important points of synergy between historical archaeologists and ethnographers or documentary historians. I would like to close with the important question, which was addressed directly in some of the chapters, about the broader relevance of these research agendas to local stakeholders.

By the 1990s, non-Mayan Mayanist ethnographers such as Kay Warren (1998) found themselves being challenged by Indigenous public intellectuals and activists who demanded anthropological research that was more immediately relevant to contemporary political struggles. In the decades that have followed, non-Mayan ethnographers have sought to reconcile the demands of their own positioning within neoliberal academic markets at home with research agendas that can have greater relevance for the communities that they study. Parallel processes are evident in archaeological research, where there has been more of a trend toward developing collaborations with local stakeholder communities and with diffusing and repatriating archaeological knowledge in ways that are relevant to local communities (Watkins 2001; Hodder 2003; Cojti Ren 2006; McAnany and Parks 2012).

Still, I would argue that archaeologists face a more difficult task in this regard than cultural anthropologists and historians, for the simple reason that their work involves interaction with spaces and objects that fall of the jurisdiction of heritage agencies. This point brings me to the chapter by Diserens Morgan (chapter 11), which explores the ethical and political complexities of heritage regimes that stress the indefinite preservation of sites and objects. Like "folk-urban" continuums, objects-as-heritage are constructs of scholars and policy makers and are often only tangentially linked to how historical sites and artifacts are used by living descendant communities. As Diserens Morgan notes, the insistence of permanence that is promoted by these formal statutes can disrupt the cycles of quotidian life in which long-occupied structures are transformed or even demolished.

The cyclical nature of site use is an aspect of material culture that links together several of the broad rubrics that I have described in the earlier sections. Ancient patterns of lowland forest horticulture entailed significant mobility. The Caste War and its aftermath accentuated this mobility, displacing large populations and creating "empty" spaces that were occupied by subsequent generations of settlers. Insofar as these historical legacies shaped the quotidian experience of generations of people in the Maya lowlands, the processes through which sites are occupied, repurposed, and used for subsistence form an important part of the intangible cultural heritage of the communities studied by anthropologists and archaeologists (Armstrong-Fumero and Hoil Gutierrez 2017). This series of cultural legacies is difficult to reconcile with formal statutes for the preservation of tangible cultural heritage, and the tensions that Diserens Morgan documents in residential architecture tend to reproduce themselves in sites across a vast agricultural and habitational landscape (see Armstrong-Fumero 2012, 2018a).

A few anecdotes from my own field sites highlight the often-ironic clashes that emerge between laws that are aimed to "preserve" heritage and the practices through which rural Maya speakers reproduce ancestral patterns of using the lived landscape. About a decade ago, a Maya-speaking family in a very small village in the municipality of Chan Kom built a traditional thatched-roofed home on top of a small, probably early postclassic platform. This happened to be the most consistently dry spot on a flood-prone plot of land that they owned. The family received a legal censure from Mexican authorities, was forced to remove the home that they had been living in for close to a year, and was threatened with a range of other possible legal repercussions. Adding insult to injury, the precedent of legal action by the Instituto Nacional de Antropología e Historia (INAH; National Institute of Anthropology and History) made their already flood-prone property practically impossible to sell. A Yucatecan archaeologist that I have known for many years commented that that eviction, based on the alteration of a piece of national patrimony, was somewhat ironic. Except for the electrical cables and satellite dish woven into the thatched roof, the illegal house was probably not *too* different from the perishable structure that had once existed on top of the house mound.

I could have added that what this family had done was not too different from what has been done by their ancestors during the century that followed the Caste War. In 2008 and 2009, Julio Hoil and I documented a number of historical sites within the Ejido de Xcalakdzonot. The residents of these communities had arrived as part of the migrations that gradually repopulated the area south of Valladolid in the late nineteenth century. Oral narratives that we recorded suggest that the ancestors of the contemporary *ejidatarios* were not the first settlers to come after the Caste War, and several sites near cenotes seem to have been populated and abandoned several times in the late nineteenth century. Each time, settlers took advantage of the pottery, grindstones, and house foundations left behind by their predecessors, as well as of the pre-Hispanic structures that were also clustered around the cenotes, to build their own habitational sites (Armstrong-Fumero and Hoil Gutierrez 2010).

As Diserens Morgan's contribution to this volume (chapter 11) reminds us, preservation for the sake of preservation can prove disruptive to the very cultural legacies that heritage laws seek to protect. This scenario is often the case when the history of a people has been so marked by repeated cycles of reoccupying places and repurposing the artifacts left behind by previous inhabitants. Clearly, laws for the preservation of heritage sites play an important social role, particularly for local communities that often derive many benefits from tourism that takes place at those sites. But finding new ways to reconcile these laws with the needs and quotidian practices of descendant communities is one of the biggest ethical and intellectual challenges confronting archaeology today. In facing these challenges, it might be possible to develop practices of research and preservation that are more seamlessly integrated into the very historical processes that archaeologists study.

References

Armstrong-Fumero, Fernando. 2012. "Tensiones entre el patrimonio tangible e intangible en Yucatán, México: La imposibilidad de re-crear una cultura sin alterar sus características." Guest-edited volume of *Chungara: Revista de Antropología Chilena* 44 (3): 435–443.

Armstrong-Fumero, Fernando. 2018a. "Artifactual Surface and the Limits of Inclusion: Blurring the Boundary between Materiality and Intangible Heritage." *Anthropological Quarterly* 91 (4): 1303–1328.

Armstrong-Fumero, Fernando. 2018b. "How Culture Became Infrastructure: Tourism and the Spatial Re-orientation of the Yucatán Peninsula after the 1960s." Paper resented at the Reunion Internacional de Historiadores de Mexico, Guadalajara, Jalisco, October 18.

Armstrong-Fumero, Fernando, and Julio Hoil Gutierrez. 2010. "Community Heritage and Partnership in Xcalakdzonot, Yucatán." In *Handbook of Postcolonial Archaeology*, edited by Uzma Rizvi and Jane Lydon, 391–397. Walnut Creek, CA: Left Coast Press.

Armstrong-Fumero, Fernando, and Julio Hoil Gutierrez. 2017. "Settlement Patterns, Intangible Memory, and the Institutional Entanglements of Heritage in Modern Yucatan." In *Legacies of Space and Intangible Heritage*, edited by Fernando Armstrong-Fumero and Julio Hoil Gutierrez, 15–32. Boulder: University Press of Colorado.

Baños Ramírez, Othón. 1989. *Yucatán: Ejidos sin campesinos*. Mérida: Ediciones UADY.

Cojti Ren, Avexnim. 2006. "Maya Archaeology and the Political and Cultural Identity of Contemporary Maya in Guatemala." *Archaeologies* 2 (1): 8–19.

Fabila, Alfonso.1941 "Exploración económico-social del Estado de Yucatán." *Trimestre Económico* 8 (30): 205–252.

Ford, Annabelle, and Ronald Nigh. 2015. *Maya Forest Garden*. New York: Routledge.

Gabbert, Wolfgang. 2004. *Becoming Maya: Ethnicity and Social Inequality in Yucatan since 1500*. Tucson: University of Arizona Press.

Grant, Cedric H. 2008. *The Making of Modern Belize: Politics, Society, and British Colonialism in Central America*. Cambridge: Cambridge University Press.

Hervik, Peter. 1999. *Maya People within and beyond Boundaries: Social Categories and Lived Identity in Yucatan*. Amsterdam: Harwood Academic Publishers.

Hodder, Ian. 2003. "Archaeological Reflexivity and the 'Local' Voice." *Anthropological Quarterly* 76 (1): 55–69.

McAnany, Patricia A., and Shoshaunna Parks. 2012. "Casualties of Heritage Distancing: Children, Ch'orti' Indigeneity, and the Copán Archaeoscape." *Current Anthropology* 53 (1): 80–107.

Mediz Bolio, Antonio. 1974. *La desintegración del Yucatán auténtico*. Mérida: Talleres Zamna.

Redfield, Robert. 1941. *The Folk Culture of Yucatan*. Chicago: University of Chicago Press.

Redfield, Robert, and Alfonso Villa Rojas. 1934. *Chan Kom: A Maya Village*. Washington, DC: Carnegie Institute of Washington.

Restall, Matthew. 1997. *The Maya World: Yucatec Culture and Society, 1550–1850*. Stanford, CA: Stanford University Press.

Rugeley, Terry. 1996. *Yucatán's Maya Peasantry and the Origins of the Caste War*. Austin: University of Texas Press.

Strickon, Arnold. 1964. "Hacienda and Plantation in Yucatan." *América Indígena* 25 (1): 35–63.

Sullivan, Paul R. 2004. *Xuxub Must Die: The Lost Histories of Murder on the Yucatan*. Pittsburgh, PA: University of Pittsburgh Press.

Warren, Kay. 1998. *Indigenous Movements and Their Critics: Pan-Maya Activism in Guatemala*. Princeton, NJ: Princeton University Press.

Watkins, Joe. 2001. *Indigenous Archaeology: American Indian Values and Scientific Practice*. Walnut Creek, CA: AltaMira Press.

Page numbers followed by *f* indicate figures. Page numbers followed by *n* indicate endnotes.

maritime life, 27
markets, 51, 179
marriages, Africans, 59
Masca, 251, 254, 258
material culture, 14, 49, 213, 257, 261, 272; Afro-descendant, 61, 68, 69, 70; haciendas, 202–4; and identity, 151, 253–54; San Pedro Maya, 155, 156–57, 158–59, 160–61, 163f–64, 165; Tikal Village, 181–85, 186–87
materiality, 14, 173
Mathews, Jennifer P., *Chicle*, 5
Maudslay, Alfred, 173, 178
Maya, 9, 10, 69, 81, 113, 152, 156, 229, 239, 265; as captives, 94–95; in Caste War, 130–31, 141–42; in logging industry, 176–77; negotiations, 258–59; political agency, 270–71; rebels, 128, 133, 139; and tourism, 212–13. *See also various groups by name*
Mayab, 270
Maya Forest Garden (Ford and Nigh), 268
Mayaness, 212
Maya Riviera, 52
Mediz Bolio, Antonio, 270
Melchor de Mencos, 179
Méndez, Modesto, 173, 175, 178
mercantilism, and piracy, 85
Mérida, 51, 94, 95, 217, 267; paths to, 91, 98n6
mestizaje, 61
Mestizos, 229, 267
metates, 120, 161, 203, 207n15; as core objects, 118–19; in Tihosuco ejido, 114, 115
Mexican Navy, in Caste War, 134–36
Mexicans, as hacienda labor, 199
Mexican War for Independence, 217
Mexico, 10, 111, 113, 130, 174, 265; Afro-descendants in, 60–61, 260; heritage management, 242–43; Indigenous populations in, 250–51; national identity, 70–71; slavery heritage sites, 71–72
Mexico City, multiethnicity of, 62, 260
Meyers, Allan, *Outside the Hacienda Walls*, 5
middens, Tahcabo, 46–47
Middle Colonial period, 4, 11–12, 27; Tahcabo, 44–45
Middle Preclassic period, 36
migration, 52, 266; Caste War, 133, 271–73; war-induced, 12, 104, 111, 133
Miles, Suzanne, 25
military, military campaigns, 12, 26, 42, 91, 113; anti-pirate activities, 94, 95; architecture, 134–40; during Caste War, 128–30, 131–32, 271
militia, in Beneficios Altos, 91, 93

milpa, 204, 268, 271; San Pedro Maya, 147, 151, 164, 165, 180
Miskito, 250
missionization, 8, 26
mobility: as food and livelihood security, 33–34, 46, 269; in Yucatán, 40–42
Moctezuma, 136
modernity, 6, 7, 8, 265, 266
Moholy-Nagy, Hattula, at Tikal, 5, 179
Montejo, Francisco de, 65
Montilla, Balthazar, 198, 207n10
Morelos, José María, 61
Mosquito Shore, 96
Mosquito-Zambo people, 95, 96
Mujeres, Isla, 84
mules, chicle industry railroads, 220
multiethnic/multiracial society, 12, 27; archaeological evidence, 59–60; hospitals and, 62–64; Mexico, 70–71, 72
Muñoz, Juan, 91

Nabalam, 40
National Guard of Yucatán, in Caste War, 130, 138–39
National Institute of Statistics and Geography (INEGI), census, 70–71
nationalism, Mexican, 251, 260, 265
National Program for Afrodescendant and Cultural Diversity Research, 71
National Register, and historic preservation, 244, 245
nationhood, 26
neighborhoods, in congregated towns, 43
Netherlands, pirates from, 95
new materialisms, 121
New Philology, 4
New Spain, Viceroyalty of, 108
Nigh, Ronald, *Maya Forest Garden*, 268
Nohbec, 135
Nohpop, 139
noni (*Morinda citrifolia*), 46
Northern Line, 131, 133, 134, 271
nuclear families, 36; resource access, 42–43; Tahcabo, 44–45
Nuestra Señora de Guadalupe de Los Morenos de Amapa, 70
Nuevo River, 94

Ojeda, Jorge Victoria, *San Fernando Aké*, 5
Okop, 138–39f
Omoa, 254, 255, 259, 261
oral histories/narratives, 213, 257–58, 275

Fernando Armstrong-Fumero is a sociocultural anthropologist specializing in research in political anthropology, oral history, and multiculturalism in Mexico and Latin America. He has a long-term research project on the intellectual history of anthropology in the Americas.

Alejandra Badillo Sánchez holds a PhD in history from the Centro de Investigaciones y Estudios Superiores en Antropología Social (CIESAS). She received her MA in anthropology from the Universidad Nacional Autónoma de México–Facultad de Filosofía y Letras (UNAM-FFyL), and a BA in archaeology from the Escuela Nacional de Antropología e Historia (ENAH). She has been a member of the Cochuah Regional Archaeological Survey since 2010. She focuses her research on the Maya area using historical documents, material remains, oral history, archival methods, and field work to critically analyze the outcomes of the Maya Social War, specifically the participation of Yucatecan armed forces at the end of the nineteenth and beginning of the twentieth centuries and its impact on the people of the region. Currently she is exploring how the historical and living memory of said war circulates.

Adolfo Iván Batún Alpuche, a professor at the Universidad de Oriente in Valladolid, Yucatán, studies the agrarian practices of pre-Hispanic Maya peoples, and contemporary perceptions of self-identity within Maya communities. Theoretically, he follows a collaborative and decolonizing approach. He received his *licenciatura* (bachelor's degree) in archaeology from the Universidad Autónoma de Yucatán (UADY) and his MA and PhD from the University of Florida.

Brooke Bonorden, MA, RPA, is a principal investigator with Pape-Dawson Engineers in North Houston, Texas. As a cultural resource management professional, Ms. Bonorden specializes in mid-nineteenth-to-twentieth-century artifact analysis and archival research, both skills she previously put to use investigating the San Pedro Maya at Kaxil Uinic village for her thesis. She is currently engaged in projects across the greater Houston, Austin, and San Antonio metropolitan areas.

Maia Dedrick, Hirsch Postdoctoral Associate at Cornell University, studies food, agriculture, and colonialism in rural Yucatán. Her dissertation research involved archaeological study in collaboration with residents of Tahcabo, Yucatán, through the Proyecto Arqueológico Colaborativo del Oriente de Yucatán (PACOY). She received her MA and PhD from the University of North Carolina at Chapel Hill.

Kasey Diserens Morgan is a doctoral candidate in anthropology at the University of Pennsylvania. She studies cultural heritage, politics, and historic preservation in rural Quintana Roo, Mexico. She has been a part of the Tihosuco Heritage Preservation and Community Development Project since 2014.

Scott L. Fedick received his MA and PhD in anthropology from Arizona State University. He is currently an Emeritus Professor of Anthropology at the University of California, Riverside, where he taught for twenty-five years. His research interests focus on ancient Maya agriculture, resource use, and settlement patterns, with an emphasis on multidisciplinary approaches. He has conducted archaeological research in Mexico, Belize, and Guatemala, as well as in California, Washington, and Arizona. He served as director of the Yalahau Regional Human Ecology Project, in Quintana Roo, Mexico, from 1993 to 2014, and is currently involved with research on the ethnobotany and physiology of Indigenous food plants of the Maya lowlands.

Tiffany C. Fryer is an assistant professor of anthropology at the University of Michigan and assistant curator of historical and contemporary archaeology at the University of Michigan Museum of Anthropological Archaeology. Her work on colonialism in the Americas has been supported by various sources including the Princeton Society of Fellows, the National Science Foundation, and the Ford Foundation. She has contributed to the Tihosuco Heritage Preservation and Community Development Project, based in Quintana Roo, Mexico, since 2013.

Fior Daliso García Lara is a PhD candidate in borderlands history at the University of Texas–El Paso. Her current research compares the formation of the southern and northern borders of eighteenth-century New Spain. She earned an MA in Caribbean, Latin American, and Latino studies from the State University of New York at Buffalo, and her dissertation is on the history of illegal trade in Darien, Panama, in the eighteenth century.

John R. Gust received his BA (University of Colorado, Colorado Springs) and MA and PhD (University of California, Riverside) in anthropology with an emphasis in Maya archaeology. He is a principal investigator and project manager at Cogstone Resource Management in Orange, California. His research interests include historical archaeology, Maya archaeology, political economy, and commodity flows.

Brett A. Houk is a professor at Texas Tech University and the director of the Belize Estates Archaeological Survey Team. He is the author of *Ancient Maya Cities of the Eastern Lowlands* (2015) and the lead editor of *Approaches to Monumental Landscapes of the Ancient Maya* (2020). His team has been investigating the historic San Pedro Maya of northwestern Belize since 2012.

Rosemary A. Joyce is a professor of anthropology at the University of California, Berkeley, and received her PhD in Anthropology from the University of Illinois, Urbana-Champaign, in 1985. She conducted field research in Honduras from 1977 to 2009 and continues research on colonial archives and museum collections pertaining to Honduras and Central America.

Gertrude B. Kilgore, MA, completed her thesis at Texas Tech University on a Late Classic Maya household at Chan Chich, Belize. Her research interests are ancient Maya households and socioeconomic stratification with a focus on community-engaged approaches.

Jennifer P. Mathews received a BA (San Diego State University), MA, and PhD (University of California, Riverside) in anthropology, with a specialization in Maya archaeology. She has conducted archaeological fieldwork in Quintana Roo, Mexico, since 1993, and her research interests include ancient Maya architecture, archaeological tourism, and historical archaeology on commodities in Mesoamerica. She is department chair and a professor of anthropology at Trinity University in San Antonio, Texas, where she teaches undergraduate courses in archaeology and physical anthropology. She is the author or editor of five books on the ancient Maya and historical Maya commodities.

Patricia A. McAnany, Kenan Eminent Professor and chair of the Anthropology Department at the University of North Carolina at Chapel Hill, is codirector of Proyecto Arqueológico Colaborativo del Oriente de Yucatán—a community-archaeology project at Tahcabo, Yucatán. She cofounded and directs InHerit: Indigenous Heritage Passed to Present, a UNC program that generates collaborative research and education projects on topics of cultural heritage with communities in North Carolina and the Maya region. She is the author of several books, notably *Maya Cultural Heritage: How Archaeologists and Indigenous Peoples Engage the Past*, and journal articles.

James Meierhoff is a PhD candidate from the University of Illinois at Chicago. Trained in Classic Maya archaeology, he has recently focused his research on Indigenous responses to incipient globalization and the post-Independence formation of nation-states in nineteenth-century Central America. Meierhoff is currently finishing his PhD dissertation titled "Where Voices Are Heard; Historic Archaeology and the Refugee Experience at Tikal, Guatemala."

Fabián Alberto Olán de la Cruz is an archaeologist. He has worked principally on the Puuc region in pre-Hispanic sites for INAH Yucatán. He is particularly interested in the historical archaeology of the Maya area, through the Colonial period. Currently, he is working toward an MA in History at Centro de Investigaciones y Estudios Superiores en Antropología Social (CIESAS) Peninsular, Mérida.

Julie K. Wesp is an assistant professor of anthropology and faculty affiliate of the Science, Technology, and Society program at North Carolina State University. Her research draws on bioarchaeological methods to reconstruct the daily life of people in the past. Current research projects examine the impact of sociopolitical changes during the Colonial period in Mexico and Colombia.